Starting and Operating a Business in New York

A Step-by-Step Guide

By Michael D. Jenkins and the
Entrepreneurial Services Group of Ernst & Young

The Oasis Press® / PSI Research
Grants Pass, Oregon

Published by The Oasis Press
© 1985, 1991 by Michael D. Jenkins and Ernst & Young

This publication is designed to provide accurate and authoritative information
in regard to the subject matter covered. It is sold with the understanding that
the publisher is not engaged in rendering legal, accounting, or other
professional service. If legal advice or other expert assistance is required, the
services of a competent professional person should be sought.
> *—from a declaration of principles jointly adopted by a committee of
> the American Bar Association and a committee of publishers.*

The principal author and technical editor of the entire *Starting and Operating a
Business* series is Michael D. Jenkins. The co-author of the state chapter of
Starting and Operating a Business in New York is Jacob Weichholz of Ernst &
Young.

Administrative Editor: Rosanno Alejandro

Series Editor: Scott Crawford

Assistant Editor: Vickie Reierson

Page Design & Typography: Constance C. Dickinson

Please direct any comments, questions, or suggestions regarding this book to
The Oasis Press, Editorial Department at the address below.

The Oasis Press offers PSI Successful Business Software for sale.
For information, contact:

> PSI Research
> 300 North Valley Drive
> Grants Pass, OR 97526
> (503) 479-9464

The Oasis Press is a Registered Trademark of Publishing Services, Inc.,
a Texas corporation doing business in Oregon as PSI Research.

Library of Congress Catalog Card Number: 90-64365

ISBN 1-55571-101-4 (paperback)
ISBN 0-916378-62-4 (binder)

Printed in the United States of America
Third edition 10 9 8 7 6 5 4 3 2 1 0   Revision Code: A

 Printed on recycled paper when available.

Table of Contents

Foreword

User's Guide

Foreword

Much is heard today about how individual initiative is on the wane in the United States and how economic activity is becoming concentrated in ever fewer hands as giant corporations increasingly dominate the business scene. Notwithstanding these gloomy assessments, which would suggest that small businesses are becoming a thing of the past, more than 400,000 new and independent businesses spring up each year in this nation. While many of these fledgling enterprises fail to make it in the marketplace and fold in a few months or years, many others survive and eventually become thriving enterprises, making an important contribution to our national economic well-being. Furthermore, ownership of a successful small business still remains the chief avenue for becoming a millionaire in America, and thousands of entrepreneurs reach that goal every year.

Thus, to paraphrase Mark Twain, the reports of the demise of small business in this country are greatly exaggerated. To the contrary, there is a strong tide running in the direction of self-employment in America. By 1970, the percentage of working Americans who were self-employed had dropped to only 7%. By 1985, the percentage who were in business for themselves had risen to 9%, and demographers expect this to increase to about 15% by the middle of the 1990s and to continue to increase well into the next century.

Researchers say this shift toward self-employment is mainly due to the fact that most people prefer working for themselves. Surveys have consistently shown that self-employed people are much more likely to be happy with their jobs than other people. Also, with the information gathering and processing roles of middle managers increasingly being taken over by computers, white-collar workers are being automated out of jobs by large companies almost as rapidly as blue-collar workers. In addition, the explosive growth of the "information society" creates an economic environment that is almost perfectly suited to the small, specialized, technically-oriented firm.

In the course of advising small and large businesses over the years, first as an economic and management consultant, then later as an attorney and more recently as a CPA, I have long been keenly aware of the need for a single authoritative and practical "cookbook" that would serve as a guide both to persons starting and operating their own businesses in a particular state and to their professional advisers. While most bookstores contain any number of books that purport to advise the reader how to become successful and rich by starting a business, what has been conspicuously absent from the bookshelves is a nuts and bolts practical guide through the maze of mostly government-created red tape with which virtually all small businesses must cope.

Like the weather, everyone complains about the excessive red tape and Kafkaesque complexity that even the smallest business must cope with, but no one does very much about it. Small business owners who want to know the ground rules for playing in this maze have very few options available in terms of getting useful information and advice. If small business owners want to know what basic legal requirements will apply to their business, they must consult an attorney and hope that they find one with a good business law background. If small business owners want to know how to structure the business to minimize taxes, they must find and consult a good tax accountant or tax lawyer; if they want some practical advice or pointers on the basics of buying or starting a business, they need to hire a management consultant who can tell them what to look for and to look out for.

Unfortunately, most people with a good idea for a business, but not a great deal of money, cannot or will not expend the time, energy, and expense involved in seeking out and consulting a whole team of specialized experts and consultants. Accordingly, most small business owners find out much of what they need to know in connection with running their businesses by the trial and error method, which is a hard and often costly way to learn.

Thus, I was particularly receptive when my friend and publisher, Emmett Ramey, approached me early in 1980 with the idea of writing this book for the state of California. His idea was to create an operating manual that would draw together, in a readable, usable, and nontechnical format, the practical facts of life one must know — to stay out of legal trouble with the government — when establishing a business in California. This manual would also explain in layperson's language many of the key financial, tax, and legal pitfalls and planning opportunities a person should be aware of before embarking on a business venture.

As a result of the highly enthusiastic reception the California edition has enjoyed from academics, lawyers, accountants, business advisers, and particularly from small business owners, we decided several years ago to develop a separate state edition for each of the 50 states, each co-authored with local experts in the respective states. As of early 1991, all

50 states and the District of Columbia editions are either in print or in the process of being published.

This book has been designed as a self-help tool for the business owner who wants an up-to-date guide to the basic financial, legal, and tax ground rules that apply to most businesses operating in his or her state. It is also intended to be a highly-useful reference source to the attorney who has only a limited knowledge of business taxation and the basic regulatory requirements of a large number of federal, state, and local government agencies. The accountant, who is often the only outside professional adviser to a small business client and who has only a limited knowledge of government regulations — other than tax laws — would also find this book a useful resource for laws affectng his or her clients.

While the book provides an authoritative discussion of many legal and tax matters of interest to small business, it is not intended to be a substitute for professional legal or tax advice. To the contrary, it is designed to assist the small business owner in focusing on key tax and legal points that should be explored in depth with a professional adviser and thus, should help the reader to more efficiently utilize the services of professional advisers.

The first chapter is designed to aid in and sharpen the focus of the decision process one typically goes through while a new business is still in the idea stage.

The second chapter describes the various legal forms in which a business may be operated — sole proprietorships, partnerships, corporations — and outlines the most significant advantages and disadvantages of each. Chapter 3 can be skipped unless you are considering buying an existing business or opening a franchised operation. Chapters 4 through 7 describe the various tax authorities and other governmental agencies that most or all businesses must deal with. Chapter 8 describes in nontechnical terms a number of the major income tax benefits that even a small business may be able to enjoy, while Chapters 9 and 10 describe miscellaneous business pointers and sources of information and guidance that are made available to small businesses by government agencies and private institutions. Chapter 11 deals specifically with the laws, taxes, and business conditions in this state.

For those who would like to further research many of the legal references used in preparing the information presented, footnotes for all chapters appear at the end of each chapter.

The appendix provides useful checklists and a number of official government forms and sources of publications needed by many businesses. Since the individual starting in business has much better uses for his or her time than going from government office to government office requesting forms — a number of agencies we contacted in connection with preparing this book would not simply mail us a form in response to a phone call. The forms and publications provided here in one place should save the reader considerable time and money, as well as shoe leather.

Although we originally intended to provide copies of all the numerous government posters (legal notices) required for the typical small business, a number of governmental bodies were unwilling to provide multiple copies of some of the posters which might be most useful. The posters were free, so the agencies could not sell multiple copies to us; a typical Catch-22 situation in dealing with bureaucracies.

Thus, we have provided those forms which were available or readily reproducible. In addition, we have provided for the user's convenience a preaddressed post cards for additional forms, posters, and publications we felt most small businesses would want or need to get started. In some instances, the post cards allow the sender to request a single publication or form; in other cases, to select those which are appropriate to the particular business. We sincerely hope that you will find this new edition to be an even more practical and useful tool in your business or professional practice than the preceding editions, which have been so well received.

The author and publisher welcome any suggestions or constructive criticisms from readers that may assist us in refining or expanding future editions. A form, as well as post cards, are also included at the back of the book to order related resources for your business.

Michael D. Jenkins

February, 1991

Acknowledgments

To my good friends and publishers, Emmett and Ardella Ramey, whose tireless efforts, creative energy, and constant support have contributed so much to making this book a reality . . . and to America's entrepreneurs, those thousands of tenacious, courageous men and women for whom this book is written, whose contribution to the variety, richness, and quality of our life is immeasurable.

User's Guide

0.1 Getting the Most Out of this Book

To most effectively use this book in your business — or in your practice, if you are a professional adviser — we suggest you become acquainted with the many helpful features this book provides.

0.2 Numbered Section Heads Correspond to Table of Contents and Index

Textual Material

This book's material ranges from explaining how to start and operate your business to discussing such practical issues as insurance, marketing, cash flow management, internal financial controls, and much more. In non-technical language, the book also discusses — and regularly updates — the various federal, state, and tax laws you will need to know about.

Topics Noted in Margins

We have tried to make the information in this workbook easily accessible to busy people. Within each numbered section, the primary topics discussed are identified by "sideheads" in the margin beside the text.

Smaller Heads for Subtopics

When subsections of primary topics are discussed, the sideheads are smaller and lighter.

Important Notes!

Information that is critical to remember, be cautious about, or act on is identified by the small, bold margin headings.

Lists

- This small bullet allows you to easily locate lists of requirements, qualifiers, things to do, and aspects of a particular subject or law.

Checklists

☐ Small boxes encourage you to enter a check, so that you can clearly see those items you've considered and dealt with — and those left to do.

Worksheets

> **Where the Action Begins**
>
> There are a number of worksheets provided for you to answer questions and fill in numbers that form the basis for action plans, self-evaluation, budgeting, personnel policies, marketing feasibility studies, and the like.
>
> The worksheets are set apart by boxes to clearly show where your interaction is required to focus your thoughts, record information, and create the plans and reports that will help you establish and guide your business.

Resources

Sources and Data   Helpful resources are set in tabular form to reduce the time you have to spend accessing the information you want.

Contacts
Addresses
Phone Numbers
(listed in directory style)

Table of Contents

The detailed table of contents will help you quickly find any specific section of the book you wish to refer to. The first digit of the chapter–section number indicates the chapter, followed by a period and the section number.

Footnotes

The footnotes follow each chapter and are provided primarily to assist attorneys, tax accountants, and other professionals who wish to access specific statutes, cases, and regulations and to use this book as a starting place for legal research.

Index

The subject-matter index referenced by chapter–section (not page) numbers helps you find important topics in the text quickly and easily.

Related Resources

At the back of this book — and in the pockets, if you have a binder edition — you'll find a compendium of useful information that will further ease your journey through the red tape jungle. From helpful business tools to a list of additional resources, this section will assist you in your business activities and save you valuable time and money.

Appendix

The appendix features: 1) Checklists of Tax and Various Other Major Requirements for Most Businesses; and 2) Checklist of Official Government Posters and Notices Required to be Displayed by a Business.

Forms

Since many business requirements depend on submitting specific forms to various government agencies, we have included some samples of the forms that may affect your business. You can review these samples to see what information you will have to gather.

Post Cards

At the back of this book, you will also find post cards preaddressed to government agencies and other sources so you can request additional information, posters, and forms that you may need.

*"Whatever you can do, or dream you can, begin it.
Boldness has genius, power, and magic in it."*

— Goethe

Part I

Preliminary Considerations

Chapter 1

Making the Decision to Go into Business

"Being boss doesn't make you right; it only makes you boss."

— Milton Metz

1.1 Introduction

Neither this book nor any other book can tell you whether or not you should take the plunge and go into business for yourself. That is a difficult decision that you and you alone must make. Before you make the decision, however, there are a number of very basic questions that you should have first considered very thoroughly, which may help you to decide whether or not you are ready to start a particular business. This introductory chapter is designed to alert you to a number of key points you may not have considered yet, as well as assist you in dealing successfully with some of these initial problems you will face.

To get started in most kinds of new businesses, a major financial risk must be taken. Once you have committed yourself, it will not be a simple or easy thing to change your mind and back out.

In evaluating the risks, you should be aware that there is a high failure rate among new businesses. According to statistics of the U.S. Small Business Administration, about 1,000 new businesses are started each business day. Of these new firms, fully 55% will fail in five years. Year in and year out, statistics show that a very high percentage of business failures result from poor management.

Poor or ineffective management is usually a lack of balanced experience and competence in three areas:

- Marketing knowhow — which means knowing what kind of product or service to sell, how to target and reach your customers, and how to sell your product or service at a price that maximizes your profits.

- Technical knowhow — which simply means that you must be able to get the work done and do it right, so you will have satisfied customers. If you are going into the auto repair business, for example, you had better know a lot about how to keep cars running right, or you will not be in business very long.

- Financial knowhow — while you do not necessarily have to be a financial wizard, you do need to know how to plan and control your business' cash flow and how to raise or borrow money you will need to start your business and get through tight periods without being caught short of cash. A certain amount of financial sophistication is becoming more and more important in today's increasingly complex financial world, even for the small business owner.

If you are seriously deficient in one or more of these three critical areas, the odds of your business becoming one of the relatively few that succeeds are greatly reduced.

In addition, there are many other facts that will influence the odds of your succeeding or failing in your own business. For example, the magazine *Canadian Business* reported on a survey conducted by Thorne Riddell, a large Canadian accounting firm, of 2,000 sole proprietorships started in Canada. In a follow-up survey three years later, they found, interestingly enough, that only 25% of the firms with male owners had survived, while 47% of the ones started by women were still around. Keeping in mind that the Canadian economy is somewhat different from that of the United States, it is still worthwhile to note the four major factors that seemed to separate the winners from the losers in the Thorne Riddell study:

Factor	Successful Firms	Failures
Degree of Preparation	Spent 6 to 10 months to research and prepare for their ventures.	Spent less than 4 months to prepare for start-up.
Use of Advisers	90% utilized professional advisers such as lawyers and accountants in starting up.	Only 25% sought professional help at an early stage.
Business Education, Reading	Almost 70% had taken business-related courses before starting business and also regularly read business books and magazines.	Only 10% had attended business courses or now took time to read business material.
Expectations of Income	More than half said they started with modest expectations, typically about $12,000 a year (Canadian) and were prepared to be patient for signs of success.	36% said they fully expected to make barrels of money within 3 years. The anticipated level of annual earnings they most often quoted was $40,000 (Canadian).[1]

More recent research, using the much larger U.S. Small Business Data Base, indicates that failure rates are lower than commonly believed and reveals a tie between growing firms (defined as those adding at least one job every two years) and success. In this study of 458,000 firms, of those businesses which did not add at least one job every two years, about 30% failed within two years after start-up, and a total of 73% had failed after six years. However, firms that grew by at least one job every 24 months experienced a much greater survival rate; only 8% closed within two years, and only 34% after six years.[2] Although the ability of a firm to generate jobs is not the sole factor in reducing the failure rate, it often increases the firm's flexiblity in weathering periods of economic contraction.[3]

This introductory chapter is designed with the intention of engaging you in the process of realistically evaluating your entrepreneurial strengths and weaknesses, your likes and dislikes. It is also intended to cause you to focus on some of the typical start-up problems and choices you are likely to face, as well as assist you in dealing effectively and rationally with those issues.

Where we have provided worksheets, we strongly urge you to pick up a pencil and write in your responses. For many people, the simple process of writing down your thoughts on specific problem areas may provide significant new insights that may suddenly seem terribly obvious to you once you have raised them to the level of conscious thought.

1.2 Advantages and Disadvantages of Owning Your Own Business

Have you realistically considered both the advantages and the disadvantages of owning and operating your own business? If not, the time to do so is before, not after, you have committed yourself.

Advantages

If you are actively considering going into business for yourself, it is likely that you have already thought about the potential advantages, such as:

- Being your own boss, not having to report to some superior.
- Having the independence and power to make your own business decisions, for better or worse. For many entrepreneurs, this is one of the major payoffs of having their own businesses.
- Direct contact with customers, employees, suppliers, and others.
- The personal satisfaction and sense of achievement that comes with being a success, plus the recognition that goes with it. For most successful entrepreneurs, money is not the real goal, but merely a way of keeping score in the game of business.
- The opportunity to create substantial wealth and job security for oneself.

- The opportunity to be creative, to develop your own idea, product, or service; the chance to make a living doing something you truly enjoy.
- Doing something that contributes to others, whether it be providing an excellent product or service, providing employment, paying dividends to stockholders, or doing something else that is useful or that creates value.

Disadvantages

You may not have thought much about the downside, if you are like most people. Awareness of the potential disadvantages should not discourage you from your goal of going into business for yourself, if you have a strong commitment to that goal. However, forewarned is forearmed and it will not be helpful for you to view the real world of business through rose-colored glasses.

Seriously consider whether you and your family are prepared to handle the disadvantages inherent in being an entrepreneur:

- In a lot of ways, you are still not your own boss. Instead of having one boss, you will now have many — your customers, the government agencies to whom you must report, and, in some cases, your key suppliers.
- There is a large financial risk. The failure rate is high in new businesses, and you may lose not only your own money but also that of your friends and relatives who may have bankrolled you.
- The hours are long and hard. When you start your business, you will no longer be working nine to five. Count on working 10- to 12- or even 15-hour days, often six or seven days a week.
- You will not have much spare time for family or social life. And you can forget about taking any long vacations for the next few years, since the business is unlikely to run itself without your presence for any great length of time.
- Your income will not be steady, unlike a salary. You may make more or less than you could working for someone else, but in either case your income will fluctuate up and down from month to month.
- The buck stops with you. If a problem arises, there is no boss you can take it to and say "What do we do about this?" You are the boss now, and all the responsibility is yours. If anything goes wrong, the cost comes out of your pocket.
- You may be stuck for years doing work you do not like. Unlike an employee, you cannot simply quit and look for a better job. It may take you years to sell the business or find some other way to get out of it without a major financial loss, if you should decide you don't like it.

1.3 Typical Characteristics of the Successful Entrepreneur

A good deal is known about what it takes to be a successful entrepreneur. For the most part, it seems that the one overriding factor that is most often found in highly successful entrepreneurs is a tremendous need to achieve. In short, attitude seems to have almost everything to do with success in business, while factors such as intelligence, education, physical appearance, and a pleasing personality are much less important. Characteristics of the typical successful entrepreneur include:

- An overpowering need to achieve, as opposed to a need to be liked, or to exercise power. The form in which different individuals measure their achievement varies widely, ranging from amassing wealth to building a larger organization to creating a better mousetrap than anyone else.
- The trait of following through on a commitment, not quitting half-way through when the going gets tough. In short, perseverance.
- Positive mental attitude, or the ability to remain optimistic in new and unfamiliar situations, which essentially grows out of being self-confident about one's abilities.
- Objectivity. The ability to accurately weigh and assess risks associated with a particular course of action, as well as being realistic about one's own abilities and limitations.
- A respectful attitude toward money, but a tendency to look upon money as a means for accomplishing things, or a way of keeping score in the game of business, rather than as a thing to be sought as an end in itself.
- The tendency to anticipate developments and to make things happen, rather than constantly reacting to problems as they arise.
- Resourcefulness. The ability to solve unique problems in unique ways — to be able to handle things that come up for which the entrepreneur has no previous experience to rely on as a guide.
- Personal relations. The successful entrepreneur usually has an emotionally stable personality, is cheerful, cooperative, and usually gets along well with (without necessarily being close to) employees and associates.
- Communication skills are well-developed, both in oral and written presentations.
- Technical knowledge is usually well-rounded, and the successful entrepreneur generally is knowledgeable about the physical process of producing goods and services or at least can effectively utilize information regarding the physical process.

How do your personal characteristics stack up against the foregoing profile of the typical successful entrepreneur? If that profile doesn't sound very much like you, maybe you had better give some long, hard thought as to whether you are cut out for making it as a business owner.

Running a business is not like working for someone else. There is no one to tell you what to do when something goes wrong. You are responsible for everything. Are you capable of handling that kind of total responsibility? Are you a self-starter, capable of planning, organizing, and carrying out projects on your own? If not, you may find that starting and running a successful business is not for you. Running a business demands a great deal in the way of initiative, hard work, self-discipline and resourcefulness. On the other hand, solving the problems that arise from day to day and making it all work out can be a source of immense satisfaction, as well as be financially rewarding.

Before reading further, get a pencil and complete Worksheet 1, which is a useful questionnaire that may help you to get a better idea of your suitability for playing the role of entrepreneur in the real world.

Worksheet 1
Self-evaluation Checklist for Going into Business

Under each question, check the answer that says what you feel or comes closest to it. Be honest with yourself.

Are you a self-starter?

☐ I do things on my own. Nobody has to tell me to get going.

☐ If someone gets me started, I keep going all right.

☐ Easy does it. I don't put myself out until I have to.

How do you feel about other people?

☐ I like people. I can get along with just about anybody.

☐ I have plenty of friends — I don't need anyone else.

☐ Most people irritate me.

Can you lead others?

☐ I can get most people to go along when I start something.

☐ I can give the orders if someone tells me what we should do.

☐ I let someone else get things moving. Then I go along if I feel like it.

Can you take responsibility?

☐ I like to take charge of things and see them through.

☐ I'll take over if I have to, but I'd rather let someone else be responsible.

☐ There's always some eager beaver around wanting to show how smart he is. I say let him.

How good an organizer are you?

☐ I like to have a plan before I start. I'm usually the one to get things lined up when the group wants to do something.

☐ I do all right unless things get too confused. Then I quit.

☐ You get all set and then something comes along and presents too many problems. So I just take things as they come.

How good a worker are you?

☐ I can keep going as long as I need to. I don't mind working hard for something I want.

☐ I'll work hard for a while, but when I've had enough, that's it.

☐ I can't see that hard work gets you anywhere.

Can you make decisions?

☐ I can make up my mind in a hurry if I have to. It usually turns out okay, too.

☐ I can if I have plenty of time. If I have to make up my mind fast, I think later I should have decided the other way.

☐ I don't like to be the one who has to decide things.

Can people trust what you say?

☐ You bet they can. I don't say things I don't mean.

☐ I try to be on the level most of the time, but sometimes I just say what's easiest.

☐ Why bother if the other fellow doesn't know the difference?

Can you stick with it?

☐ If I make up my mind to do something, I don't let anything stop me.

☐ I usually finish what I start if it goes well.

☐ If it doesn't go right away, I quit. Why beat your brains out?

How good is your health?

☐ I never run down!

☐ I have enough energy for most things I want to do.

☐ I run out of energy sooner than most of my friends seem to.

Now count the checks you made.

How many checks are there beside the first answer to each question? _____

How many checks are there beside the second answer to each question? _____

How many checks are there beside the third answer to each question? _____

If most of your checks are beside the first answers, you probably have what it takes to run a business. If not, you're likely to have more trouble than you can handle by yourself. Better find a partner who is strong on the points you're weak on. If many checks are beside the third answer, not even a good partner will be able to shore you up.

Source: U.S. Small Business Administration.

1.4 Knowing Your Market

One of the most important questions you should ask yourself is whether you feel that you know and understand the market for the particular kind of products or services you intend to sell. Do you know who your competition is and whether the particular market you intend to appeal to is large enough for both you and the existing competition? Also, how will your products or services measure up against those of your competitors in terms of quality and price?

It is very important, if your product or service is something new or unusual, to have a sense of whether you will be selling an item that is wanted and needed in the marketplace. Or, even if you intend to sell a product or service that you know there is a need for, you should be satisfied in your own mind that you are going to be making it available at the right place at the right time. Few sights are sadder than the boarded-up mom-and-pop store or restaurant, in which the owners have sunk their life savings, that never got off the ground for some obvious reason, such as lack of visibility from the street, lack of substantial foot traffic by its doors, or some other fatal flaw that the inexperienced owners overlooked.

In order for your business to succeed, you must find the right business opportunity. If you do not have a clear idea of what business you want to go into and where you want to operate it, you will need to do some intelligent investigation of all possible opportunities that might be suitable for you. If you already have a concept of what you want to do, you will still need to do a great deal of investigating to make sure it is as good an opportunity as it appears to be. In either case, a lot of initial research and footwork is going to be advisable, unless you want to close your eyes and indulge in wishful thinking. As the Canadian study mentioned earlier in this chapter indicated, most of the successful new ventures they surveyed had gotten started only after six to ten months of careful investigation and planning.

Determining Market Feasibility

In other words, to quote a well-known brokerage firm, "Investigate before you invest." What this often entails is doing your own marketing feasibility study before you commit yourself to opening a new business. On the other hand, if you have several thousand dollars to spend, you can hire a professional economist or marketing consultant to do a feasibility study if you have a well-defined idea of what it is you want to do. In almost any major city, there are a number of such firms that can do a thorough marketing and demographic study for you. Such a feasibility study can be quite valuable, but will also be fairly expensive. Most people starting a new business will probably prefer to do their own marketing feasibility study.

A couple of key points should be borne in mind in choosing a business to go into:

- If you see that a particular business is doing quite well and you want to go in and compete head-to-head with them, don't make the mistake of adopting a me-too approach and going in with the assumption that you can take away a lot of their business by competing on a price basis. You had better have a lot of good reasons other than price why you think their customers will switch over to you, such as a distinctly better product, better service, more convenient location or the like.

- Keep your eyes open for developing social, economic, and technological trends that will create new markets that you can move into at an early stage. It will help if you are a voracious reader of magazines such as *Time*, *Newsweek* (social trends), *Forbes*, *Business Week* (economic trends), *Omni* or *Discover* (technological innovations). An example of how observation of social trends can translate into profits — in this case stock market profits — is the case of an investment analyst in the sixties who noticed the trend toward mini-skirts, correctly anticipated that the spread of mini-skirts among women would create a boom market for panty hose and made a killing by buying stocks of panty hose makers. A more cynical — and probably spurious — example, again from the investment world, is the story of a group of investment analysts who were discussing over lunch a recent report that heroin addiction was increasing by 30% a year in the United States One quick-thinking analyst immediately asked the others, "Who makes the hypodermic needles?"

So how do you go about analyzing the market for your product or service once you have focused on a particular business you might want to start into? Worksheet 2 (on the next page) will be of help to you in pinpointing the kind of information you need to develop to satisfy yourself that a good market exists for whatever it is you are planning to sell. Take out a pencil and paper now and spend some time writing down your responses to each of the items in Worksheet 2, before you read any further.

Market Data Resources

Once you have identified who your potential customers are most likely to be, you will need to find out how to locate your business or structure and to direct your advertising and promotional efforts to most efficiently reach them. Fortunately, there is a great deal of published data you can use if you need to do this type of research.

One of the best is *Sales Marketing and Management Magazine*, which publishes *Survey of Buying Power* each year, giving breakdowns as to population, households, retail sales by type of business, and total purchasing dollars for each county in the United States, and for cities of more than 10,000 population.

Another excellent source is the 1990 U.S. census data, which gives vast amounts of detailed information on the U.S. population and its buying habits by individual census tract. You may want to obtain a couple of useful pamphlets from your nearest U.S. Small Business Administration field office. Ask for the pamphlet entitled *Researching Your Market* for guidance on how to do your own marketing research and the pamphlet entitled *Choosing a Retail Location.*

Finding the Optimum Site

Even more important in your local community may be studies and future projections as to population and income trends that have been done by local groups such as your local chamber of commerce or, in some areas, the local planning commission. If finding the optimum site to locate is important to your marketing effort, do the following:

- Talk to a knowledgeable person at your local chamber of commerce about business and other trends in the area where you intend to locate.
- Talk to a staff person at your local planning commission about census tract projections of future population growth, income trends, and economic development in the area you are considering. Also, they (or some other local agency, such as a traffic or streets department) will usually have done traffic counts showing how many cars pass certain points every day, which can be very useful if you are opening a retail business. Also, consult any trade association serving your business, which may have available information tailored exactly to your needs in some cases.

Worksheet 2
Marketing Feasibility Study Checklist for Your Product or Service

---

Your Product

Describe briefly the nature of the product or service you will offer. _____
_____
_____

Most products or services have a life cycle, beginning with very rapid growth in the introductory stage, which slows down in the maturity stage, flattens out in the saturation stage, and finally begins shrinking in the declining stage. Which stage of its market cycle do you believe your product or service is in?

☐ introductory (high growth)　　　☐ saturation (little or no growth)
☐ maturity (slower growth)　　　　☐ declining (negative growth in demand)

If you believe your product is in one of the earlier, faster growing stages of its life cycle, what edge do you believe your product will have over similar products that may be introduced by new competitors who may come into the field? ____
_____
_____

If you are entering at a fairly late stage of the product marketing cycle, why is it you believe that you can succeed in taking away others' market share with your product? _____
_____
_____

How is your product differentiated from what is already on the market, in terms of quality and price? _____
_____
_____

Is there good reason to believe that your customers will recognize the difference? _____ If so, why? _____
_____
_____

What is different about your marketing strategy or distribution strategy that will enable your product or service to succeed in a market where there is little, if any, growth? _____
_____
_____

Your Customers

Not everyone is a potential customer. Certain age groups, income levels, geographic areas, ethnic groups, and educational levels will be more likely than others to be your customers. You need to focus on who will need your product and be most likely to buy it and then where to locate your business or how to structure your marketing approach to reach those segments of the market that you are most interested in reaching. Spell out below, as clearly as you can, who your customers are most likely to be.

The particular area from which I will be able to draw most of my customers is: _____
_____
_____

In addition, I should draw a significant number of customers from the following area or areas: _____
_____
_____

My plan or strategy for reaching potential customers in the above areas can be summarized as follows: _____
_____
_____

The chief market for my product, in terms of age and sex groups, should be among the following persons (describe):
_____
_____
_____

In terms of income groups, my particular product should appeal primarily to people in the following income levels:

☐ Under $25,000 a year household income

☐ $25,000 – $35,000 a year

(Continued: over)

(Continued)

☐ $35,000 – $50,000 a year

☐ $50,000 – $75,000 a year

☐ $75,000 – $100,000 a year

☐ More than $100,000 a year

My product or service is likely to be more in demand by certain social, cultural, and ethnic groups than others. The groups that are most likely to be customers, if any, are: _____

_____

_____

The groups that are least likely to be customers are: _____

_____

_____

Your Competition

Even though you may have done a great job in pinpointing and studying your market segment, the job isn't done until you have considered your competition.

My main competitors in my market area are (list firms by name):

(1) _____

(2) _____

(3) _____

(4) _____

(5) _____

(6) _____

Based on my market research of statistical data, such as *Sales Management Magazine*, the amount of buying power per business represented in my area for this kind of business is $_____.

If I can generate that amount of sales, it: will ☐, will not ☐, be sufficient for me to operate successfully.

Five reasons why customers would buy from me rather than my competitors are:

(1) _____

(2) _____

(3) _____

(4) _____

(5) _____

Five weaknesses my business will have, in comparison to my competitors, are:

(1) _____

(2) _____

(3) _____

(4) _____

(5) _____

In order to overcome these weaknesses, I will: _____

_____

_____

1.5 Knowing the Business

Do you have any experience in the area of business in which you will be engaged? Of course it is possible to learn while doing, but it helps a great deal to know the business before you start. Often the most successful businesses are started by people who have worked in a particular line of business for years for someone else, and who finally decide that they know the ropes well enough to leave their employer and start their own similar operation. It helps to have experience in the particular business you propose to enter, but in most cases, your experience working in some other line of business will also have considerable carryover value. If you have neither type of experience, you may find that you have a lot to learn once you commence.

As we have noted already, one of the major management weaknesses that causes business to fail is a lack of technical ability, that is, an inability to get the job done, do it right, on time, and efficiently enough to charge a competitive price for your product or service and still make a profit. For example, you may have done a lot of market research and decided that, with the tremendous proliferation of personal computers, a great business to go into is repairing small computers. You may be absolutely right, but unless you have the technical capability to do such repairs, or the ability to properly select and hire employees who can do the job, you had better look for some other kind of business to go into.

In many cases, if you know you lack the technical experience you need to open a particular kind of business, your best approach will be to get a job in that industry and work for someone else a few years until you learn what you need to know. This may require a lot of patience, but is definitely preferable to getting into a business you do not know well and losing your shirt in the process.

Worksheet 3
Estimated Cash Inflow From Sales for Year _____

Item: Month:					
Gross Sales for Month					
Less: Credit Sales Made					
Sub-total: Cash Sales					
Plus: Collections on Prior Credit Sales					
Less: Bad Debts*					
Total: Net Cash Flow from Monthly Sales					

* Consider using some percentage, say 1% or 2% of credit sale collections, to estimate your uncollectible debts.

1.6 Money

Can you afford to start a full-time business, if it will mean giving up your current employment and income? Many small businesses never really have a chance to succeed, because the owners run out of money before the business becomes a viable operation. As a result, the owners often wind up having to go back to work for someone else again, disappointed and broke.

As in politics, money is the mother's milk of business. You should carefully calculate and schedule out, in as much detail as possible, the income and expenses that you can reasonably expect for at least the first year of operation, as well as your living expenses and a reserve for emergencies.

Important Note!

Be sure that you have enough money to last until the business reaches the point where you expect to make enough profit to live on.

Remember that there are a lot of expenses involved in starting up almost any kind of business, and that most businesses start out operating in the red for a time.

Completing Worksheets 3 through 5 will help you plan out your cash flow for the crucial first year of business. Worksheet 3 will help you to project your sales revenue, in terms of actual cash to be received, for each month. Worksheet 4 is for projecting your operating expenses each month for the first year of business, plus one-time start-up expenses. Worksheet 5 is a schedule of your estimated personal living expenses during that first year.

Once you have completed Worksheets 3 through 5, enter the bottomline figures from each on Worksheet 6, which is a summary of your cash

							Annual Totals

needs that will show you how much cash you will have to put into the business each month — and on a cumulative basis — during the first year of business. Once you have completed Worksheet 6, you should have a pretty good handle on how much money it's going to take you to get the business started and approximately when you will need it.

If, under your most realistic projections, you are still running a deficit in cash flow each month at the end of the first year, you may want to do a similar projection out into the second year of operation.

If it appears that you will need to borrow or otherwise raise money to keep the business operating until it gets into the black, the time to find out whether (and how much) you will be able to raise is well in advance and not when you have almost run out of funds. If you plan to borrow, do you know how to put together a strong presentation to demonstrate to the prospective lender how you will be able to repay the loan? If not, see Chapter 10 for sources of information and help in obtaining financing for a small business and in putting together an impressive loan application package.

Note for Computer Owners!

PSI Successful Business Software has developed affordable and easy-to-use software programs, perfect for small businesses. Many of the programs, such as *Financial Templates for Small Business* or *Small Business Expert*, go hand-in-hand with this *Starting and Operating a Business* book. For more information, contact your book source or call The Oasis Press, (800) 228-2275.

Worksheet 4
Estimated Cash Flow from Sales for Year _____

Item: Month:					
Monthly Expenses					
Rent					
Salaries and wages (except owner)					
Payroll taxes					
Advertising and promotion					
Insurance					
Federal estimated income tax					
State estimated income tax					
Owner's FICA or SE tax					
Telephone and utilities					
Inventory replacement purchase					
Interest on loans					
Maintenance					
Legal and accounting fees					
Office supplies					
Delivery expense					
Miscellaneous					
One-time Expenses					
Fixtures and equipment					
Decorating and remodeling					
Initial stock of inventory					
Utility and lease deposits					
Licenses and permits					
Other					
Total Expenses for Month					
Plus: Loan principal payment					
Less: Purchases on credit					
Plus: Payment on prior credit					
Net Monthly Cash Outlay					

							Annual Totals

Worksheet 5
Estimated Personal and Living Expenses for Year _____

Item: Month:					
Regular Payments					
Rent or house payment					
Property taxes					
Condo owner's dues					
Car payments					
Furniture and appliance payments					
Loan payments					
Health insurance					
Other insurance					
Household Expenses					
Food — restaurants					
Food — at home					
Telephone and utilities					
Water					
Personal Expenses					
Clothing and laundry					
Medical, dental, and drugs					
Education					
Dues and subscriptions					
Gifts and charity					
Gasoline and auto					
Entertainment and travel					
Miscellaneous spending					
Total Personal Expenses (Draw required)					

							Annual Totals

Worksheet 6
Summary of Estimated Cash Requirements for Year _____

Item: Month:					
Net cash for month from sales - Worksheet 3					
Less: Net monthly cash outlay - Worksheet 4					
Subtotal: Net operating cash flow (or deficit)					
Less: Owner's draw for living & personal expenses - Worksheet 5					
Add: Money borrowed					
Add (or subtract): Equity capital paid in (or withdrawn) from the business					
Total: Net cash flow (or deficit) for month					
Cumulative* cash flow (or deficit)					

* Add this month's net cash flow to the previous month's cumulative total.

1.7 Signing a Lease

If you will need to lease space to operate your business in, have you located a suitable place that is available? If so, there are a number of critical points you need to consider before you sign a lease with the landlord.

Remember that a lease is a binding legal contract, and that if you agree to pay rent of $1,000 a month for two years, you are on the hook for $24,000, unless you can sublease or assign the lease to someone else, which the lease, or the landlord, may make difficult or impossible to do. Key points to consider include:

- What are the terms of the lease? Most businesses tend to start off by either growing rapidly or quickly folding. Thus, except in a retail or service business, you will probably be better off leasing initially on a month-to-month basis or for as short a lease term as you can get, such as three or six months, even if the monthly rent is higher than for a longer lease. You will already have enough financial problems if your business fails, without being saddled with a long-term lease obligation.
- Can you put up the kind of sign you must have, as large as you need, on the building? A business like a restaurant can be devastated if the landlord doesn't permit a sign that is sufficiently visible to passersby.
- Will the landlord permit you to make necessary improvements and alterations to the leased premises?

							Annual Totals

- Will the local health department, fire and police departments, air pollution control authorities, and zoning rules permit operation of your particular type of business at the location you have chosen?
- Is your location in a high-crime area that will require expensive burglary insurance and security precautions?
- Is there is enough parking nearby or good public transit access for customers?
- Is the location appropriate to the kind of business you will conduct? There is usually no need to locate a manufacturing operation in a busy, high-traffic area. On the other hand, retail businesses are usually heavily dependent on the number of people passing nearby on foot or by car. For example, the Pillsbury Company reportedly selects its sites for Burger King fast food restaurants by looking for locations that have at least 16,000 cars passing by each day at an average speed of about 30 miles per hour.[4]
- Does the lease provides you an option to renew — and at what rental price? — after the initial term expires?
- If the lease is for more than just a few months, do you have the right to sublease or assign the lease? If so, under what conditions or restrictions?

1.8 Will You Hire Employees?

In the initial start-up phases, and perhaps even afterwards, at least in certain kinds of businesses, you may be able to operate without employees, either doing all your work yourself, or perhaps with the help of family members, or contracting out certain functions to independent outside contractors. To the extent you can do so, you will probably find your life is much simpler. Once you hire even one employee, you will learn that you have a great many responsibilities as an employer, over and above meeting a payroll every week or two.

In this section, we will review some of the legal restrictions on your hiring practices and provide you with a working outline of what you will need to consider in the way of personnel policy, once your business reaches the point where you will have to hire employees, which may be immediately. See Section 5.9, regarding new U.S. Immigration Law restrictions on hiring.

Hiring Practices

The whole area of hiring people is an extremely touchy one in our society, and there are a broad array of state and federal laws designed to prevent the employer from hiring on the basis of discriminatory factors, such as age, sex, race, religion, or other factors that are considered irrelevant. Most of these laws affect all but the smallest employers, so you will have to be alert to most of these rules to avoid even the appearance of discrimination in your hiring practices. While these anti-discrimination rules apply to promotions, job assignments, firing, and other aspects of the employment relationship as well as to hiring, we will focus here mainly on hiring practices. That is the area where most small business owners are likely to stumble into trouble, even when they have no intention to discriminate.

Things Not to Do

There are many things you must be very cautious to avoid in your process of hiring people. All questions or information you put out should relate to job qualifications only, and not to extraneous factors such as age, race, sex, or physical size or condition. If there are special occupational requirements — for example, hard physical labor that might preclude hiring certain handicapped individuals — be sure to carefully document such unusual situations or requirements.

In "Help Wanted" Ads

Use the lists below to guide your company's interaction concerning prospective employees.

- Do not mention race or national origin in your ads, or any attribute of national origin, such as native language.
- Do not refer to sex classifications in your ads, such as "girl wanted."
- Avoid any type of reference to age, such as "young boy" or "recent high school graduate."

SAMPLE EMPLOYMENT APPLICATION FORM

Employment Application

Personal Data

Name: _____
           (last)   (first)   (middle)

Present address: _____
                        (street address)   (city)   (state)   (zip)

Telephone numbers: _____ _____
                             (home)   (work)

Education

High School: _____ Graduated? Yes ☐ No ☐ Location: _____

College or University: _____ Graduated? Yes ☐ No ☐ Degree(s): _____

_____ _____

Other (specify type): _____ Graduated? Yes ☐ No ☐ Certificate(s): _____

_____ Graduated? Yes ☐ No ☐ Certificate(s): _____

Work Experience

List below all present and previous employment, starting with the most recent.

Company name: _____ From (mo/yr): _____ Type of work: _____

Address: _____ To (mo/yr): _____ Name of Supervisor: _____

_____ Reason you left: _____

Company name: _____ From (mo/yr): _____ Type of work: _____

Address: _____ To (mo/yr): _____ Name of Supervisor: _____

_____ Reason you left: _____

Company name: _____ From (mo/yr): _____ Type of work: _____

Address: _____ To (mo/yr): _____ Name of Supervisor: _____

_____ Reason you left: _____

Company name: _____ From (mo/yr): _____ Type of work: _____

Address: _____ To (mo/yr): _____ Name of Supervisor: _____

_____ Reason you left: _____

May we contact the employers above? Yes ☐ No ☐ If yes, list any employers you do not wish us to contact:

_____

Remarks: _____

_____

_____

Applicant's Signature: _____ Date _____ , 19__

On Job Application Forms

Your employment application forms (see sample on previous page) should avoid any of the following kinds of questions:

- Arrest record;
- Whether the applicant has ever filed for unemployment benefits;
- Place of birth or where parents were born;
- Physical characteristics, such as height or weight;
- Social Security number;
- Marital status;
- Labor union affiliation;
- Request for photograph;
- Religious affiliation;
- Mode of transportation to work;
- Sex;
- Race or national origin;
- Clubs or organizations, unless you instruct the applicant not to list organizations that indicate race or national origin;
- Native language or how applicant learned a foreign language?

In Employment Interviews

Refrain from asking questions, such as:

- Whether applicant is a U.S. citizen;
- When the applicant attended grade school, high school, or college;
- Whether the applicant has children, and who will care for them while the applicant is working;
- Existence of any physical handicap;
- What applicant's spouse does, whether they are likely to move elsewhere;
- Whether applicant's religion would prevent him or her from working on holidays or certain days of week?

Note that federal law now generally bans the use of any kind of lie detector tests in most private employment situations, except for drug manufacturers and distributors and security firms.[5] State laws are even more stringent in many states.

In addition, questions on possible felony convictions, previous military service, and drug or alcohol addiction are not necessarily illegal in all cases but may entail difficulties and probably should be avoided, as a general rule.

When Checking References

You should note, as a general rule, that former employers have no legal obligation to give you any information about a former employee. As a practical matter, however, most former employers will at least verify the former employee's employment and the date of employment. Since a former employer can get into trouble for giving you negative information that they cannot substantiate, don't expect them to volunteer much information or to put anything negative in writing. For that reason, you should generally do reference checks by phone. Acceptable questions would include the following:

- Verifying information given by the applicant;
- Asking about applicant's principal strong points, weak points, and degree of supervision needed;
- Asking about applicant's attitude;
- Asking how applicant's performance compared with others;
- Asking if the applicant would be rehired.

This section includes a sample employment application (on a previous page) you may use. If you wish to add additional questions to it, be careful not to indirectly request anything that would reflect on the applicant's race, religion, sex, age, marital status, national origin, or physical condition. Because state laws differ, check with your legal adviser or state employment department before preparing your employment application.

Personnel Policies

Even before you hire your first employee for your business, you will need to have outlined in your own mind some basic personnel policies. Better yet, if you write down your policies on matters such as hours, vacation time, and sick leave and can give such a written summary to new employees, it will greatly help to clarify the employment relationship. Perhaps it will even prevent a misunderstanding that could lead to legal action against you by an employee.

Worksheet 7 provides a series of questions that will help you to focus on different personnel policies that are typical in a small- to medium-sized business. For a more thorough treatment of this area, if you wish to develop a personnel policies manual for your business, you may want to obtain a copy of *A Company Policy and Personnel Workbook* (The Oasis Press, 1989).

Related Information

This book contains several other sections that you may want to read now, in conjunction with this section on hiring employees. These following sections will help you to better place this section in perspective:

- Employee or Independent Contractor? – Section 9.11
- Fair Employment Practices – Section 5.8
- Immigration Law Restrictions on Hiring – Section 5.9
- Hiring Your Spouse as an Employee – Section 8.12
- Employee Wage & Hour and Child Labor Laws – Section 5.7

In addition, you should at least scan through the rest of Chapter 5 right now, to get an overview of other legal obligations that come with the territory when you have employees.

Worksheet 7
Defining Your Company's Personnel Policies

Working Hours

Describe briefly the policy you will set for working hours, including:

Starting time? _____

_____

How much time will be allowed for lunch? _____

_____

Quitting time? _____

_____

Which days of the week employees will be expected to work? _____

_____

If, like many companies these days, you want to adopt some kind of "flex-time" system, spell out how that will work.

_____

_____

_____

Overtime

Outline your policy on overtime work. Refer to Section 5.7 of this book for legal requirements for paying overtime premiums. See also Section 11.5 regarding state wage laws. Points to consider here include:

Will you pay exempt employees (administrative or professional) overtime if they work extra hours? _____

_____

Will you require employees to obtain permission to work overtime? _____

_____

Compensation

Make a list of the job positions in the company other than your own and the compensation level for each. On a separate piece of paper, write out a specific job description for each position, outlining duties and responsibilities. Refer to Sections 5.7 and 11.5 of this book for a description of hourly minimum wage requirements.

Position	Hourly wage	Salary	Total monthly pay
_____	_____	_____	_____
_____	_____	_____	_____
_____	_____	_____	_____
_____	_____	_____	_____
_____	_____	_____	_____
_____	_____	_____	_____
_____	_____	_____	_____
_____	_____	_____	_____

Vacation Policy

Describe how much paid vacation employees will have and how this may increase after a certain number of years of service. _____

_____

Will vacation time and sick leave time off be combined into a single category for employees (as some companies now do to reward employees who do not abuse sick leave and to discourage others from using sick leave as additional vacation by playing hooky)? _____

_____

Will you pay employees who terminate for unused vacation? (The laws of many states require you to do so.) _____

_____

Sick Leave Policy

Outline your policy for both paid sick leave and unpaid sick leave, or whichever you choose to provide, if not both. (Note: Sick pay is no longer exempt from FICA tax, in general.)[6]

Sick leave _____

_____

Unpaid sick leave _____

_____

Leaves of Absence

What will your policy be towards employees who request unpaid leaves of absence? _____

_____

Time Off with Pay

Will you provide other time off with pay for such eventualities as funerals or emergencies in an employee's immediate family?

Funerals or family emergencies? _____

_____

Jury duty? _____

_____

Birth of a child? _____

_____

Promotions and Evaluations

Outline your policy for evaluating employees' performance and determining when promotions will be made. _____

_____

_____

_____

_____

_____

Fringe Benefits

Consider which of the following employee fringe benefits you will provide and indicate in specific terms what your policy will be for each that is to be provided.

Medical Insurance: _____

_____

Long-term Disability Insurance: _____

_____

Life Insurance: _____

_____

Dental Insurance: _____

_____

Medical Expense Reimbursement: _____

_____

Child Care Benefits: _____

_____

Maternity Benefits: _____

_____

Pension or Profit-Sharing Plans: _____

_____

Paid Holidays: _____

_____

Automobiles or Allowances: _____

_____

Expense Accounts: _____

_____

Employee Discounts on Purchases: _____

_____

Stock Options (if incorporated): _____

_____

Incentive Bonus Plan: _____

_____

Placement Fees

If you hire employees through a personnel agency or "headhunting" firm, will you pay the placement fee?_____

_____

1.9 Other Questions You Need to Ask

- Will you advertise? Should you? If you do, you need to decide what kind of advertising will be the most cost-effective for your business, whether it be newspaper ads, direct mail, radio, posters, handbills, or other forms of advertising and promotion.

- Do you understand what will be involved in purchasing, managing, and restocking your inventory of goods?

- How will you go about selling? Will you hire sales clerks or outside salespeople, or will you do most of the selling yourself?

- Will you sell to customers on credit? If so, how will you protect yourself from bad credit risks and outright deadbeats?

- How much of your personal savings are you putting at risk by going into business? Are you willing to risk losing all of it if the business is a failure?

- Can you run the business alone — or with help from family members — or would you do better with one or more partners or business associates to provide additional capital and skills and to divide up some of the responsibilities of running the business?

The hard questions posed in this chapter are not intended to discourage you from going ahead with starting the business you are considering. Chances are, you have already considered most of the points raised in this chapter, and are reasonably confident that you will be able to do what is necessary to make your business work. If so, many of the questions raised above probably seem rather elementary and obvious to you as they will to most individuals seriously considering going into business, and you will now want to proceed to the more substantive discussion in the remainder of this book.

If you have not previously given serious thought to most of the above points that are relevant to the type of business you are planning to start, now is the time to take a long, hard look at whether you are adequately prepared to embark upon such a venture.

Footnotes

1. Cook, *Women: The Best Entrepreneurs*, CANADIAN BUSINESS (June, 1982). Reproduced with permission.
2. *The State of Small Business, A Report of the President*, Wash. D.C. Superintendent of Documents (1989).
3. Phillips and Kirchoff, *Analysis of New Firm Survival and Growth*, J. SMALL BUS. ECON. (Winter 1989).
4. San Francisco Chronicle, Aug. 3, 1980.
5. The Employee Polygraph Protection Act, 29 U.S.C. 2001, *et seq.*
6. Internal Revenue Code (I.R.C.) § 3121 (a)(4).

Chapter 2

Choosing the Legal Form of the Business

"The hardest thing in the world to understand is Income Tax."

— Albert Einstein

2.1 General Considerations

There are many ways in which a business venture can be structured;
however, the law classifies businesses so that most fall into one of three
legal forms — the sole proprietorship, the partnership, or the corporation.
As we shall see, there are also certain variations on some of these basic
legal forms of doing business.

The person who is planning to start a business should be actively considering the following kinds of questions in deciding upon the legal form
under which the business will operate.

- Will someone else share in ownership of the business? If so, it will not
  be a sole proprietorship. Thus, the choice will be between a partnership
  arrangement and a corporation.

- How important is it to be able to limit personal liability for debts or
  claims against the business? If this is a major consideration,
  incorporating the business would generally be the best means of
  limiting your liability.

- Which form of business organization will result in the least taxes?
  While there is no universal answer to this question, the rest of this
  chapter explains the types of circumstances in which it will generally
  be more beneficial to incorporate and when it will save more taxes not
  to be incorporated.

- What legal form of business will be the simplest and least expensive to establish and maintain? A sole proprietorship is generally the simplest, least regulated form of business, and can usually be initiated without any formalities. If you simply start doing business without a partner, the law will classify your business as a sole proprietorship. You do not need a lawyer or approval of any government agency to create a sole proprietorship.

A partnership can also be started with a minimum of formalities. A partnership need not be more than a handshake agreement with your business partner, but it is generally advisable to have a written partnership agreement defining your respective rights and responsibilities, and that usually means incurring fairly significant legal fees. A limited partnership, in which the liability of one or more of the partners is limited, is much more involved, as discussed in Section 2.3 of this chapter.

Of the three basic categories, the corporation is the most formalized and regulated form of business entity, and, therefore, the costs of establishing and maintaining the legal status of a corporation are generally greater than for a sole proprietorship or partnership.

How difficult is it to change from one legal form to another? As a broad generalization, it is usually a simpler matter to change from a sole proprietorship to a partnership, or to change from a sole proprietorship or partnership to a corporation, than it is to move in the opposite direction. For example, converting a business that is operated as a corporation into a sole proprietorship or partnership may result in substantial individual and corporate-level taxes when the corporation is liquidated. This would happen if the value of the business transferred to the owners of the stock of the corporation were greater than their cost or tax basis for such stock or if any corporate assets have values in excess of their tax basis. While there are almost always some expenses and complications in changing the legal form in which a business is carried on, such changes are quite routine transactions. Many businesses start off as sole proprietorships, develop into partnerships and later incorporate, if tax and other considerations indicate that it no longer makes good business sense not to be incorporated. Thus, the choice of one legal form when starting a business should not be considered a final choice.

2.2 Advantages and Disadvantages of Sole Proprietorships

The great advantage of operating a new business as a sole proprietorship is that it is simple and does not require any formal action to set it up. You can start your business today as a sole proprietorship — there is no need to wait for an attorney to draft and file documents or for the government to approve them. Of course, you will need a business license — and a few states require even a sole proprietor to register to do business. A sole proprietor is the sole owner of his or her business. If married, however, one's spouse will usually have a one-half interest in the business in a state which has community property laws.

As the owner of the business, the sole proprietor will be personally liable for any debts or taxes of the business or other claims, such as legal damages resulting from a lawsuit. This is one reason why many entrepreneurs who have substantial wealth that could be lost if their business were to fail prefer to use a corporation rather than a sole proprietorship. Unlimited personal liability is perhaps the major disadvantage of operating a business in the form of a sole proprietorship.

Personal Liability

All of the profit or loss from a sole proprietor's business belongs to the owner and must be reported on the owner's income tax return, usually on *Schedule C, Income (or Loss) from a Business or Profession,* of *Form 1040.* This can either be an advantage or a disadvantage for income tax purposes, depending on the circumstances. If operating the business results in losses or significant tax credits, the sole proprietor may be able to use the tax losses or tax credits to reduce taxes on income from other sources. Or, if the sole proprietorship generates modest profits for the owner, but not more than about $60,000 to $75,000 a year, overall taxes may be less than if incorporated, assuming the owner needs most of the income to live on.

As a general rule of thumb, however, once a business begins to generate more than about $75,000 a year in taxable income to the sole proprietor (or to each partner in a partnership), this author generally counsels clients to strongly consider incorporating in order to reduce taxes, among other reasons, provided that the business would not be a "personal service corporation."

When to Consider Incorporating

There are several reasons why a sole proprietorship may become disadvantageous tax-wise if the business becomes highly profitable. One reason is that all of the income of a sole proprietorship is taxed to the owner, which may push the owner into high tax brackets; however, after the Tax Reform Act of 1986 and the Omnibus Budget Reconciliation Act of 1987 (OBRA), a sole proprietorship is now less likely to become disadvantageous as compared to a corporation on account of tax rates. For one thing, the highest corporate tax rate for 1991 is 34% (39% on income between $100,000 and $335,000), which is higher than the maximum nominal individual tax rate of 31%. Thus, corporate tax rates are no longer lower than individual rates, except that the first $50,000 of corporate income is taxed at only a 15% rate and the next $25,000 at 25%. If a corporation (not an S corporation), however, is considered to be a personal service corporation, such as a medical or law firm, all of its taxable income is taxed at a flat rate of 34%, for tax years beginning after 1987.[1]

**Splitting Income
With Your Corporation**

By using a corporation, it may be possible to split the overall profit between two or more taxpayers, so that none of the income gets taxed in the highest brackets. For example, with an overall economic profit of $100,000, an incorporated business may be able to reduce its taxable income to $50,000 by paying (and deducting) a $50,000 salary to its owner, as an officer–employee of the corporation. The corporation would pay tax only on the remaining $50,000 profit, at a maximum federal tax rate of only 15%, while the owner would pay tax on the $50,000 salary received. Because of the progressive tax rate structure under the federal income tax laws, the tax on the $100,000 income divided between the owner and his or her corporation would typically be much less than if the whole $100,000 were taxable to the owner. In 1991, for example, a single individual would pay $26,876 in federal income taxes on $100,000 of taxable income, while if the income were split evenly between the owner and his or her corporation, the corporation's tax would be $7,500 and the owner's $11,376, a saving of $8,000 — assuming the corporation is not a personal services corporation subject to a 34% flat rate of tax.

**Splitting Income Among
Family Members**

Another way to split the income of a business between multiple taxpayers is for the owner to make his or her children part owners of the business. (Ideally, the children should be given an interest in the business when it is started, since the value of the gifts to them will often be minimal for gift tax purposes at that time.) This sharing of ownership with family members can sometimes be done with a sole proprietorship, by converting it into a family partnership where the children — even if they do not work in the business — share in the profits of the business.

As you may have already guessed, the Internal Revenue Service (IRS) will generally take a dim view of such a family partnership and may seek to tax all the income to the parents, if they are the ones carrying on the business.[2] In certain cases, where much of the income of the business is generated by large investments of capital, rather than the services of the parents, such a family partnership may succeed in effectively splitting the business' income among several family members; however, such an arrangement should not be attempted without consulting a competent tax adviser. By contrast, it is frequently more feasible to split the income of a corporation with the owner's children, by giving them some of the stock of the corporation. This approach, however, will work only if the corporation has filed an election on *Form 2553* with the IRS to be taxed as an S corporation (formerly called a Subchapter S corporation). As is discussed later in this chapter, the taxable income of a corporation that qualifies as an S corporation is taxable to its shareholders — in proportion to the stock they own in the corporation — and is generally not taxed to the corporation. By giving a number of shares of stock in such an S corporation to one or more of the owner's children, part of the taxable income of the business can often be shifted to the children[3] and taxed at their low tax brackets — assuming, as is usually the case, that the children do not have a lot of taxable income from other sources.

Under the Tax Reform Act of 1986, shifting significant income to one's children will not work if the children are under 14 years of age.[4]

Caution!

As a sole proprietor, you are not considered to be an employee of your business. As a result, you will avoid having to pay unemployment taxes on your earnings from the business.

Both the state and the federal governments impose unemployment taxes on wages or salaries but not on self-employment income. For 1991, the federal unemployment tax rate is effectively 0.8%[5] of the first $7,000[6] of wages paid each employee ($56 maximum per employee). Refer to Section 11.2 regarding the state unemployment taxes you must pay for each employee. As a sole proprietor, your income would not be subject to either of these taxes. Note that a corporation would normally get an income tax deduction for the unemployment tax it paid on your salary, so that the actual after-tax savings from operating as a sole proprietorship would be somewhat less than the unemployment taxes you would avoid paying.

Unemployment Taxes

Another advantage of a sole proprietorship is that you can shift funds in and out of your business account or withdraw assets from the business with few tax, legal, or other limitations. In a partnership, you can generally withdraw funds only by agreement and, in the case of a corporation, a withdrawal of funds or property will usually be taxable as a dividend or capital gain and may violate the state's corporation laws in some instances.

A major disadvantage of sole proprietorships and partnerships is that they cannot obtain a number of significant tax benefits regarding group term life insurance benefits, long-term disability insurance coverage, and medical insurance or medical expense reimbursements. Corporate retirement plans still offer some advantages over Keogh retirement plans for self-employed persons, but most of the major differences were eliminated as of the beginning of 1984. To qualify for favorable tax treatment in connection with such fringe benefit plans, it is necessary to incorporate. This important subject is discussed in more detail in Chapter 8.

Limited Tax Savings for Fringe Benefits

As we shall later see in this chapter, one of the most important reasons for incorporating in the past, the special advantages of corporate pension and profit-sharing plans, have largely been eliminated, starting in 1984. As of now, there are virtually no differences in the tax treatment of self-employed (Keogh) plans of sole proprietorships and partnerships, as compared with corporate retirement plans.

See the table at the end of this chapter summarizing the key characteristics of sole proprietorships, partnerships, and corporations.

2.3 Advantages and Disadvantages of Partnerships

A business partnership is much like a sole proprietorship in many respects, except that it has two or more owners. Creating a partnership can be a very simple matter, since the law does not require any formal written documents or other formalities for most partnerships. As a practical matter, however, it is much sounder business practice for partners in a business to have a written partnership agreement that, at a minimum, spells out their agreement on such basic issues as:

- How much and what kind of property each partner will contribute to the venture;
- What value will be placed on the contributed property;
- How profits and losses will be divided among the partners;
- When and how profits will be withdrawn;
- Whether or how certain partners will be compensated for their services to the partnership or for making capital available to the partnership; and
- How changes in ownership of interests in the partnership will be handled.

A written partnership agreement should be prepared by an attorney and, if possible, should be reviewed by a tax accountant before it is put into effect.

Partnerships are a bit like marriages — they usually start out with a great deal of trust and have a high break-up rate. And like marriages, it has been said, partnerships are easy to get into, require a lot of patience and understanding to live with, and are often costly and painful to get out of.

Liability of Partners

Each partner is an agent for the partnership and can do anything necessary to operate the business, such as hire employees, borrow money, or enter into contracts on behalf of the partnership. Each partner (except for a limited partner in a limited partnership, discussed below) has personal liability for the debts, taxes, and other claims against the partnership. If the partnership's assets are not sufficient to pay creditors, the creditors can satisfy their claims out of the individual partners' personal assets. In addition, when a partner fails to pay personal debts, the partnership's business may be disrupted if his or her creditors seek to satisfy their claims out of his or her interest in the partnership, by seeking what is called a charging order against partnership assets.

State and Federal Tax Requirements

While a partnership must file federal and usually state information returns (*Form 1065* is the federal form), it generally pays no income tax. Instead, it reports each partner's share of income or loss, tax credits, etc. on the information return, and each partner reports the income or loss on *Schedule E* of his or her individual tax return. However, 1987 tax legislation allowing partnerships and S corporations to elect to retain their fiscal tax year (rather than change to a calendar year, as the 1986 Tax Reform Act generally mandated), requires the partnership or S Corporation itself to report and pay a tax directly each year under an extremely complex formula — as long as there is a tax-deferral benefit to their partners or shareholders. This is the price for retaining a fiscal tax year.[7]

In addition, since 1985, partnerships have been required to file a special report with the IRS (*Form 8308*) regarding so-called hot assets each time a sale or exchange of an interest in the partnership occurs.[8] See Section 11.2 regarding state tax return filing requirements for a partnership.

Like a sole proprietor, a partner is not generally considered an employee of the partnership for income tax and payroll tax purposes. The income tax advantages and disadvantages of a sole proprietorship, discussed in Section 2.2 of this chapter, are equally applicable to a partnership, since a partner's share of income from a partnership is treated essentially the same as income from a sole proprietorship. For example, a partner's income from a partnership may be subject to federal self-employment tax, but not to federal and state unemployment taxes, as is discussed in Section 2.2.

Unless a partnership agreement provides otherwise, a partnership usually terminates when any partner dies or withdraws from the partnership. This is in contrast to a corporation which, theoretically, has perpetual existence. Under the laws of most states, bankruptcy of a partner or the partnership itself will cause the dissolution of the partnership, regardless of any agreement.

Limited Partnerships

The law provides for a special kind of partnership, the limited partnership, in which the limited partners have limited personal liability. The limited partnership entity is more regulated than the common garden variety general partnership discussed above, but it allows investors who will not be actively involved in the partnership's operations to become partners without their being exposed to unlimited liability for the debts of the business if it goes under. The limited partner risks only his or her investment, but must allow one or more general partners to exercise control over the business. In fact, if the limited partner becomes involved in the partnership's operations, he or she may lose his or her protected status as a limited partner. The general partners in a limited partnership are fully liable for the partnership's debts. Every limited partnership must have one or more general partners as well as one or more limited partners.

State law requires certain formalities in the case of a limited partnership that are not required for other partnerships. To qualify for their special status, such partnerships must usually file a *Certificate of Limited Partnership* with the secretary of state or other state or county offices. Establishing a limited partnership also requires a written partnership agreement. See Section 11.2 regarding special filing requirements for partnerships under state law.

2.4 Advantages and Disadvantages of Incorporating

A corporation is an artificial legal entity that exists as a separate legal person apart from the people who own, manage, control, and operate it. It can make contracts, it pays taxes, and is liable for its debts. Corporations exist only because state statutory laws allow these entities to be created. A business corporation issues shares of its stock, as evidence of ownership, to the person or persons who contribute the money or business assets which the corporation will use to conduct its business. Thus, the persons who own the stock are the owners of the corporation, and they are entitled to any dividends the corporation pays and to receive all the corporation's assets (after all creditors have been paid) if the corporation is liquidated.

Limited Personal Liability

The main reason most businesses incorporate is to limit the personal liability of the owners for the debts, taxes, and other liabilities of the business to the amount they have invested in it. Generally, stockholders in a corporation are not personally liable for claims against the corporation and are, therefore, at risk only to the extent of their investment in the corporation. Likewise, the officers and directors of a corporation are not normally liable for the corporation's debts, although in some cases an officer whose duty it is to withhold federal income tax from employees' wages may be liable to the IRS if the taxes are not withheld and paid over to the IRS as required.

Problems with Thin Corporations

The advantage of limited liability is not always completely available through incorporation. For example, one must beware of starting a corporation on a shoestring. If a corporation is capitalized too thinly with equity capital (owner's money) as compared to debt capital (borrowed money), the courts may determine that it is a thin corporation and hold the shareholders directly liable to creditors. Failure to observe corporate formalities and the separate legal existence of the corporation can have a similar result. This is called "piercing the corporate veil by the courts," meaning that if a corporation is not adequately capitalized and properly operated to protect the interests of creditors, the courts will take away the veil of limited liability that normally protects the shareholders.

Piercing the corporate veil is relatively uncommon. A much more frequent problem is that many banks and other lenders will not loan money to a small incorporated business unless someone, usually the stockholders of the corporation, personally guarantees repayment of the loan. Despite this common business practice, the feature of limited liability can still be an important protection from personal liability for other debts, such as accounts payable to suppliers and others who sell goods or services to the corporation on credit, typically without requiring any personal guarantee of payment by the owners. Even this partial protection is a significant advantage of incorporating most small businesses. In addition, being incorporated can also protect you in many cases from personal liability from lawsuit damages not covered by your corporation's liability insurance policies if, for example, someone slips on a banana peel in your store and sues the corporation for $10 million.

Unlike a sole proprietorship or partnership, a corporation has continuous existence and does not terminate upon the death of a stockholder or a change of ownership of some or all of its stock. Creditors, suppliers, and customers often prefer to deal with an incorporated business because of this greater continuity of the enterprise that is provided by the corporate form. Naturally, like other forms of business organization, a corporation can be terminated by mutual consent of the owners or even by one shareholder in some instances.

To set up a corporation, the prospective stockholders must make application to the state office that grants corporate charters by filing articles of incorporation for approval. See Section 11.2 for a discussion of where to file in this state and for applicable fees and taxes payable upon incorporation.

Note: Set Up Is Costly

Legal fees usually run between $500 and $1,000, even for a simple incorporation, and if it is necessary to obtain a permit from the state to issue stock or securities, legal fees can be much more. Refer to Section 11.2 regarding any exemptions for small or closely-held corporations issuing stock in this state.

Thus, it should be apparent that one of the disadvantages of incorporating is the cost involved, which will be substantial even for the simplest incorporation. In addition to the costs of establishing a corporation, there will be recurring costs, often including annual franchise or corporate income taxes (see Section 11.2) and federal corporate income taxes.

Certain "qualified personal service corporations," generally those engaged in law, medicine, architecture, accounting, engineering, actuarial science, performing arts, or consulting, where substantially all the stock is owned by certain employees, are subject to a flat 34% tax rate[9] on all corporate taxable income for tax years beginning in 1988 or later.

Federal Corporate Income Taxes

Taxable Income	Tax Rate
Under $50,000	15% of taxable income
$50,000 to $75,000	25% of excess over $50,000
$75,000 to $100,000	34% of excess over $75,000
$100,000 to $335,000	39% of excess over $100,000
More than $335,000	34% of excess over $335,000

In addition, many corporate actions must or should be formalized by board of directors' resolutions or shareholders' meetings and must be recorded in written form in the corporate minute books, which takes valuable time — or money if the corporation's attorney assists with such corporate housekeeping. An out-of-state corporation usually must pay a qualification fee to qualify to transact business in the state. See Section 11.9 regarding qualification fees.

The owners who operate the business will usually draw salaries from the corporation, which will be subject to FICA (Social Security) taxes, and state and federal unemployment taxes, as is explained in Section 2.2 above. These unemployment taxes are not imposed on the owner's income from a sole proprietorship or partnership. FICA taxes, in 1990 and subsequent years, are generally the same (in total) on the wages of a corporate employee–owner as would be the self-employment tax on the same amount of business income if the owner were a sole proprietor or a partner in a partnership. For certain types of unincorporated businesses, however, such as a firm whose income is from interest or real estate rentals or both, there is no self-employment tax on the income, which could make not incorporating such a firm advantageous for tax purposes.

Double Taxation of Income Distributed to Shareholders

Another potential disadvantage of a corporation is the double taxation of its income that is distributed to its shareholders. If a corporation has taxable income, pays corporate income taxes on it, and the shareholders withdraw money in the form of a dividend, they will also pay tax on the dividend, as a rule. Thus, the use of a corporation can obviously be disadvantageous if it results in this double taxation of the business' income. Most incorporated small businesses, however, with good tax planning, can avoid double taxation and can instead often use the corporation to save taxes.

As was noted above, except for qualified personal service corporations, corporate tax rates now start at 15% on the first $50,000 of taxable income, and the total federal corporate income tax on $75,000 of taxable income is only $13,750 for a corporation, as compared to $19,126 for a single taxpayer or $16,580 for a married couple filing jointly (in 1991). Since double taxation occurs only if a corporation pays out money or property that is taxable as dividend to its stockholders, most small corporations never, or rarely, pay dividends. Instead, they retain the lightly-taxed profits in the business. This is ideal for a business that needs funds to invest in expansion of operations. Note, however, that the highest corporate tax rate is now higher than the maximum individual rate. Thus, many highly profitable businesses may be better off as S corporations or unincorporated.

Accumulated Earnings Tax

Even where the business does not need to retain the profits, the corporation can still safely accumulate up to $150,000 of after-tax profits over a period of years, which can be invested by it in stocks, bonds, real estate, etc., without fear of incurring an accumulated earnings tax.[10] This exemption is $250,000 for most businesses except that only a $150,000 exemption is allowed for certain incorporated professional service firms, such as physicians, lawyers, accountants, performing artists, architects, and consultants. Any accumulation of profits, however, in excess of $150,000 or $250,000 that is not needed for use in the business may be hit by the accumulated earnings tax, which is a penalty tax in additon to the regular corporate income tax.

The penalty tax is 28% of the improperly accumulated earnings, which are specially defined and not necessarily the same as net profits for accounting purposes or taxable income.[11] This penalty tax is designed to keep corporations from accumulating large amounts of profits at low corporate tax rates, unless they need to accumulate the profits to reinvest in their business. You should consult a tax adviser as to what constitutes a legitimate business purpose for your corporation to accumulate profits beyond the $150,000 or $250,000 exemption, since the law in this area is quite complex. The key point to remember is that under present law your corporation can generally accumulate up to $150,000 or $250,000 in profits without incurring an accumulated earnings tax. This can make it an excellent tax shelter.

Income-Splitting

As a separate taxpaying entity, a corporation can be used to split a given amount of business income between itself and its shareholder or shareholders. For example, take a corporation with only one stockholder, who is also its only employee. If the business of the corporation earns a $100,000 profit for the year, before salary, it could split the $100,000 between itself and the owner by paying $50,000 to the owner as salary (assuming that $50,000 was not an unreasonable salary), while the corporation would retain the remaining $50,000 of income and pay tax on it. Thus, neither the corporation nor the owner would be pushed into an excessively high tax bracket in the example given, and the savings could be substantial, as noted in Section 2.2.

Retirement Plans

For many years, corporations — except for S corporations — have had very significant tax advantages over unincorporated businesses with respect to pension and profit-sharing plans, primarily because much larger tax-deductible contributions could be made to corporate retirement plans on behalf of high-income individuals than to Keogh plans for partners or sole proprietors. In fact, the advantages of corporate retirement plans were a main reason why many high-income professional people and profitable small businesses incorporated in recent years. Since 1984, the main differences between corporate retirement plans and Keogh plans have been eliminated.

The Tax Equity and Fiscal Responsibility Act of 1982, known as TEFRA, cut back considerably on the tax advantages of corporate retirement plans, while at the same time liberalizing the tax rules for Keogh plans effective in 1984. The intention behind the TEFRA changes was to create parity between the two types of plans. In large measure, the TEFRA legislation did just that, although there are still a few, relatively minor advantages that corporate plans retain compared to Keogh plans.

Perhaps the most significant remaining difference is that an owner–employee who participates in a Keogh plan, or a shareholder–employee in the retirement plan of an S corporation, cannot borrow money from the plan without incurring a prohibited transactions excise tax on such a loan,[12] while a participant in a regular corporate retirement plan may be able to borrow up to as much as $50,000 from the plan, if various tax requirements are met. In addition to covering oneself under a corporate or Keogh retirement plan — or even if one is not covered under either type of plan — it is also possible for an owner of a business, whether or not incorporated, to create his or her own individual retirement account or IRA. Since only a $2,000[13] a year deduction ($2,250 if one has a non-working spouse) can be taken for contributions to an IRA, it will not be possible to build up a very large retirement fund or to shelter much income from tax with an IRA — although it is better than having no tax-qualified retirement plan at all, and can be a useful supplement to a corporate or Keogh plan.

After 1986, the law no longer allows deductions for contributions to IRA plans if an individual or spouse is also an active participant in a corporate or Keogh qualified retirement plan and if adjusted gross income exceeds $35,000 for a single person or $50,000 for a married couple filing jointly.[14] The maximum $2,000 or $2,250 deduction phases out between income levels of $25,000 and $35,000 for single taxpayers and between $40,000 and $50,000 for married couples.[15]

Tax Advantages

The primary tax advantages of all three types of tax-qualified retirement plans, corporate, self-employed (Keogh), and IRA, are these:

- Amounts contributed to each type of plan, up to certain limits, are deductible from the income of the corporation or individual taxpayer.[16] For a corporate retirement plan or Keogh plan, the annual deductible contribution that can be made for an individual in the case of a defined contribution plan, such as a "money purchase" pension plan, can be as much as 25% of the individual's compensation for the year (not counting the plan contribution) or $30,000, whichever is less. Or, in the case of a defined benefit pension plan, the contribution can be much more, depending on the age and earnings of the participant and other factors. In the case of high-income individuals in their late 40s or 50s, annual contributions of $100,000 or more are possible, depending on actuarial factors, including how aggressive your actuary is.

- The funds contributed can be invested by the trust that holds the funds on a tax-free basis.[17] The qualified retirement trust that usually holds retirement funds is exempt from state and federal income taxes on its income or capital gains from investments in stocks, bonds, savings accounts, gold, silver, real estate, and other passive investments.[18] Note, however, that gold, silver, and other collectibles can no longer be purchased as investments by individually-directed retirement plans or by an IRA except for certain gold and silver coins minted by the United States after 1986.[19]

- When trust funds are paid out to you at retirement, you may be in a lower tax bracket than when you made the contributions to the plan.

Thus, not only do you get to defer payment of any tax on amounts contributed to the plan until you retire, but the tax you finally pay at retirement is apt to be at a lower rate than you would have paid when you were working.

- Receipt of all your retirement plan funds in a lump sum at retirement, or in certain other circumstances, may often qualify for special low tax rates if the distribution is from a corporate or Keogh plan but not from an IRA.[20]

- Until 1985, payment of your retirement funds to your spouse or other designated beneficiary other than your estate at your death generally exempted up to $100,000 of the funds from federal estate taxes, if certain requirements were met.[21] But don't count on getting any tax benefit from this law unless a wealthy relative died on or before December 31, 1984, because after this date, the $100,000 exemption is generally repealed. You may, however, still leave all your pension benefits or any other property, free of federal estate tax, to your surviving spouse, unless you leave your spouse a large amount — approximately $750,000 or more. Therefore, repeal of the $100,000 exemption will only affect you if you are planning to leave your pension plan benefits to someone other than your spouse in the event of your death. See Section 8.10 for related information.

Exceptions from Estate Tax

The Tax Reform Act of 1986 retroactively amended certain exclusions from estate tax for pension plan benefits. Under these amendments, an individual who separated from service before January 1, 1983 and was receiving benefits on December 31, 1982 is considered as having made an irrevocable election as to the type of benefits to be received and the value of such benefits may be completely exempt from estate tax, if the form of benefits is not changed before his or her death. A similar rule applies to any person who separated from service before January 1, 1985 and was receiving benefits on December 31, 1984, if the form of benefits is not changed. Such individuals will still qualify for the $100,000 estate tax exclusion for pension benefits.

Note!

If you are receiving pension benefits and come within either of the above categories, don't change the form in which your benefits are being paid!

It has often been said that the corporate retirement plan is the last great tax shelter. As should be apparent from reading the above discussion, that may not be an exaggeration, but since 1984, Keogh plans have had nearly all of the tax advantages that corporate plans have. Thus, if you are considering incorporating for the mere purpose of obtaining better retirement plan tax treatment, you may want to reconsider. Incorporation now only makes sense if there are nontax reasons for doing so, or if you want to accumulate income inside the corporation as an income-splitting device, or utilize other corporate fringe benefits discussed in the following paragraphs.

Other Fringe Benefit Plans

The tax law permits corporate employers to provide a number of different fringe benefits to employees on a tax-favored basis. Generally, the employer is allowed to deduct the insurance premiums or other payments it makes on behalf of the employee, while the employee is not taxed on the value of the benefit provided. This is much more favorable than payments of salary to an employee, which are fully taxable.

In an unincorporated business, the payments made on behalf of the sole proprietor or partners for such benefits are generally not deductible as expenses of the business, in contrast to fringe benefits paid for by a corporation for its stockholder–employees. So the tax benefits of employee fringe benefits, such as those described below, are another reason for incorporating your business and becoming an employee of the corporation.

Note, however, that if your corporation is an S corporation, it will be treated like a partnership for fringe benefit purposes.[23] That means it will not be allowed a deduction for fringe benefits described below for any 2% or greater shareholder. The major types of fringe benefit plans, other than retirement plans, that allow for tax deductions to the corporation and no taxable income to the employee are described below.

Medical Insurance Plans

The corporation that maintains a medical insurance plan, such as Blue Cross, or prepaid health care plan is permitted to deduct the premiums it pays to the insurer, and the employee is not required to include either the cost of the premiums[24] or the benefits[25] provided by the insurer in his or her taxable income, as a general rule. Note that for the tax years 1987–1991 a self-employed individual is allowed to deduct 25% of his or her health insurance in computing adjusted gross income.[26]

Self-Insured Medical Reimbursement Plans

A corporation can set up a plan under which the corporation directly reimburses employees for medical expenses or even for such expenses as dental care, orthodontic work, and prescription eyeglasses or contact lenses.[27] If the plan satisfies tax law requirements prohibiting discrimination in favor of highly-paid employees,[28] the reimbursements paid can be deducted by the corporation and are not taxable to the recipients. Such plans are often set up in addition to medical insurance plans, either to cover deductibles that the insurance does not pay or to cover particular types of medical or dental costs that the insurance plan does not provide for. Note that costs of cosmetic surgery are no longer deductible as medical expenses after 1990.

In the past, it was possible to set up a self-insured medical reimbursement plan so that it covered only the officers of the corporation. As the tax law now stands, such a plan would probably be considered discriminatory in most cases, and the reimbursements paid to the officers would, therefore, be taxable to them. Under present law, it will usually be necessary for a self-insured medical plan to cover most of the corporation's employees to qualify for favorable tax treatment.

Payment by a corporation of disability insurance premiums is deductible by the corporation and is not taxed to the employees covered by the insurance.[29] Sole proprietorships and partnerships may not deduct premiums on disability coverage for the sole proprietor or partners.[30]

Disability Insurance

If an employee becomes disabled and receives disability benefits under a policy that the employer has paid the premiums for, the benefits will be included in the employee's income for tax purposes. Note that if an individual, such as a sole proprietor or partner, has paid his or her own premiums for disability insurance, any disability benefits received are tax-free.[31]

An employer, such as a corporation, may set up a group-term life insurance plan and deduct the insurance premiums it pays on behalf of its employees. To the extent the life insurance coverage on an employee does not exceed $50,000 under the plan during the taxable year, the premiums paid by the employer are not taxable income to the employee.[32] Even to the extent an employee's coverage exceeds $50,000, the amount the employee must include in taxable income from the additional insurance premiums paid by the employer for the excess coverage is sometimes considerably less than the premium actually paid and deducted by the employer.

Group-Term Life Insurance

The owner or owners of an unincorporated business cannot deduct the premiums for their own coverage under a group life insurance plan, since they are not considered employees of their businesses for tax purposes.

Another important tax advantage of a corporation (other than for an S corporation discussed in the next section of this chapter) is that, in general, it can deduct 70% of the dividends it receives from stock investments from its federal taxable income.[33] Thus, if you use your corporation to accumulate profits at low corporate tax rates, as was suggested previously in this chapter, you may want to consider investing some of those accumulated funds in common stock or preferred stock of publicly-traded U.S. corporations, since the dividends received by your corporation will be 70% tax-free in most cases or 80%, if your corporation owns 20% or more of the stock of the company paying the dividend. For example, if your corporation receives $1,000 in dividends from an investment in General Motors stock, only $300 would be taxable for federal income tax purposes. Even if your corporation were in the 34% corporate tax bracket, the federal tax on those dividends would be 34% of $300, or $102, which is a maximum effective tax rate of only 10.2% on the dividends received.

Tax Break for Dividends Received by a Corporation

Note, however, that this deduction will be reduced if your corporation borrows money, on which it pays interest, to purchase dividend-paying stocks.[34]

Important Note!

Many states' corporation tax laws also permit a deduction for dividends received by a corporation. Refer to Section 11.2 regarding the corporate dividends received deduction in this state.

Corporate Income Tax Disadvantages

While this chapter has outlined a number of important tax advantages of incorporating a business, the picture is not all that one-sided. There are also a number of significant potential tax problems that corporations may face, and which you would not need to worry about if you did not incorporate. The potential disadvantages include:

- A maximum corporate tax rate that is now generally higher than the individual tax rate;
- Difficulties in withdrawing profits from the business without incurring double taxation, a problem discussed earlier in this section;
- The accumulated earnings tax that may apply — also discussed above briefly in this section — if profits are not withdrawn from the corporation or plowed back into the business; and
- The personal holding company tax, a 28% tax that may apply to the undistributed income of certain corporations that have too much passive income.[35]

Each of these potential tax disadvantages of corporations is discussed in more detail in Chapter 8, Section 8.9. Note that most of the above disadvantages are not applicable if you elect S corporation status, as described in Section 2.5 below. The decision whether to incorporate in this state or elsewhere is covered in Chapter 9, Section 9.12.

2.5 Subchapter S Corporations

The first thing to understand clearly about Subchapter S corporations (now usually referred to as S corporations) is that they are no different than any other corporation under state law in terms of corporate law requirements, limited liability of shareholders, or any other aspect except tax treatment. In fact, some states do not even recognize S corporation elections for tax purposes. An S corporation is simply a regular corporation that meets certain requirements and which has to be treated somewhat like a partnership for federal tax purposes. See Section 11.2 for a discussion of how S corporations are taxed in this state, if at all.

Once a corporation has made an election with the IRS to be treated as an S corporation, its shareholders will generally report their share of the corporation's taxable income or loss on their individual tax returns. That is, the corporation "passes through" its income or loss and tax credits to the shareholders in proportion to their stock holdings in the corporation, much like a partnership. The S corporation does not usually pay tax on any of its income.[36] Profits are deemed to be distributed to the shareholders on the last day of the corporation's tax year, whether or not the profits are actually distributed.[37] Thus, if profits of an S corporation are distributed as dividends, the distribution itself is ordinarily not taxable, so that there is no double taxation of distributed profits.

The Tax Reform Act of 1986 has made S corporations a much more attractive form of doing business than before, due primarily to the fact that, for the first time within memory, the top corporate tax rate of 34% (or 39%) is higher than the top individual tax rate of 31% — top rates vary, see Sections 2.4 and 2.6. Accordingly, an S corporation election is advisable for many more corporations now than in previous years.

S Corporation Requirements

To qualify for S corporation treatment, a corporation must meet the following requirements:

- It must be a domestic corporation, i.e., incorporated in the United States.[38]
- No shareholder can be a nonresident alien individual.[39]
- All of its shareholders must generally be individuals, although certain trusts, called Qualified Subchapter S Trusts and Grantor Trusts, may hold stock under certain circumstances. No shareholder can be a corporation or a partnership.[40]
- The corporation can have only one class of common stock and no preferred stock.[41]
- There cannot be more than 35 shareholders.[42] For this purpose, a husband and wife who are both stockholders will be counted as only one stockholder, whether or not they hold the stock in joint ownership.[43]
- The corporation cannot be a member of an affiliated group of corporations.[44] If it owns stock in a subsidiary that is considered an affiliate, it may not be able to qualify under the S corporation provisions.
- If more than 25% of the gross receipts during three successive tax years are from passive sources such as interest income, dividends, rent, royalties, or proceeds from the sale of securities, a corporation will not qualify as an S corporation for subsequent tax years.[45] The passive income limit does not apply at all for a brand new corporation or an existing corporation that has no accumulated earnings and profits when it elects S corporation status.[46]

Electing S Corporation Status

To become an S corporation, a company that meets the above requirements must file an election on *Form 2553* with the IRS. The election must be signed by all of the corporation's shareholders,[47] including a spouse who has a community property interest in stock that is in the name of the other spouse. The election must be filed during the first two months and 15 days of the corporation's tax year for which the election is to go into effect or at any time during the preceding tax year.[48]

Since a newly-formed corporation that wants to start out as an S corporation does not have a preceding tax year, it has to file an election in the two-month and 15-day period after it is considered to have begun its first tax year. Its first tax year is considered to start when it issues stock to shareholders, acquires assets, or begins to do business, whichever occurs first. Filing of articles of incorporation with the secretary of state usually does not begin the first taxable year.

Care must be taken to file the election at the right time, which can be tricky, since it is sometimes difficult to determine when a corporation first began to do business. Otherwise, there can be some horrendous tax consequences if you operate the corporation as though it were an S corporation, and it is not because the election is later determined to have been filed too early or too late. Fortunately, the law was amended several years ago so that if an election turns out to be filed too late for the year it was intended to apply to, it will at least become effective during the next year.[49] Under prior law, if the election was not filed at the right time, it never became effective.

Potential Tax Traps

After 1986, extreme care must also be taken if a regular C corporation elects to change over to S corporation status — this should not be done without consulting a competent tax adviser. A regular corporation that elects after December 31, 1986 to become an S corporation will generally be subject to an eventual corporate-level tax on any "built-in gains" on its assets (assets with a value greater than their tax basis), if assets are sold for a gain within 10 years. This tax on built-in gains is not imposed on capital-gains type property if a corporation elected S corporation status before January 1, 1989, provided more than 50% of the stock (by value) of the company is owned by 10 or fewer "qualified" persons; the company's stock outstanding is worth less than $5 million; and certain other technical requirements are met. If the stock is worth between $5 million and $10 million, this exclusion gradually phases out, becoming zero at a value of $10 million or greater. Any built-in gains, however, on ordinary income property will be fully taxable to any C corporation changing over to S corporation status after 1986, if disposed of within 10 years. Careful planning and analysis is needed before electing S corporation status.

Also, 1987 tax legislation created a new and potentially costly trap for changeovers from C corporation to S corporation status. Any C corporation that has been using the LIFO method of accounting for inventories (see Section 8.8) and that elects S corporation status after December 17, 1987 (with some minor exceptions) must "recapture" the difference between its LIFO inventory value and a higher inventory value that would have resulted if using FIFO.[50] The tax on this LIFO recapture is computed on the corporation's final C corporation tax return but can be paid in four annual installments. This can be a severe deterrent to making an S corporation election, if a corporation has been using the LIFO method of inventory accounting.

Terminating an S Corporation Election

If it becomes desirable to revoke or terminate S corporation status after a few years, as is often the case, this can be done if shareholders owning more than half the stock sign and file a revocation form.[51] A revocation is effective for the tax year it is filed, if it is filed during the first two months and 15 days of that tax year.[52] If it is filed later in the year, it does not become effective until the next year.[53]

Doing anything, however, that causes the corporation to cease to qualify as an S corporation will also terminate the election, effective on the first day after the corporation ceases to qualify as an S corporation. In that case, the company must file two short-period tax returns for the year, the first — up to the date it ceased to qualify — as an S corporation, the second as a regular taxable corporation. Once a corporation terminates an S corporation election, it cannot re-elect S corporation status for five years, unless it obtains the consent of the IRS.[54]

Reasons for Electing S Corporation Status

For a corporation, electing S corporation status can be very advantageous in some instances, and less so, or even disadvantageous in other situations. An S corporation election should not be made without the advice and assistance of a tax professional, since it is a very complex and technical area of the tax law, even though it no longer contains as many pitfalls for the unwary or the unsophisticated as it previously did.

Electing S corporation treatment for a corporation is usually most favorable in these types of situations:

- Where it is expected that the corporation will experience losses for the initial year or years of doing business and where the shareholders will have income from other sources that the "passed through" losses can shelter from tax. Note that if S corporation losses are passive losses, they can only be used to offset your passive activity income.

- Where, because of the low tax brackets the shareholders are in, there will be tax savings if the anticipated profits of the corporation are passed through to them, rather than being taxed at higher corporate tax rates. This is particularly true for personal service corporations after 1987, since all of the taxable income of such a C corporation is now taxed at a flat 34% rate.

- Where the nature of the corporation's business is such that the corporation does not need to retain a major portion of profits in the business. In this case, all or most of the profits can be distributed as dividends without the double taxation that would occur if no S corporation election were in effect.

- An S corporation election can be particularly useful where a corporation is in danger of incurring an accumulated earnings penalty tax for failure to pay out its profits as dividends.

- An old Subchapter S corporation formerly had an advantage over a partnership in that it could select a tax year that ends any month of the year. Generally, a partnership must adopt the calendar year as its tax year if its partners are individuals. By adopting a January 31 tax year, a Subchapter S corporation was able to defer the shareholder's tax on its profits for up to 11 months. Since 1983, this flexibility has been taken away for corporations newly electing S corporation status, so now most S corporations will have to adopt the calendar year for tax purposes. The Tax Reform Act of 1986 required even pre-existing S corporations to change over to a calendar year beginning in 1987,[55] but 1987 tax legislation allowed such S corporations to elect in 1988 to retain their old fiscal year by agreeing to a prepayment of tax that eliminates any tax-deferral benefits of retaining the fiscal year.[56]

It should be apparent from the above that it will often be advantageous for a corporation to operate as an S corporation in its early years, when losses can be passed through to shareholders, or when income is not so great as to push the shareholders into high tax brackets. Also, the nontax advantage of being incorporated and protected from personal liability if the business fails is generally most important during the early years of operation, when the risk of failure is highest, so that S corporation status is often preferable to operating as a partnership.

Thus, many businesses initially start off as S corporations, obtaining the advantage of limited liability while being taxed much like an unincorporated business. Later, when or if the profit from the business becomes very substantial, the S corporation election can be terminated, and the C corporation can be used to split income between the corporation and its stockholder–employees, if not a qualified personal service corporation.

Disadvantages of S Corporation Election

While there are some significant advantages to operating as an S corporation, the S corporation election is frequently not advisable, depending on the circumstances. Some of the possible disadvantages of operating your business in the form of an S corporation are:

- Changing over a regular corporation to S corporation status may eventually result in a large corporate-level tax on built-in gains or an immediate LIFO recapture tax, as discussed above.
- The tax law regarding S corporations is very complex. (The name "Subchapter S" came from the whole subchapter of the Internal Revenue Code that deals with these corporations.) As a result, it is almost imperative that you have good and continuing tax advice and assistance if your corporation elects S corporation status. Thus, you should expect to pay fairly substantial additional legal or accounting fees to your tax adviser, compared to what would be necessary with a regular corporation. Otherwise, there is a strong chance that you will fall into one of the remaining traps and pitfalls of Subchapter S. In short, don't try to go through the S corporation jungle without a trusted guide!
- S corporations are now treated almost exactly like regular corporations with respect to pension and profit-sharing plans in which there are

shareholder–employees participating, thanks to the parity provisions of TEFRA enacted in 1982. A shareholder–employee is any employee of an S corporation who directly or indirectly is considered as owning more than 5% of its stock.[57] One important difference remains, however — a shareholder–employee participating in an S corporation's pension or profit-sharing plan is prohibited from borrowing from the plan, unlike a participant in a regular corporation's retirement plan.[58]

- Certain built-in gains of an S corporation may be taxed to the corporation and the shareholder for federal tax purposes.[59] For example, if a C corporation is a cash-basis taxpayer, its accounts receivable have a zero basis. If it converts to an S corporation, collection of those receivables will, of course, be taxable income to the shareholders, and, in addition, will be a built-in gain on which the S corporation itself must pay tax.

- Fringe benefit payments for medical, disability, and group-term life insurance for 2% shareholders are no longer deductible.[60] Effective since 1983, S corporations are treated like partnerships or sole proprietorships with regard to such fringe benefits for 2% shareholders.

- Unlike many regular corporations, very few newly-electing S corporations may now have a fiscal tax year that ends earlier than September.[61]

- For your convenience, a sample of *Form 2553, Election by a Small Business Corporation*, is provided on the following pages.

For More Information

2.6 Summary of the Key Characteristics of the Various Legal Forms of

	Proprietorship	General Partnership
Simplicity in Operation and Formation	Simplest to establish and operate.	Relatively simple, informal, but is usually desirable to have formal written agreement between partners.
Liability for Debts, Taxes, and Other Claims	Owner has unlimited personal liability.	Partners all have unlimited personal liability.
Federal Income Taxation of Business Profits	Taxed to the owner at individual tax rates of up to 31% or more, depending on exemptions and deductions which may phase out.	Taxed to partners at their indivividual tax rates.
Double Taxation if Profits Withdrawn from Business	No.	No.
Deduction of Losses by Owners	Yes. May be subject to "passive loss" restrictions.	Yes. Limited partner's deductions generally cannot exceed the amount he or she has invested in a limited partnership interest (except for real estate, in some instances). Also, may be subject to "passive loss" restrictions.
Social Security Tax on Earnings of Owner from Business	15.3% of owner's self-employment earnings in 1991 on first $53,400 of income, plus 2.9% on earnings between $53,400 and $125,000, half of which is now deductible for income tax purposes.	15.3% of each partner's share of self-employment earnings from the business in 1991 on up to $53,400 in earnings, plus 2.9% on earnings between $53,400 and $125,000, half of which is now deductible for income tax purposes on the partner's individual income tax return.
Unemployment Taxes on Earnings of Owner from Business	None.	None.
Retirement Plans	Keogh plan. Deductions, other features now generally the same as for corporate pension and profit-sharing plans. But proprietor cannot borrow from Keogh Plan.	Keogh plan. Same as for proprietorships. A 10% partner cannot borrow from Keogh Plan.
Tax Treatment of Medical, Disability, and Group-Term Life Insurance on Owners	Not deductible, except part of medical expenses may be an itemized deduction on owner's tax return, including medical insurance premiums. But 25% of medical insurance on owner now allowed as a deduction from adjusted gross income.[62] (At least until December 31, 1991.)	Not deductible, except part of medical expenses may be an itemized deduction on owner's tax return, including medical insurance premiums. But 25% of medical insurance on owner now allowed as a deduction from adjusted gross income.[62] (At least until December 31, 1991.)
Taxation of Dividends Received on Investments	Dividends received on stock investments are fully taxable to owner.	Dividends taxable to individual partners. See proprietorship.

Business Organization

Limited Partnership	Regular Corporation	S Corporation
More complex and expensive to establish than other unincorporated forms of business. Requires written agreement and filing of certificate. Managed by general partners only.	Requires most formality in establishment and operation, generally.	Same as a regular corporation but requires close oversight by a tax adviser (an additional cost).
General partners are personally liable; limited partners are liable only to the extent of their investment, generally.	Stockholders are not generally liable for corporate debts, but often have to guarantee loans, as a practical matter, if the corporation borrows money. Also, corporate officers may be liable for failure to withhold and pay over to IRS, withholding taxes on employees' wages.	Stockholders are not generally liable for corporate debts, but often have to guarantee loans, as a practical matter, if the corporation borrows money. Also, corporate officers may be liable for failure to withhold and pay over to IRS, withholding taxes on employees' wages.
Taxed to partners at their individual tax rates.	Taxed to the corporation, at rates higher than those of individuals (maximum of 34% or 39% in 1991).	Taxed to individual owners at their individual rates (but certain gains are taxable to the corporation as well).
No.	Yes, but not on reasonable compensation paid to owners who are employees of the corporation.	No, in general.
Yes. Limited partner's deductions generally cannot exceed the amount he or she has invested in a limited partnership interest (except for real estate, in some instances). Losses generally restricted by "passive loss" rules.	No. Corporation must carry over initial losses to offset future profits, if any.	Yes, in general, for federal tax purposes. But not for state tax purposes in all states. Loss for a shareholder limited to investment in stock plus amount loaned to the corporation. Losses may be subject to "passive loss" restrictions.
15.3% of each partner's share of self-employment earnings from the business in 1991 on up to $53,400 in earnings, plus 2.9% on earnings between $53,400 and $125,000, half of which is now deductible for income tax purposes on the partner's individual income tax return.	Owner–employee of corporation pays 7.65% on his or her salary and corporation pays 7.65%. Total Social Security (FICA) tax on employer and employee is 15.3% of employee's first $53,400 of wages (in 1991). Employee and corporation each pay 1.45% on wages above $53,400, up to limit of $125,000.	Owner–employee of corporation pays 7.65% on his or her salary and corporation pays 7.65%. Total Social Security (FICA) tax on employer and employee is 15.3% of employee's first $53,400 of wages (in 1991). Employee and corporation each pay 1.45% on wages above $53,400, up to limit of $125,000.
None.	Yes. State and federal unemployment taxes apply to salaries paid to owners.	Yes. State and federal unemployment taxes apply to salaries paid to owners.
Keogh plan. Same as for proprietorships. A 10% partner cannot borrow from Keogh Plan.	Corporate retirement plans no longer significantly better than Keogh plans. Deduction limits same now as for Keogh, but participants can borrow from plan.	Plans now essentially identical to regular corporate retirement plans, except that shareholder–employee (5% shareholder) of S corporation cannot borrow from plan.
Not deductible, except part of medical expenses may be an itemized deduction on owner's tax return, including medical insurance premiums. But 25% of medical insurance on owner now allowed as a deduction from adjusted gross income.[62] (At least until December 31, 1991.)	Corporation may be able to deduct corporation medical insurance premium or reimbursements paid under medical reimbursement plan. Generally not taxable to the employee, even if employee is an owner. Similar treatment for disability and group-term life insurance plans.	Fringe benefits for 2% shareholders not deductible by corporation (same as for partnership or proprietorship).
Dividends taxable to individual partners. See Proprietorship.	Dividends are taxable to the corporation. However, 70% of the dividends received are generally free of federal income tax (unless stock is purchased with borrowed money), an important tax advantage.	Dividends taxable to individual shareholders of the S corporation, as in the case of a partnership.

**Department of the Treasury
Internal Revenue Service**

Instructions for Form 2553

(Revised October 1989)

Election by a Small Business Corporation

(Section references are to the Internal Revenue Code unless otherwise noted.)

Paperwork Reduction Act Notice.—We ask for this information to carry out the Internal Revenue laws of the United States. We need it to insure that you are complying with these laws and to allow us to figure and collect the right amount of tax. You are required to give us this information.

The time needed to complete and file this form will vary depending on individual circumstances. The estimated average time is:

Recordkeeping	.6 hrs., 42 min.
Learning about the law or the form	.3 hrs., 16 min.
Preparing, copying, assembling, and sending the form to IRS	.3 hrs., 32 min.

If you have comments concerning the accuracy of these time estimates or suggestions for making this form more simple, we would be happy to hear from you. You can write to the **Internal Revenue Service,** Washington, DC 20224, Attention: IRS Reports Clearance Officer, T:FP; or the **Office of Management and Budget,** Paperwork Reduction Project (1545-0146), Washington, DC 20503.

General Instructions

A. Purpose.—To elect to be treated as an "S Corporation," a corporation must file Form 2553. The election permits the income of the S corporation to be taxed to the shareholders of the corporation, except as provided in Subchapter S of the Code.

B. Who May Elect.—Your corporation may make the election to be treated as an S corporation only if it meets all of the following tests:

1. It is a domestic corporation.

2. It has no more than 35 shareholders. A husband and wife (and their estates) are treated as one shareholder for this requirement. All other persons are treated as separate shareholders.

3. It has only individuals, estates, or certain trusts as shareholders. See the instructions for Part III regarding qualified subchapter S trusts.

4. It has no nonresident alien shareholders.

5. It has only one class of stock. See sections 1361(c)(4) and (5) for additional details.

6. It is not an ineligible corporation as defined in section 1361(b)(2).

7. It has a permitted tax year as required by section 1378 or makes a section 444 election to have a tax year other than a permitted tax year. Section 1378 defines a permitted tax year as a tax year ending December 31, or any other tax year for

which the corporation establishes a business purpose to the satisfaction of the IRS. See the instructions for Part II for details on making a section 444 election.

8. Each shareholder consents as explained in the instructions for Column K.

See sections 1361, 1362, and 1378 for additional information on the above tests.

C. Where To File.—File this election with the Internal Revenue Service Center where the corporation will file **Form 1120S,** U.S. Income Tax Return for an S Corporation. See the Instructions for Form 1120S for Service Center addresses.

D. When To Make the Election.— Complete Form 2553 and file it either: (1) at any time during that portion of the first tax year the election is to take effect which occurs before the 16th day of the third month of that tax year (if the tax year has 2½ months or less, and the election is made not later than 2 months and 15 days after the first day of the tax year, it shall be treated as timely made during such year), or (2) in the tax year before the first tax year it is to take effect. An election made by a small business corporation after the 15th day of the third month but before the end of the tax year is treated as made for the next year. For example, if a calendar tax year corporation makes the election in April 1988, it is effective for the corporation's 1989 calendar tax year. See section 1362(b) for more information.

E. Acceptance or Non-Acceptance of Election.—The Service Center will notify you if your election is accepted and when it will take effect. You should generally receive a determination on your election within 60 days after you have filed Form 2553. If the Q1 box in Part II is checked on page 2, the corporation will receive a ruling letter from IRS in Washington, DC, which approves or denies the selected tax year. When Item Q1 is checked, it will generally take an additional 90 days for the Form 2553 to be accepted.

Do not file Form 1120S until you are notified that your election is accepted. If you are now required to file **Form 1120,** U.S. Corporation Income Tax Return, or any other applicable tax return, continue filing it until your election takes effect.

You will also be notified if your election is not accepted.

Care should be exercised to ensure that the election is received by the Internal Revenue Service. If you are not notified of acceptance or nonacceptance of your election within 3 months of date of filing (date mailed), or within 6 months if Part II, Item Q1, is checked, you should take follow-up action by corresponding with the Service Center where the election was filed. If filing of Form 2553 is questioned by IRS,

an acceptable proof of filing is: (1) certified receipt (timely filed); (2) Form 2553 with accepted stamp; (3) Form 2553 with stamped IRS received date; or (4) IRS letter stating that Form 2553 had been accepted.

F. End of Election.—Once the election is made, it stays in effect for all years until it is terminated. During the 5 years after the election is terminated under section 1362(d), the corporation can make another election on Form 2553 only if the Commissioner consents. See section 1362(g) for more information. See sections 1362(d), (e), and (f) for rules regarding termination of election.

G. User Fee.—Corporations filing Form 2553 and requesting a fiscal year under section 6.03 of Revenue Procedure 87-32, 1987-2 C.B. 396, must pay a user fee ($150 when these instructions were revised). Payment of the fee (check or money order) should not be made with or attached to Form 2553 when it is filed. The Service Center sends Form 2553 to the IRS in Washington, DC, who, in turn, notifies the taxpayer that the fee is due. See Revenue Procedure 89-4, 1989-3 I.R.B. 18.

Specific Instructions

Part I.—Part I must be completed by all corporations.

Name and Address of Corporation.—If the corporation's mailing address is the same as someone else's, such as a shareholder's, please enter this person's name below the name of the corporation. Enter the true corporate name as set forth in the corporate charter or other legal document creating it. If the corporation has changed its name or address since applying for its EIN (filing Form SS-4), be sure to check the box in item E(2) of Part I.

A. Employer Identification Number.—If you have applied for an employer identification number (EIN) but have not received it, enter "applied for." If the corporation does not have an EIN, you should apply for one on **Form SS-4,** Application for Employer Identification Number, available from most IRS or Social Security Administration offices. Send Form SS-4 to the IRS Service Center where Form 1120S will be filed.

B. Principal Business Activity and Principal Product or Service.—Use the Codes for Principal Business Activity contained in the Instructions for Form 1120S. Your principal business activity is the one that accounts for the largest percentage of total receipts. Total receipts are gross receipts plus all other income.

Also state the principal product or service. For example, if the principal business activity is "grain mill products," the principal product or service may be "cereal preparation."

C. Name and Telephone Number.—Enter the name and telephone number (area code and seven digit number) of a corporate officer or legal representative of the corporation who IRS may contact to resolve questions (or obtain additional information) that may arise when the corporation's Form 2553 is reviewed.

D. Effective Date of Election.—Enter the beginning effective date (month, day, year) of the tax year that you have requested for the S corporation. Generally, this will be the beginning date of the tax year for which the ending effective date is shown in item I, Part I. For a new corporation (first year the corporation exists) it will generally be the date shown in item H, Part I. The tax year of a new corporation starts on the date that it has shareholders, acquires assets, or begins doing business, whichever happens first. If the effective date for item D for a newly formed corporation is later than the date in item H, the corporation should file Form 1120, or Form 1120A, for the tax period between these dates.

I. Selected Tax Year.—If a corporation selects a tax year ending other than December 31 (excluding a 52-53-week tax year with reference to the month of December), the corporation must complete Part II in addition to Part I.

Temporary Regulations section 1.441-2T(e)(3) grants automatic approval for the S corporation to use a 52-53-week tax year with reference to the month of December.

Column K. Shareholders' consent statement.—Each shareholder who owns (or is deemed to own) stock at the time the election is made must consent to the election. If the election is made during the corporation's first tax year for which it is effective, any person who held stock at any time during the portion of that year which occurs before the time the election is made, must consent to the election although the person may have sold or transferred his or her stock before the election is made. Each shareholder consents by signing and dating in column K or signing and dating a separate consent statement described below. If stock is owned by a trust that is a qualified shareholder, the deemed owner of the trust must consent. See section 1361(c)(2) for details regarding qualified trusts that may be shareholders and rules on determining who is the deemed owner of the trust.

An election made during the first 2½ months of the tax year is considered made for the following tax year if one or more of the persons who held stock in the corporation during such tax year and before the election was made did not consent to the election. See section 1362(b)(2).

If a husband and wife have a community interest in the stock or in the income from it, both must consent. Each tenant in common, joint tenant, and tenant by the entirety also must consent.

A minor's consent is made by the minor or the legal representative of the minor, or by a natural or adoptive parent of the minor if no legal representative has been appointed. The consent of an estate is made by an executor or administrator.

Continuation sheet or separate consent statement.—If you need a continuation sheet or use a separate consent statement, attach it to Form 2553. The separate consent statement must contain the name, address, and employer identification number of the corporation and the shareholder information requested in columns J through N of Part I.

If you wish, you may combine all the shareholders' consents in one statement.

Column L.—Enter the number of shares of stock each shareholder owns and the dates the stock was acquired. If the election is made during the corporation's first tax year

for which it is effective, do not list the shares of stock for those shareholders who sold or transferred all of their stock before the election was made. However, these shareholders must still consent to the election for it to be effective for the tax year.

Column M.—Enter the social security number for shareholders who are individuals. Enter the employer identification number for estates. Enter the social security number or employer identification number for shareholders that are qualified trusts.

Column N.—Enter the month and day that each shareholder's tax year ends. If a shareholder is changing his or her tax year, enter the tax year the shareholder is changing to. If a shareholder is changing his or her tax year, an explanation should be attached to Form 2553 indicating the present tax year and the basis for the change (e.g., automatic revenue procedure or letter ruling request).

If the election is made during the corporation's first tax year for which it is effective, you do not have to enter the tax year of shareholders who sold or transferred all of their stock before the election was made but who still must consent to the election for it to be effective for the tax year.

Signature.—Form 2553 must be signed by the president, treasurer, assistant treasurer, chief accounting officer, or other corporate officer (such as tax officer) authorized to sign.

Part II

Item P.—Item P is completed by a corporation that selects a fiscal year, and that qualifies under section 4.01(1) or 4.01(2) of Revenue Procedure 87-32, 1987-2 C.B. 396. In addition, if the corporation selects a fiscal year that qualifies under section 4.01(1), then it must attach a statement to Form 2553, showing the amount of gross receipts for the most recent 47 months (show each month separately) as required by section 4.03(3)(b) of the revenue procedure. Sections 4.01(1) and 4.01(2) provide for expeditious approval of certain corporations' requests to adopt, retain, or change to a fiscal year. The representation statements highlight the requests provided for in section 4 of the revenue procedure. A corporation adopting, retaining, or changing its accounting period under the procedure must comply with all applicable conditions of the procedure.

Form 1128, Application for Change in Accounting Period, should not be used to request a tax year for or during the 1st year the corporation elects to be an S corporation.

Item Q.—Item Q is completed as follows:

Box Q1.—The corporation checks box Q1 to make a request as specified in section 6.03 of Revenue Procedure 87-32. The taxpayer must attach a statement to Form 2553 pursuant to the ruling request requirements of Revenue Procedure 89-1, 1989-1 I.R.B. 8. (Changes to this revenue procedure are usually incorporated annually into a new revenue procedure as the first revenue procedure of the year.) The statement must show the business purpose for the desired tax year. See Revenue Ruling 87-57, 1987-2 C.B. 117, for examples of business purpose. Also, submit

figures showing monthly gross receipts from sales or services (and monthly inventory figures, if applicable) for the 36 months immediately preceding the effective date of the Form 2553. If the corporation has been in existence for less than 36 months, submit figures for the period of existence.

Box Q2.—The corporation checks box Q2 to show its intention to make a back-up section 444 election. The back-up section 444 election is made in addition to the request for a fiscal year based on business purpose. The back-up election applies in the event the IRS does not approve the corporation's request for a tax year based on business purpose. **Caution: If the corporation makes a back-up section 444 election for which it is qualified, then the election must be exercised in the event the business purpose request is denied.**

Under certain circumstances, the tax year requested under the section 444 back-up election may be different than the tax year requested under business purpose. See the instructions for Form 8716 for details on making a back-up section 444 election.

Box Q3.—The corporation checks box Q3 to make a calendar year back-up election. The calendar year back-up election applies if: (a) the corporation's business purpose request is denied, or (b) the business purpose request was denied and the section 444 back-up election was made, but later the corporation was not eligible to make the election. In certain cases, the corporation will not be eligible to make the section 444 election when it becomes a member of a tiered structure.

Item R.—Item R is completed as follows:

Box R1.—The corporation checks box R1 to show that it is making or intends to make the section 444 election. The corporation makes the election when filing Form 2553 by completing Form 8716 and attaching it to Form 2553. Form 8716 can also be completed and filed after Form 2553 is filed. See the instructions for Form 8716 for details on filing Form 8716.

Box R2.—The corporation checks box R2 to make a back-up calendar year election.

If the corporation is not qualified to make the section 444 election after making the item Q2 section 444 back-up election or indicating its intention to make the election in item R1, and therefore it later files a calendar year return, it should write "Section 444 Election Not Made" in the top left corner of the 1st calendar year Form 1120S it files.

Part III

Certain Qualified Subchapter S Trusts (QSSTs) may make the QSST election required by section 1361(d)(2) in Part III. Part III may be used to make the QSST election only if corporate stock has been transferred to the trust on or before the date on which the corporation makes its election to be an S corporation. However, a statement can be used in lieu of Part III to make the election.

Note: *Part III may be used only in conjunction with making the Part I election (i.e., Form 2553 cannot be filed with only Part III being completed).*

The deemed owner of the QSST must also consent to the S corporation election in column K, page 1, of Form 2553. See section 1361(c)(2).

☆U.S. Government Printing Office: 1989-261-157/00021

Form **2553**
(Rev. October 1989)

Department of the Treasury
Internal Revenue Service

Election by a Small Business Corporation
(Under section 1362 of the Internal Revenue Code)
▶ For Paperwork Reduction Act Notice, see page 1 of instructions.
▶ See separate instructions.

OMB No. 1545-0146

Expires 2-28-91

Notes: 1. This election, to be treated as an "S corporation," can be accepted only if all the tests in General Instruction B are met; all signatures in Parts I and III are originals (no photocopies); and the exact name and address of the corporation and other required form information are provided.
2. Do not file Form 1120S until you are notified that your election is accepted. See instruction E.

Part I Election Information

Name of corporation (see instructions)	A Employer identification number (see instructions)	B Principal business activity and principal product or service (see instructions)
Number and street	C Name and telephone number of corporate officer or legal representative who may be called for information	
City or town, state, and ZIP code	D Election is to be effective for tax year beginning (month, day, year)	

Please Type or Print

E (1) Is the corporation the outgrowth or continuation of any form of predecessor? ☐ Yes ☐ No

If "Yes," state name of predecessor, type of organization, and period of its existence ▶ . . . .

F Date of incorporation

G State of incorporation

(2) Check here ☐ if the corporation has changed its name or address since applying for the employer identification number shown in item A above.

H If this election takes effect for the first tax year the corporation exists, enter month, day, and year of the **earliest** of the following: (1) date the corporation first had shareholders, (2) date the corporation first had assets, or (3) date the corporation began doing business. ▶

I Selected tax year: Annual return will be filed for tax year ending (month and day) ▶ . . . .

See instructions before entering your tax year. If the tax year ends on any date other than December 31, except for an automatic 52–53-week tax year ending with reference to the month of December, you must complete Part II on the back. If the date you enter in item I is the ending date of an automatic 52–53-week tax year, write "52–53-week year" to the right of the date. See instructions.

J Name of each shareholder, person having a community property interest in the corporation's stock, and each tenant in common, joint tenant, and tenant by the entirety. (A husband and wife (and their estates) are counted as one shareholder in determining the number of shareholders without regard to the manner in which the stock is owned.)	K Shareholders' Consent Statement We, the undersigned shareholders, consent to the corporation's election to be treated as an "S corporation" under section 1362(a). (Shareholders sign and date below.)*	L Stock owned		M Social security number or employer identification number (see instructions)	N Shareholder's tax year ends (month and day)
		Number of shares	Dates acquired		

*For this election to be valid, the consent of each shareholder, person having a community property interest in the corporation's stock, and each tenant in common, joint tenant, and tenant by the entirety must either appear above or be attached to this form. (See instructions for Column K, if continuation sheet or a separate consent statement is needed.)

Under penalties of perjury, I declare that I have examined this election, including accompanying schedules and statements, and to the best of my knowledge and belief, it is true, correct, and complete.

Signature and Title of Officer ▶

Date ▶

See Parts II and III on back.

Form **2553** (Rev. 10-89)

Part II Selection of Fiscal Tax Year (All corporations using this Part must complete item O and one of items P, Q, or R.) (See instructions for information about a user fee, if applicable, required attachments, and other details.)

O   Check the applicable box below to indicate whether the corporation is:

☐ A new corporation adopting the tax year entered in item I, Part I.

☐ An existing corporation retaining the tax year entered in item I, Part I.

☐ An existing corporation changing to the tax year entered in item I, Part I.

P   Check the applicable box below to indicate the representation statement the corporation is making as required under section 4 of Rev. Proc. 87-32, 1987-2 C.B. 396.

☐ Under penalties of perjury, I represent that shareholders holding more than half of the shares of the stock (as of the first day of the tax year to which the request relates) of the corporation have the same tax year or are concurrently changing to the tax year that the corporation adopts, retains, or changes to per item I, Part I. I also represent that the corporation is not described in section 3.01(2) of Rev. Proc. 87-32.

☐ Under penalties of perjury, I represent that the corporation is retaining or changing to a tax year that coincides with its natural business year as defined in section 4.01(1) of Rev. Proc. 87-32 and as verified by its satisfaction of the requirements of section 4.02(1) of Rev. Proc. 87-32. In addition, if the corporation is changing to a natural business year as defined in section 4.01(1), I further represent that such tax year results in less deferral of income to the owners than the corporation's present tax year. I also represent that the corporation is not described in section 3.01(2) of Rev. Proc. 87-32. (See instructions for attachments required by section 4.03(3) of Rev. Proc. 87-32.)

Note: *If you do not use item P and the corporation wants a fiscal tax year, complete either item Q or R below. Item Q is used to request a fiscal tax year based on business purpose and to make a back-up section 444 election. Item R is used to make a regular section 444 election.*

Q   Business Purpose—To request a fiscal tax year based on business purpose, you must check box Q1. You may also check box Q2 and/or box Q3.

1. Check here ☐ if the fiscal year entered in item I, Part I, is requested under the provisions of section 6.03 of Rev. Proc. 87-32. Attach to Form 2553 a statement and other necessary information pursuant to the ruling request requirements of Rev. Proc. 89-1, 1989-1 I.R.B. 8. The statement must include the business purpose for the desired fiscal year.

2. Check here ☐ to show that the corporation intends to make a back-up section 444 election in the event the corporation's business purpose request is not approved by the IRS.

3. Check here ☐ to show that the corporation agrees to adopt or change to a tax year ending December 31 if necessary for the IRS to accept this election for S corporation status in the event: (1) the corporation's business purpose request is not approved and the corporation makes a back-up section 444 election, but is ultimately not qualified to make a section 444 election, or (2) the corporation's business purpose request is not approved and the corporation did not make a back-up section 444 election.

R   Section 444 Election—You must check box R1 and you may also check box R2.

1. Check here ☐ to show the corporation will make, if qualified, a section 444 election to have the fiscal tax year shown in item I, Part I. To make the election, you must complete **Form 8716**, Election To Have a Tax Year Other Than a Required Tax Year, and either attach it to Form 2553 or file it in accordance with the instructions for Form 8716.

2. Check here ☐ to show that the corporation agrees to adopt or change to a tax year ending December 31 if necessary for the IRS to accept this election for S corporation status in the event the corporation is ultimately not qualified to make a section 444 election.

Part III Qualified Subchapter S Trust (QSST) Election Under Section 1361(d)(2)**

Income beneficiary's name and address	Taxpayer identification number
Trust's name and address	Taxpayer identification number

Date on which stock of the corporation was transferred to the trust (month, day, year) ▶

In order for the trust named above to be a QSST and thus a qualifying shareholder of the S corporation for which this Form 2553 is filed, I hereby make the election under section 1361(d)(2). Under penalties of perjury, I certify that the trust meets the definition requirements of section 1361(d)(3) and that all other information provided in Part III is true, correct, and complete.

_____   _____
Signature of income beneficiary or signature and title of legal representative or other qualified person making the election   Date

**Use of Part III to make the QSST election may be made only if stock of the corporation has been transferred to the trust on or before the date on which the corporation makes its election to be an S corporation. The QSST election must be made and filed separately if stock of the corporation is transferred to the trust after the date on which the corporation makes the S election.

☆ U.S. Government Printing Office 1989-261-557/00008

Footnotes

1. I.R.C. § 11(b)(2).
2. I.R.C. § 704(e).
3. However, if the parents attempt to shift too much income to the children by drawing no salary or too little salary from the corporation, the IRS has the power to reallocate the corporation's income to the parents to reflect the value of services rendered to the corporation. I.R.C. § 1366(e).
4. I.R.C. § 1(g).
5. The basic FUTA rate is 6.2% in 1990. I.R.C. § 3301(1). A credit of up to 5.4% for state unemployment tax paid is allowed against the FUTA tax. I.R.C. § 3302(b). Thus, the credit for state unemployment taxes results in an effective FUTA tax rate of 6.2%– 5.4% = 0.8% in most states.
6. I.R.C. § 3306(b)(1).
7. I.R.C. §§ 444 and 7519.
8. I.R.C. § 6050K.
9. I.R.C. § 11(b)(2).
10. I.R.C. § 535(c)(2).
11. I.R.C. § 531.
12. I.R.C. § 4975(d) (last paragraph).
13. I.R.C. § 219.
14. I.R.C. § 219(g).
15. I.R.C. § 219(g)(3).
16. I.R.C. §§ 219 and 404(a).
17. I.R.C. § 501(a).
18. But investments in active businesses or purchases of assets with borrowed funds will cause the exempt trust to be taxed on the income from those sources. I.R.C. §§ 511(a) and 514. However, real estate investments can be financed, generally. I.R.C. § 514(c)(9).
19. I.R.C. § 408(m).
20. I.R.C. § 402(e).
21. I.R.C. § 2039(c), (d), (e), and (g). (Repealed after 1984.)
22. Tax Reform Act of 1984 § 525.
23. I.R.C. § 1372(a).
24. I.R.C. § 106.
25. I.R.C. § 105.
26. I.R.C. § 162(l).
27. I.R.C. § 105(b).
28. I.R.C. § 105.
29. I.R.C. § 106.
30. I.R.C. § 105(g).
31. I.R.C. § 104(a)(3).
32. I.R.C. § 79(a).
33. I.R.C. § 243(a).
34. I.R.C. § 246A.
35. I.R.C. § 541.
36. However, in certain instances an S corporation may be subject to tax on "built-in gains." I.R.C. § 1374.
37. I.R.C. § 1366.
38. I.R.C. § 1361(b).
39. I.R.C. § 1361(b)(1)(C).
40. I.R.C. § 1361(b)(1)(B).
41. I.R.C. § 1361(b)(1)(D).
42. I.R.C. § 1361(b)(1)(A).
43. I.R.C. § 1361(c).
44. I.R.C. § 1361(b)(2)(A).
45. I.R.C. § 1362(d)(3).
46. I.R.C. § 1362(d)(3)(B).
47. I.R.C. § 1362(a)(2).
48. I.R.C. § 1362(b).
49. I.R.C. § 1362(b)(3).
50. I.R.C. § 1363(d).
51. I.R.C. § 1362(d)(1)(B).
52. I.R.C. § 1362(d)(1)(C)(i).
53. I.R.C. § 1362(d)(i)(C)(ii).
54. I.R.C. § 1362(g).
55. I.R.C. § 1378.
56. I.R.C. §§ 444 and 7519.
57. I.R.C. § 1379(d). (Before amendment.)
58. I.R.C. § 4975(d).
59. I.R.C. § 1374(a).
60. I.R.C. § 1372(a).
61. I.R.C. § 1378(a).
62. I.R.C. § 162(l).

Chapter 3

Buying an Existing Business

3.1 General Considerations

Obviously, it may not be necessary for you to build your business from the ground up. A person who wishes to go into a particular type of business will often find that it is possible to buy an existing business of that type. Doing so can have considerable advantages over starting from scratch, and one of the most important of these is the chance to start out with an established customer base. It is also sometimes possible to have the seller stay on as an employee or consultant for a transitional period to help familiarize the new owner with the operation of the business.

Other advantages of purchasing a going business include these:

- You may be able to take a regular draw or salary right from the start, if it is a profitable operation. This is usually not the case in a start-up operation, which typically starts off losing money.

- Your risk is frequently less when you buy an established, profitable business. You know that it has a viable market if it is already profitable. Your main risks are that something will change, such as new competition or obsolescence of product, that will adversely affect the business after you acquire it. Another risk is that you will mismanage it.

- Getting started is simpler. By buying an established business, you can focus your attention on giving good service and operating profitably. Since most facilities, operating systems, and employees will already be in place, your efforts will not be diluted by remodeling the premises, trying to hire employees, setting up accounting systems, acquiring initial inventory, and the like. With an existing business, in most cases, you should be able to step right into an operation that has already been broken in by someone else.

- While there are some definite advantages to buying an established business, as compared to starting up a new business from nothing, it can also be a lot more complicated and involves many potential pitfalls that you must avoid. The watchword in buying any kind of business should be caveat emptor — let the buyer beware.

- Because the process of buying and selling businesses is very complicated even for experts, one should not attempt it without retaining the services of a reliable attorney and, usually, a good accountant. Even skilled professionals, however, can generally only protect you from certain legal, financial, or tax pitfalls that arise in connection with the purchase of a business. Many of the potential problems that would not become obvious until it is too late can be spotted in advance, if at all, only by the exercise of your good judgment and as a result of your doing the necessary homework — whatever that turns out to be — regarding the particular business you are looking over. Important pitfalls you should look out for in connection with buying an existing business are discussed in Section 3.3.

3.2 Finding a Business for Sale

How do you go about finding a business that is up for sale? There are a number of ways to approach the problem, none of which are ideal, so you will probably want to use two or more of the approaches discussed below to find and buy an existing business.

Advertisements

The business opportunities section of your local newspaper or a regional magazine or trade association journal can be a major source of leads to businesses that are for sale. Such ads often do not tell you very much about the nature of the business that is for sale, but at least they can be a starting point in your search. In many cases, the ads will have been placed by a business broker rather than the owner. This is not necessarily bad, however, since the business broker will often be representing people who are seeking to sell their business.

Business Brokers and Realtors

Business brokers and realtors can be excellent sources to contact in your search for a business that is for sale. The main drawback of going through a business broker or realtor is that their fee (paid by the seller) is usually a percentage, often 10%, of the sales price of the business, so that they, like the seller, are trying to get the highest possible price for the business. At the same time, the seller will usually want more than he or she would if the sale were made without a broker, since he or she knows that the broker will take a healthy commission out of the negotiated sale price.

Your local chamber of commerce can usually tell you a great deal about the local business community and provide free leads to firms that are for sale that you would be interested in.

Local Chambers of Commerce

Often these professionals can be the best sources of leads to good businesses that may be coming up for sale, even before they are on the market. Frequently, a business client will tell his CPA, attorney, or banker that he or she is planning to sell out or retire, long before making any formal attempt to put the business up for sale. So, if you have friends who are CPAs, bankers, or business lawyers, take one or more such persons to lunch and tell them what you have in mind. Typically, they will have a vested interest in finding a friendly buyer for a retiring client's business, since they may fear losing that account if the firm is sold to strangers who have their own CPA, lawyer, or banker already.

Accountants, Attorneys, and Bankers

Certified public accountants can be excellent sources of leads. Not only will they usually not charge you any kind of finder's fee, but they usually know which businesses of their clients are little gold mines. In some cases, a CPA who has a very profitable client who wishes to sell out may even want to go into the business with you as a financial partner, leaving the day-to-day operations to you. In those cases, you can generally be sure that if the CPA is putting up his or her money, he or she has studied the client's business carefully and feels that it is a real money-maker. In short, the CPA will have already done much of the prescreening for you in such a case, at his or her own expense.

Often, if you see a small business that you think you might like to buy, the simplest approach will be to talk to the owner and see if he or she is interested in selling. While they may have had no serious thoughts about selling the business before, the appearance of an interested potential buyer is not only somewhat flattering, but may even cause them to decide to sell out to you. Many businesses are bought and sold in just this way.

The Direct Approach

3.3 What To Look for Before You Leap

Perhaps the first question you should ask someone who is offering to sell their business to you is why they want to sell. Often the response will be that the owner wants to retire or is in poor health. While such an explanation may be true in many cases, it is also quite likely to be a well-rehearsed cover story in many instances. The real reason may be that the business is in a declining neighborhood, and the owner has been robbed several times recently and wants out. Or the owners of a profitable little corner grocery store may be anxious to sell out while they can because they have learned that a major chain-store supermarket will be opening

Why Is the Business for Sale?

in the neighborhood in a few months. Another common reason behind a planned sale is that the business is either losing money or is not sufficiently profitable to make continuing worthwhile.

Whatever the real reason is behind the owner's attempt to sell the business, you are unlikely to discover it without rolling up your sleeves and doing some independent and in-depth investigation.

Perhaps the best way to find that needle in the haystack is to talk to a number of other business people in the vicinity of the business you are investigating, particularly competitors in the same business as the target firm or its suppliers. Even if you are very diligent and thorough, you may not be able to discover the hidden reason — if there is one — underlying the owner's desire to sell out. You may simply have to rely on the smell test in deciding whether the seller's alleged reason for getting out of the business is the real reason. Just remember that a good and profitable small business is not something that most people walk away from, in most cases, unless there is a very good reason to do so or the price offered for it is too good to turn down.

What Kind of Reputation Does the Firm Have?

One of the great advantages of taking over an existing business can be the opportunity to enjoy the reputation and goodwill that the existing owner has built up with customers and suppliers over the years. On the other hand, you may be much better off starting your own business from scratch than acquiring a business that has a poor reputation because of inferior work or merchandise or that has a history of sleazy service. It could take you years of hard work and reduced profits to overcome a former owner's bad reputation.

Even if the present owner has an excellent business reputation, you will want to know whether or not that goodwill is based on personal relationships built up between the owner and customers, which won't be easy to transfer to you. This is particularly important if the business relies heavily on a few key customers with whom the owner has very favorable business arrangements based on personal relationships; when you attempt to take the owner's place, those business arrangements may be lost. In short, satisfy yourself that the goodwill you are buying is not just a handful of air.

How Profitable Is the Business Now?

Unless you have some very good reasons to believe that you can operate the business more profitably than the current owner, you should not purchase a going business that does not produce a satisfactory profit under its current ownership. Thus, it is extremely important to find out how the business has fared financially for the last few years. This is where the services of a good accountant, who has knowledge of the particular type of business, will be invaluable.

You should insist on having the seller make available the business' financial and business records to your accountant. (Be particularly wary of a business that keeps poor records.) Often the most reliable sources of financial information can be the income tax and sales tax returns filed by the owner in past years, since it is not very likely that a business owner will report more income than actually earned, for tax purposes. If the seller is not willing to make financial records available, you should make it clear that you are not willing to negotiate any further. Buying a business is a lot like buying a used car — you want to make sure it runs before you pay for it.

Assets and Liabilities

You will need to review the assets of the business, both tangible and intangible, to see if they are worth the price you will be paying and also to determine just what assets you will be acquiring under the sale agreement. You should personally inspect the business premises, looking for things like obsolete or unsalable inventory, out-of-date or rundown equipment, or furniture or fixtures that you may have to repair or replace. Also, determine whether the business is able to expand at its present location or if it is already too cramped. What you determine might require you to buy or lease additional facilities if you wish to expand.

Review the terms of any leases. One reason some businesses close is the imminent expiration of a favorable long-term lease, when the landlord plans to either raise the rent drastically or not renew the lease at all when the current lease expires.

If you will be acquiring the accounts receivable of the business as part of the purchase, review them in detail. An aging of the accounts should be performed to determine how long various receivables have been outstanding. As a general rule, the longer a given receivable has been outstanding, the more likely it will prove to be uncollectible. If a few large accounts of credit customers make up a significant portion of the receivables, you will want to particularly focus on those accounts and perhaps even have credit checks run on those customers. The bankruptcy of a major credit customer can ruin an otherwise successful business.

Part of your job in investigating a business that you want to buy is to find out what makes it tick — and make sure you will be getting that, whatever it is. For example, a business which has well-developed customer or mailing lists, should ordinarily include those lists in the sales agreement; if there is a favorable lease, make sure it can and will be assigned to you; if patents, trade marks, trade names, or certain skilled employees are vital to the business, be sure that you will get them as part of the package. You also need to be aware of potential problems with the government that the seller is experiencing or expects to experience in the near future, such as zoning problems or new environmental restrictions that may hamper the business' profitability.

Liabilities of the business may not always show up on its accounting records. There may be any number of hidden claims against the business, such as security agreements encumbering the accounts receivable, inventory, or equipment, unpaid back taxes of various kinds, undisclosed lawsuits or potential lawsuits, or simply unpaid bills. If you are going to assume liabilities of the business, the written agreement of sale should specify exactly which liabilities are being assumed and the dollar amount of each.

Hidden Liabilities

Other examples of hidden liabilities to look out for are:

- Pension liabilities — You may be taking on significant termination liability as a successor employer if the seller maintains or contributes to a pension fund and has unfunded pension fund liabilities.

- Vacation liability — If, as purchaser of a business, you are a successor employer, you may be liable for accrued but unpaid vacation leave of employees, which can be a significant hidden liability in some cases.

- Environmental problems — In many instances, current trend in the law is to impose liability for past environmental abuses on current land owners or lessors, a severe and potentially devastating financial problem that many banks and S&L's have recently learned about the hard way, after foreclosing on land which had been contaminated over the years by toxic substances and being held liable for clean-up costs as the contamination problems came to light. Many companies, when buying land or other companies that own land, now require the sellers to make detailed representations and warranties concerning environmental matters and to undertake extensive and costly environmental audits as a condition to buying a business.

If the business you intend to buy is operated in corporate form, you will generally be well-advised to buy the business assets from the corporation rather than purchase the stock of the corporation itself. The latter approach will subject the business to all hidden or contingent liabilities of the old corporation, whether or not you have agreed to pay for any liabilities of the corporation that predated the sale. One exception to this general rule would be a corporation that had substantial tax loss or tax credit carryovers that you might be able to utilize if you bought the stock of the corporation rather than the assets. Be aware, however, that the tax law is a mine field when it comes to taking over someone else's tax loss or credit carryovers, so be certain before you do so that you seek good tax advice from a tax attorney or tax accountant, or you may find that the carryovers you thought you were acquiring have evaporated like a mirage.

Note that under the provisions of the Tax Reform Act of 1986, a mere change in ownership of more than 50% of the stock of a corporation in a three-year period will generally result in a severe restriction on the amount of its prior net operating losses that can be deducted in any subsequent taxable year.

3.4 Should You Consider a Franchise Operation?

Many small businesses, particularly fast food restaurants and print shops, are operated under franchises from a large national company. There can be substantial advantages in operating a franchised business, such as the benefits of national advertising, training programs, and assistance in setting up and running the business. If the business you are investigating operates under a franchise, it will be vitally important to determine whether the franchise can be transferred to you, and if so, to provide for the transfer as part of the sale in the sale agreement. You will also want to carefully review the franchise agreement (with the help of your attorney) to determine whether the franchisor must approve the transfer, what the costs of operating under the franchise are and the other terms of the agreement. If the franchisor is not a well-known and respected company, you should contact your local Better Business Bureau or an appropriate state agency to see if they have any information regarding the ethics and reputation of the franchisor. You do not want to sign on with one of the less-than-reputable franchising operations that charge substantial franchising fees for very little in the way of useful services.

In addition, as a potential purchaser of a franchised business, you need to be aware that there are franchising laws and regulations of the Federal Trade Commission and in a number of the major states that offer protections to you, by mandating the timing and content of the various disclosures which the franchisor must make to you as the franchisee. You or your attorney should make sure that you ask for all of these disclosures on a timely basis, and you should be wary of any franchisor who does not provide these disclosures to you unless you ask for them.

A number of excellent publications can be obtained to help you evaluate various franchise opportunities. Refer to Section 10.10 for a list.

Franchise Bible: A Comprehensive Guide, by Erwin J. Keup, explains in detail what the franchise system entails and presents the perspectives of both the franchisor and the franchisee. It is available from your book source or from The Oasis Press, (800) 228-2275.

Tax Hint

If you do acquire a franchise, either from the franchising company or as a transfer from another franchisee, you may be able to amortize (write off) the cost of acquiring the franchise, under certain circumstances, for federal income tax purposes. Consult your tax adviser as to whether or not this will be possible in your case. If it is amortizable, you may want to allocate a significant part of the purchase price for the business to the cost of the franchise, which could save you major tax dollars in the long run; however, 1989 tax law changes have somewhat limited these benefits.

For evaluating a franchise operation, you will find the following checklist useful — once you've focused on a particular franchise opportunity.

Checklist for Evaluating a Franchise

The Franchise

YES NO

☐ ☐ Did your lawyer approve the franchise contract you are considering after he studied it paragraph by paragraph?

☐ ☐ Does the franchise call upon you to take any steps which are, according to your lawyer, unwise or illegal in your state, county, or city? _____

_____

_____

☐ ☐ Does the franchise give you an exclusive territory for the length of the franchise? or

☐ ☐ Can the franchisor sell a second or third franchise in your territory?

☐ ☐ Is the franchisor connected in any way with any other franchise company handling similar merchandise or services?

If the answer to the last question is "yes," what is your protection against this second franchisor organization?

_____

_____

Under what circumstances can you terminate the franchise contract and at what cost to you, if you decide for any reason at all that you wish to cancel it? _____

_____

_____

☐ ☐ If you sell your franchise, will you be compensated for the goodwill you have built into the business?

The Franchisor

How many years has the firm offering you a franchise been in operation? _____

☐ ☐ Has it a reputation for honesty and fair dealing among the local firms holding its franchise?

☐ ☐ Has the franchisor shown you any certified figures indicating exact net profits of one or more going firms?

☐ ☐ Have you personally checked these with the franchisor?

Will the firm assist you with:

☐ ☐ A management training program?

☐ ☐ An employee training program?

☐ ☐ A public relations program?

☐ ☐ Capital?

☐ ☐ Credit?

☐ ☐ Merchandising ideas?

☐ ☐ Will the firm help you find a good location for your new business?

☐ ☐ Is the franchising firm adequately financed so it can carry out its stated plan of financial assistance and expansion?

YES NO

☐ ☐ Is the franchisor a one-person company? or

☐ ☐ Is the franchisor a corporation with an experienced management trained in depth (so that there would always be an experienced person at its head)?

Exactly what can the franchisor do for you which you cannot do for yourself? _____

_____

_____

☐ ☐ Has the franchisor investigated you carefully enough to assure itself that you can successfully operate one of their franchises at a profit both to them and to you?

☐ ☐ Does your state have a law regulating the sale of franchises? and

☐ ☐ Has the franchisor complied with that law?

You – The Franchisee

How much equity capital will you have to have to purchase the franchise and operate it until your income equals your expenses? _____

Where are you going to get it? _____

_____

☐ ☐ Are you prepared to give up some independence of action to secure the advantages offered by the franchise?

☐ ☐ Do you really believe you have the innate ability, training, and experience to work smoothly and profitably with the franchisor, your employees, and your customers? _____

_____

_____

_____

☐ ☐ Are you ready to spend much or all of the remainder of your business life with this franchisor, offering its product or service to your public?

Your Market

☐ ☐ Have you made any study to determine whether the product or service which you propose to sell under franchise has a market in your territory at the prices you will have to charge?

Will the population in the territory given you increase ☐, remain static ☐, or decrease ☐ over the next five years?

Will the product or service you are considering be in greater demand ☐, about the same ☐, or less demand ☐ five years from now than today?

What competition exists in your territory already for the product or service you contemplate selling:

From nonfranchise firms? _____

From franchise firms? _____

Source: *Franchise Opportunities Handbook*, U.S. Department of Commerce (Washington, D.C.: 1982).

3.5 Negotiating the Purchase

The Purchase Price

Neither this book nor any other can tell you how much you should pay for the business you are planning to buy. You are on your own on that one; however, if you have done your homework thoroughly in investigating the business in question and have talked to bankers and other business people about what the normal purchase price for a business of that type and size should be, you should have a fairly good basis for determining whether the purchase price is a reasonable one. For example, you may find that small businesses of the type you are considering generally sell for about one and one-half times their annual gross sales. That could be very important to know if the seller is asking three times last year's gross sales.

Even if you conclude that the purchase price is a fair one, or even a bargain, you still must decide whether the price is one you can afford. Assuming that you can get the purchase price together, will it so deplete your liquid resources that you will not have enough working capital to make the business go or put you in a bind if income from the business drops off while you are at the learning stage? Or, if you are financing a substantial part of the purchase price, will your operating budget be able to stand the cost of making the payments on the debt and still leave enough for you to live on? Remember that just because the price is right and you can get the purchase price or down payment together does not necessarily mean that you can afford to buy a particular business that is for sale.

Disclosure of Financial Information

At an early stage in the negotiations, specify that you want access to tax returns, books of account, and other financial records of the business, and make it clear that you have no interest in continuing the negotiations unless the seller cooperates fully in this respect. Also, be sure that this condition is expressed in any informal "memorandum of understanding" or letter agreement between you and the seller that is written up prior to the final contract of sale.

Allocation of Purchase Price

One very important item that is often omitted in business sale agreements, perhaps because it is not absolutely necessary, is a provision in the agreement that shows how the parties agree to allocate the purchase price between the various assets that are being acquired. For tax purposes, however, it is often very important to both purchaser and seller to have a written allocation agreement. Since a purchaser and seller usually have opposing interests in making an agreed allocation, the courts and the IRS have generally been willing to abide by any allocation agreement between the parties.

The Tax Reform Act of 1986, however, has clamped down on sale price allocations rather severely for businesses sold after May 6, 1986.[1] The new law requires that both seller and purchaser abide by an allocation formula that works as follows:

- First reduce the purchase price by the amount of any cash or cash equivalents.
- Next, allocate part of the purchase price to assets like certificates of deposit, government securities, readily marketable stocks or securities and foreign currencies, up to the fair market value of each such asset.
- Any remaining unallocated portion of the purchase price is then allocated to tangible and intangible assets (land, improvements, equipment, inventories, patents, etc.), but not to exceed the fair market value of such assets.
- If there is still any portion of the purchase price left to be allocated, it must then be allocated to goodwill and going concern value, which cannot be deducted, depreciated or amortized by the purchaser. This part of the formula is the zinger in the new law.

In the past, purchaser and seller were often pitted against each other in allocating the purchase price, with the seller seeking to allocate as much as possible of the sales price to capital gain assets, such as goodwill or land, and the purchaser seeking a larger allocation to assets that can be depreciated or otherwise written off, such as a covenant not to compete, or to depreciable improvements, such as buildings, rather than goodwill or nondepreciable land. Accordingly, whatever the parties were finally able to agree to as a sales price allocation was usually difficult for the IRS to challenge, since they were bargaining at arm's-length.

This game is now largely over. On the other hand, the Tax Reform Act of 1986 has opened up some new opportunities for purchasers, since a corporate seller will no longer be very motivated to seek capital gain treatment (allocations to goodwill, land, and other capital assets) now that capital gains of corporations are taxed at the same rate as other income. In short, it should now be easier to get a corporate seller to go along with a purchase price allocation that you have proposed.

Thus, notwithstanding the government's new four-step formula for allocating the purchase price upon sale of a business, it appears that there will still be some good reasons for having a purchase price allocation agreement when you buy an existing business.

The main advantage will be to create a rationale for allocating at least some part of the purchase price to intangible assets that can be amortized or otherwise written off over some period of time. For example, you may purchase a business for a price well in excess of the value of its specific, easily identifiable assets. This is particularly likely to be the case in some service businesses where the value of the receivables and a few tangible assets such as office equipment, furniture, and supplies may be only a small fraction of the price paid for the business. In those cases, it clearly will not be possible to allocate $50,000 of the purchase price to a $5 supply of paper clips.

Instead, you should consider provisions in your agreement of sale with the seller to allocate part of the purchase price to some of the following types of assets.

Customer Lists

For some types of businesses, it may be appropriate to create a list of customers whom you are buying and an agreed value for each. In recent years, the courts have frequently allowed purchasers of businesses to deduct the price paid for customer accounts on some rational basis, such as writing off the amount agreed to be the value of a particular customer account in the year that customer is lost,[2] or on some other basis.

Other Intangible Assets

Similar advantageous tax treatment for you as the purchaser (and possibly with capital gains treatment to the seller, if that is of importance to the seller) may be gained from allocating part of the purchase price to items, such as a very favorable lease with several years left to run or to items like blueprints or technical knowhow that have a limited useful life.[3]

Covenant Not to Compete

If the agreement includes a covenant by the seller not to compete with you for some period of time (which you may want to have regardless of tax considerations), you should seek an allocation in the agreement of a substantial part of the excess purchase price to the covenant, which, if the value assigned is reasonable, you should be able to amortize — deduct in part each year over the term of the covenant. In the past, a seller would have fiercely resisted such an allocation, since the covenant payments would have all been taxable to him or her as ordinary income; this is less of an issue now that capital gains are taxed at ordinary income rates. Remember that if there is no agreement as to the value of the covenant not to compete, you lose taxwise, since the IRS generally treats the value of such a covenant as zero unless the parties have agreed that it has a particular value.[4]

Important!

Please note that new tax regulations require both purchaser and seller to file *Form 8594* with the IRS any time a business is bought or sold. *Form 8594* reports certain information about the purchase price allocation.[5] Penalties for failure to file this form can be extremely large! Needless to say, the information on the two *Forms 8594* that are filed by you and the seller should be identical, or you will both be inviting IRS audits. Also, recent 1990 legislation now makes any agreement as to the value of an asset in a contract of sale between purchaser and seller binding upon both parties for tax purposes, in most cases. Thus, it is very important, from a tax standpoint, to negotiate the best possible allocation of the purchase price among the assets you acquire, and have that allocation reflected in the contract of sale.[6]

3.6 Closing the Deal

As has already been noted, the legal procedures involved in buying an existing business are rather complex. To ensure that you are protected under the law as fully as possible from liabilities you have not agreed to assume, you should see to it that someone, most likely your attorney, has taken the steps described below.

In most states, the purchaser of a retail or wholesale establishment or certain other types of businesses must prepare a Notice to Creditors of Bulk Transfer and file it in counties where the business operates and also publish it in a general circulation newspaper prior to the purchase of the business. If this is not properly done, the seller's unsecured creditors may be able to attach the property that you thought you were buying free and clear. See Section 11.3 for specific requirements under the bulk sale law in this state.

Before closing the purchase, your attorney should check with the secretary of state's office to determine whether anyone has recorded a "security interest" — a lien or chattel mortgage — against the personal property of the seller's business. Naturally, if the transaction involves a purchase of real property, you will also have a title search performed to see if the seller has good title and if there are any recorded mortgages or other claims against the property that the seller has not disclosed to you. For a fee, the secretary of state's office will provide a listing of any security interests that have been recorded as a lien against the assets of the business you are buying. See Section 11.3 for information on how to check for recorded security interests or liens.

As the purchaser of the business, you should require as a condition of the sale that the seller obtain the required form or certificate from the state agency that collects payroll taxes, certifying that all employment taxes due the state have been paid by the seller. Otherwise, if you fail to withhold enough of the purchase price to cover unpaid employment taxes, you may be liable to the state for those taxes if the seller has not made all necessary payments. See Section 11.3 for specifics.

Similarly, you should insist that the seller obtain and provide you a sales and use tax certification showing that all outstanding sales and use tax payments due have been made by the seller, so that you do not unwittingly subject yourself to exposure for paying the seller's unpaid sales or use taxes. See Section 11.3 on this point.

File *Form 8594* with the IRS regarding the purchase price allocation and other information in connection with the transaction. The penalty for intentional disregard of this filing requirement is 10% of the amount that was not correctly reported, which could mean up to 10% of the entire purchase price! Don't forget to file *Form 8594*!

If there is any one thing discussed in this book that you should not attempt to do, it is buying or selling a business without the assistance of

Legal Steps in Buying a Business

File Transfer Notice

Check Security Interests

Get Tax Releases

File with IRS

Retain a Lawyer

an attorney in reviewing and structuring the deal. Preferably, the attorney should be one who specializes in business law practice rather than a litigation specialist or general practitioner. You will also need competent tax advice, either from your attorney or from an accountant, in negotiating and structuring such aspects of the deal as the allocation of the purchase price (discussed in the previous section) and the disposition of any employee benefit plans carried on by the seller for the employees of the business.

Use an Escrow

In general, both purchaser and seller will be protected if an escrow is used to handle a sale of a business from the time the sale agreement is signed until the deal closes. The escrow holder, which is usually an escrow company or escrow department of a financial institution, will hold the agreement, escrow instructions, funds, and important documents until all conditions for closing the deal or releasing the funds or documents are fulfilled. At that time, it will disburse the funds to the seller and deliver the documents of title to the purchaser if the deal closes, or make such other disposition as is called for by the escrow instructions if the deal falls through. Your attorney or the seller's attorney may also act as escrow holder, but you probably will not want the seller's attorney to act in that role in most cases, for obvious reasons.

Build in Holdbacks

If the seller has made misrepresentations to you in the contract of sale regarding assets that do not exist, or the like, you may always seek satisfaction by suing for damages. However, in view of the cost, delay, and uncertainty in bringing a lawsuit, you would generally be far better off if there were some simple way you could merely offset any such overstated asset or understated liability against the purchase price, retroactively. To make this possible, you should seek to structure the deal so that part of the purchase price is held back for some period, say a year, just in case such a contingency arises. Then, if you discover false representations as to assets or liabilities, it will be relatively simple — compared to bringing a lawsuit against a seller who may have skipped town — to have your claim deducted from the amount held back. Discuss with your attorney the possibilities of structuring the transaction so that you either (a) give the seller a note as part of the purchase price, with a right to reduce the principal amount of the note if certain contingencies occur, or (b) have part of the cash payment price held in escrow for six months or more after the sale occurs.

3.7 Summary Checklist for Buying an Existing Business

☐ Why does the present owner want to sell the business?

☐ Will the reputation of the business be helpful or harmful if you take it over?

☐ Obtain tax returns, bank deposit records, and other financial records. Don't buy a pig in a poke.

☐ If the business is not currently very profitable, why do you think you can run it more profitably than the present owner?

☐ Thoroughly investigate the business' financial records and history, its reputation, and any factors that might unfavorably impact on its future. You may need the help of an accountant or other experts.

☐ Review or have reviewed the provisions of key contracts, leases, franchise agreements, or any other legal arrangements which have a significant effect on the business. Be sure you are not assuming an unfavorable lease or contract or losing the benefits of a favorable one.

☐ Make sure that the purchase price is fair. Even if it is, can you afford it? Will you have enough working capital to run the business properly after you pay the purchase price?

☐ Insist on getting accurate financial information and access to the supporting data, early in the negotiations.

☐ Push for an allocation of the purchase price to specific assets in the sale agreement. Seek to maximize the amounts allocable to depreciable assets and any noncompetition covenant; seek to minimize allocations to goodwill or land purchased.

☐ Look for hidden liabilities, such as pending lawsuits, accrued vacation liabilities, unfunded pension plan liabilities, or potential exposure to environmental cleanup costs.

☐ Retain an attorney to participate in drawing up the sale agreement.

☐ Comply with the requirements of the Bulk Transfer Act if it applies to the particular type of business being acquired.

☐ Be sure that acquired property is not subject to any recorded security interests or other liens beyond those disclosed by the seller.

☐ Have the seller obtain and furnish a certification that all employment taxes due have been paid.

☐ Have the seller obtain and furnish a certification that all sales and use taxes due have been paid.

☐ Seek to hold back part of the purchase price as security to indemnify you for any misrepresentations as to assets or liabilities by the seller.

☐ Prepare *Form 8594* and file it with the IRS.

☐ See Section 11.3 for state law considerations.

Other Tax Considerations

☐ Determine whether the sale of the business will result in a sales tax liability with respect to part or all of the purchase price. If so, is there a way to reshape the transaction to reduce or avoid sales tax? For example, allocate more of the purchase price to assets not subject to sales tax, less to assets that are.

☐ If you are buying a corporation that has not been paying income taxes because it has carryovers of net operating losses or investment tax credits, be aware that you may be able to use only a small portion of those carryovers to shelter the income of the business once you become the owner. After 1985, in general, if there is more than a 50% change in the ownership of the stock of a corporation that has net operating loss carryovers, only a certain amount of those carryovers, equal to the yield on long-term tax-exempt bonds (about 7% at this writing) multiplied by the value of the "loss" corporation, may be used each year to offset taxable income for all tax years ending after the change in ownership.[7]

☐ If the seller has a favorable experience rating for unemployment tax purposes, make sure you act promptly so that you can succeed to that rating as a successor employer. See Section 11.3 on how and when this should be done.

☐ If you are acquiring a franchise, trademark, or trade name as part of the purchase, be aware that you may be able to amortize the cost of such franchise, etc. over a period of years,[8] although 1989 tax legislation has limited such deductions.

Footnotes

1. I.R.C. § 1060(a).
2. *Holden Fuel Oil Co.* v. *Commissioner*, 479 F.2d 613 (6th Cir. 1973); Rev. Rul. 74-456, 1974-2 CB 65; *Computing and Software, Inc.*, 64 T.C. 223 (1975).
3. *U.S. Mineral Products*, 52 T.C. 177 (1969) (Acq.). (Sale of technical know- how eligible for capital gain.)
4. *George Bacon*, 36 T.C. Memo 1977-52.
5. Temp. Regs. 1.1060-1T.
6. I.R.C. § 1060(a).
7. I.R.C. § 382.
8. I.R.C. § 1253.

Part II

Starting the Business

Chapter 4

A Trip through the Red Tape Jungle: Requirements that Apply to Nearly All New Businesses

"The difference between a taxidermist and a tax collector is that the taxidermist leaves the skin."

— Ancient American proverb

4.1 General Considerations

The purpose of this chapter is to outline the most common governmental requirements and other red tape that virtually everyone starting a new business must attend to. The requirements discussed in this chapter will also generally apply if you have bought an existing business, unless you have acquired the stock of an incorporated business.

This chapter assumes that your business has no employees. If you expect to have one or more employees, a large number of additional legal requirements will affect your business immediately. Chapter 5 covers the additional requirements that apply to new businesses that have employees. This chapter does not discuss the special licenses that many types of businesses are required to have. If you do not know whether the type of business you are considering going into requires a special license or licenses from federal, state, or local government agencies, refer to Chapter 6.

In the following chapters, we have described specific, widely-used government forms and indicated whether the form is provided for your use in the back of this book.

4.2 Choosing a Name for the Business

The name you choose for your business can be important from a business image standpoint and also in communicating to the public what you have to offer. Most small businesses should select a name that, at least in part, clearly describes the product or service provided. If you ignore this basic common-sense rule, you run the risk of losing many potential customers for the simple reason that they will pass right by without realizing what you do. A fanciful or whimsical name is fine from an image standpoint, but it should also give the public a clear idea of what it is your business provides in the way of goods or services. For example, if you call your restaurant "The Comestible Emporium," a lot of hungry people will probably drive right by without realizing that you serve food. It is advisable, however, from the standpoint of protecting your business' name as a trademark or service mark under federal or state law, to adopt a name that is also partially arbitrary or nondescriptive, in conjunction with a name that is descriptive of the services or goods provided. An example would be the "21 Club Restaurant." The reason for selecting a name that is partially whimsical or arbitrary is that trademarks or service marks that are merely descriptive of the goods or services cannot be legally protected from use by others unless it can be proven that the name has acquired a secondary meaning, which is very difficult to establish for a new small business.[1]

You also need to think of the possible consequences of putting your name out before the public, however satisfying that might be to your ego. You may want to consider using some sort of fictitious name (see Section 4.10 of this chapter) for your business, rather than your name. There is nothing illegal or shady about using a fictitious business name. If you put your name on the business and the venture goes belly up, as so many new businesses do, many people in the community will automatically associate your name with the defunct or bankrupt business, which may make it very difficult for you if you try to start another business or obtain credit in the same community in the future.

Once you have settled on a name for your business, you or preferably your attorney, should find out whether the same name, or a confusingly similar name, has already been pre-empted by someone else. This involves making an inquiry with the state's secretary of state to find out whether the name is already being used in the state by a local corporation or an out-of-state corporation that has qualified to do business in the state. Inquiry should also be made of the county clerk in each county where you will do business, to see if another business is already using the same or a confusingly similar name in the county and has filed a fictitious business name statement. If so, you may have to choose a different name to do business under. See Section 9.5 for more information on trademark protection.

4.3 Local Business Licenses

Almost every business will need city or county business licenses, or both. These licenses can be obtained at the local city hall or county offices. Failure to obtain a license when you start business will usually result in a penalty when the local government eventually catches up with you; therefore, obtaining the necessary licenses should be among the first steps taken when you start a business.

Some cities and counties impose a gross receipts, income, or payroll tax on most businesses. Certain types of businesses, such as restaurants, may also be required to obtain special permits from local health authorities and fire or police departments.

If your business will construct its own building, it will be necessary to consult your local city or county zoning ordinances. A building permit must be obtained for both new construction and remodeling in most areas.

In addition, whether or not you plan to carry on any construction activity or do any remodeling, you will need to make certain that the business activity you intend to carry on does not violate any zoning regulations or any ordinances regarding hazardous activities. You may also be required to obtain a use permit from the city or county planning commission.

4.4 State Licenses

Most states impose license fees or taxes on a wide range of businesses, occupations, and professions. The fees often vary widely among the different types of businesses and occupations, ranging from relatively nominal to substantial amounts or rates, depending upon the activity. The many different types of licenses and permits are usually granted based on some combination of requirements such as registration, bonding, education, experience, and passage of licensing examinations. Since you may not legally operate any of these regulated businesses or professions without being licensed, you should find out whether there is a state licensing requirement for the business you plan to start. If so, determine whether and how you will be able to comply with the licensing requirements. See Section 11.6 for a partial listing of businesses, occupations, and professions that must be licensed under the laws of this state.

4.5 Federal Licenses

Most new small businesses are unlikely to require any type of federal permit or license to operate, unless they are engaged in rendering investment advice, making alcohol or tobacco products, preparing meat products, or making or dealing in firearms. Federal permits or licenses would also be necessary to commence certain large-scale operations, such as a radio or television station or a common carrier, or to produce drugs or biological products. If you wish to engage in any of the foregoing activities, all of which are heavily regulated, you should consult an attorney well in advance regarding regulatory requirements.

4.6 Estimated Taxes

As a sole proprietor or partner in a partnership, you will have to make advance payments of estimated federal — and possibly state — income taxes and federal self-employment tax once your business begins to turn a taxable profit. Individual estimated tax payments are due in four annual installments on April 15, June 15, September 15, and January 15 of the following year for an individual whose tax year is the calendar year. Any remaining unpaid federal tax is due with your tax return on April 15 of the following year (which is also the date when the first estimated tax installment is due for that year). An individual files *Form 1040-ES* with his or her federal estimated tax payments. Note that you must pay 90% of your estimated tax during the year rather than the 80% previously required before 1988.[2]

If your business is incorporated, the corporation will generally have to make corporate estimated tax payments, if it has taxable income, as early as the fourth month of its first tax year. Federal estimated tax payments should be computed on *Form 1120-W* (which can be obtained, along with other federal tax forms, from any IRS office) and must be deposited in a bank that is authorized to accept federal tax deposits. The corporate estimated tax deposits must be accompanied by federal tax deposit coupons. Your corporation will be issued one coupon book which contains 23 coupons per book, preprinted with your corporate tax identification number. These coupons can be used for deposits of all types of federal taxes.

On each coupon you must indicate, by checking the applicable box, the kind of tax being deposited and the quarter to which payroll tax deposits are to be applied. The boxes on the coupon indicate the form name for the type of tax being paid.

Federal Tax Deposits

Type of Tax	Box to Check on Coupon
Payroll tax deposits	941
Federal unemployment tax	940
Corporate income tax estimates (and year-end payments)	1120

For deposits of corporate estimated income tax you must indicate the quarter which most closely corresponds to your fiscal year end, not the calendar quarter to which the payment relates. Example: If your corporate year end is May 31, you would check the "1120" box and darken the box which indicates 2nd quarter. For each of the four quarterly estimates, 2nd quarter would be indicated on each deposit coupon.

Tax Periods

Fiscal Year Ends	Applicable Quarter
January, February, March	1st quarter
April, May, June	2nd quarter
July, August, September	3rd quarter
October, November, December	4th quarter

The coupon books will be sent to you automatically when you file *Form SS-4*, requesting a tax identification number for the corporation. When you receive your coupon book, a reorder form, *Form 8109A*, will be provided, so you can request additional coupon books for the current year, if needed.

Important Notice!

A penalty may be imposed for failure to make deposits directly to an authorized government depository bank. In the recent past, when tax deposit cards were unavailable, it was common practice to mail payments to the Internal Revenue Service accompanied by a letter indicating the nature of the tax payment and requesting additional tax deposit cards. This method of paying business taxes is no longer acceptable. Thus, it is important to mail the reorder form in time to receive additional coupon books before you run out; however, the IRS will sometimes send you blank coupons to use temporarily.

Refer to Section 11.4 regarding state filing requirements for individual and corporate estimated income taxes.

4.7 Miscellaneous Tax Information Returns

Reporting Payments to Individuals

As a general rule, every person engaged in a trade or business must report to the IRS any payments of $600 or more made to any person during the calendar year, for items such as rent, compensation for services, commissions, interest, and annuities, plus other items of fixed or determinable income.[3] In addition, there are a number of additional new tax reporting requirements you need to be aware of — since there are stiff new penalties for failure to comply.

Obtaining Social Security Numbers

Recently enacted laws make it necessary to obtain the name and Social Security number or other tax identification number of anyone to whom you make payments that you must report. There is a $50 penalty for failure to obtain their tax identification number, unless you have a reasonable excuse, such as their refusal to give you the number.[5] If they do refuse to give you the number, you must withhold 20% of whatever amount you owe them and deposit it with the IRS, or you will be subject to a penalty for failure to withhold.[6]

Reporting Sales to Direct Sellers

You must now report sales of $5,000 or more of consumer products to any individual who is engaged in direct selling (that is, selling in any way other than through a permanent retail establishment).[4] This will mainly apply to sales made to people in direct sales organizations, such as Tupperware, Amway, or Shaklee. It would also apply in many other situations, such as where the person you sell to sells the goods by mail order. Use *Form 1099-MISC* to report these sales.

1099 Forms

These types of payments are usually reportable on information return *Form 1099-MISC* or *Form 1099-INT* (for interest) for each payee, and a duplicate must be sent to the payee. In addition, you must prepare and file a *Form 1096* return summarizing all the information on the 1099-MISC forms and on the other forms in the 1099 series. Each of these forms is due by February 28 each year, for the prior calendar year, and a copy must also be sent to the recipient of the payment by January 31.

Payments of compensation to nonemployees — independent contractors — are reportable on *Form 1099-MISC*.

Penalties

There are now much stiffer IRS penalties for not filing the above 1099 forms. Until a few years ago, the penalty for not filing or not giving a 1099 to a payee was only $1 per incident. Now it is $50 per failure, and since there is a separate penalty for not giving a copy of the 1099 to the payee as well as for not filing a copy with the IRS, it can cost you $100 for each person for whom you fail to prepare 1099s.[7] However, 1989 tax law changes have reduced the $50 penalty for late-filed 1099s and certain other information returns to $30, if filed more than 30 days late but before August 1 of the year due, or to only $15, if filed within 30 days after the due date.

Independent Contractors

In addition, if you erroneously, but in good faith, treat a person as an independent contractor, and it is later shown that the person was actually an employee, you will only be liable as an employer for 20% of the employee's Social Security tax that should have been withheld, and for income tax withholding equal to 1.5% of what you paid the individual provided that you properly filed *Form 1099-MISC* with the IRS.[8] If you failed to file *Form 1099-MISC* for that person, the amount of withholding tax you are liable for is doubled.[9]

Fortunately, there are a number of important exemptions from the 1099 filing requirements that will eliminate most of the people or companies to whom you are likely to make payments of $600 or more. You do not have to report:

- Payments to corporations (except certain corporations in the medical field).[10]
- Payments of compensation to employees that is already reported on their W-2s.[11]

- Payments of bills for merchandise, telegrams, telephone, freight, storage, and similar charges.[12]
- Payments of rent made to real estate agents.[13]
- Expense advances or reimbursements to employees that the employees must account to you (the employer) for.[14]
- Payments to a governmental unit.[15]

Businesses now have to report royalty payments of $10 or more to any person — a rule that went into effect in 1987.

Reporting Dividends and Interest

If your business is incorporated, it will also have to file a *Form 1099-DIV* for each person to whom it pays dividends[16] of $10 or more each year and *Form 1099-INT* for each person, if any, to whom it pays $10 or more ($600 for interest payments, in general) in interest[17] on bonds, debentures, or notes issued by the corporation in "registered form." *Form 1099-DIV* or *Form 1099-INT* is also required for any other payment of dividends or interest on which you are required to withhold tax. Payments reported on *Form 1099-DIV* and *Form 1099-INT* must also be reported on the *Form 1096* summary. *Form 1099-S* must be given to recipients of the proceeds from the sales of real estate, in general.

Reporting Large Cash Transactions

Any business that receives a payment of more than $10,000 in cash, in cash equivalents, or in foreign currency in one transaction, or in two or more related transactions, is required to report the details of the transactions within 15 days to the IRS[18] and to furnish a similar statement to the payor by January 31 of the following year.[19] The form for reporting such "suitcase" transactions is *Form 8300*. The penalties for noncompliance are generally the same as for not filing 1099s, except that in cases of intentional failure to file, there is an additional penalty equal to the higher of $25,000 or the amount of the cash or cash equivalent received in the transaction, up to $100,000.[20]

In addition to the requirement that you file 1099s with the IRS, you may have to file similar forms with the state.

Reporting Mortgage Interest Received

Federal law now requires that you give *Form 1098* to any individual from whom you receive $600 or more in mortgage interest during the year, in the course of your trade or business. *Form 1098* has the same filing requirements as *Form 1099*.[21]

Reporting on "Magnetic Media"

Note that the IRS permits you to file *Form 1098* and *Form 1099*, as well as certain other information returns, on "magnetic media" (computer tapes or disks) rather than the actual paper forms, if very specific formats for the computer tape or disk are met. The IRS requires that certain information returns be filed on magnetic media, if your business files 250 or more such returns for a calendar year.[22] These include *Form 1098*, all of the 1099 series and W-2 series of information returns, and various others such as *Form 5498* and *Form 8027*.

A "hardship waiver" to excuse you from having to file in magnetic media format may be granted if you file a request on *Form 8508* at least 90 days in advance of the due date, under certain circumstances.

Failure of a taxpayer to file an information return on magnetic media — or on a machine-readable form where magnetic media filing is not required — when required to do so is treated as a failure-to-file and can result in the imposition of applicable penalties for failure to file, as noted above.

If your firm finds that it will be required to file information returns on magnetic media, there are many data processing firms and computer programs you can buy that will encode the data for you in a way that meets the IRS' highly-technical specifications, at a relatively small cost.

4.8 Sales and Use Tax Permits

With a limited number of exceptions, every business that sells tangible personal property, such as merchandise, to customers must obtain a seller's permit from the state sales tax agency. Usually, a separate permit must be obtained for each place of business where property subject to tax is sold.

See Section 11.4 for a discussion of the state's sales and use tax laws and permit requirements. Some states have a gross income or a gross receipts tax rather than a sales tax.

In general, as a wholesaler or manufacturer, you will not have to collect sales tax on goods you sell to a retailer for resale, if the retailer holds a valid seller's permit and provides you a "resale certificate" in connection with the transaction.

Likewise, if your business, as a retailer, buys goods for resale, you need not pay sales tax to the wholesalers if you provide them with resale certificates. You may also buy blank resale certificate forms at most stationery stores in states where such certificates are required.

The sales and use tax laws typically require that a business that sells or leases tangible personal property keep complete records of the gross receipts from sales or rentals whether or not the receipts are believed to be taxable. You must also keep adequate and complete records to substantiate all deductions claimed on sales and use tax returns and of the total purchase price of all tangible personal property bought for sale, lease, or consumption in the state.

4.9 Real Estate Taxes

As a rule, you do not need to worry about contacting the county tax assessor's office regarding payment of any real property taxes on real property acquired for your business. They will usually contact you by mailing a property tax bill to the owner of record. See Section 11.4 for a general description of how state or local real property and personal property taxes are assessed and collected.

Property Taxes

In addition to local property taxes, American citizens and other U.S. residents who acquire U.S. real estate — including partnership interests or stock in certain firms owning U.S. real property — from foreign persons must withhold up to 10% of the purchase price and remit it to the IRS under the Foreign Investment in Real Property Tax Act (FIRPTA). If you fail to withhold the tax, you are liable for it. This is a potentially dangerous tax trap for unsuspecting American buyers of real estate, since it is often difficult to determine whether a seller is a foreign person.

FIRPTA Withholding Tax on Purchase of Real Property

While there is an exception for residences costing $300,000 or less, if you will live in it for at least 50% of the time for two years, it is far safer to obtain a *Certificate of Non-Foreign Status* from the seller if there is any possibility that the seller is a nonresident alien or a foreign company.

To protect yourself when purchasing real estate — or your client, if you are in the real estate business — you should require, as a condition of closing the transaction, that the seller provide you with an affidavit certifying that the seller is not a nonresident alien or a foreign company.

If the seller refuses to sign the affidavit and provide the required information, you should withhold 10% of the gross purchase price and transmit it to the IRS within 10 days of the sale along with IRS *Form 8288* and *Form 8288-A*. This can be a real problem in a highly-leveraged deal where less than 10% of the purchase price is paid in cash at the closing. Note that some states have recently adopted similar withholding provisions with regard to purchases of real estate within such states where the seller is a nonresident of the state.

If the seller is a foreign person, you will owe the IRS 10% of the purchase price if you fail to withhold the tax, unless you received a *Certificate of Non-Foreign Status* from the seller.

Remember!

4.10 Fictitious Business Name Statement

Every state has laws requiring any person who regularly transacts business in the state for profit under a fictitious business name to file and publish a fictitious business name statement. For a sole proprietorship or partnership, a business name is generally considered fictitious unless it contains the surname of the owner or all the general partners and does not suggest the existence of additional owners. Use of a name that includes words like "company," "& Associates," "Group," "Bros.," or "& Sons" will suggest additional owners and will make it necessary for a business to file and publish a fictitious business name statement. Putting a name that would be considered a fictitious name on your company letterhead, on your business cards, in advertising, or on your products will be considered a use of the name.

Many newspapers will provide the form for filing, publish the notice, and file the required affidavit. See Section 11.4 regarding specific requirements for filing a fictitious business name statement in this state.

4.11 Insurance — A Practical Necessity for Businesses

Insurance, like death and taxes, is an inevitable necessity for the owner of any small business. For almost any business, even one that has no employees, insurance coverage for general liability, product liability, fire and similar disasters, robbery, theft, and interruption of business should be considered. If the business will have employees, workers' compensation insurance is usually mandatory under state law, and employee life, health, and disability insurance are virtual necessities in many businesses and professions, if you wish to be competitive with other firms in hiring and retaining capable employees. Fidelity bonding should be considered for employees who will have access to the cash receipts or other funds of the business. If you have an employees' pension or profit-sharing plan subject to the Employee Retirement Income Security Act of 1974 (ERISA), employees involved in administering the plan or handling its funds must be covered by a fidelity bond, under ERISA.[23]

Faced with a bewildering number of choices between insurance companies, rates, and types of coverage, the typical small business owner simply picks an insurance agent out of the phone book or calls an acquaintance in the insurance business to help set up the business with insurance. Since the agent or broker's fee tends to increase if the insurance coverage is greater, or if the premium rates are higher, some agents may be less than entirely objective in advising you as to what kind and how much insurance coverage you need. Thus, the chances are that you may wind up paying a lot more for insurance for your business than you should, if you rely on an agent to tell you what you need and what carrier to buy it from, unless that agent is both knowledgeable and trustworthy.

Insurance Agents

Since it isn't realistic to expect you to become a sophisticated comparison shopper for insurance while you are trying to get a business off the ground, you should put considerable emphasis on seeking out and finding a good insurance agent whom you can trust and rely upon to give you good advice. There is no easy way to find such an agent, just as there is no foolproof way of finding a good lawyer or accountant. In general, the best approach will be to ask friends, lawyers, accountants, or other business people you know to refer you to a topflight insurance agent. Agents who have earned the Chartered Life Underwriter (CLU) designation will as a rule be more experienced and capable than those without the CLU credential. This can be an additional factor to consider when selecting your insurance agent. Agents who deal primarily in property and casualty insurance will not usually have CLU on their business cards. Instead, they may have the initials CPCU — Chartered Property/Casualty Underwriter — after their name, which is a similar mark of distinction in the field of property/casualty insurance.

Insurance Consultants

If you cannot find an agent with whom you feel comfortable, the author suggests the following, somewhat unorthodox, approach. Call an insurance consultant. Ask if — and satisfy yourself that — the consultant is a member of the Insurance Consultants Society or the Institute of Risk Management Consultants. To belong to either group, the individual or firm cannot be an insurance broker. These consultants are insurance experts and can give you their unbiased opinions on exactly what insurance you need. The usual hourly fees may seem high, but most new businesses probably will not need more than an hour of their time. Most will bill in quarter-hour increments. You will probably recoup the consultant's fee several times over in premium savings in just the first year alone. You should, however, be wary of a consultant who wants to increase the number of hours by offering to create specifications and provide additional services.

Once you have met with an independent consultant and know what is needed, shop for the insurance you need from insurance brokers. Don't let them bid up the amount of coverage or add on additional types of insurance. Use the insurance consultant as you would an attorney or physician — follow his or her advice.

An inexpensive way to become a better shopper for insurance is to use The Oasis Press' book titled *Risk Analysis: How to Reduce Insurance Costs* by Gary Robinson. This book provides help in analyzing your risks and shows you how to prepare a request for proposal that will help you compare insurance prices. It includes many ideas about selecting an agent and suggests ways of putting more responsibility on the agent for helping you obtain the proper insurance.

4.12 Requirements Specific to the Legal Form of the Business

Sole Proprietorships

There are no significant government regulatory requirements that apply specifically to sole proprietorships; however, as a sole proprietor of a business, you will need to attach a *Form Schedule C* to your individual federal tax return, on which you will report the income or loss from the business. Also, if your sole proprietorship shows a profit, you will usually have to pay a self-employment tax equal to 15.3% of your net self-employment income from the business or at least on the first $53,400 of such income, plus an additional 2.9% on self-employment income of more than $53,400, up to $125,000, in 1991. The self-employment tax is computed on *Schedule SE*, which must also be attached to your federal income tax return. See Section 11.4 for how to report business profits on your state income tax return.

Partnerships

As in the case of a sole proprietorship, a partner must pay self-employment tax on his or her share of the partnership's self-employment income, which is reported on *Schedule SE* of the partner's individual federal income tax return.

In addition, the partnership must file a partnership information return, federal *Form 1065*, reporting the partnership's income and each partner's share of income and other items. Each partner reports his or her share of partnership income or loss on *Schedule E* of the partner's federal personal income tax return. The partnership must also file *Form SS-4* with the IRS to obtain a federal employer identification number, even if it has no employees. See Section 11.4 for state partnership return filing requirements.

When a partner buys, sells, or exchanges a partnership interest, the partnership must file a special information return if the partnership's assets include unrealized receivables or substantially appreciated inventory that might cause the seller to have ordinary gain, rather than all capital gain, on the sale or exchange.[24] Statements also have to be sent to the partners involved in the transaction.[25]

A limited partnership, to qualify as such, is usually required to file a *Certificate of Limited Partnership* with the secretary of state or other state agency. In most states, a limited partnership should also file certified copies in each county where it does business or owns real estate.

Corporations

Corporations are subject to the following requirements not applicable to other legal forms of business organization:

- Filing articles of incorporation.
- Adopting a set of bylaws.
- Observing other corporate formalities on a regular basis, such as the

election of directors by shareholders and appointment of officers by action of the board of directors.

- Filing federal income tax returns on *Form 1120* (or *Form 1120-S* for an S corporation) and state income or franchise tax returns in most states where they do business. See Section 11.4 for various filings, taxes, and fees required of corporations that are incorporated or doing business in this state.

- If assets other than cash are transferred to the corporation at the time its stock is issued, in a transaction that is nontaxable under Section 351 of the Internal Revenue Code, certain specified information regarding the transfer must be reported on the corporation's income tax return for that tax year.[26]

- Filing *Form SS-4* with the IRS to obtain an employer identification number, even if there are no employees.

- If the corporation was organized under the laws of another state, the corporation will have to qualify with the secretary of state to do business.

4.13 Checklist of Requirements for Nearly All New Businesses

☐ Obtain local business licenses.

☐ Check on local zoning ordinances, regulations, and other land use restrictions.

☐ Determine if your particular business requires a state license to operate.

☐ Determine whether any type of federal permit or license is required. See Chapter 6.

☐ Be prepared to make estimated income tax payments almost immediately after starting business or incorporating.

☐ Apply for a sales and use tax seller's permit if you will sell tangible personal property. See Section 4.6 and the forms provided with this book.

☐ File sales and use tax returns, if sales or use tax must be collected on your sales.

☐ File with the county clerk and publish a fictitious business name statement if the business operates under a fictitious name, and then file an affidavit of publication with the county clerk (in most states).

☐ Locate a good insurance agent or retain and meet with an insurance consultant regarding fire, accident, liability, theft, and other types of commercial insurance you need. Then obtain the necessary insurance coverage.

☐ If you purchase real estate, you must withhold up to 10% of the purchase price and remit it to the IRS if the seller is a foreign individual or foreign-owned company, under the Foreign Investment in Real Property Tax Act.[27] Otherwise, you should insist upon receiving an affidavit that the seller is not a nonresident alien, with his or her taxpayer identification number, unless you are certain that he or she is a U.S. citizen or resident.

☐ For a sole proprietorship, report any self-employment income on *Schedule SE* of federal *Form 1040*, and report income or loss on *Schedule C* of *Form 1040*.

☐ A partnership files *Form 1065* reporting partnership income. Each partner reports his or her share of self-employment income on *Schedule SE* of *Form 1040* and income or loss from partnership operations on *Schedule E* of *Form 1040*.

☐ For a limited partnership, file a *Certificate of Limited Partnership* with the secretary of state and copies in counties where the partnership has places of business or real estate (in most states).

☐ For a corporation, file articles of incorporation, adopt bylaws, and observe necessary corporate formalities. File federal income tax return *Form 1120* (*Form 1120-S* for an S corporation). If property is transferred to the corporation tax-free under IRC Section 351, report required information relating to the transfer on the corporation's income tax return for that year.

☐ For a corporation or a partnership, apply for a federal employer identification number on *Form SS-4*, even if the business has no employees. See sample at the end of this chapter.

☐ File annual tax information returns, *Form 1096* and the *Form 1099* series, for payments of $600 or more for items such as rent, interest, and compensation for services, and send 1099s to the payees. File *Form 1098* for mortgage interest of $600 or more your business receives in a year from an individual. Also, report any cash payments or cash equivalents of more than $10,000 that you receive to the IRS within 15 days. Such filing may have to be done on computer-readable magnetic media.

☐ If your business is a corporation, be sure to obtain an adequate supply of federal tax deposit coupons in time to make your estimated tax payments.

See Section 11.4 for a checklist of additional state law requirements that apply to nearly all new businesses.

Note!

The above requirements apply to any business, whether it has employees or not. There are many additional requirements for businesses that do have employees, and these are covered in the next chapter.

4.14 Securities Laws

Inherent in the choice of the legal form of the business is the potential application of federal and state securities laws, if the new business is to have more than one owner, or should it become necessary to raise capital for an existing business. Because of the potentially dire consequences of violating federal or state securities laws, it is important to consult with your attorney as early as possible when considering issuing or transferring a security. Corporate stock and limited partnership interests generally are considered securities, and even a general partnership interest can be a security in appropriate circumstances, as can certain types of debt instruments.

Since the Securities Act of 1933, federal law has required registration as a prior condition to the issuance or transfer of securities. The law exempts various types of securities and certain types of transactions. The most important of these exemptions for small businesses have been the exemption for securities sold to persons residing within a single state and transactions by an issuer not deemed to involve any public offering. The Securities and Exchange Commission from time to time has issued regulations exempting small securities issues, attempting to balance the needs of small businesses to raise capital against the public policy of protecting investors. In 1982, the commission adopted Regulation D as its primary method of regulation of securities offerings by small businesses, although not to the exclusion of other exemptions which might apply.

Registration of Securities

Rule 504[28] under Regulation D exempts the issuance of securities by an entity if the aggregate offering price of all exempt securities sold by the entity during a twelve-month period does not exceed $1 million — not more than $500,000 of securities can be offered and sold without registration under one or more states' securities laws. The securities cannot be offered or sold by any form of general solicitation or general advertising, and the securities so acquired cannot be resold without registration or an exemption from registration. This rule does not require any specific information to be given to the purchasers of the securities; however, since the anti-fraud provisions of the securities laws apply even though the transaction is exempt from registration, it is helpful to memorialize in writing the material information regarding the offering.

Rule 504 Exemption

Rule 505[29] exempts offers and sales of securities if the offering price for all exempt securities sold over a twelve-month period does not exceed $5,000,000. To obtain this exemption, the issuer must reasonably believe that there are not more than 35 purchasers exclusive of accredited investors.

Rule 505 Exemption

Examples of accredited investors include: banks, insurance companies, a natural person whose net worth at the time of purchase exceeds $1,000,000, or a person who has individual income in excess of $200,000 — or $300,000 jointly with a spouse — in each of the two most recent years and expects the same in the current year, or an individual who purchases at least $150,000 of the securities offered, if the total purchase price does not exceed 20% of that purchaser's net worth at the time of the sale. Exceptions are also made for certain large investors, including corporations, partnerships, or business trusts with total assets in excess of $5 million, unless formed for the specific purpose of acquiring the securities.

For purposes of Rule 505, the issuer must furnish extensive information and certified financial statements to the investors, unless securities were sold only to accredited investors. The prohibition against advertising and solicitation applies to this rule, as do the anti-fraud provisions of the securities laws.

Rule 506 Exemption

Rule 506[30] is similar to the exemptions provided by Rule 505, except that the $5 million limitation does not apply. The 35 purchaser limitation does apply, with the exception for accredited investors, but a separate limitation requires that the issuer must reasonably believe immediately prior to making any sale to a nonaccredited investor that such investor either alone, or with a representative, has such knowledge and experience in financial and business matters that he or she is capable of evaluating the merits and risks of the prospective investment. The prohibition against advertising and solicitation applies to this rule, as do the anti-fraud provisions of the securities laws.

Issuers utilizing any of the above exemptions must file *Form D* with the Securities and Exchange Commission generally no later than 15 days after the first sale of securities and at other specified times thereafter. New Rule 507 disqualifies any issuer found to have violated the *Form D* filing requirement from future use of the Regulation D exemptions, if the issuer has been enjoined by a court for violating the notice filing requirement — but apparently will not disqualify prior issuances of securities merely due to failure to file *Form D*.[31]

It should be kept in mind that the exemptions available under the federal securities laws are more liberal than those available under the securities laws of many states. In connection with any issuance or transfer of securities, it is necessary to consider the possible application of securities laws in the state where the business entity is established or operates, and, if different, the states where purchasers of the securities live. See Chapter 11 for further information concerning state securities laws.

Form **SS-4**
(Rev. August 1989)
Department of the Treasury
Internal Revenue Service

Application for Employer Identification Number

(For use by employers and others. Please read the attached instructions before completing this form.) Please type or print clearly.

EIN

OMB No. 1545-0003
Expires 7-31-91

SAMPLE

1 Name of applicant (True legal name) (See instructions.)

2 Trade name of business, if different from name in line 1

3 Executor, trustee, "care of name"

4a Mailing address (street address) (room, apt., or suite no.)

5a Address of business. (See instructions.)

4b City, state, and ZIP code

5b City, state, and ZIP code

6 County and state where principal business is located

7 Name of principal officer, grantor, or general partner. (See instructions.) ▶

8a Type of entity (Check only one box.) (See instructions.)

☐ Individual SSN _____
☐ REMIC   ☐ Personal service corp.
☐ State/local government   ☐ National guard
☐ Other nonprofit organization (specify)_____
☐ Other (specify) ▶

☐ Estate
☐ Plan administrator SSN _____
☐ Other corporation (specify) _____
☐ Federal government/military

☐ Trust
☐ Partnership
☐ Farmers' cooperative
☐ Church or church controlled organization

If nonprofit organization enter GEN (if applicable)_____

8b If a corporation, give name of foreign country (if applicable) or state in the U.S. where incorporated ▶

Foreign country

State

9 Reason for applying (Check only one box)
☐ Started new business
☐ Hired employees
☐ Created a pension plan (specify type) ▶_____
☐ Banking purpose (specify) ▶

☐ Changed type of organization (specify) ▶_____
☐ Purchased going business
☐ Created a trust (specify) ▶_____
☐ Other (specify) ▶

10 Date business started or acquired (Mo., day, year) (See instructions.)

11 Enter closing month of accounting year. (See instructions.)

12 First date wages or annuities were paid or will be paid (Mo., day, year). **Note:** *If applicant is a withholding agent, enter date income will first be paid to nonresident alien. (Mo., day, year).* ▶

13 Enter highest number of employees expected in the next 12 months. **Note:** *If the applicant does not expect to have any employees during the period, enter "0."* ▶

Nonagricultural	Agricultural	Household

14 Does the applicant operate more than one place of business? . . . . ☐ Yes ☐ No
If "Yes," enter name of business. ▶

15 Principal activity or service (See instructions.) ▶

16 Is the principal business activity manufacturing? . . . . ☐ Yes ☐ No
If "Yes," principal product and raw material used ▶

17 To whom are most of the products or services sold? Please check the appropriate box.   ☐ Business (wholesale)
☐ Public (retail)   ☐ Other (specify) ▶   ☐ N/A

18a Has the applicant ever applied for an identification number for this or any other business? . . . . ☐ Yes ☐ No
Note: *If "Yes," please complete lines 18b and 18c.*

18b If you checked the "Yes" box in line 18a, give applicant's true name and trade name, if different than name shown on prior application.

True name ▶

Trade name ▶

18c Enter approximate date, city, and state where the application was filed and the previous employer identification number if known.

Approximate date when filed (Mo., day, year)

City and state where filed

Previous EIN

Under penalties of perjury, I declare that I have examined this application, and to the best of my knowledge and belief, it is true, correct, and complete.

Telephone number (include area code)

Name and title (Please type or print clearly.) ▶

Signature ▶

Date ▶

Note: *Do not write below this line.*   For official use only.

Please leave blank ▶	Geo.	Ind.	Class	Size	Reason for applying

For Paperwork Reduction Act Notice, see attached instructions.

☆U.S. Government Printing Office: 1989-242-315/80163

Form **SS-4** (Rev. 8-89)

Footnotes

1. *Armstrong Paint and Varnish Works v. New and U-Enamel Corp.* 305 U.S. 315 (1938): *Carter-Wallace, Inc. v. Proctor and Gamble Co.* 434 F.2d 794 (9th Cir. 1970). The author wishes to acknowledge Henry C. Bunsow, esq. of the San Francisco patent and trademark law firm of Townsend and Townsend for alerting him to this important point.

2. I.R.C. §6654.

3. I.R.C. §6041(a).

4. I.R.C. §6041A(b).

5. I.R.C. §6724(d)(3).

6. I.R.C. §3406(a).

7. I.R.C. §§6721 and 6722.

8. I.R.C. §3509(a).

9. I.R.C. §3509(b).

10. Treas. Regs. §1.6041-3(c).

11. Treas. Regs. §1.6041-3(a).

12. Treas. Regs. §1.6041-3(d).

13. Treas. Regs. §1.6041-3(e).

14. Treas. Regs. §1.6041-3(i).

15. I.R.C. §6041(a) requires filing of information returns for payments made to another "person." As defined in IRC §7701(a)(1), "person" does not include governmental bodies.

16. I.R.C. §6042(a).

17. I.R.C. §6049(a).

18. I.R.C. §6050I.

19. I.R.C. §6722.

20. I.R.C. §6721.

21. I.R.C. §6050H.

22. Rev. Proc. 89-42, 1989-29 I.R.B. 14.

23. 29 U.S.C. §1112 (§412 of ERISA).

24. I.R.C. §6050K(a).

25. I.R.C. §6050K(b).

26. Treas. Regs. §1.351-3.

27. I.R.C. §1445(a).

28. 17 C.F.R. §230.504.

29. 17 C.F.R. §230.505.

30. 17 C.F.R. §230.506.

31. Rule 507, as interpreted in Securities Act Release No. 6825, March 14, 1989 (17 C.F.R. §230.507).

Chapter 5

The Thicket Thickens: Additional Requirements for Businesses with Employees

"If anything can go wrong it will. Nature always sides with the hidden flaw."

— Murphy's Law

"Murphy was an optimist."

— O'Toole's Law

5.1 General Considerations

As the previous chapter indicated, there is a considerable amount of governmental red tape involved in starting almost any new business. If your business will have any employees — even if it is incorporated and you are the only employee — the level of government regulation and red tape will multiply several times over in the typical case. This chapter outlines the bases you must cover, in addition to those described in Chapter 4, if you start a business that will have employees.

5.2 Social Security and Income Tax Withholding

Once you go into business and begin paying salary or wages to employees, you will find that you have been appointed, as an agent of the government, to collect taxes from your employees. The most significant taxes you will be required to collect, in dollar terms, are income taxes and Social Security (FICA) tax withheld from employees' wages, which are discussed below in this section. You will also find in this and subsequent sections of this chapter that there are payroll taxes imposed directly on the employer, as payer of wages.

Employer Identification Number

The first thing you must do in this connection is to apply for a federal Employer Identification Number. This number will be used to identify your business on payroll and income tax returns and for most other federal tax purposes. To apply for a number, you need to file a completed *Form SS-4* at the earliest possible time, if your business has employees.[1] Corporations and partnerships must file *Form SS-4* even if they have no employees.[2] A sample of this form is located at the end of Chapter 4.

As a new employer, you should obtain a business tax kit from your local IRS office. At the same time, you can obtain *Circular E, Employer's Tax Guide*, an IRS publication that explains federal income tax withholding and Social Security tax requirements for employers. *Circular E* also contains up-to-date withholding tables that you must use to determine how much federal income tax and Social Security tax is to be withheld from each employee's paycheck.

Employer Social Security Tax

In addition to withholding Social Security tax from an employee's paycheck at the rate of 7.65% on gross wages up to $53,400, 1.45% on wages more than $53,400, with a $125,000 limit in 1991, the employer must also pay an equal amount of employer's Social Security tax. The withheld federal income tax, withheld employee Social Security tax, and employer's Social Security tax are all lumped together and paid over to the government at the same time. In some cases, these taxes can simply be mailed in with your payroll tax return (*Form 941* series) at the end of the calendar quarter or year; however, if you have significant amounts of the above taxes to pay, you will generally be required to deposit the taxes with a federal tax deposit form, a precoded coupon, at an authorized commercial bank or a Federal Reserve Bank. As a rule, the greater the amount of the taxes due, the sooner they must be paid. The rules as to how and when federal income and Social Security taxes are to be mailed in or deposited are summarized briefly as follows:[3]

Undeposited Federal Income and FICA Taxes	Deposit with Bank Is Due by:
Less than $500 at the end of a calendar quarter.	Last day of the following month (or mail in payment with *Form 941* return).
$500 or more, but less than $3,000 undeposited at end of any eighth-monthly period (a period ending on the 3rd, 7th, 11th, 15th, 19th, 22nd, 25th, or last day of any month).	15th day of the following month.[4]
$3,000 or more undeposited at the end of an eighth-monthly period.	3rd banking day after the end of the eighth-monthly period in which undeposited taxes reach $3,000.[5]
$100,000 or more undeposited at the end of any day.	1st banking day following.[6]

Thus, very large employers may have to make payroll tax deposits very frequently. For an employer making eighth-monthly deposits, no penalty for underdeposits will be made if at least 95% of the tax due is deposited when required each month. For a more detailed explanation of federal tax deposits, see IRS *Notice 109*.

Note!

Deposits of payroll and withholding taxes may be mailed to a depository bank, if postmarked at least two days prior to the tax deposit due date. But tax deposits of $20,000 or more by employers making more than one deposit a month must reach the bank by the due date, regardless of postmark date.[7]

New Employees

When a new employee is hired, you must furnish to the employee a federal *Form W-4* which he or she must complete and return to you. *Form W-4*, when completed, will give you the employee's Social Security number and the number of withholding exemptions the employee is claiming, which is used to determine how much income tax you must withhold from his or her wages. *Form W-4* is to be retained by an employer, and neither it nor the information on it is filed with the IRS, except in the case of an employee who claims more than 10 withholding exemptions, or who claims exemption from income tax withholding.

By January 31 of each year, you must furnish each employee with copies of *Form W-2, Annual Wage and Tax Statement*, showing the taxable wages paid to the employee during the preceding calendar year and the taxes withheld, including state income tax. By the last day of February, the original of each W-2 and a summary form (*Form W-3*) should be filed with the IRS.

Independent Contractors

Not all individuals who perform services for your business will necessarily be employees. In many cases it is possible to structure your legal relationships with persons who provide services to you so that they are considered to be independent contractors for tax and other legal purposes. From your standpoint as an employer, it is much preferable to be able to treat someone as an independent contractor rather than an employee of your business. If a person is considered to be an independent contractor, you do not have to pay Social Security tax or federal or state unemployment taxes with respect to his or her compensation. The independent contractor is considered to be self-employed for tax purposes and pays self-employment tax. In addition, you are relieved from the obligation to withhold income and payroll taxes from payments made to independent contractors or to file payroll tax returns with respect to their compensation. You must, however, file a *Form 1099-MISC* for each independent contractor (with certain exceptions) to whom you make payments of $600 or more during a calendar year, or, in the case of a direct seller of consumer goods, for each such direct seller to whom you sell $5,000 of goods during a year.

Because of the obvious advantages to employers of treating their employees as independent contractors, the IRS has been very aggressive in attempting to reclassify so-called independent contractors as employees where they perform functions in a manner that is more typical of an employer–employee relationship. Requiring businesses to file *Form 1099-MISC* is an attempt by the IRS to identify those businesses that may be improperly treating employees as independent contractors.

Before you decide to treat anyone who works for you as an independent contractor, you should consult your tax adviser, since there can be serious consequences if those individuals are reclassified as employees by the IRS. See Section 9.11 for a discussion of the risks involved.

State Withholding Taxes

Turn to Section 11.5 for a complete description of the state withholding tax requirements, if any, for an employer in this state.

5.3 Unemployment Taxes

With relatively few exceptions, all businesses with employees must pay both federal and state unemployment taxes. These taxes are imposed entirely on the employer. The federal unemployment tax is nominally 6.2% of the first $7,000 of annual wages per employee.[8] In practice, however, the federal rate is usually only 0.8%, since a credit for up to 5.4% is given for state unemployment taxes paid, or if the employer has a favorable experience rating for state unemployment tax purposes.[9]

The state unemployment tax rate for an employer can be either more or less than the basic rate, depending upon the amount of unemployment claims by former employees of the particular employer. The more unemployment benefits claimed by your former employees, the higher your unemployment tax rate will be, within certain limits. See Section 11.5 for specifics on state unemployment tax and other state payroll taxes, if any.

Federal Unemployment Tax

Your business will be required to pay federal unemployment tax (FUTA) for any calendar year in which it pays wages of $1,500 or more[10] or if it has one or more employees for at least a portion of the day during any 20 different calendar weeks during the year.[11] Needless to say, this will cover almost any business that has even one employee, even part-time.

If the FUTA liability during any of the first three calendar quarters is more than $100, you must deposit the tax with a federal tax deposit coupon, *Form 8109*, at an authorized bank during the month following the end of the quarter. If the tax is $100 or less, you are not required to make a deposit, but you must add it to the taxes for the next quarter. For the fourth quarter, if the undeposited FUTA tax for the year is more than

$100, deposit the tax with a tax deposit coupon at an authorized bank by January 31. If the balance due is $100 or less, either deposit it with the coupon or mail it in with your federal unemployment tax return, *Form 940,* by January 31. *Form 940* is not due until February 10 if all of the FUTA tax for the prior year has already been deposited when due.

The state also imposes an unemployment tax which meshes closely with the federal unemployment tax. Refer to Section 11.5 for details on the state unemployment tax, rates, returns, registration as an employer, etc.

State Unemployment Tax

5.4 Workers' Compensation Insurance

A business is generally required by state law to obtain workers' compensation insurance for its employees. This means that you, as an employer, may have to immediately seek out and obtain a workers' compensation insurance policy covering all your employees, or you will be subject to possible legal sanctions. Workers' compensation insurance coverage provides various benefits to an employee who suffers a job-related injury or illness.

There are many insurance companies that offer workers' compensation coverage. Many such companies, however, may be reluctant to write a policy that covers only one or a few employees, unless it is tied to other types of insurance policies. See Section 11.5 for a description of other formal requirements applicable to employers under the workers' compensation laws.

5.5 Compliance with ERISA — Employee Benefit Plans

If you have employees and provide them with fringe benefits, such as group insurance (other than workers' compensation), other types of employee "welfare plan" benefits, or if you adopt a pension or profit-sharing retirement plan, you will almost certainly have to comply with at least some aspects of the Employee Retirement Income Security Act of 1974 popularly — or unpopularly — known as ERISA. There are criminal penalties for willful failure to comply with two types of ERISA requirements: reporting to government agencies and disclosure to employees.[12] In addition, there are a number of different types of civil penalties which are incredibly numerous and complex, for unintentional failures to comply with ERISA requirements.[13] In short, compliance with ERISA is a nightmare.

This section is an attempt to lay down some relatively simple and straightforward guidelines you, as a layperson, can follow in trying to recognize when you might have an ERISA compliance obligation, so that you will know when to call your attorney, CPA, or benefit consultant for help.

ERISA deals with two kinds of employee benefit plans — pension plans and welfare plans. Pension plans[14] under ERISA are pretty much what you might expect — tax qualified retirement plans including both pension and profit-sharing plans (including Keogh plans), plus other types of benefit programs that defer payments until after employment has terminated. The ERISA reporting and disclosure requirements for pension plans are quite extensive, and if your business adopts any such plans, you will most definitely need professional assistance in meeting the ERISA requirements that may apply. These are summarized later in this section.

Welfare Plans

Welfare plans[15] under ERISA include most other types of employee benefit plans that are not considered pension plans. These include typical fringe benefit plans adopted by small firms, such as health insurance, long-term disability, group-term life insurance, and accidental death insurance plans. ERISA compliance for welfare plans is usually less of a burden than for pension plans, but is required for almost every business that provides any kind of benefits for employees of the type mentioned above. Note that a number of so-called fringe benefits that are in the nature of payroll practices, such as paid holidays, vacation pay, bonuses, overtime premium pay, and most kinds of severance pay arrangements, usually are not considered to be either pension or welfare plans under ERISA.[16] Thus, these kinds of payroll practices are not subject to ERISA at all.

Compliance requirements for reporting and disclosure under ERISA are briefly discussed below.

Summary Plan Description

The one ERISA compliance requirement that applies to almost all small businesses is the requirement that an employer prepare a Summary Plan Description (SPD) for distribution to all employees covered by any type of welfare plan sponsored by the employer, such as typical health, accident, life, or disability insurance plans.[17] An SPD must contain more than 20 specific items of information listed in U.S. Department of Labor Regulations,[18] including an ERISA Rights Statement which must be copied more or less verbatim from the regulations.

An SPD must be prepared for each plan and distributed to covered employees within 120 days after the plan is first adopted.[19] Each new employee must be given a copy of the SPD within 90 days after becoming a participant in the plan.[20] Since an SPD must be prepared for each employee plan subject to ERISA, even a very small business may find that it has to produce three or four of these documents, each of which must meet detailed technical requirements. One important consideration in taking out insurance coverage for employees should be a firm commitment from the insurance company or brokers that they will prepare the necessary SPDs for the insurance plans they are selling you. Otherwise, you may need to have your attorney or benefit consultant prepare the SPDs, which can result in substantial professional fees. Other than the need for an employer to prepare SPDs and distribute them to employees, there are no significant ERISA requirements that apply to most kinds of insured-type welfare plans that cover fewer than 100 employees.[21] You must, however, make available the insurance policies and other plan documents for inspection by your employees and you must furnish copies to them upon request.[22]

If your business should grow to have 100 or more employees who are covered by a plan, or if you adopt any type of uninsured funded welfare plan, you will suddenly become subject to a whole array of additional ERISA requirements, including:

Additional ERISA Requirements

- Filing a copy of the SPD with the Department of Labor;[23]
- Filing an Annual Return/Report or Registration (*Form 5500* series) with the IRS each year;[24]
- Preparing and distributing a Summary Annual Report to covered employees each year;[25]
- Preparing a Summary of Material Modifications of the plan (if necessary) and filing it with the Department of Labor and distributing it to covered employees;[26] and
- Filing a terminal report if the plan is terminated.[27]

The ERISA compliance requirements for a pension or profit-sharing plan of even a very small business are very onerous, complex, and expensive, despite numerous attempts by the IRS and Department of Labor to simplify the reporting requirements in recent years, in response to a barrage of criticism from small businesses. Because these compliance requirements are so very complex and are constantly in a state of flux, no attempt to spell them out in detail is made here. Instead, the basic ERISA compliance requirements for most pension and profit-sharing plans are summarized as follows:

Pension Plans

Item	Provided to	
Summary Plan Description	Department of Labor; participants; beneficiaries	**Summary of Basic ERISA Compliance Requirements**
Annual Return/Report (*Form 5500, 5500-EZ, 5500-C or 5500-R*)	IRS (now required even for a simple one-person Keogh plan)	
Schedule A, Form 5500 series (insurance information)	IRS	
Schedule B, Form 5500 series (actuarial information prepared and signed by an enrolled actuary for "defined benefit" plans only)	IRS	

Continued

ERISA Requirements (continued)	Item	Provided to
	Schedule SSA, Form 5500 series (registration statement)	IRS
	Form W-2P (report of periodic plan benefit payments made during the year)	IRS; recipient of distribution
	Form 1099-R (report of total distribution of benefits during the year)	IRS; recipient of distribution
	Form W-3 or *W-3G* (transmittal of forms W-2P and 1099-R)	IRS
	Form PBGC-1 (premium payment of required plan termination insurance — for "defined benefit" plans only)	Pension Benefit Guaranty Corporation (a government agency that insures pension plans of corporate employers)
	Summary Annual Report	Participants; beneficiaries
	Individual Deferred Vested Benefit Statement to Separated Employee	Former participant in plan
	Summary of Material Modifications (to a plan)	Department of Labor; participants; beneficiaries
	Terminal Report (when plan is terminated)	Department of Labor; participants; beneficiaries
	Written explanation of Joint and Survivor Annuity and financial effect of not electing to receive it (if plan provides benefits in the form of an annuity)	Participants
	Written explanation of reasons for denying benefit claim and description of appeal procedures	Person claiming entitlement to plan benefits
	Various documents and information to be provided on request	Department of Labor; participants
	Various formal notices upon occurrence of certain events	IRS; Department of Labor; Pension Benefit Guaranty Corporation; participants

If your business maintains a pension or profit-sharing plan, it should be obvious from the above that you need some expert help from an attorney, accountant, or pension consulting firm — or all of them — if you are going to be able to properly comply with the requirements of ERISA and avoid potential fines and other civil and criminal penalties.

While the author has long been a strong proponent of qualified retirement plans for saving taxes and motivating employees, the cost of maintaining these plans has unfortunately multiplied several times over since the passage of ERISA in 1974, followed by a labyrinth of ERISA regulations issued by several different federal agencies. In short, unless you make substantial contributions to, and obtain significant tax savings from, an employee retirement plan, it may not be worth having because of the heavy costs of compliance with ERISA.

Besides the ERISA reporting and disclosure requirements discussed above, there are two other points you should be aware of regarding ERISA — the bonding requirement and withholding requirements on pension or profit-sharing plan distributions. All employees who are deemed to handle assets of a pension or welfare plan that is subject to ERISA must be covered by fidelity bond.[28] You should consult your attorney or benefit consultant regarding the amount and extent of bonding required, if any, with regard to benefit plans you maintain for your employees, particularly if you have a pension or profit-sharing plan.

Bonding and Withholding Requirements

Secondly, withholding is now mandatory on distributions of pension and profit-sharing benefits,[29] unless the recipient elects in advance not to have any tax withheld.

In addition to reporting and disclosure requirements under ERISA, there are other federal reporting and recordkeeping requirements for certain types of fringe benefit plans.[30] For example, employers maintaining educational assistance programs, group legal services plans, and so-called cafeteria plans are currently required to file annual reports with the IRS on *Form 5500*, *Form 5500-C*, or *Form 5500-R* and to maintain records to show, if needed, that those plans qualified for tax purposes for each year after 1984.[31]

5.6 Employee Safety and Health Regulations

As has been discussed in Section 5.4 above, employers are required by state law in many states to carry workers' compensation insurance for the protection of employees who develop job-related illnesses or who are injured on the job. In addition, there are comprehensive and far-reaching federal laws that set safety standards designed to prevent injuries arising out of unsafe or unhealthy working conditions. The primary federal law regulating job safety is the Occupational Safety and Health Act of 1970 (OSHA).

Over the years, the Occupational Safety and Health Administration has issued reams of regulations and standards for workplace safety that employers, or their attorneys, are somehow supposed to understand and obey. This book is not intended to be a legal or engineering treatise on the substantive safety requirements of OSHA. Instead, the following summary highlights a number of exemptions and formal requirements you should be aware of, as a small business owner, in relation to OSHA.

Federal OSHA

If you have employees, you will need to consult an attorney, preferably one with OSHA expertise, to determine what, if any, steps you must take to comply with federal and state safety standards at your place of business. Otherwise, you may be subject to fines and other legal sanctions if any employee is injured on the job or OSHA inspectors find that you are not in compliance with applicable safety standards at your place of business.

The Federal Occupational Safety and Health Act of 1970 (OSHA) imposes reporting and recordkeeping obligations on an employer that can be briefly summarized as follows:

Notices to Employees

OSHA requires that you post a permanent notice to employees regarding job safety.[32] In addition, OSHA rules require the posting of a second official poster regarding the rights of employees who are punished for objecting to unsafe working conditions.

Recordkeeping Requirements

Under OSHA, it is necessary to keep a log of industrial injuries and illnesses.[33] The federal *Form 200* can be used to satisfy this requirement.[34] The information in the log must also be summarized and posted prominently in your workplace from February 1 to March 1.[35] This requirement was eliminated January 1, 1983 for most retail, financial, insurance, and service firms,[36] but not for the following:

- Building material and garden supply stores
- General merchandise stores
- Foodstores
- Hotels and other lodging places
- Repair, amusement, and recreation services
- Health services[37]

Under OSHA, a Supplementary Record must be prepared after a recordable injury or illness occurs, using federal *Form 101* or any of the substitutes state law permits to be used for this purpose.[38]

Neither of the above recordkeeping forms are ordinarily filed with the government. Instead, these records must be retained and kept available for inspection for five years.[39]

In addition, special recordkeeping requirements will generally apply if your employees are exposed to toxic substances, asbestos, radiation, or carcinogens on the job. You may obtain more detailed information on OSHA recordkeeping requirements by calling the nearest OSHA office (usually listed in the phone book under U. S. Government — Department of Labor) and asking for the booklet entitled *Recordkeeping Requirements for Occupational Injuries and Illnesses*.

Exemption from Recordkeeping

The federal act exempts small employers from most of the reporting and recordkeeping requirements and treats any employer with 10 or fewer

employees during the previous year as a small employer.[40] The requirements, however, of keeping a log and reporting fatalities and multiple
injuries are not exempted.

Federal OSHA reporting requirements include the following:

Reporting Requirements

- The Bureau of Labor Statistics may require certain selected employers,
  including small employers, to report certain summary information on
  job-related injuries and illnesses annually on *Occupational Injuries
  and Illness Survey Form.*[41]
- In the event of a fatality or an accident resulting in the hospitalization
  of five or more employees, an employer must notify the area director
  of OSHA within 48 hours, describing the circumstances of the
  accident, the extent of any injuries, and the number of fatalities.[42] There
  are penalties in the event you fail to give notice as required.[43]

See Section 11.5 for a discussion of laws your state may have that govern
employee health and safety.

**State Employee Safety and
Health Regulations**

5.7 Employee Wage & Hour and Child Labor Laws

Not all businesses nor all employees of a given business are covered by
federal and state wage and hour and child labor laws. The coverage of
these laws is a crazy quilt patchwork of exceptions and exceptions to
exceptions. Thus, there is no simple way to tell you whether your business will be subject to one or more of the federal and state laws relating
to minimum wage, overtime pay, and child labor, or, if it is, which
employees are covered and which are not. You will have to find that out
for yourself, with the help of your attorney, the local wage and hour
offices, or both. This section outlines some of the basic requirements of
these laws that you must be aware of as an employer in this state.

The Federal Fair Labor Standards Act (FLSA) includes a number of
requirements regarding compensation of employees covered under the
act. There are two major requirements you need to know about.

**Federal Wage and Hour
Laws**

The minimum wage provisions of the FLSA set an hourly minimum
wage that an employer can pay to an employee. For 1991, the federal
minimum wage is $3.80 per hour until April 1, 1991, when it will increase
to $4.25 an hour .[44] Certain states provide for a minimum wage in excess of
the federal requirement or that applies to some employees who are not covered under the federal minimum wage law (refer to Section 11.5).

Minimum Wage Requirement

Overtime Pay Requirement

This rule requires an employer to pay a covered employee at one and one-half times the employee's regular hourly rate for any hours worked in excess of 40 in a week.[45] The regular rate cannot be less than the minimum wage. For the overtime pay requirement, the FLSA takes a single workweek as its measuring period and does not permit averaging of hours over two or more weeks. For example, if an employee works 30 hours one week and 50 hours during the next, he or she must receive overtime compensation (time and a half) for the 10 overtime hours worked in the second week, even though the average number of hours worked in the two weeks is 40. Note that the FLSA only requires overtime pay based on the number of hours worked during a week and not for working long hours on a particular day.

The above rules generally apply to salaried workers as well as to those paid on an hourly basis. To determine the hourly rate for a salaried employee, it is necessary to divide the number of hours in the employee's regular workweek (40 or less) into his or her weekly salary.

Employee Exemptions

Executives, administrators, professionals, and outside salespeople are not covered and thus are not entitled by law to any pay for overtime hours worked.[46] The theory behind this exemption is apparently the view that these types of employees are independent and sophisticated enough to take care of themselves and do not need to be protected by the government from exploitation by their employers.

Retail & Service Exemptions

Employees of certain retail and service establishments that are not engaged in commerce are exempt from coverage.[47] What this really means, translated from the legalese, is that retail and service businesses that do not affect the flow of goods and services in interstate commerce are exempt. As you might guess, the Department of Labor interprets this exemption very narrowly, so that many types of businesses that seem local in nature are considered to be engaged in commerce and therefore are not exempt from the FLSA requirements. If your retail or service business, however, does less than $362,500[48] in annual gross sales and more than 50% of its sales are made within the state, it will generally be exempt from FLSA overtime and minimum wage requirements.[49] Note that even where an employer is exempt from the FLSA wage and hour rules, state wage and hour laws may apply. Because of numerous, sometimes overlapping rules, it is frequently unclear whether a particular retail or service business is exempt. Employers sometimes seek an opinion in writing from the local Department of Labor, Wage and Hour office when their attorneys cannot give them a definite answer as to whether they are covered by the FLSA provisions.

There are numerous other exemptions·from the wage and hour laws based on the type of business, the nature of the work performed by the employee, where the work is done, and other factors.[50] Before you assume that your employees are covered by the FLSA, you should consult your attorney, or at least call the local wage and hour office on an anonymous basis and ask for an informal and nonbinding opinion over the phone.

Probably the most important thing you should be aware of, if you have employees subject to FLSA standards, is the need to keep detailed records of hours worked, the type of work, and wages or salary paid. Under the law, if an employee files a claim against you for alleged failure to pay required wages in the past, you will need to be able to produce proof that you met the statutory requirements. Keeping detailed pay and work records for each employee is the only way to protect yourself against such claims for back pay. In addition, the FLSA requires employers to preserve such records.

Detailed Records Required

If you have employees whose wages, hours, and working conditions are subject to FLSA regulations, you will need to post the official wage and hour poster provided by the Department of Labor.

Poster Requirement

Refer to Section 11.5 for a discussion of the basic wage and hour and other significant labor law requirements under state law.

State Wage and Hour Laws

Both the FLSA and various state laws regulate or prohibit the employment of children in businesses, with very few exceptions. If you intend to hire children to work in your business — other than hiring your own children, which is usually permitted, except in hazardous situations — you need to be aware of the following basic child labor law provisions.

Child Labor Laws

As a general rule, the FLSA prohibits the employment of children under 16 years of age,[51] although there are a number of exceptions to this rule.[52] All children under age 18, however, are excluded from certain occupations that are designated as hazardous by the secretary of labor.[53]

Federal Child Labor Law

Children under 16 years of age cannot be hired under any of the following circumstances:

- To work in any workplace where mining, manufacturing, or processing operations take place.
- To operate power machinery, other than office equipment.
- To operate or serve as a helper on motor vehicles.
- To work in public messenger services.
- To work in the following occupations: (1) transportation; (2) warehousing or storage; (3) communications or public utilities; or (4) construction (except sales or office work).[54]

Children 14 or 15 years of age can be hired in other occupations not considered to be hazardous, but there are numerous limitations on the hours and times when they may work, particularly when schools are in session. A few occupations, such as delivering newspapers and doing theatrical work, are exempt from the federal child labor laws, even for children under 14 years of age.[55]

State Child Labor Law

Most states also strictly regulate the employment of children. See Section 11.5 regarding state child labor laws in this state.

Thus, if you intend to employ children under 18 years of age in a business, you will probably need legal guidance as to the conditions under which they may work, if at all, under federal and state child labor laws.

5.8 Fair Employment Practices

As an employer, you will also need to be alert to your obligations under a number of federal and state laws that prohibit discrimination in employment on the basis of sex, age, race, color, national origin, religion, or on account of mental or physical handicaps. These anti-discrimination laws are not just limited to hiring practices, but relate to almost every aspect of the relationship between employer and employee, including compensation, promotions, type of work assigned, and working conditions.

In addition to outlawing discrimination in employment, companies contracting for business with the federal government are generally required to adopt affirmative action programs in employment of minorities, women, the handicapped, and Vietnam veterans. Affirmative action programs are employment programs that go beyond elimination of discrimination. Under such programs, employers consciously make an effort to hire more women and minority group members and to upgrade the pay and responsibility levels of women and other groups that have historically been subject to patterns of discrimination. Affirmative action programs are generally not required in the case of businesses that are not government contractors — they are only required to refrain from discriminating in employment.

Federal Government Anti-Discrimination Laws

There are several anti-discrimination requirements that, as a small business owner, you should be aware of; however, if your small business employs less than 15 employees and is not working on government contracts or subcontracts, the federal anti-discrimination laws listed below generally do not apply to you. The one exception to this would be the Equal Pay Act of 1963 which provides equal pay for equal work for women. This act is applicable to employers with two or more employees.

Name of Law	Employers Who Are Covered	What the Law Requires	Employers Subject to Federal Anti-Discrimination Laws
Title VII of the Civil Rights Act of 1964	Employers with 15 or more employees during 20 weeks of a calendar year	No discrimination in employment practices based on race, religion, or national origin	
Pregnancy Discrimination Act	Same as for Title VII above	Equal treatment for pregnant women and new mothers for all employment-related purposes, including fringe benefits	
Executive Order 11246 as amended	Employers with federal contracts or subcontracts of $10,000 or more	No discrimination in employment practices based on race, sex, color, religion, or national origin	
Equal Pay Act of 1963	Nearly all employers with two or more employees	Equal pay for women	
Age Discrimination in Employment Act of 1967	Employers with 20 or more employees, 20 or more weeks in a calendar year	No discrimination in hiring or firing on account of age, for persons age 40 to 70	
Rehabilitation Act of 1973	Employers with federal contracts or subcontracts of $2,500 or more	No discrimination in employment practices on account of mental health or physical handicaps	
Vietnam Era Veteran Readjustment Assistance Act of 1974	Employers with federal contracts or subcontracts of $10,000 or more	Affirmative action programs for certain disabled veterans	

Employers who violate any of the above laws may be sued by either the complaining individuals or by the various government enforcement agencies, or both.

Formal Compliance Requirements

Small businesses are not required to do a lot of paperwork and filling out of forms when it comes to federal anti-discrimination laws. An employer with more than 100 employees, however, must file *Form EEO-1* with the Equal Employment Opportunity Commission (EEOC) each year.[56] In addition, as an employer you are required to keep detailed records — and should anyway, for your own protection — as to reasons for hiring or not hiring, promoting or not promoting, any employee or job applicant, in the event it is ever necessary to demonstrate that your firm has not discriminated against any group or individual member of a group in violation of federal laws.

Besides the above requirements, there are a number of official posters you may be required to post in your place of business. These are summarized in the table on the following page.

Required Display Posters

Type of Poster	Who Must Post	Source of Poster
Poster regarding sexual, racial, religious, and ethnic discrimination (*WH Publication 1088*)	Employers with 15 or more employees during 20 weeks of the year or with federal contracts or subcontracts of $10,000 or more[57]	EEOC offices, the nearest Office of Compliance
Age Discrimination poster	Employers with 20 or more employees who work 20 or more weeks a year[58]	EEOC offices
Notice to employees working on government contracts (*WH Publication 1313*)	Any employer performing government contract work subject to the Service Contract Act or the Public Contracts Act	U.S. Department of Labor, Employment Standards Division
Poster required under the Vietnam Era Veterans Readjustment Assistance Act	Employers with federal contracts or subcontracts of $10,000 or more	From the federal contracting officer administering the contract

State Government Anti-Discrimination Laws

Refer to Section 11.5 for a discussion of the relevant anti-discrimination provisions of the laws of this state.

5.9 Immigration Law Restrictions on Hiring

The Immigration Reform and Control Act of 1986 represents a major new governmental requirement regarding the relationship between employer and employee. Under the new law, employers are prohibited from hiring illegal aliens and are subject to fines of $250 to $20,000 for each illegal alien hired after November 6, 1986, depending on the number of prior violations by the employer. At the same time, the new act also prohibits employment discrimination on the basis of citizenship status and national origin. Employers may not fire or fail to hire anyone on the basis of foreign appearance, language, or name.

For all employees hired after November 6, 1986, employers are required to verify their eligibility for employment within three business days of each new hire. As an employer, you will need to fill out a fairly simple one-page I-9 form. The employee fills out the top portion of the form, indicating whether he or she is (1) a citizen or national of the United States, (2) an alien lawfully admitted for permanent residence, or (3) an alien authorized by the Immigration and Naturalization Service (INS) to work in the United States.

As employer, you must fill out the bottom portion of the I-9 form, which consists of three lists of identity and employment eligibility documents.

You must check off the documents you have examined, such as passport, Certificate of Naturalization, etc., which must include either one document in List A or one each in Lists B and C. Both employer and employee must sign the form under penalty of perjury, and the employer must retain the completed form and make it available if the INS or Department of Labor requests it in an inspection.

You may obtain copies of *Form I-9* and a related *Employer's Handbook* from the nearest office of the U.S. Immigration and Naturalization Service. A sample *Form I-9* is also included at the end of this chapter. For more information on employer responsibilities, call toll-free: (800) 755-0777 and request category #3.

For More Information

5.10 Restrictions on Layoffs of Employees

The WARN Act

If your business grows to the size where you have 100 or more full-time employees — or the equivalent, based on 40-hour workweeks — at a single location, you may be subject to the potentially onerous provisions of the Plant Closing bill that was enacted by Congress in 1988 and went into effect on February 4, 1989. This new law, called the Worker Adjustment and Retraining Notification Act, or WARN Act,[59] would affect you if you laid off 50 or more employees, or one-third of the work force, in a 30-day period. It applies to virtually any plant closing or major layoff for any reason, with a few obvious exceptions, such as due to an earthquake or flood, or due to a labor dispute, eg. a strike or lockout, for which no notice need be given.

A "layoff" under this act includes any of the following:

- A permanent termination of employment;
- A layoff of an employee for more than six months; or
- A loss of half the employees' working hours for six consecutive months.

In case of any major layoff or shutdown, the law requires you to give at least 60 days advance notice. If you give less than that, you are required to pay the laid-off workers for 60 days minus the actual number of days' notice you gave. The law requires you to notify the labor union that represents the employees, or, if none, the individual employees by mailing the notice to their last known address or including it in their pay envelope. You must also notify the local city or county government and state labor agency of the planned shutdown or cutback.

The WARN Act doesn't generally prohibit a company from making layoffs or shutting down a money-losing plant, but it makes it more costly for the employer to do so, and also gives local unions and politicians time to find some way to attempt to coerce a company into maintaining an antiquated facility that is no longer economically viable.

Count on being on the local evening news if you try to shut down your business or part of it, if you have become a major local employer.

The WARN law does impose stiff restrictions on a firm's ability to sell off, reorganize, merge, or consolidate operations, if such a decision would adversely affect the jobs of 50 or more employees. In other words, if your Japanese competition renders your plant obsolete, you will not be allowed to sell it off to a competitor if doing so would cost 50 or more employees their jobs. Instead, it appears that your only option would be to simply board up the plant and go broke. So much for the claim by its sponsors that WARN would somehow make American business more competitive against foreign competition. Instead, it has made it much more costly to take a risk on building a plant in the United States — if it fails, you may have to go down the tubes with it rather than restructuring or selling it off.

The unintended consequence of this supposed job-saving legislation will be to make any employer think long and hard about hiring employees and to start trying to find a way to automate every phase of its business.

This new law should create a great deal of employment for lawyers, however, if that is any consolation. There is expected to be a great deal of litigation over what does and does not constitute a mass layoff or shut-down under WARN. Let the good times roll!

EMPLOYMENT ELIGIBILITY VERIFICATION (Form I-9)

1 **EMPLOYEE INFORMATION AND VERIFICATION:** (To be completed and signed by employee.)

Name: (Print or Type) Last	First	Middle	Birth Name
Address: Street Name and Number	City	State	ZIP Code

Date of Birth (Month/Day/Year)	Social Security Number

I attest, under penalty of perjury, that I am (check a box):

☐ 1. A citizen or national of the United States.

☐ 2. An alien lawfully admitted for permanent residence (Alien Number A _____).

☐ 3. An alien authorized by the Immigration and Naturalization Service to work in the United States (Alien Number A _____ .
or Admission Number _____ , expiration of employment authorization, if any _____).

I attest, under penalty of perjury, the documents that I have presented as evidence of identity and employment eligibility are genuine and relate to me. I am aware that federal law provides for imprisonment and/or fine for any false statements or use of false documents in connection with this certificate.

Signature	Date (Month/Day/Year)

PREPARER/TRANSLATOR CERTIFICATION (To be completed if prepared by person other than the employee). I attest, under penalty of perjury, that the above was prepared by me at the request of the named individual and is based on all information of which I have any knowledge

Signature	Name (Print or Type)		
Address (Street Name and Number)	City	State	Zip Code

2 **EMPLOYER REVIEW AND VERIFICATION:** (To be completed and signed by employer.)

Instructions:

Examine one document from List A and check the appropriate box, **OR** examine one document from List B **and** one from List C and check the appropriate boxes. Provide the **Document Identification Number** and **Expiration Date** for the document checked.

List A Documents that Establish Identity and Employment Eligibility	List B Documents that Establish Identity	and	List C Documents that Establish Employment Eligibility
☐ 1. United States Passport	☐ 1. A State-issued driver's license or a State-issued I.D. card with a photograph, or information, including name, sex, date of birth, height, weight, and color of eyes. (Specify State)_____)		☐ 1. Original Social Security Number Card (other than a card stating it is not valid for employment)
☐ 2. Certificate of United States Citizenship			☐ 2. A birth certificate issued by State, county, or municipal authority bearing a seal or other certification
☐ 3. Certificate of Naturalization	☐ 2. U.S. Military Card		
☐ 4. Unexpired foreign passport with attached Employment Authorization	☐ 3. Other (Specify document and issuing authority)		☐ 3. Unexpired INS Employment Authorization Specify form
☐ 5. Alien Registration Card with photograph	_____		# _____
Document Identification	**Document Identification**		**Document Identification**
# _____	# _____		# _____
Expiration Date (if any)	**Expiration Date (if any)**		**Expiration Date (if any)**
_____	_____		_____

CERTIFICATION: I attest, under penalty of perjury, that I have examined the documents presented by the above individual, that they appear to be genuine and to relate to the individual named, and that the individual, to the best of my knowledge, is eligible to work in the United States.

Signature	Name (Print or Type)	Title
Employer Name	Address	Date

Form I-9 (05/07/87)
OMB No. 1115-0136

U.S. Department of Justice
Immigration and Naturalization Service

Employment Eligibility Verification

> **NOTICE:** Authority for collecting the information on this form is in Title 8, United States Code. Section 1324A, which requires employers to verify employment eligibility of individuals on a form approved by the Attorney General. This form will be used to verify the individual's eligibility for employment in the United States. Failure to present this form for inspection to officers of the Immigration and Naturalization Service or Department of Labor within the time period specified by regulation, or improper completion or retention of this form, may be a violation of the above law and may result in a civil money penalty.

Section 1. Instructions to Employee/Preparer for completing this form

Instructions for the employee.

All employees, upon being hired, must complete Section I of this form. Any person hired after November 6, 1986 must complete this form. (For the purpose of completion of this form the term "hired" applies to those employed, recruited or referred for a fee.)

All employees must print or type their complete name, address, date of birth, and Social Security Number. The block which correctly indicates the employee's immigration status must be checked. If the second block is checked, the employee's Alien Registration Number must be provided. If the third block is checked, the employee's Alien Registration Number *or* Admission Number must be provided, as well as the date of expiration of that status, if it expires.

All employees whose present names differ from birth names, because of marriage or other reasons, must print or type their birth names in the appropriate space of Section 1. Also, employees whose names change after employment verification should report these changes to their employer.

All employees must sign and date the form.

Instructions for the preparer of the form, if not the employee.

If a person assists the employee with completing this form, the preparer must certify the form by signing it and printing or typing his or her complete name and address.

Section 2. Instructions to Employer for completing this form

(For the purpose of completion of this form, the term "employer" applies to employers and those who recruit or refer for a fee.)

Employers must complete this section by examining evidence of identity and employment eligibility, and:
- checking the appropriate box in List A *or* boxes in both Lists B and C;
- recording the document identification number and expiration date (if any);
- recording the type of form if not specifically identified in the list;
- signing the certification section.

NOTE: Employers are responsible for reverifying employment eligibility of employees whose employment eligibility documents carry an expiration date.

Copies of documentation presented by an individual for the purpose of establishing identity and employment eligibility may be copied and retained for the purpose of complying with the requirements of this form and no other purpose. Any copies of documentation made for this purpose should be maintained with this form.

Name changes of employees which occur after preparation of this form should be recorded on the form by lining through the old name, printing the new name and the reason (such as marriage), and dating and initialing the changes. Employers should not attempt to delete or erase the old name in any fashion.

RETENTION OF RECORDS.

The completed form must be retained by the employer for:
- three years after the date of hiring; or
- one year after the date the employment is terminated, whichever is later.

> Employers may photocopy or reprint this form as necessary.

U.S. Department of Justice
Immigration and Naturalization Service

OMB #1115-0136
Form I-9 (05/07 87)
☆ U S G P O 1987- 183-918/69085

For sale by the Superintendent of Documents, U.S. Government Printing Office
Washington, D.C. 20402

Footnotes

1. To ensure that you will get tax deposit coupons in time, for depositing federal payroll taxes or corporate income tax.
2. Per instructions on *Form SS-4*.
3. Treasury Decision 7701, 1980-28 I.R.B. 20.
4. Treas. Regs. §31.6302(c)-1(a)(1)(i)(a).
5. Treas. Regs. §31.6302(c)-1(a)(1)(i)(b).
6. I.R.C. §6302(g).
7. I.R.C. §7502(e)(3).
8. I.R.C. §§3301(1) and 3306(b)(1).
9. See footnote 5 to Chapter 2.
10. I.R.C. §3306(a)(1)(A).
11. I.R.C. §3306(a)(1)(B).
12. 29 U.S.C. §1131.
13. 29 U.S.C. §1132; I.R.C. §§4971, 4975, 6057–6059, 6652.
14. 29 U.S.C. §1002(2); 29 C.F.R. §2510.3-2.
15. 29 U.S.C. §1002(1); 29 C.F.R. §2510.3-1.
16. 29 C.F.R. §2510.3-1(b); 29 C.F.R. §2510.3-2(b).
17. 29 C.F.R. §2520.104b-2.
18. 29 C.F.R. §2520.102-3.
19. 29 C.F.R. §2520.104b-2(a)(2).
20. 29 C.F.R. §2520.104b-2(a)(1).
21. 29 C.F.R. §2520.104-20.
22. 29 U.S.C. §1024(b)(4); 29 C.F.R. §2520.104b-1.
23. 29 C.F.R. §2520.104a-3.
24. 29 C.F.R. §2520.104a-5.
25. 29 C.F.R. §2520.104b-10.
26. 29 C.F.R. §§2520.104a-4 and 2520.104b-3.
27. 29 U.S.C. §1021(c).
28. 29 U.S.C. §1112.
29. I.R.C. §3405(a).
30. I.R.C. §6039 D.
31. Announcement 86-20, I.R.B. 1986–7, 34.
32. 29 C.F.R. §1903.2.
33. 29 C.F.R. §1904.2.
34. 29 C.F.R. §1904.10.
35. 29 C.F.R. §1904.5.
36. 29 C.F.R. §1904.16.
37. 29 C.F.R. §1904.12.
38. 29 C.F.R. §1904.4.
39. 29 C.F.R. §1904.6.
40. 29 C.F.R. §1904.15.
41. 29 C.F.R. §§1904.15 and 1904.21.
42. 29 C.F.R. §1904.8.
43. 29 C.F.R. §1904.9.
44. 29 U.S.C. §206(a)(1).
45. 29 U.S.C. §207(a)(1).
46. 29 U.S.C. §213(a)(1).
47. 29 U.S.C. §213(a)(2).
48. 29 U.S.C. §203(s). (For years after 1981.)
49. Note 45, above.
50. 29 U.S.C. §213.
51. 29 U.S.C. §§203(1) and 212.
52. 29 U.S.C. §213.
53. 29 C.F.R. §570.50–570.71.
54. 29 C.F.R. §570.33.
55. 29 U.S.C. §213(c) and (d).
56. 29 C.F.R. §1602.7.
57. 29 C.F.R. §1601.30.
58. 29 U.S.C. §627 and 29 C.F.R. §1627.10.
59. 29 U.S.C. §2101–2109.

Chapter 6

Businesses that Require Licenses to Operate

*"The bureaucrat who smiles when something serious has gone
wrong has already found someone to blame it on."*

— Anonymous

6.1 General Licensing

Almost any kind of business activity you engage in will require a city or
county business license, which is usually fairly simple to obtain. In addition, a few kinds of businesses will have to obtain licenses from the federal government to operate. Many kinds of businesses, occupations and
professions are also licensed and regulated by the state. While there are
tremendous variations in the kind and extent of requirements for obtaining necessary federal and state licenses, these requirements generally
relate to educational attainments, experience in the particular field, passage of examinations, submission of detailed applications, meeting financial or bonding requirements, or some combination of the foregoing, plus
payment of a licensing fee or tax.

In addition to the federal and state licensing requirements discussed in
this chapter, you need to be aware of certain local city or county permits
that you may have to obtain, such as from the county health department
if you will be in the food business, from the fire department if your business may have large crowds on the premises or various permits for construction or remodel.

Before you begin to operate any kind of business, you need to find out
whether you will be required to obtain any special government licenses
or permits, since in most cases you must obtain the particular license
before commencing operation.

This chapter and Section 11.6 provide a partial listing of federal and state licensing requirements you are most likely to encounter as a small business owner. Because the number of activities that may require federal or state licenses is so large, no attempt has been made to try to list all of them in this book. Obviously, the reader of this book is not likely to be planning to engage in some grandiose or exotic project like building a dam or operating a nuclear reactor. If you were, you could expect to need dozens of licenses and permits from government agencies and would probably require the services of a battalion of lawyers in the licensing process.

Thus, the lists of licensing agencies and businesses that require licenses found in this chapter and in Chapter 11 should be helpful in alerting you, as a small business owner, to possible licensing needs, but you should remember that these lists are not complete and are not a substitute for individualized legal advice.

6.2 Federal Licenses

If you are starting a small business, it is relatively unlikely that you will need any type of license or permit from the federal government; however, the following is a list of the federal licensing requirements you might possibly encounter:

Federal Licensing Requirements

Activity	Federal Agency
Rendering investment advice	Securities and Exchange Commission
Providing ground transportation as a common carrier	Interstate Commerce Commission
Preparation of meat products	Food and Drug Administration
Production of drugs or biological products	Food and Drug Administration
Making tobacco products or alcohol	Treasury Department, Bureau of Alcohol, Tobacco, and Firearms
Making or dealing in firearms	Treasury Department, Bureau of Alcohol, Tobacco, and Firearms
Radio or television broadcasting	Federal Communications Commission

6.3 State Licenses

For a partial listing of businesses and professions required to be licensed in this state, see Section 11.6.

Remember!

Your business may have to obtain several different licenses from various federal, state, and local government agencies.

Part III

Operating the Business

Chapter 7

Excise Taxes

"Taxation without representation is tyranny."
— Patrick Henry

"Taxation with representation is worse."
— Will Rogers

7.1 General Considerations

Both federal and state tax laws impose excise or similar taxes on a number of different types of businesses, products, services, and occupations. These taxes are usually imposed without any assessment or notice to the taxpayer. Thus, it is up to you to find out if you are subject to any of these taxes and if so, to obtain the proper tax return forms and pay the tax on time. It is not uncommon for a small business to operate for several years without the owner ever being aware of the need to pay excise taxes. Then comes the day of reckoning, when a formal notice is received from the government demanding immediate payment of several years' worth of back taxes on some particular item subject to excise tax, plus interest and penalties for not filing the returns and not paying the tax. This can be a disastrous surprise, especially since the business owner has not factored into the price of his or her goods or services the cost of paying the excise.

Therefore, this chapter is designed to alert you in advance to the types of federal and state excise — and similar — taxes that a small business owner may need to know about. Some excise taxes, such as those on telephone service and insurance companies, are not discussed below since they are passed along or absorbed by the telephone company, insurance company, or other large institution with which your business may deal, and you have no obligation to file any returns or make any direct payment to the government of such taxes.

7.2 State Excise and Miscellaneous Taxes

See Section 11.7 for a summary of various state excise taxes that may affect your business.

7.3 Federal Excise Taxes

Federal excise taxes on many products and transactions have been repealed over the last 20 years, so these taxes are much less pervasive now than in the past. The excise tax that the largest number of small businesses are likely to be subject to is the motor vehicle highway use tax on vehicles of more than 55,000 pounds gross weight.[1] If you want information about the highway use tax, you should request a copy of IRS *Publication 349* from any IRS office. The federal government imposes a number of excise taxes on various types of business activities. Some excise taxes are on the production or sale of certain goods. Some are on services or the use of certain products or facilities. Still others are imposed on businesses of a certain type. Most federal excise taxes are reported on *Form 720, Quarterly Federal Excise Tax Return*, the most common excise tax form. *Form 2290* must be filed by owners of trucks and buses subject to the highway use tax. Environmental taxes on petroleum and 42 designated chemical substances went into effect on April 1, 1981. *Form 6627* is used to report these taxes and is attached to *Form 720*. The windfall profits tax on crude oil was repealed by Congress in 1988.

Federal excise taxes can be broken down into several major categories:

- The motor vehicle highway use tax. This tax is imposed on vehicles of more than 55,000 pounds gross weight.[2]
- Retailers taxes on certain fuels.[3] The federal gasoline tax is now $0.14 (14 cents) per gallon on gasoline, and the tax on diesel is $0.20 (20 cents) per gallon. In addition, both of the taxes are increased by $0.01 ($1/10$ of a cent) per gallon to create a Leaking Underground Storage Tank Trust Fund. A reduced tax rate applies to qualified methane and ethanol fuel.
- Other retail excise taxes are now imposed on sales of:
  - Heavy trucks and trailers[4]

- Tires and tubes[5]
- Recreation equipment such as bows, arrows, fishing rods, reels, lures, and creels[6]
- Firearms and ammunition[7]

- Transportation taxes on air transportation.[8] If you are in the business of transporting people by air, you may have to collect an excise tax.
- Communications taxes on telephone and teletype services.[9]
- Wagering taxes.[10]
- Tax on coal mined in the United States.[11]
- Environmental taxes on petroleum products, various chemicals, and hazardous wastes.[12]
- Taxes on alcohol, firearms, ammunition, and tobacco products.[13]
- Manufacturer's Excise Tax on Vaccines. As of January 1, 1988, certain vaccines manufactured or imported into the United States are subject to a new excise tax in order to create a Vaccine Injury Compensation Trust Fund, a no-fault program for compensating persons who are injured by, or die from, certain vaccines.[14]

In addition, the Revenue Reconciliation Act of 1989 has:

New Excise Taxes

- Created a new excise tax on ozone-depleting chemicals;
- Increased the oil spill liability excise tax to five cents a barrel; and
- Accelerated its collection to January 1, 1990.[15]

So-called luxury taxes, which were all repealed in 1965, have come back to life in the Revenue Reconciliation Act of 1990. In general, the newly enacted luxury taxes apply to retail purchases of certain items after December 31, 1990 and apply at a rate of 10% of the amount by which the retail price exceeds certain exempt amounts.[16] The new luxury taxes are as follows:

Luxury Taxes

- Automobiles — The 10% tax applies to the portion of the retail purchase price in excess of $30,000. It does not apply to vehicles of more than 6,000 pounds unloaded gross weight, or to any vehicle, such as a taxicab, that is used exclusively in the active conduct of a trade or business of transporting people or property for compensation or hire.
- Boats — The 10% tax applies to the portion of the retail purchase price that exceeds $100,000, but not to boats used commercially for fishing or transporting persons or property for compensation or hire.
- Aircraft — The 10% tax applies to the portion of the retail purchase price that exceeds $250,000. The tax can be avoided if the aircraft is to be used at least 80% for business.
- Furs and Jewelry — The 10% tax applies to the portion of the retail purchase price that exceeds $10,000, per item.

The new luxury taxes, which are collected by the retailer who sells the item, apply only to the first retail sale of an item. Thus, for example, if you buy a used $50,000 automobile, there is no luxury tax on the purchase.

For More Information

For further information on excise taxes and other federal taxes, you may wish to obtain IRS *Publication 334, Tax Guide for Small Business* or, for more detailed information on excise taxes, IRS *Publication 510, Excise Taxes.*

Footnotes

1. I.R.C. § 4481(a).
2. Id.
3. I.R.C. §§ 4041, 4081, and 4091.
4. I.R.C. § 4051.
5. I.R.C. § 4071(a).
6. I.R.C. §§ 4161(a) and (b).
7. I.R.C. § 4181.
8. I.R.C. §§ 4261(a) and 4271(a).
9. I.R.C. § 4251.
10. Including tax on wagers and on the occupation of wagering. I.R.C. §§ 4401 and 4411.
11. I.R.C. § 4121(a).
12. I.R.C. §§ 4611 and 4661.
13. I.R.C. §§ 5001, 5041(b), 5801–5822, and 5701.
14. I.R.C. §§ 4131 and 4132.
15. I.R.C. §§ 4611(c)(2) and 4681.
16. I.R.C. §§ 4001–4012.

Chapter 8

Planning for Tax Savings in a Business

"The words of such an act as the income tax merely dance before my eyes in a meaningless procession: cross-reference to cross-reference, exception upon exception — couched in abstract terms that offer no handle to seize hold of — leave in my mind only a confused sense of some vitally important, but successfully concealed, purport, which it is my duty to extract, but which is within my power, if at all, only after the most inordinate expenditure of time. I know that these monsters are the result of fabulous industry and ingenuity, plugging up this hole and casting out that net against all possible evasion; yet at times I cannot help recalling a saying of William James' about certain passages of Hegel: that they were no doubt written with a passion of rationality; but that one cannot help wondering whether to the reader they have any significance save that the words are strung together with syntactical correctness."

— Judge Learned Hand
referring to the 1939 Internal Revenue Code, a statute which was almost childlike in its simplicity compared to our current tax law.

8.1 General Considerations

One of the most shocking and unpleasant realizations of many successful small business owners comes when they finally grasp the fact that they have acquired an unwanted silent partner — a partner who contributes nothing to the business but who often lays claim to half or more of the owner's hard-earned profits. That silent partner, of course, is the government income tax collector, and this chapter is a summary of many of the best and most effective legal ways to reduce that silent partner's share of the profits from your business.

This chapter is not intended to be a substitute for professional tax advice regarding your individual situation. Because the tax laws are so enormously complex, a technique that may work brilliantly in most cases might be useless or even disastrous in your particular tax situation, due to the interrelationships between the many tax rules and the way they may apply in different circumstances. What this chapter will do is provide you with a working understanding, from a layperson's standpoint, of some of the key ways to plan for tax savings and to avoid tax pitfalls in your business.

After you have read this chapter, you will probably want to talk to your tax adviser about one or more of the ideas discussed here that you feel might be useful to apply in your business. Your tax adviser should be able to tell you whether the particular idea will work in your situation. If it will, he or she can help you implement it.

Tax attorneys and accountants, particularly the most competent ones, often have a very heavy workload and a large number of clients to serve. An unfortunate result of this situation is that your tax adviser may tend to spend most of the time responding to inquiries by clients and meeting tax deadlines rather than taking the initiative in seeking out ways to minimize your taxes. Thus, to the extent you have some understanding of what you would like to do in the way of reducing taxes on your business income, you can propose ideas to your tax advisers and maximize the effectiveness of their expert knowledge and advice. In tax planning, as in so many areas of life, it pays to be assertive. "The wheel that squeaks is the one that gets the grease."

8.2 Using a Corporation as a Tax Shelter

One of the simplest and best ways to reduce your taxes is, in many cases, to incorporate your business. Incorporation is most likely to be advantageous if the business is generating about $75,000 or more in annual profits and salary for the owner — or per owner, if there is more than one. There are three basic ways, other than through adopting employee fringe benefit plans, incorporation can reduce your taxes on business income.

Leaving Profits in the Corporation

One way is by leaving profits in the corporation to be taxed at low corporate rates. These tax rates will often be much lower than if you were unincorporated and all of the business' profits — or your share, if a partnership — were taxed to you at individual federal income tax rates up to

31% or slightly more. Federal corporate income tax rates are only 15% on the first $50,000 of taxable income, 25% on the next $25,000, 34% on the next $25,000, 39% on the next $235,000, and 34% on income more than $335,000.[1]

Please note, however, that after 1987 there are no low corporate tax rates for qualified personal service corporations, whose income is now taxed at a flat 34% tax rate. Thus, you will now be able to take advantage of low corporate tax rates on the first $75,000 of corporate income only if your corporation is not considered such a qualified personal service corporation. See discussion of this definition in Chapter 2.

See Section 2.4, and Sections 8.5 and 8.9 of this chapter regarding some of the potential benefits and risks of allowing profits to accumulate in your corporation.

Income-Splitting

Splitting income between you and the corporation is done by paying yourself a salary and leaving the remaining profit after salary in the corporation, so it can be taxed at corporate rates. Thus, both you and the corporation may be taxed at relatively low tax brackets on the business income, as explained in more detail in Section 2.4.

Investing in Stocks

By investing accumulated corporate funds in dividend-paying stocks, you can take advantage of the 70% deduction corporations are entitled to on dividends they receive.[2] Because this special deduction makes most dividends received by a corporation — other than an S corporation — practically tax-free to the recipient corporation, your incorporated business can be an excellent place to hold stocks you wish to invest in, if you do not personally need the dividend income to live on currently. See the discussion of this corporate tax break in Section 2.4.

Before you get too excited about putting your whole stock portfolio into your incorporated business, you should be aware of several potential drawbacks:

- If you decide to later withdraw from your corporation the dividends from stocks it holds, or the stocks themselves, the withdrawal will usually be taxable to you as ordinary income[3] or perhaps, if you liquidate the corporation, as capital gains.[4] After 1990, capital gains are taxed at a maximum rate of 28% for individuals.[5]

- If you should accumulate more than $250,000 — $150,000 for a professional services firm — in after-tax earnings in your corporation, including the 70% of dividends that the corporation doesn't pay income tax on, and invest part of those earnings in liquid, nonbusiness investment assets like stocks, you may be inviting an IRS audit and a potential penalty tax[6] for unreasonably accumulating earnings and profits in the corporation. See the discussion of the accumulated earnings tax in Section 8.9.

- If too much of your corporation's income is in the form of dividends and other passive types of investment income, the corporation may be classified as a personal holding company[7] for tax purposes, and this can have drastic tax consequences, as outlined at Section 8.9. As long as more than 40%[8] of your corporation's gross income is from sales of goods and services, however, you should not have to be concerned about personal holding company taxes, as a general rule.

- Putting your personal assets that are not needed in the business into your corporation will subject those assets to the risk of the business. That is, anything you put into the corporation will be subject to the claims of the corporation's creditors if it goes bankrupt. If you put all of your assets into the corporation, you will in effect have given up the limited liability that the corporate form of doing business can afford you.

- If your corporation borrows money to invest in or carry stock investments, the 70% dividend exclusion will be reduced in part by the interest paid on the borrowed funds.[9]

Your accountant will probably be the best person to consult in determining how and whether you can use a corporation to reduce taxes on your business profits and how to split income between salary — compensation — and retained corporate profit to achieve the best overall tax results, consistent with your personal financial needs and the financial requirements of your business.

8.3 Retirement Plans and Other Fringe Benefits

One of the great advantages of being your own boss, either as a sole proprietor, a partner, or a shareholder of a closely-held incorporated business, is the opportunity to be able to set up a Keogh plan or corporate retirement plan structured according to your ability and desire to put away pre-tax income free of current taxes. In an incorporated business, other than an S corporation, you can obtain insurance and other important fringe benefits as an officer and employee of the corporation on a tax-favored basis. At this point, you may wish to refer to Section 2.4, where retirement plans for businesses and corporate fringe benefits are discussed in greater detail.

Up until a few years ago, corporate retirement plans offered very substantial tax and practical advantages to owners of incorporated businesses compared to the Keogh plans available to owners of unincorporated businesses. Since 1984, it has become a whole new ball game. You should be aware that corporate and Keogh retirement plans are now almost identical under the tax law in all major respects, except for the ability to borrow one's retirement funds from the plan, which still will be subject to an excise or penalty tax in the case of a Keogh. The key point you need to get is that it no longer pays to incorporate your business just for pension and profit-sharing plan purposes.

If you decide to establish a retirement plan, there are several practical points you should consider before reaching a decision.

Model SEP Plans from Financial Institutions

If you are setting up an Simplified Employee Pension (SEP) plan for yourself, or a Keogh plan, you should consider obtaining a "canned" plan from a bank, savings and loan, insurance company, or mutual fund. Usually, their preapproved plans will be suitable for you unless you have a significant number of employees to cover under your Keogh, in which case you probably should be incorporated anyway. The great advantages of getting a canned SEP or Keogh plan from a financial institution are cost and simplicity.

Most such institutions will charge you only $10–$25 to adopt their plan; their profit comes from investing your funds for a management fee (in the case of a mutual fund) or obtaining your deposits in interest-bearing accounts (in the case of a bank or savings and loan). Hiring a lawyer or benefit consultant to draw up a personalized SEP or Keogh plan for you could cost anywhere from a few hundred to a few thousand dollars in fees. In addition, since the pension laws seem to be rewritten every time Congress meets, you may find yourself paying hundreds or even thousands of dollars each year to your attorney or benefit consultant to revise or amend a custom-designed plan, just to keep it in compliance with the never-ending changes in the tax and other laws affecting pension plans.

Model SEP Plans from Stockbrokerages

If you are not content to invest your SEP or Keogh funds in or with a financial institution, you can still participate in a canned plan offered by some stockbrokerage firms. These plans usually permit you to direct your own stock and bond investments. See Chapter 10 for information on where to write or call about setting up such a plan.

Model Corporate Plans

If you are setting up a corporate retirement plan, it also is possible to obtain canned prototype plans from banks, if you allow them to act as trustee, or from insurance companies, if you buy their insurance or managed fund accounts through the plan. These plans usually have variable terms that can be tailored somewhat to suit your needs, unless you want to do something out of the ordinary, such as allow each participant to direct the investment of his or her portion of the plan's funds. Other institutions, such as stockbrokerages and mutual funds, also offer corporate plans.

Customized Plans

Even if you do need something unusual that requires a customized retirement plan for your corporation, you will probably find it more cost-effective to have a benefit consulting firm draw up the plan for you. This way, your attorney would only be involved in reviewing the plan and obtaining approval of the plan from the IRS. Typically, benefit consultants or pension consultants will charge only a fraction of what a law firm would charge to draw up the plan, and the larger benefit consulting firms are generally quite competent. Most of their fees come from helping you administer the plan under ERISA after it is set up — a service you will need anyway.

Saving with SEPs

Simplified Employee Pension (SEP) plans have gotten very little use since they were created by Congress several years ago; however, they now offer most of the attractive features of typical Keogh and corporate plans with virtually no administrative costs, unlike a Keogh or corporate plan that may cost up to $2,000 or $3,000 a year to maintain for only five or ten employees.

A SEP is basically a glorified IRA, but it is one where the employer contributes to each employee's IRA account an amount of up to 15% of an employee's compensation with a maximum of $30,000.

The amount contributed is not taxed to the employee and can be invested in any type of IRA account the employee chooses. SEPs can be set up by corporations, partnerships, or sole proprietorships. Participants can still contribute up to $2,000 a year to their SEP/IRA or to another IRA plan.

SEP participants, however, with taxable income in excess of $25,000 (single) or $40,000 (married filing jointly) will have their IRA deductions reduced or eliminated.

The main existing drawback of an SEP is that any distributions from the plan at retirement are taxed as ordinary income. The special five-year averaging for lump sum distributions from a Keogh or corporate qualified plan is not available for IRAs or SEPs. Even so, they strongly merit consideration as an alternative to Keogh or corporate retirement plans, due to their relative simplicity.

8.4 Sheltering Profits on Export Sales

Many small and large American businesses have an unfortunate tendency to look at the United States as their only market and to ignore the vast potential markets for their products or services that lie outside the borders of this country. One way in which Congress has taken constructive steps to encourage more exports and to make American goods and services more competitive in foreign markets is to provide a form of indirect tax subsidy to American firms that export.

While this export subsidy has not succeeded in stemming the unfavorable trend in the balance of trade the U.S. has experienced in recent years, it does provide a very attractive tax benefit for U.S. companies that export.

If your business is one of the many small firms that does sell its goods or services overseas, you may be able to qualify for this tax incentive by setting up either a Domestic International Sales Corporation (DISC) or a new type of entity permitted by the Tax Reform Act of 1984, called a Foreign Sales Corporation (FSC). In general, a DISC will allow you to accumulate profits earned from export sales in a specially-treated corporation, free of U.S. taxes until you eventually choose to distribute the deferred income. An FSC will allow you to accumulate such income free of U.S. corporate taxes (in part), whether or not distributed.[10]

The 1984 tax changes largely obsolesced DISCs for large companies, since DISC gross receipts in excess of $10 million are fully taxable in 1985 and after. For small companies, however, DISCs may often be preferable — as well as much simpler to operate — to the new FSCs, at least for the first few years of operation.

DISCs — In a Nutshell

A DISC is usually just a dummy corporation that has no employees and does not carry on any sort of business, except on paper.

The tax law allows a U.S. firm that has qualified export receipts to set aside part of its profits on the export transactions by paying a so-called sales commission to a DISC.[11] As a corporation without any employees, the DISC does not actually do anything to earn the commissions; your firm pays the DISC the largest commission permitted by the tax law on each qualifying export sale. It is usually advisable to have a written commission agreement between your firm and the DISC for legal purposes, although not required for tax purposes. The commission that can be paid to the DISC on an export sale is the larger of 4% of the gross sales price or 50% of the profit on the sale[12] — so long as the commission does not create a loss on the sale for your firm.[13] In addition, the DISC's commission income can be increased by 10% of certain export promotion expenses, if any, incurred by the DISC.[14] As you might suspect, there are some fairly elaborate tax accounting rules[15] which determine how much profit you have on an export sale, for purposes of computing the DISC's maximum commission.

The tax benefits for your business arise from the fact that you or your business owns the DISC stock, and the commissions your business pays to the DISC are deducted from the business's taxable income, while the DISC pays no tax on income it receives.

However, about 6% (or $1/17$) of the DISC's income each year is taxed to its corporate (but not individual) shareholders,[16] so the DISC will usually pay about 6% of its income back as a dividend to the business that owns the stock of the DISC (which is usually, but not necessarily, as we shall see, your corporation that paid the DISC the commissions). Thus, 94% (or $16/17$) of the income that is shifted to the DISC as export sales commissions escapes federal income tax indefinitely, until the DISC either pays out the accumulated income as dividends or is disqualified and loses its status as a DISC.[17] For deferred DISC income that accumulates after 1984, however, each DISC shareholder must compute the amount of additional tax it would pay each year if all the deferred DISC income were taxed and pay the IRS interest on the deferred tax.[18] This interest will apparently be tax-deductible if paid by a corporation. The interest rate is based on the going rate for one-year T-bills.

Conceptually, having a DISC can be thought of as taking $100 of pre-tax income out of your left-hand pocket and putting it in your right-hand pocket, then putting $6 back into the left-hand pocket. You do not have to pay tax on the $94 that remains in the right-hand pocket as long as you leave it there. In fact, there are even legal ways in which you can borrow the $94 and put it back in the left-hand pocket (your business) without paying tax on it — another example of having your cake and eating it, too. But as long as you keep the $94 in the right-hand pocket, you pay interest on the tax saved.

Example of DISC Benefits

A simplified example will illustrate how an incorporated business that has $2 million a year in gross sales, all from exports, would benefit by having a DISC. Assume that the business, XYZ Corporation, has a pre-tax profit (all from exports) equal to 5% of gross sales, or $100,000. Under a typical DISC commission agreement, XYZ would pay DISC a commission equal to 4% of gross sales ($80,000), or 50% of export profits (50% x $100,000), whichever is greater; that is, an $80,000 commission. Assuming that XYZ owns all the stock of DISC, XYZ's taxable income and federal income tax would compute as follows:

Example of the Benefits of Having a DISC	With DISC	Without DISC
Pre-tax profit	$100,000	$100,000
Less: DISC commission	–80,000	- 0 -
Net income before DISC dividend	=$20,000	$100,000
Add: DISC dividend equal to 6% of DISC commission	+4,800	- 0 -
Taxable income	$24,800	$100,000
Federal income tax of corporation	$3,720	$22,250

Note: By using DISC, the corporation has saved (deferred) $18,530 tax. However, the IRS charges DISC shareholders interest on the deferred tax. In this example, the interest (at 9%) on the deferred $18,530 would be $1,668. This amount is reported by shareholders on *Form 8404* and paid when shareholders' individual income tax returns are filed.

The above example assumes that XYZ owns all the stock of DISC, so that the dividend of 6% (or $1/17$) of its income that DISC pays out (or should pay out, since that amount is deemed to be paid out, whether or not it actually is) goes back into XYZ's corporate income. However, this does not necessarily have to be the case — the shareholders of XYZ Corporation could own the stock of DISC directly, so that there would be no "deemed dividend distribution" of $1/17$ of the DISC's income to individual shareholders. And, of course, the portion of DISC's income that is retained tax-free could in effect be loaned back to XYZ, if certain formalities are observed.[19]

An even more interesting possibility would be for some or all of the stock of DISC to be given to children of the XYZ shareholders when the DISC is incorporated. In that case, part of the income of XYZ could be skimmed off as, in effect, deductible dividend — like payments by distributing part of the deferred DISC income and could be split and shifted to children in low tax brackets, a classic estate-planning maneuver. Recent tax reforms, however, require children under 14 years of age to pay taxes at their parents' marginal tax bracket rate.

Income-Splitting

Another advantage of having a DISC is that the DISC can continue to accumulate its undistributed profits year after year without fear of incurring an accumulated earnings tax, since a DISC is exempt from the accumulated earnings tax as well as the regular federal income tax.[20]

The new Foreign Sales Corporation (FSC) entity that is permitted after 1984 is somewhat similar to a DISC, but will probably be too great of an administrative burden for it to be worthwhile for a small business to consider.

FSCs — In a Nutshell

Unlike a DISC, an FSC cannot be a dummy or paper corporation set up in the United States. Instead, it must meet all of the following requirements:

- It must be a foreign corporation, incorporated in a foreign country that, in general, has arrangements to swap tax information with the IRS, or in a U.S. possession.
- There can be no more than 25 shareholders in an FSC.
- An FSC cannot issue preferred stock.
- An FSC must maintain a foreign office, at which there is a permanent set of tax records, including invoices.
- The FSC's board of directors must include at least one person who is not a resident of the United States — although the nonresident member can apparently be a U.S. citizen.
- An FSC cannot be part of a controlled group of corporations that also includes a DISC. That is, you can set up either an FSC or a DISC, but not both.[21]

Large FSCs are also subject to additional stringent requirements such as being managed outside the United States and satisfying various tests with respect to carrying on economic activities outside the United States.[22] Fortunately, these foreign management and foreign economic process requirements do not apply to small FSCs,[23] which are FSCs with $5 million or less in foreign trade gross receipts per year.

Additional FSC Requirements

The amount of export income that can be shifted to an FSC is usually limited to 1.83% of gross foreign trading receipts — versus 4% for a DISC — or 23% of the combined profit of the U.S. parent company and the FSC on an export sale — versus 50% for a DISC — whichever is greater. However, the profit under the gross receipts method is limited to twice the amount of the combined profit.[24]

Once the FSC's taxable income for the year has been determined under the above rule, $5/23$ of such income is treated as exempt, and is not taxable,[25] even if it is distributed to the parent U.S. corporation.[26] Tax must be paid by the FSC on the remaining $8/23$ of its taxable income.

Summary

To summarize this section on DISC and FSC tax benefits:

- If your business will be engaged or is engaged in selling goods or services abroad, you should consult your tax adviser as to the advisability of establishing a DISC or FSC to shelter a large portion of your export profits.

- If you decide to set up a DISC corporation, consider placing partial ownership of the DISC stock in your children's hands for estate and income tax planning purposes or else hold its stock directly.

- Both DISCs and FSCs are extremely complex entities to establish and administer, although a DISC will probably be much less of a headache for a small business to operate than an FSC. In either case, you will need to hire some very sophisticated accounting talent, so unless you earn some fairly substantial export profits, the administrative costs of having a DISC or FSC may well exceed any tax savings you will generate. State tax treatment of DISCs and FSCs is discussed in Section 11.8.

8.5 Planning for Withdrawal of Corporate Funds with Minimum Tax Cost

Because of the many tax and other advantages of operating in corporate form, there is a good chance you will choose, either initially or later on, to incorporate your business. If you do, and your business becomes profitable to the extent that it has significant profits even after paying you the largest salary that can be justified as "reasonable compensation" under the circumstances,[27] you will eventually be faced with the problem of how to remove the accumulated profits from the corporation without excessive tax costs. That is, unless you decide to liquidate the corporation at some point and operate as an unincorporated business, or decide to sell your stock to someone else. The proceeds you receive from liquidation or selling your stock would probably result in capital gains tax in most cases, in addition to a tax at the corporate level upon liquidation.

If the corporation simply pays dividends to you, that will normally be a tax disaster, since the dividends you receive will probably be taxable to you as ordinary income at federal income tax rates up to 31% or somewhat more. Since the corporation will have already paid tax on the money it distributes to you as dividends, double taxation will result. If both you and the corporation are in the maximum tax brackets, the result can be an effective tax rate of approximately 58% (federal corporate and individual taxes) on the income that is paid out as dividends and an even higher rate if there are also state income taxes. There are better ways to get the money out of the corporation.

Personal Loans from the Corporation

Your corporation can often serve as a bank for your short-term financial needs; however, if you continually borrow from your corporation, the IRS can in some cases treat the loans as dividends to you, which is just what you want to avoid. Or, if your corporation has an accumulated earnings problem, as described in Section 8.9 of this chapter, the existence of loans to shareholders can make it very difficult to argue that the corporation is accumulating earnings for the reasonable needs of the business. So, while a loan from your corporation can be a very good way to tap its funds on a temporary basis, it is not a long-term solution.

If you do borrow, you should normally pay interest if the loan is greater than $10,000. The interest rate should not be less than the applicable federal rate established by the IRS.[28] This rate is announced by the IRS each month of the year for transactions that occur during the following month.

Preliminary Structuring

A number of different ways of structuring your corporation at its inception can give you a great deal of potential flexibility in getting money out of the corporation to yourself or family members later at no tax cost or, at worst, as only partially taxable. Some of these approaches can also make it possible to keep a great deal of the value of the corporation's stock out of your taxable estate for estate tax and inheritance tax purposes.

Generally, the structuring of your corporation should be discussed with your tax adviser before the corporation is formed. Some of the possible approaches you should explore are discussed below.

Putting Stock in Names of Spouse & Children

When the corporation is formed, consider putting a substantial part of the stock in the name of your spouse or children, or both. Later, when or if the business has prospered and the stock has become valuable, it may be possible to bail out a large chunk of the corporation's accumulated profits at a child's lower tax rates by having the corporation redeem (purchase) all of the stock of your spouse or child. The redemption will usually be treated as a sale for a capital gain if your spouse or child agree to notify the IRS if he or she reacquires any interest in the corporation within 10 years after the redemption.[29] Working as an employee of the corporation would be an "interest" that would prevent the spouse or child from receiving favorable capital gains treatment. So if you want your son or daughter to work for you in the business, do not count on being able to redeem his or her stock as a capital gain.

Note that while capital gains are taxed at only slightly lower rates than ordinary income after 1990, it is still very desirable to have a stock redemption qualify for capital gains treatment, since part of the money received will be a nontaxable recovery of the shareholder's tax basis in the stock that is being redeemed. This is usually not the case if the redemption payment is treated as an ordinary income dividend.

Such redemption of stock as a capital gain could even be made on an installment basis.[30] For example, if your daughter had all her stock redeemed by the corporation for, say $150,000, the corporation could pay the $150,000 price, plus interest, in 15 annual installments of $10,000 each, so that your daughter would not have a "bunching" of all the capital gain on the sale in one tax year. Instead, the capital gains tax would be spread over a 15-year period, and the corporation should be able to deduct interest paid on the note held by the daughter.

Constraints in Community Property States

Unfortunately, this tactic does not work as well in community property states if you attempt to redeem your spouse's stock. Under the community property laws, half of your stock will generally be treated as owned by your spouse, so that it is difficult to completely terminate his or her interest, unless all of the stock that is community property is first split in half between you by agreement, so that you each own your shares as separate property.

Even in that case, your spouse may be considered to have reacquired a community property interest in your separately-owned stock if you continue to work for the corporation and the value of the stock increases on account of your efforts. Thus, if you live in a community property state, you probably should not count on trying to redeem your spouse's interest in the corporation as a capital gain. The states that have community property laws are California, Texas, Louisiana, New Mexico, Arizona, Nevada, Washington, Idaho, and Wisconsin.

Gifts of Stock to Children

Even if the corporation never redeems your children's stock, it is useful to put some of the stock in their names when you form the corporation, at a time when a gift to them of the stock will be subject to little or no gift tax because of its low value. When you die many years later, the stock owned by your children may then be very valuable and will not be included in your estate in most instances, which could save a great deal in the way of estate and inheritance taxes. The federal gift tax laws now permit you to make gifts worth up to $10,000 per child per year free of federal gift tax. If you are married, you and your spouse can jointly make gifts of up to $20,000 per year per child; however, you may be subject to state gift taxes in some states.

Until the Revenue Reconciliation Act of 1989 was passed, it was considered astute tax planning, when setting up a new corporation, to capitalize the company with both equity capital (stock) and debt capital (an interest-bearing note from the corporation to you).

Now, in many instances, such a tactic can be a tax trap. This type of structuring can still be done without adverse tax consequences, but only if the assets you are transferring to the corporation are cash or other assets on which you would not have a taxable gain if sold at current fair market value — otherwise, under the new law, any notes or other debt capital you take back from the corporation will cause you to have to pay tax on appreciated assets (land, equipment, etc.) that you transfer to the corporation in return for the stock and debt instruments.

If, however, the only asset you are putting in the corporation to start it up is, for example, cash, you will not be affected by the 1989 tax law change mentioned in the preceding paragraph. As an illustration, if you plan to put $10,000 in the corporation to get the business started, you might take back stock for $5,000 and a $5,000 note when the corporation is set up, rather than having the corporation issue you stock for the whole $10,000. While the note is outstanding, you will be able to siphon off some funds from the corporation as interest on the note, which the corporation can deduct. By contrast, if the corporation distributed profits to you as dividends on its stock, it would result in double taxation of those profits, since the corporation cannot deduct dividends it pays, unlike interest.

More importantly, when the note becomes due, the corporation will repay you the $5,000 principal of the note, and you should pay no tax on that $5,000 if things have been handled properly. In contrast, if the corporation attempted to return part of your investment in the stock, whatever you received would probably be fully taxable to you as a dividend, even if you surrendered some of your stock in a redemption. Lending the corporation part of its start-up capital allows you to withdraw part of your investment without paying tax.

Thus, there are considerable advantages in partially capitalizing your corporation with debt in the form of a note or notes that you will hold from the corporation. You will need competent tax advice before you do so, however, since there are hundreds of court cases that have tried to define when debt instruments will be considered debt, and when they will be considered stock. For example, if you capitalize your corporation with more than about $3 of debt for each $1 of stock, say a $8,000 note and $2,000 of stock, the note (debt) may be treated as though it were stock for tax purposes. Thus, if the corporation paid you interest or principal on the note, whatever payments you received would be treated as dividends to you, and the corporation's deduction for the interest payments would be disallowed. So you must tread very lightly in lending money to your corporation. See the discussion of the distinction between debt and equity for tax purposes in Section 8.9 of this chapter.

Post-Incorporation Planning

Whether or not you take advantage of the above planning suggestions at the time you incorporate, there are a number of other ways you can get cash out of your corporation at a low tax cost later on.

Leasing to the Corporation

One way is to lease real property or equipment to the corporation. Instead of putting enough of your own money into the corporation for it to buy property it needs for its business, keep the money outside the corporation, buy the property yourself and lease it all at a reasonable rental to the corporation. This way, you will be able to directly obtain the tax depreciation and other benefits of owning the property. At the same time, by keeping the property out of the corporation, you will be putting less of your assets at risk in the business, in case the corporation goes broke. Also, if the leased property is real estate, it will probably appreciate in value, and you can personally and directly benefit from that appreciation, including the increased rent you will be able to charge the corporation as inflation continues. Furthermore, if you have used straight-line depreciation and sell the property at a gain, all of the gain will be capital gain. By contrast, if the corporation sells real property at a gain, 20% of the straight-line depreciation is recaptured as ordinary income.[31] Although a corporation's capital gains are currently taxed at the same rate as ordinary income, Congress restored preferential tax rates for capital gains in 1990 tax legislation, and may do the same for corporations in the near future, if regular corporate tax rates are increased.

Trusts for Your Children

You could make a gift of business property, or the funds to buy it, to a trust and have a bank or other independent trustee negotiate a reasonable lease of the property to the business, with the rental income going to the trust for distribution to your children. Upon the trust's termination, the property can be distributed to the children, can revert to the trust grantor, or can be distributed in accordance with the trust terms.

This can be a useful way of taking cash out of the corporation for the benefit of your children, who have lower tax brackets; however, since the IRS regularly attempts to attack these types of arrangements, you should go into this only with the help of an astute tax adviser. Be aware that the Tax Reform Act of 1986 eliminated nearly all the tax advantages of trusts for children under 14 years of age.

DISC Deferrals

Consider setting up a DISC corporation if your corporation has foreign sales. You can then hold the DISC stock yourself or give it to your children. As discussed in greater detail in Section 8.4 of this chapter, this will not only enable you to indefinitely defer federal income taxes on part of the profits from export sales, but it will also, in effect, allow you or your children to siphon off part of the profits on export sales (dividends paid by the DISC) in a manner that allows your corporation to deduct those dividends, thereby avoiding double taxation.

Consider adopting corporate pension or profit-sharing plans and various corporate fringe benefit plans. These types of benefit plans, in appropriate circumstances, can provide deferred retirement benefits or current insurance benefits to you tax-free — or on a tax-deferred basis, in the case of retirement plans — while reducing the corporation's taxable income currently. See the discussion of these kinds of employee benefit plans in Section 8.3.

Benefit Plans

8.6 Deducting Expenses Related to Your Business

One major advantage of operating your own business is the opportunity it may give you to enjoy certain luxuries as deductible business expenses. Some of the tax benefits that were available in the past, however, such as costs of attending foreign conventions[32] and treating part of your home as a business office,[33] have been severely curtailed, and there are strict recordkeeping requirements[34] for others. Some of the major remaining types of items you may be entitled to write off as business expenses for tax purposes are discussed below.

The three-martini lunch is dead. It is still possible to deduct business travel expenses, entertainment of your clients or customers, and business-related meals, but only 80% of qualifying business meals and entertainment are deductible. Long live the 2.4 martini lunch! This 80% rule considerably complicates recordkeeping for expenses. For instance, if you stay in a hotel on a business trip and charge your meals to your room, you are required to separately break out your meal expenses from the rest of your hotel bill for tax purposes, since your meal expenses are only 80% deductible.

Travel, Entertainment, and Meal Expenses

Note that if you are an employee of your business, the 20% disallowance of meal and entertainment expenses does not apply to you individually if your company reimburses you for the expenses; rather, it applies at the company level.

To claim any of these kinds of deductions, you must keep daily, detailed records of such expenditures, including bills, receipts, and the following information for each expense:

Detailed Records Required

- The relationship of the expenditure to the business;
- The time when the expense was incurred;
- Where the money was spent, and to whom it was paid;
- The amount of the expenditure; and
- The identities of the persons involved, including persons entertained.[35]

It is strongly recommended that you pick up a daily expense record book or diary at a stationery store and that you enter all expenses for travel, meals, and entertainment that you think should be deductible, including the above information for each item.

The Tax Reform Act of 1984 would have required contemporaneous written records to substantiate all such travel and entertainment expenses, beginning in 1985. The issuance of IRS regulations on October 15, 1984, provoked a massive outcry among taxpayers that was heard all the way to the District of Columbia. Senator William Roth (R-Del.) said, "I've never had an outrage at home as I've had with this legislation."

Accordingly, by mid-1985, Congress retroactively repealed the contemporaneous part of the recordkeeping requirement for travel and entertainment deductions, replacing it with the requirement that taxpayers keep "adequate records or . . . sufficient evidence corroborating the taxpayer's own statement."[36]

This is a return to the old substantiation requirements as they existed before the 1984 act, except that these substantiation requirements now also apply to local travel expenses, which was not the case in the past.

Not All Expenses Deductible

Not all expenses for entertaining clients or customers will be deductible, even if you keep meticulous records. As a general rule, your records must show that you were engaged in a substantial and bona fide business discussion during or immediately before or after the entertainment.[37] Expenses of entertaining people just to create a good impression on them, in the hope they might send some business your way someday, are classified as goodwill entertainment and are not deductible.

The rule allowing quiet business meals with clients or potential customers to be deductible, even if no business is discussed, has been repealed.[38]

Automobile Expenses

If you use an automobile more than 50% of the time for business purposes, you will generally be able to deduct a percentage of the costs of owning and operating the car, if you can substantiate the business mileage. The expenses of using the car for commuting to and from work and for personal travel are not deductible.[39] For example, if your business purchases a new car for your use as a business car, and 80% of the mileage on the car can be shown to be for business trips, and only 20% for commuting to work and other personal use, you should be able to deduct 80% of the gas, oil, insurance, and maintenance costs relating to the car. You can also depreciate the cost of the car, less 20% for personal use, over five years, or three years if the car was bought before 1987.

After December 31, 1986, the depreciation of automobiles is spread out over five years rather than three years for autos placed in service after 1986.[40] Also, for luxury automobiles placed in service after 1986, the maximum annual depreciation deduction allowed is limited to:

1987 or 1988 Acquisitions	1989 or 1990 Acquisitions	**Luxury Automobile Depreciation**
$2,560 for the first year	$2,660 for the first year	
$4,100 for the second year	$4,200 for the second year	
$2,450 for the third year	$2,550 for the third year	
$1,475 for each succeeding year[41]	$1,475 for each succeeding year	

The new rules are even more drastic for any automobile, airplane, or boat — or for a computer not kept in your place of business — if you can't establish a business-use percentage in excess of 50%. Automobile depreciation is stretched out over at least six years, straight-line: 10% the first year; 20% a year thereafter, for four years; and 10% the final year. For boats, planes, or computers, it can be stretched out for longer periods.[42]

Exempted Business Vehicles

These new restrictions don't apply to business vehicles such as ambulances, hearses, taxis, delivery vans, or heavy trucks.[43]

If you drive an inexpensive economy car on business, it may be simpler and better to elect to deduct a flat $0.26 (26 cents) for 1990 or $0.275 (27.5 cents) for 1991 per mile[44] for your business mileage rather than keep records of your various kinds of automobile expenses. You will, however, still be required to keep records to substantiate that the car was used for business purposes for the mileage you claim. If you use this method, you can still deduct tolls and parking incurred on business trips. In these times of soaring automobile prices, you will probably get much larger tax deductions if you drive an expensive car by reporting your actual expenses of operating it, plus depreciation, than by electing the mileage allowance.

Note that *Form 4562* on your 1990 tax return, due in 1991, requires you to answer questions if you claim an automobile deduction.

Questions To Be Answered If You Claim an Automobile Deduction

Total miles driven during the year: _____

Total business miles driven during the year: _____

Total commuting miles driven during the year: _____

Total other personal (noncommuting) miles driven: _____

Was the vehicle available for personal use during off-duty hours? Yes ☐ No ☐

Was the vehicle used primarily by a more than 5% owner or related person? Yes ☐ No ☐

Is another vehicle available for personal use? Yes ☐ No ☐

Do you have evidence to support the business-use percentage claimed? Yes ☐ No ☐

If yes, is the evidence written? Yes ☐ No ☐

8.7 Choosing the Best Taxable Year for a Corporation

If your business is incorporated and is neither an S corporation nor a "personal service corporation" in which the services performed are "substantially performed" by owner–employees,[45] you will have an opportunity to choose any tax fiscal year period you desire during your initial year of operation as a corporation. Otherwise, if your business is an S corporation or is considered a personal service corporation, you will generally have no choice but to operate on a calendar year basis, and you can skip over the following discussion of how to select a taxable year. There are significant tax deferral and savings opportunities in selecting the right year-end.

Unfortunately, in some cases it will be necessary to be able to project with some accuracy how much your corporation will earn or lose each month for several months to a year ahead. If you expect to have start-up losses and show an overall net profit for your first year as an incorporated business, one good rule is to cut off your first taxable year at the end of the month in which you first get back to break even for the year-to-date.

For example, assume your first tax year starts on January 1, 1991, and you show a cumulative tax loss of $20,000 at the end of June. You then have taxable income of $10,000 a month in July, August, and September, and expect profits to continue. If you chose June 30 as your tax year-end, you would have a $20,000 loss for your first tax period ending June 30, 1991. For federal income tax purposes, it's no problem, since you can carry over the loss and use it to offset $20,000 of taxable income during the next tax year. Some states, however, do not allow a carryover of losses.

Another approach would be to choose an August 31 year-end, so that you would show no taxable income for your first year, assuming the corporation continued to net $10,000 a month.

If you did not mind paying some tax earlier, it might pay, in the above example, to wait until the end of October, November, or even December to cut off the first tax year. This would enable the corporation to isolate $20,000 to $40,000 or so of profit in a tax period subject to low federal corporate income tax rates, which are only 15% on the first $50,000 of corporate income. If you do so, however, you are making an assumption that the corporation will be in a higher tax bracket in the following year, which cannot be known with any certainty. Also, the existence of tax credits would somewhat complicate the simple picture portrayed above. Obviously, your accountant can help you decide which tax year will produce the best result.

Start-up Losses Must Be Capitalized, Not Deducted

Remember, when projecting your start-up losses, that you can't immediately deduct preopening expenses, but must instead capitalize those costs and write them off (straight-line) over 60 months.[46] For example, if you are starting a restaurant and are paying salaries, etc. to a manager and to employees being trained prior to the day the restaurant opens for business, you might well think those expenses are immediately deductible. Not so! All such preopening expenses must be capitalized, and you can't begin to amortize them until opening day.

Benefits of Adopting January 31 Year-end

Another planning approach in adopting a year-end, which may sometimes conflict with the above strategy, is to adopt a January 31 year-end. If you structure your employment contract with your corporation so that you receive a substantial part of your compensation in January each year, you can, in effect, defer the bonus to your following tax year, while the corporation can deduct it (if paid in January) for its fiscal year ending just after the bonus is paid. Naturally, the corporation will be required to withhold income tax from your bonus, but at reduced rates, compared to regular monthly salary payments. Federal income tax withholding on bonuses is at a flat rate of only 20%.

Until 1984, you could achieve the same effect even if your corporation was on a calendar tax year, if it used the accrual method of accounting, simply by accruing your bonus in December and delaying payment until the following January. This is no longer possible if you are a related person, such as a stockholder, with regard to the corporation, in which case the corporation is, in effect, placed on the cash method of accounting for any expenses it owes you.[47] In the past, if your corporation elected to be treated as a Subchapter S corporation (discussed in Chapter 2, Section 2.5), it was advantageous to elect a January 31 year-end in many cases if you expected it to show profits, since your share of earnings from a Subchapter S corporation (now called "S corporations") must all be included in your income for the calendar year in which the corporation's tax year ends.[48]

Unfortunately, Congress changed the law in 1982 so that now, if you elect S corporation status, your corporation will usually have to adopt the calendar year as its tax year.[49] The Tax Reform Act of 1986 required even pre-existing S corporations and personal service corporations to switch over to a December 31 year-end.[50] However, tax legislation in 1987 allowed pre-'86 Act S corporations, personal service corporations, — not to be confused with qualified personal service corporations — and partnerships to retain their fiscal years, if they make certain tax prepayments.[51]

Seasonal Businesses

If yours is a seasonal business, you may want to select a tax year that ends just before your most profitable season begins to defer taxes. For example, if you are in the business of selling Christmas tree ornaments and do most of your business from October through December each year, you might choose a September 30 tax year. Remember, though, that tax considerations are not the only factors to take into account in choosing a fiscal year. If taking an annual inventory is a major task, consider adopting a year-end that occurs when inventory is at a low ebb and when business is slow, if possible. You may also find that you will get somewhat quicker and better service from your CPA firm for annual tax returns, audits, etc. if you pick a fiscal year that ends several months before or after December. Most CPAs are at their busiest during their annual tax season from about February to May, preparing 1040s and doing audits for their many clients who have December year-ends.

8.8 Selecting Tax Accounting Methods

You should rely on your tax accountant's advice as to which tax accounting methods you can or should adopt in your business.

This section is provided for your information in case you are not sure whether your accountant has recommended the method that will produce the best results for you.

The two overall tax accounting methods most commonly used are the cash method and the accrual method, although there are other special overall methods, plus a number of special kinds of accounting elections a business can make with regard to particular items such as installment sales, inventory valuations, and deduction of accrued vacation pay.

Cash Method

The cash receipts and disbursements method of accounting, called the cash method, is the simplest accounting method generally in use. Under this method, you include income only as it is actually or constructively received.

Likewise, you only become entitled to deductions when you actually pay expenses — except for certain special items like depreciation or amortization of certain kinds of expenditures — rather than when you receive bills for the expenses. Thus, you usually do not have to report your year-end accounts receivable in income for the year and cannot deduct your year-end accounts payable. This will normally allow you to defer some taxable income each year if your year-end receivables are larger than accounts payable and other accrued but unpaid expenses. Obviously, this gives you some flexibility, too, if you want to pay off a number of payables at year-end to reduce your taxable income for the current year.

The cash method is the method used by most individual taxpayers and by businesses in the real estate, financial, and service fields, where inventories of goods are not material factors in producing income.

Businesses with significant inventories, such as manufacturers and wholesale or retail firms, are usually required to use an accrual method of tax accounting.[52] In some cases, however, it is possible even for those businesses to use a hybrid accounting method — accounting for income and the cost of goods sold on an accrual method — while using the cash method to report selling expenses and administrative expenses.

The Tax Reform Act of 1986 has also disallowed use of the cash method for C corporations — regular corporations — and for partnerships that have C corporations as partners, except for small firms with average gross receipts of $5 million or less during the three preceding years.[53] An exception is made for larger firms in the farming business and for certain employee-owned qualified personal service corporations in fields such as law, medicine, accounting, architecture, or consulting. Sole proprietorships, S corporations, and partnerships with no C corporation partners are not affected by the new restrictions, unless they are considered tax shelters, and may remain on the cash method if that is a permissible accounting method for their particular type of business.

Firms that are forbidden from using the cash method must instead adopt the more complex accrual method of accounting.

Accrual Method

As noted above, most large corporations and businesses with significant inventories are required to report income on the accrual method of accounting for tax purposes. This method requires you to report income when income is earned rather than when you receive it. Similarly, expenses can be deducted when all events have occurred that fix the amount and the fact of your business' liability for a particular expense, even if it is paid in a subsequent tax year. However, if economic performance required of the other party does not occur until a subsequent tax year, you may not be able to deduct an accrued expense until economic performance occurs.

For example, if you sign a contract with your CPA in 1991 to prepare your tax return in 1992, "economic performance" does not occur until 1992, and you may be unable to accrue the deduction in 1991, unless you meet several requirements — recurring expenses, performance occurs within a reasonable time after the end of the tax year, etc.[54]

Important Note!

A once-in-a-lifetime tax election must be made on your first tax year after 1989 — the 1990 tax return for existing businesses. Under the economic performance rules, if you wish to deduct in advance items that you prepay under the recurring items exception, you must elect to deduct such item on the first return on which the item recurs, or you will be unable to use that exception for the item in question, forever. The new tax regulations covering this exception to the economic performance rules go into effect for tax years that begin after 1989, which means that if you have some recurring item that you are in the habit of prepaying before year-end each year, you must elect to deduct it on your 1990 tax return, or you will never again be able to deduct it in advance in any subsequent year when it has been prepaid.

Even though the accrual method may not be required for your business, you may find it preferable to use if most or all of your income is from cash sales, and you pay a large part of your expenses on a delayed credit basis. In that case, you would have few, if any, receivables at year-end, but might have substantial accrued payables you could deduct in the current year if on the accrual method, without having to actually make payment before year-end. Accrual of bonuses to employees, in an incorporated business, is a good example of a deduction that can be accelerated by a business using the accrual method. But expenses owed to you or a related owner of the business can't be deducted until actually paid.[55]

Special Accounting Methods
Long-term Contracts

If your business is engaged in heavy construction work on a long-term contract basis, it may be difficult to tell in advance whether a particular contract will result in a profit or loss, since many unforeseen difficulties may arise. The tax regulations recognize this problem and allow such contractors to utilize special methods of accounting, the percentage of completion method and the completed contract method, both of which may delay the time at which profit or loss is recognized on a long-term contract.[56] The Tax Reform Act of 1986, however, and subsequent legislation have limited, then finally eliminated, the use of the completed contract method of accounting for most large companies, except for certain ship contracts and for some home construction and other residential building contractors. Fortunately, small businesses, whose average annual gross receipts for the three preceding years do not exceed $10 million, are still allowed to use completed contract accounting for tax purposes, at least for contracts that are estimated to take no more than two years to complete.[57]

Even those completed contract method deferrals that survive the new restrictions are now mostly considered tax preference items under the alternative minimum tax rules.[58] In other words, heads you lose, tails the tax collector wins.

Installment Sales

If your business makes casual or occasional sales of personal property (other than merchandise held for sale) or makes sales of real estate it owns, the profit on any such sale can, in general, be reported on the installment basis as and when payments are received, rather than in the year of sale.[59] Also, until recently, if you were a retailer who regularly sold merchandise on the installment plan, you could adopt the installment method of reporting all such sales.[60] However, after 1987, the installment method of reporting has generally been repealed for "dealers," such as retailers, in personal or real property.

A limited exemption, however, was left for certain dealers in real property. This is an election that sellers of residential lots or time-shares may make to use the installment method. The catch is that the dealer making such an election must agree to pay interest on any tax that is deferred by using installment reporting.[61] Certain manufacturers who are dealers are still allowed to use the installment method as well.

Under the Omnibus Budget Reconciliation Act of 1987 (the '87 act) and the 1988 Revenue Act, most nondealer installment sales of personal property or real estate can still be reported on the installment method. However, in the case of nondealer sales of property for more than $150,000, if the total face amount of all installment notes exceeds $5 million for the year and at the end of the year, the seller must pay interest on the deferred tax liability.[62] Sales of personal-use property or of farm property, for any amount, are exempt from the interest-on-deferred-tax provisions.[63] The Tax Reform Act of 1986 introduced an horrendously complex new formula under which taxpayers, who have any business debts, were required to accelerate the recognition of gain on installment sales prior to actual collection. The formula also barred use of the installment method for retailers selling under revolving credit plans.[64]

Fortunately, the outcry from accountants and lawyers that the new income acceleration formula was too complex to be understood by mere mortals was heard by Congress and, in general, the '87 act repealed the formula provisions after 1987. It was replaced with the somewhat less complex but tougher provisions described above, as well as other new pitfalls, such as triggering part or all of the gain on an installment obligation if it is used as security for a loan by the taxpayer.

While an installment sale of property is still available to a number of types of taxpayers and in a number of kinds of transactions, this whole area of the tax law has become a very complex minefield. Thus, although you may still be able to reap major tax benefits from installment sale reporting in some cases, don't consider doing a major installment sale transaction without first getting some competent tax advice, or you may regret it.

Inventory Valuation Methods

If you maintain substantial inventories, discuss with your accountant the pros and cons of using the Last-In-First-Out (LIFO) method of valuing year-end inventories[65] rather than the more common and simpler First-In-First-Out (FIFO) method. In inflationary times there can be a substantial tax benefit in carrying your inventory at the lowest possible value for tax purposes. In general, the lower the value of your ending inventory each year, the higher your cost of goods sold — which means your net taxable income will be lower, all things being equal.

LIFO Method

Since the LIFO method works on the assumption that the items in your ending inventory each year are the first or oldest ones you acquired rather than the ones bought most recently, you reflect many items at the per-unit cost you were paying when the business first began buying those inventory items on a LIFO basis. Thus, the LIFO method tends to reduce the reported value of your inventory in times of rising prices and vice versa.

For example, under the LIFO method, if the very first widget you buy for inventory costs $10 in 1986, you will continue to value one widget in your inventory at $10 in 1996, even if the widgets in your ending inventory in 1996 were bought just before the end of that year and actually cost $75. Thus, the LIFO method would tend to understate the actual value of that inventory item substantially by 1996, if inflation continues as assumed in the example. This would result in a cumulative deferral of $65 of taxable income ($75 actual cost less $10 reported cost) on this one particular widget alone over a period of 10 years of inflation. Thus, the LIFO method is currently an excellent means of deferring taxation. By contrast, the FIFO method tends to reflect inventory values at near the current cost of the items in inventory and provides no such deferral.

At present, the use of the LIFO method is extremely complex, and the tax savings may more than be eaten up by additional accounting fees incurred and management time spent in attempting to comply with the LIFO tax regulations. However, once your inventories become fairly substantial in dollar terms, you should look into the possible advantages of switching over to the LIFO method. In the Tax Reform Act of 1986, Congress took some steps to simplify LIFO for small businesses with less than $5 million in sales.[66]

Cautionary Note!

If your C corporation already uses LIFO inventory accounting and elects S corporation status, the '87 act will require the corporation to pay tax, in four annual installments, on the LIFO "reserve" (tax-deferred income) at the time of the changeover to an S corporation.[67]

The Tax Reform Act of 1986 also imposed numerous new and complex rules requiring companies with inventories to allocate various types of indirect costs to inventory, even in the case of retailers and wholesalers. Fortunately, these new "uniform capitalization" rules do not apply to the inventories of small retail or wholesale firms with $10 million or less in annual gross receipts for the preceding three years.[68]

Vacation Pay Accrual Method

If you accrue employees' vacation pay for internal business purposes, you normally cannot deduct your liability for such pay except as and when employees go on vacation. Before 1988, under certain circumstances, employers were able to elect to deduct the vacation pay liability that was accrued as of the end of each year.[69] Unfortunately, the '87 act repealed this method of accounting. Vacation pay is now generally deductible only in the year it is paid — except for accrual-basis taxpayers, where it is vested at the end of a tax year and paid within two and a half months afterwards. Kiss one more loophole goodbye.

If your firm was already using the vacation pay accrual method, you must now stop using it and recognize the deferred taxable income from the vacation pay reserve over a period of up to four years in unequal installments.

Bad Debt Deductions

Before 1987, if your business extended credit to customers you could accelerate your business' bad debt deductions by electing to create a bad debt reserve for tax purposes. By doing so, you could deduct an amount that you expected to have to write off in the future currently, without waiting until the debts became uncollectible.

Since 1987, the reserve method of accounting has been abolished except for certain small financial institutions.[70] For all other taxpayers, bad debts are now only deductible when they actually become uncollectible. Companies already using the reserve method are required to take back into income one-fourth (25%) of their already existing bad debt reserve each year for the first four taxable years beginning after 1986.[71]

8.9 Tax Problems Unique to Corporations

While this book has outlined some of the many tax and other advantages inherent in operating a business in corporate form, you need to be aware that there are a number of traps in the tax law if you go overboard in trying to take advantage of the tax benefits bestowed on corporations.

For many years, the most basic goal in corporate tax planning for many high-income individuals was to leave as much profit in the corporation as possible to be taxed at the relatively low corporate tax rates and to somehow later withdraw that profit tax-free or at capital gains rates, such as by selling or having the corporation redeem the stock or by liquidating the corporation.

Corporate-Level Tax on Most Liquidations

The Tax Reform Act of 1986 changed the rules of the game somewhat so that there will now typically be a substantial corporate-level tax when a corporation is liquidated, particularly for liquidations occurring after January 1, 1989.

In addition, corporations now pay tax at a higher rate than individuals, on income in excess of $75,000, although corporate tax rates on the first $75,000 of income will still be considerably lower than individual rates, in most cases. Certain qualified personal service corporations pay tax at a flat rate of 34% on all their taxable income.[72]

Nevertheless, a corporation may still be useful as a second taxpayer, for splitting income between an owner and his or her corporation, thereby taking advantage of the lower income tax brackets for both individual and corporation.

Thus, the game is not over, although the rules have changed considerably as a result of the Tax Reform Act of 1986 and the '87 act.

The government's role in the game is to prevent the taxpayer from reaching these goals except where the corporation has good business reasons — as opposed to the individual's tax and investment reasons — for virtually everything it does. In attempting to plug up all the possible loopholes taxpayers might use to take advantage of low corporate rates, the tax law contains a whole array of penalties for corporations that unreasonably accumulate earnings[73] that are used as "incorporated pocket books" for holding personal investments[74] or that are capitalized too heavily with debt.[75]

These and other operating problems of corporations under the tax law are briefly outlined below to give you a sense of what the limits are and how far you can go in utilizing corporate tax advantages.

Tax Problems Specific to C Corporations

None of the pitfalls and problems below are of concern if your business is not incorporated or taxed as a corporation, and most of them are inapplicable or of only minor concern to corporations operating under S corporation elections.

Penalty Tax on Accumulated Earnings

The accumulated earnings tax[76] might well be called the scourge of the overly-successful small corporation, since it potentially applies to almost every corporation that accumulates over $250,000[77] in after-tax profits (with certain adjustments),[78] unless the corporation can demonstrate that it needs to retain the profits for use in its business operations.[79]

Your corporation can accumulate up to $250,000 — $150,000 for certain professional service firms — in earnings without having to be concerned about this penalty tax.[80] However, if additional accumulations cannot be justified as being made for the "reasonable needs of the business," the corporation will be faced with the choice of paying out the excess earnings as dividends or paying the accumulated earnings tax. The tax is imposed at the rate of 28% on the improperly accumulated earnings.[81] Since this is a tax that is imposed in addition to the corporate income tax, it is one you probably do not ever want to be forced to pay.

As long as you are able to keep plowing profits back into your business, buying more facilities, equipment, and inventory, and maintaining needed working capital, you will not have much cause for worry about the accumulated earnings tax. If, however, you reach a point where the corporation has more liquid funds than it needs, and you are beginning to look for places to invest the surplus cash, like real estate or the stock market, that should serve as a signal to you that there may be a potential accumulated earnings problem. In that case, you will need some good tax advice as to what you can do to protect the corporation from imposition of the penalty tax.

Justifiable Accumulations

Fortunately, there are a number of acceptable reasons that can justify accumulating funds that are not currently being used in the corporation's business. Some of the more important ones include:

- Setting up a reserve to redeem enough of the stock of a shareholder (yourself, for example) who dies, in order to enable the individual's estate to pay certain expenses related to his or her death — estate and inheritance taxes, funeral expenses, and expenses of administering the estate.[82] This reserve can only be created after the death of a shareholder.

- Creating a fund to allow for a bona fide plan to replace facilities or expand the business, including the acquisition of another business.[83]
- Creating a reasonable reserve fund to pay potential uninsured product liability claims.[84]
- Accumulating funds to retire indebtedness created in connection with the business of the corporation.[85]
- Setting up a defined benefit pension plan with an initial "past service liability" to be funded over a number of years.

A number of ways also exist to reduce the accumulated earnings without paying them out as dividends. Some typical examples would be to redeem part of the stock of the corporation, such as the stock of one of your children. This will not only reduce accumulated earnings but will reduce the amount of excess cash not needed in the business.

Another useful approach is to have the corporation purchase real estate that it might currently be leasing. This can sometimes be particularly advantageous where you are the landlord who is leasing the property to the corporation, as suggested in Section 8.5. This tactic technically will not reduce the corporation's accumulated earnings, but will use up excess cash that would otherwise raise questions by IRS auditors.

S Corporations

S corporations are not subject to the accumulated earnings tax because all their earnings are deemed to be distributed to shareholders. Thus, in some cases, an S corporation election may be a solution to the accumulated earnings problem. In the past, one frequent objection to electing Subchapter S status was that it limited pension plan contributions for shareholder–employees to the lesser limits allowed for Keogh plans. Since 1984, this has ceased to be a problem since pension and profit-sharing plans of S corporations are treated almost exactly like those of regular corporations after 1983.

Penalty Tax on Personal Holding Company Income

If a closely-held corporation gets a large proportion of its gross income, usually 60% or more, in the form of personal holding company income,[86] such as dividends, interest, rents, and royalties, it will generally be considered a personal holding company for tax purposes.[87]

Certain other nonpassive kinds of income will also be considered personal holding company income, such as income in a service business where anyone other than the corporation (the customer, for example) has the right under a contract to designate the individual who is to perform the services when the person designated owns at least 25% of the corporate stock.[88] Also, payments a corporation receives from a 25% shareholder for use of its property is personal holding company income.[89] This would put a damper on such schemes as having your corporation buy a yacht and charter it to you, for example.

If a corporation comes within the definition of a personal holding company, the tax law imposes a 28% penalty tax on any personal holding company income not distributed as a dividend,[90] as a rule.

Most actively-conducted small businesses will not need to be very concerned about being treated as personal holding companies since they will seldom get 60% or more of their gross income from passive sources like dividends and interest. The kind of small business most likely to have a personal holding company problem is the incorporated personal service business — when the corporation enters into contracts and agrees to provide the services of an employee who is a major shareholder. The best way to avoid this problem is to specify in the contract that the corporation reserves the right to designate the person who will provide the services. You will need to consult your tax adviser before entering into any such personal service contract, however, since the tax rules in this area are quite subtle and the tax penalty is very heavy if the income under the personal service contract is considered to be personal holding company income.

Another type of operating company that frequently encounters personal holding company tax problems is the developer of computer software that generates much of its income from software licensing agreements.

While the Tax Reform Act of 1986 included a special exemption from the personal holding company provisions for corporations actively engaged in the computer software business, the terms of this exception[91] are quite technical and many software firms will not be able to qualify for this relief without very careful planning.

Possible Treatment of Corporate Debt As Stock

As discussed in Section 8.5, there are two significant advantages to putting part of your investment in an incorporated business into the corporation in the form of debt, rather than all in exchange for stock. These advantages are (1) the interest paid to you is normally deductible by the corporation, unlike dividends paid on its stock, and (2) repayment to you of the money you loaned to the corporation allows you to take part of your investment out of the corporation free of tax.

Because the use of debt in structuring a closely-held corporation is so advantageous, Congress[92] has taken steps to limit the extent to which you can use debt to capitalize a corporation and still enjoy these advantages.

Over the last few years, the IRS has proposed, umpteen times, sets of new and complex regulations as to when loans to a corporation by its shareholders will be treated as equivalent to an investment in its stock — in which case interest payments will not be deductible by the corporation and principal payments would be taxable to the recipient.

These regulations raised such a storm of protest each time they were proposed that the IRS has finally withdrawn them. We are now back to a case-by-case determination of what is debt and what is stock, with hundreds of often conflicting court decisions as our only guidelines. Nevertheless, there are a few generally accepted ground rules that you should follow to avoid having corporate debt reclassified as equity (stock) by the IRS:

- The loan should not have any equity-like features, such as interest or payments pegged to the corporation's income.
- The loan should be made at a reasonable interest rate, such as the rate at which the IRS imputes interest between related parties.
- The corporation's total debts — other than trade accounts payable — should not be more than about three times its net worth, to be on the safe side.
- The loan should be documented by a written note and should have a specified maturity date. All interest and principal payments on the note should be made on time.

If you follow each of the above rules, you will generally avoid the problem of having debt reclassified as stock. If you fail to comply with one or more of those rules when lending money to your corporation, the loan may be treated as a stock investment. This can be a serious tax trap if, when the loan is to be repaid, you are unaware that the repayment to you may constitute taxable income.

Debt-Equity Distinction

The most basic tax problem resulting from incorporating a business is the possibility of double taxation of the business income if it is paid out as dividends. That is, if the corporation has any profit after payment of salaries and other expenses, it must pay tax on those profits, unless it is an S corporation. Then, if those profits left after taxes are distributed to stockholders as dividends, the stockholders must also pay tax on the dividends they receive.

Fortunately, the problem of double taxation is usually quite manageable and most small incorporated businesses never pay dividends. The owners usually are also the officers of the corporation and can take enough income out in the form of salary and fringe benefits to live on, usually leaving some profit in the corporation to be plowed back into the business.

Also, as outlined briefly in Section 8.5, there are a number of better ways to get the accumulated profits out of the corporation than by paying dividends.

Double Taxation of Corporate Income

If you own an incorporated business or own a portion of its stock and are actively involved in operating the business, you will be an employee of the corporation and will draw a salary. Drawing a large salary from the

Unreasonable Compensation

corporation may enable you to withdraw much of the profits of the business without any problem of double taxation, since the corporation can deduct reasonable compensation it pays to you as your salary.[93]

Thus, taking salary out of the corporation is clearly much preferable to taking money out in the form of dividends, since the corporation cannot deduct dividends it pays. The salary you receive, if reasonable, is deductible by the corporation; however, the key word here is reasonable. If you try to take too much income out of the corporation as salary, including bonuses and fringe benefits like pension and profit-sharing contributions, the IRS may try to treat part of your salary as unreasonable compensation. There are no hard and fast rules as to how much compensation is reasonable, but if you are taking no more than the officers in similar businesses of the same size are paid, you should not have any problem establishing that your compensation from the corporation is reasonable under the circumstances.

However, if the IRS succeeds in treating part of your compensation as excessive, there will be two serious tax consequences:

- The deduction by the corporation for the unreasonable portion of your salary will be disallowed, and
- Part of your salary will be reclassified as dividend income, and thus pension and profit-sharing plan contributions based on that salary may not be fully deductible, which could even result in disqualification of your pension or profit-sharing plan.

8.10 Estate Planning in Connection with Your Business

As the owner of part or all of even a moderately successful business, you may find that after a few years the value of your interest in the business accounts for a very large portion of your personal net worth. As such, it will probably be the most important single asset you have to be concerned with for estate planning purposes, both during your lifetime and at the time of your death.

No attempt will be made here to go into the intricacies of the estate planning possibilities that may be available to a business owner for reducing lifetime income, gift taxes, and the size of your estate that will be subject to death taxes. Instead, we have noted below several of the fundamental approaches you need to be aware of and which, at an appropriate time, you should discuss with your tax adviser and attorney.

Income-Splitting

A useful method of reducing lifetime income taxes is to split the taxable income from your business between two or more persons or entities. Usually a corporation, particularly an S corporation, is the most useful vehicle for splitting income between you and your children, if you give them stock in the corporation. A corporation that has not elected S corporation treatment can also be used to split income between you and the corporation (see Section 2.4).

Remember, however, that income-splitting only works now if your children are 14 years of age or older. Otherwise, any unearned income of your children in excess of $1,000 a year is taxed at your marginal tax bracket, eliminating any tax savings.[94]

Reducing Estate and Gift Taxes

Often the best time to remove potential wealth from your taxable estate at death is by giving your children part of the stock in your incorporated business when the business is formed — when the value of the stock is likely to be negligible. If you wait until the business has become a valuable and profitable enterprise, gifts of stock at that time may result in substantial taxable gifts for gift tax purposes, even though the tax cost of those gifts may not be felt until you die, in some cases. You can now make gifts of up to $10,000 ($20,000 if married) per year to each of your children completely free of federal gift taxes.

Assuming that you want part of your stock in your incorporated business to pass to your children at your death, it obviously makes sense to give them a portion of the stock (but not enough to affect your control of the corporation) during your lifetime, with little or no gift tax cost if it is done when the business is started. Thus, they will already own the stock when you die, and that valuable asset will have passed to them free of death taxes in most instances. Also, as noted above, lifetime gifts of stock to your children may also save income taxes.

Buy–Sell Agreements

If you have one or more partners or business associates who also own a part of the business, it is highly important that you enter into a buy–sell agreement with them that spells out what happens if one of you dies, becomes disabled, or wants to sell his or her interest in the business. Often these agreements are funded by life insurance on the owners, so that if you die, the business or the other owners will collect the life insurance proceeds and use those funds to buy out your interest in the business. Otherwise, your surviving family members might find it very difficult to sell the interest in the business they inherit from you, except at a give-away price.

Many small business owners ignore the need for buy–sell agreements or, like having a will drawn up, they keep putting it off. When one of the partners or shareholders dies, the survivors may have a problem in raising enough cash to pay the death taxes. This is only one of the problems that may arise when there is no buy–sell agreement.

The few hundred dollars you may spend in legal fees to have a buy–sell agreement with your business partners or associates drawn up is probably one of the best investments you and your associates will ever make.

Retirement Plan Exemptions

Prior to 1983, there were unlimited statutory exemptions from the estate tax for retirement plan benefits if you left your interest in any such plan or IRA to a designated beneficiary other than your estate and if certain other requirements were met.[95] Unfortunately, Congress limited the exclusion to $100,000 after 1982[96] and has repealed this exemption entirely after 1984.

Accordingly, if you have already done some estate planning based on obtaining this estate tax exemption for retirement benefits you planned to leave to a beneficiary other than your spouse, you had better go back to the drawing board now that this exemption has expired. However, if you were already receiving retirement benefits before 1984, the benefits may still be eligible for the above exclusions — if you don't change the form in which benefits are being paid.

Unlimited Marital Deduction

You should be aware that since 1982 it has been possible to leave your entire estate to your surviving spouse free of federal estate tax. While it is not always advisable to fully utilize this unlimited deduction for property left to your spouse, you should have an up-to-date will that takes the most advantageous approach for your particular circumstances.

Be aware, however, that if you leave your heirs accrued pension benefits worth more than $750,000 (more or less, the threshold amount can vary) upon your death, in general, your estate will be subject to a special 15% excise tax[97] on the excess pension benefits, even though you leave all such benefits to your surviving spouse, which otherwise should qualify for the unlimited marital deduction.

Since not all state inheritance tax laws permit an unlimited marital deduction, it can create inheritance tax problems in those states if you leave too much property to your spouse. Refer to Section 11.8 for details regarding your state's marital deduction rules under its inheritance tax laws.

Note!

If you have a will or revocable trust executed before September 13, 1981 which leaves your spouse the maximum amount of your property that qualifies for the estate tax marital deduction, your will or trust may be a ticking time bomb. Wills or trusts executed before September 13, 1981 don't benefit from the unlimited marital deduction.[98] If you have such a will or trust, have it revised and updated immediately!

8.11 Targeted Jobs Tax Credit

Are you aware that if you hire members of certain economically-disadvantaged groups, the federal government will pay you a subsidy of up to $2,400 in the form of tax credits per employee? Unfortunately, most employers, particularly small businesses, seem to be unaware of this substantial tax subsidy or else assume that it applies only if you hire ex-felons or the like.

Part of the reason so many employers fail to take advantage of this tax incentive appears to be on account of a Catch-22 in the way the program works:

To qualify for the targeted jobs tax credit for hiring a disadvantaged category person, he or she must be certified as such by a designated state employment security agency, and the certification must be received by the employer (or requested in writing) at least one day before the employee begins work.[99]

At the same time, state and federal anti-discrimination laws make it very difficult for you as an employer to ask prospective job applicants if they belong to any of the disadvantaged groups that are eligible for the targeted jobs tax credits, since to do so could be considered a discriminatory hiring practice.

Your best bet is to check first with your local state employment department or division to find out how to take advantage of state and federal job credit programs. The department will either refer you to the proper agency or organization who can assist you, or the department itself will help you find an individual who qualifies under this program and matches your specific job requirements.

The targeted group individuals for whom you can claim the jobs tax credit are:

Targeted Groups

- Vocational rehabilitation referrals. These are certain handicapped individuals who have completed rehabilitation programs. Tax credits aside, handicapped individuals often are extremely good and conscientious employees.
- Economically-disadvantaged youths. Individuals between 18–22 years of age who are certified as being members of economically-disadvantaged families.
- Economically-disadvantaged Vietnam veterans.
- SSI recipients. Persons receiving SSI payments from Social Security.
- General assistance recipients. Persons receiving state or local welfare payments.
- Economically-disadvantaged ex-convicts.
- Youths participating in a cooperative education program. Certain youths 16–20 years of age who have not finished high school.
- Eligible work incentive program employees.
- Qualified summer youth employees. Economically-disadvantaged youths 16 or 17 years old who are hired to work between May 1 and September 15, who were not previously employed by you.

On the first $6,000 you pay an eligible target group employee, you will earn tax credits of 40% of the wages. This is limited to $3,000 of wages for qualified summer youth employees during the first 90 days they work for you.

Here is how the federal targeted jobs tax credits apply for eligible and certified new employees:

Category of Employee	Federal Tax Credit	Minimum Work Period
All qualified employees as listed above	40% of wages on first $6,000 of wages or a maximum credit of $2,400 per employee	90 days or 120 hours
Qualified summer youth employees	40% of first 90 days' wages for up to $3,000 of wages or maximum credit of $1,200	14 days or 20 hours

Drawbacks

One drawback with all of these tax credits is that you must reduce the wages you can deduct dollar-for-dollar for credits you claim.[100] That is, if you pay someone $1,000 and claim a $400 targeted jobs tax credit, you can only deduct $600 for wage expense, not the full $1,000. The credit is not allowed for wages paid to strikebreakers or scabs after 1986.

Note!

The targeted jobs credit expires on December 31, 1991, but it is likely to be extended again by Congress. See Section 11.8 regarding state jobs tax credits.

8.12 Hiring Your Spouse as an Employee

If you run an unincorporated business and your spouse works with or for you, there are three ways your spouse can be treated for tax purposes:

- As an employee;
- As a partner in the firm;
- As an uncompensated employee, which is probably the most common approach.

Social Security

Until very recently, a sole proprietor could often reduce net income subject to self-employment tax by hiring his or her spouse, a parent, or a minor child as a paid employee, since the wages paid reduced the proprietorship's net income — and thus, in many cases, the self-employment tax liability — but were exempt from FICA (Social Security) tax[101] or unemployment taxes.[102] We have recommended this tactic for years in prior editions of this publication.

Unfortunately, Congress partially closed this loophole in the Omnibus Budget Reconciliation Act of 1987, ending the exemption from FICA taxes for wages paid to a spouse, parent, or minor child — with the exception of a child under 18 years of age — effective January 1, 1988. However, there are still some advantages to having your spouse be a paid employee of your proprietorship, as described below.

Individual Retirement Account for Spouse

If your spouse works for you without pay and has no other income from an outside job, the most the two of you can put into an Individual Retirement Account (IRA) is $2,250. If you start compensating your spouse, even as little as $2,000 a year, you should each qualify for a $2,000 IRA deduction or a total of $4,000 a year, rather than only $2,250. Note that IRA deductions may be limited if either of you is an active participant in another retirement plan.

Medical Insurance

If you are a sole proprietor of a business, you can deduct medical insurance coverage for employees that you pay for, but can deduct only 25% of your own medical insurance premiums. If your spouse works for you, put your spouse on the payroll and provide a medical expense reimbursement plan or medical insurance for your spouse and his or her family (which includes you), and you can deduct the payments or premiums in full since your spouse is an employee. While this might sound a bit flaky, the IRS has approved just such an arrangement in a published ruling.[103]

See Section 11.8 regarding state tax exemptions and other implications of hiring a spouse as an employee.

8.13 How to Save on Unemployment Taxes

The unemployment tax rate you pay as an employer is one of the few taxes where you have some control over the rate you pay. The state maintains a reserve account for each employer, in which it monitors the unemployment taxes you pay in and the unemployment benefits it pays out to your former employees. The more benefits the state pays to your former employees, the higher your individual company's tax rate will be and vice versa. So it pays for you to have as few former employees as possible who are collecting unemployment benefits, since these are charged to your reserve account.

To succeed in keeping down the unemployment claims charged to your account, you need to challenge any former employees' claims that appear to be unjustified. Often you will be surprised to learn that an employee you had fired for stealing or who had quit on you has filed for benefits and has lied about his or her reasons for leaving. In general, an ex-employee can't collect unemployment based on his or her work for you if the employee left your employment for one of these reasons:

- Refusal to work;
- Voluntarily quitting;
- Inability to continue work due to illness, injury, etc; or
- Misconduct, such as theft, not showing up for work, or the like.

Tips on Reducing Claims

An employee who leaves your employ for virtually any other reason, such as being fired for incompetence, can generally collect benefits, which will cost you money by raising your unemployment tax rate. The following are some tips on how you can keep down the number of unemployment claims filed against your account.

- Be aware, when you are hiring, of the cost if you have to lay people off. You may hire a number of new employees for an expansion or new project with the view that if things don't work out as planned, you will simply lay them off and cancel the project with no further cost. Count the cost. Remember that if you do have to lay them off, you may be paying a much higher unemployment tax rate for several years as a result.

- Document in writing your reasons for firing an employee, if for reasons such as theft, insubordination, absence, or intoxication on the job. This will buttress your argument that the fired employee is not entitled to benefits if he or she should file a claim.

- Be aware that if you change an employee's hours of work and he or she quits as a result, it will be considered involuntary dismissal and the employee will probably be eligible for benefits. So it pays to have a written agreement signed by the employee to work any shift, hours, weekends, etc., that are required, if needed. Then if the employee quits it will not be due to a change in job conditions, in the eyes of the law.

- If you decide to fire someone for misconduct, do it on the spot. If you keep them on at your convenience until you find a replacement, it will not usually be considered a discharge for misconduct, and the fired employee will most likely be eligible for benefits.

- If new employees do not work out, consider firing them before they have worked three months. In most states, a person has to work for you at least three months before they can earn unemployment benefits that are chargeable to your reserve account.

In general, it pays to keep a close eye on your employer reserve account and be aware of who is filing benefit claims that will cost you money. Contest any claims that you do not feel are legitimate.

8.14 Deductions for Office-in-the-Home Expenses

If you use part of your residence for business purposes, you may be able to deduct part of your office-in-the-home expenses; however, the rules are rather stringent, and the general rule is that office-in-the-home expenses are not deductible for tax purposes, unless you meet a number of quite technical requirements.

There are several types of situations under which you may be able to claim deductions for part of your rent or expenses related to ownership of your residence, as well as other occupancy expenses, despite the home–office deduction limitations.

If you use part of your residence exclusively for business purposes and on a regular basis, you may be able to claim office-in-the-home deductions, if you also qualify under one of the following tests:[104]

Exclusive-Use Tests

- Principal Place of Business — you use a portion of your home as your principal place of business; or
- Use as a Place to Meet or Deal with Clients, etc. — you use your home as a place to meet clients, customers, patients, etc.; or
- Separate Structure Not Attached to Dwelling Unit — your home office is a separate structure that is not attached to your house or living quarters.

Two special exceptions are made where part of a home is regularly, but not exclusively, used for business purposes.

Nonexclusive Uses that Qualify

- Storage of Inventory — a wholesaler or retailer who uses part of a home to store inventory that is being held for sale; only, however, if the dwelling unit is the taxpayer's sole fixed location of the trade or business.
- Day Care Facility — part of the home is used for day care of children, physically and mentally handicapped persons, or individuals age 65 or older.

If you can show that a portion of your residence qualifies as a home office, you have cleared the first hurdle. But note that, even if you don't meet any of the above requirements, these rules will not disallow your deductions that are otherwise allowed for tax purposes, such as interest on your home mortgage, real estate taxes, or casualty losses from damage to your residence. Also, business expenses that are not home-related, such as business supplies, cost of goods sold, wages paid to business employees, and other such operating expenses, are not affected by the limitation on home office-related deductions.

If the business use of your home qualifies under one of the above tests, then you may be able to deduct part of the home office expenses that are allocable to the portion of your home that is used in your business, in addition to home mortgage interest, property taxes, and casualty losses.

For example, if 15% of your home is used exclusively and regularly as your principal place of business you could possibly deduct up to 15% of your occupancy costs, such as gas, electricity, insurance, repairs, and similar expenses, as well as 15% of your rent or depreciation expense on 15% of the tax basis of your house. The IRS and the Tax Court don't agree on the deductibility of certain other types of expenses, e.g., lawn care.

Deductions Limited to Income

Note, however, that the amount of qualifying home office expense you can actually deduct for the year is limited to the gross income from your home business, reduced by regular operating expenses (wages, supplies, etc.) and an allocable portion (15% in the above example) of your mortgage interest, property taxes, and casualty loss deductions. If you still have net business income after taking those deductions, then you may deduct the allocable portion of your home office expenses, up to the amount of such net income.

Any portion of your home office expenses that aren't deducted due to the income limit in one year can be carried over to future years until usable, if ever. Thus, it pays to keep track of any such disallowed expenses, in case your home-based business becomes more profitable in the future, and you are then able to deduct the carried-over expenses from earlier years.

Cautionary Note

The downside of taking home office deductions is a potential tax bite when you sell your home. For example, if 15% of your home has been used for business and you sell your home for a gain, you will have to pay tax on 15% of the gain, even if you reinvest in a new house, or even if you qualify for the once-in-a-lifetime $125,000 exclusion of gain (for persons over age 55) when you sell the house. Thus, a few hundred dollars of home office deductions now could result later in many thousands of dollars of tax on the "business" part of your house when sold for a gain a few years down the road.

Footnotes

1. I.R.C. §11.
2. I.R.C. §243(a).
3. I.R.C. §§301 and 302(d).
4. I.R.C. §331.
5. I.R.C. §1(h).
6. I.R.C. §531.
7. I.R.C. §542.
8. I.R.C. §542(a)(1) provides that a corporation may be a "personal holding company" if at least 60% of its "adjusted ordinary gross income" (as defined) constitutes "personal holding company income."
9. I.R.C. §246A.
10. For a FSC, the exempt foreign trade income will not even be taxed when paid out as a dividend, if the shareholder is a corporation. I.R.C. §245 (c)(1).
11. I.R.C. §991–997.
12. I.R.C. §994(a).
13. Treas. Regs. §1.994-1(e).
14. I.R.C. §994(a).
15. Treas. Regs. §1.994.
16. I.R.C. §995(b)(1)(F)(i) (as amended by The Tax Reform Act of '86).
17. I.R.C. §995.
18. I.R.C. §995(f).
19. A direct loan is usually out of the question (except for a "producer's loan" as defined in §994(d), which is of limited usefulness). However, it is possible to achieve the same result as a loan by having the DISC enter into an agreement to purchase export accounts receivable from XYZ at a discount, so that all of DISC's cash is, in effect, loaned to XYZ all of the time. The IRS accepts this type of arrangement. Rev. Rul. 75-430, 1975-2 CB 313; Rev. Rul. 76-284, 1976-2 CB 236.
20. Treas. Regs. §1.991-1(a).
21. I.R.C. §922(a)(1).
22. I.R.C. §924(b)(1).
23. I.R.C. §924(b)(2).
24. I.R.C. §925.
25. I.R.C. §923(a)(3) makes 16/23 of the income exempt from tax. But I.R.C. § 291(a)(4) reduces this exempt fraction to 15/23 for an FSC with a corporate shareholder.
26. An FSC's export profits computed under the "gross receipts" or "combined income" pricing rules are free of tax if paid out as dividends to the U.S. parent corporation. I.R.C. §245. But if the U.S. owner of the FSC is not a corporation, the dividends are fully taxable to the recipient.
27. See the discussion of "unreasonable compensation" at Section 8.9 of this chapter.
28. I.R.C. §7872.
29. I.R.C. §302(c)(2) permits the complete termination of the interest of a family member in a corporation by means of a stock redemption to qualify for capital gains treatment, if certain conditions are met.
30. I.R.C. §453(g).
31. I.R.C. §291(a).
32. I.R.C. §274(h). Deductions for foreign conventions are now completely disallowed, unless you can show that it was just as reasonable for the convention to be held abroad as it would have been to hold it in North America. Deductions for conventions or seminars on cruise ships are limited to $2,000, and other travel by "luxury water transportation" is deductible only up to certain per diem amounts. I.R.C. §274(m)(1).
33. I.R.C. §280A. In order to claim any deductions for an office in your home, you must use a part of your home exclusively for business, and your home office must either (a) be your principal place of business for the business you operate (which can include a "moonlighting business"), or (b) be used regularly by clients, customers, etc. as a place where you deal with them. Even if you pass these tests, you cannot take any home office deductions except to the extent the income from your home-based business exceeds other expenses. In short, you generally cannot deduct any loss on a home-based business.

Continued

34. I.R.C. § 274(d).

35. I.R.C. § 274(d).

36. I.R.C. § 274(d), as amended by Pub. L. No. 99-44.

37. I.R.C. § 274(a)(1)(A).

38. I.R.C. § 274(e)(1) (Repealed as of 1-1-87.)

39. I.R.C. § 262.

40. I.R.C. § 168(e)(3)(B).

41. I.R.C. § 280F(a)(2)(A) as amended in 1986 by Pub. L. No. 99-514.

42. I.R.C. § 280F(b)(2).

43. I.R.C. § 280F(d)(5)(B).

44. Rev. Proc. 89-66, 1989-2CB 792.

45. I.R.C. § 441(i).

46. I.R.C. § 195.

47. I.R.C. § 267(a)(2).

48. I.R.C. § 1373 (b) (before amendment).

49. I.R.C. § 1378(b).

50. I.R.C. §§ 1378(a) and 441(i).

51. I.R.C. §§ 444 and 7519.

52. Treas. Regs. § 1.446-1(c)(2)(i).

53. I.R.C. § 448.

54. I.R.C. § 461(h).

55. I.R.C. § 267(a)(2).

56. Treas. Regs. § 1.451-3.

57. I.R.C. § 460.

58. I.R.C. § 56(a)(3).

59. I.R.C. § 453(b).

60. I.R.C. § 453(a) (before 1987 amendment).

61. I.R.C. §§ 453(1)(2)(B) and 453(1)(3).

62. I.R.C. § 453A(b).

63. I.R.C. § 453A(b)(3).

64. I.R.C. §§ 453C and 453(j).

65. I.R.C. § 472.

66. I.R.C. § 474.

67. I.R.C. § 1363(d).

68. I.R.C. § 263A(b)(2)(B).

69. I.R.C. § 463(a). (Repealed by '87 Act.)

70. The Tax Reform Act of 1986 § 805.

71. The Tax Reform Act of 1986 § 805 (d).

72. I.R.C. § 11(b)(2).

73. I.R.C. § 531.

74. I.R.C. § 541.

75. I.R.C. § 385.

76. I.R.C. § 531.

77. I.R.C. § 535(c)(2). This limit has been increased to $250,000, but remains at $150,000 for various professional service businesses (law firms, architects, physicians, etc.).

78. I.R.C. § 535(a) and (b).

79. I.R.C. § 537(a).

80. I.R.C. § 535(c)(2).

81. I.R.C. § 531.

82. I.R.C. § 537(a)(2).

83. Treas. Regs. §§ 1.537-1(b)(1) and 1.537-2(b)(2).

84. I.R.C. § 537(b)(4).

85. Treas. Regs. § 1.537-2(b)(3).

86. As defined in I.R.C. § 543.

87. I.R.C. § 542.

88. I.R.C. § 543(a)(7).

89. I.R.C. § 543(a)(6).

90. I.R.C. § 541.

91. I.R.C. § 543(d).

92. I.R.C. § 385.

93. I.R.C. § 162(a)(1).

94. I.R.C. § 1(g).

95. I.R.C. § 2039(c) and (e). (Repealed after 1984.)

96. I.R.C. § 2039(g). (Repealed after 1984.)

97. I.R.C. § 4980A(d).

98. § 403 (e)(3) of the Economic Recovery Tax Act of 1981 (Public Law 97-34).

99. I.R.C. § 51.

100. I.R.C. § 280C(a).

101. I.R.C. § 3121(b)(3)(A).

102. I.R.C. § 3306(c)(5).

103. Rev. Rul. 71-588, 1971-2 CB 91.

104. I.R.C. § 280A(c)(1).

Chapter 9

Miscellaneous Business Pointers

"Money is not the root of all evil. The lack of money is the root of all evil."

— Reverend Ike

9.1 General Considerations

This chapter sets forth a number of general pointers and suggestions in connection with operating a small business, some of which may be of interest to you in your particular business.

9.2 Accounting — Some Basics

Accounting Systems

Maintaining good accounting records is a must for any small business. Without accurate and up-to-date records, you will be operating your business without vitally important information, since meaningful financial statements can be prepared only if the underlying records of transactions are accurate and current.

It may help to think of your accounting system as being like an airplane's radar system. If you are not getting current and correct feedback from either system, you will not have enough time to react to prevent a potential crash.

Single-Entry Method

While most schools and colleges teach only the double-entry method of bookkeeping, which provides a series of checks and balances in recording income and expenditures, some small business owners get by adequately using a single-entry method of accounting. If you are not knowledgable about double-entry bookkeeping and handle most of the funds directly yourself, you may find that a single-entry system is acceptable for your needs and much simpler to use. The single-entry method is only slightly more involved than keeping a checkbook record of cash income and disbursements and usually consists of three basic records:

- A daily cash receipts summary, which may come from a cash register tape or sales slips. This will give you not only a total of your daily cash receipts but will break down your sales by product, by salesman, by store, etc., depending on how much detail you need.
- A monthly cash receipts summary, which is simply a summary of the daily summaries.
- A monthly cash disbursements report of expenses and other payments, such as debt repayments, purchases of capital assets or distributions of profits.

A number of simplified write-it-once systems for all different kinds of businesses are available at office supply stores or from firms, such as Safeguard Business Systems, which is one of the most popular sellers of such systems.

Double Entry Method

You should be aware that while a single-entry system is easy to use, it is not a complete accounting system, since it focuses mainly on profit and loss and does not provide a balance sheet. For all but the very smallest businesses, a single-entry accounting system is likely to be inadequate, and even if your business is very small, but expected to grow, it will usually be advisable to start out with a full set of books, kept on the double-entry method, rather than changing over to it later as the size of your business expands. You can avoid many future problems if you get a CPA to help you set up the accounting system for your business. He or she will tailor a chart of accounts to your specific needs, and build in internal controls to record all transactions and to reduce the possibilities of employee theft or embezzlement that might go undetected with a poorly-designed system. If you use a personal computer in your business, there are any number of general ledger accounting software packages you can buy if your accounting needs are fairly straightforward and if you have a reasonable understanding of how double-entry accounting works. For a very small business, there are software packages available for under $100 that are adequate.

Financial Accounting Guide for Small Business, published by The Oasis Press, is a valuable resource for the beginning small business owner, manager, or accountant. It explains the why as well as the how of all aspects of small business accounting, from preparing financial statements to interpreting the numbers. To obtain this book, contact your book source or The Oasis Press, (800) 228-2275.

Accounting Firm Services

If you are going to use an outside accounting firm to prepare financial statements, you need to be aware of the three different levels of service that they will provide.

Audits

An audit is invariably the most involved and most expensive level of service in connection with financial statements. An accounting firm that audits financial statements must not only verify that your financial statements are presented fairly and in accordance with generally accepted accounting principles (GAAP), but also checks and verifies some or all of the actual accounts to satisfy itself that they are for real. It does this, for instance, by requesting confirmations of bank accounts, receivable and payable account balances from banks, customers, and vendors to uncover possible errors or fraud in recordkeeping. Because audits are relatively expensive, many small businesses elect to have review or compilation statements done; however, lenders or bonding companies often insist that you have a certified audit.

Reviews

A review involves some limited analysis or testing of the financial records, but the CPA expresses only a very limited opinion as to the accuracy of the information in the financial statements. A review is thus somewhat less expensive than an audit, but more expensive than a compilation. Most small businesses hire a CPA firm to do a review only if their bankers or other lenders or financial backers insist on a review rather than a compilation.

Compilations

Most financial statements prepared for small businesses are compilations for the simple reason that a compilation is far less expensive than an audit or review. In a compilation, the outside accountant has no obligation to do any investigation unless he or she becomes aware of something that looks suspicious or that could be misleading. Generally, all an accountant is required to do in preparing compilation statements is to take the financial data you give him or her and present it in a manner that conforms with GAAP — or in some other form, such as income tax basis accounting, if he or she discloses what method of accounting is being used. In a compilation, the accountant expresses no opinion on the accuracy of the information presented. The accountant is simply taking what you gave him or her and putting it in a proper financial statement format. It is important for you to remember that regardless of what type of assurance your accountant expresses, they are your financial statements, and it is your ultimate responsibility to see that they are accurately prepared.

Depreciation — A New Ballgame after 1986

The Tax Reform Act of 1986 has effectively repealed the highly favorable ACRS tax depreciation system that was in force from 1981 until the end of 1986. As of January 1, 1987, taxpayers must learn to live with another whole new complex system of depreciation. Unfortunately, it is still necessary to know the old ACRS rules for assets acquired during the

1981–1986 period as well as the old depreciation rules for items acquired before 1981, in order to compute current depreciation on those assets. Since many readers may still be depreciating pre-1987 assets for a number of years, we have included the ACRS depreciation tables and a description of how the old ACRS system worked in this subsection. The Modified ACRS depreciation system that became effective in 1987 is summarized briefly below.

The Modified ACRS System

The new Modified ACRS law does not provide depreciation tables, unlike the old ACRS system. Instead, all assets placed in service after 1986 (with a few special exceptions) are assigned to 3-, 5-, 7-, 10-, 15-, or 20-year recovery period categories, except for real estate, which must be depreciated over 31.5 years — 27.5 years for residential rental property.[1]

Under the new system, all personal property is depreciated under the 200% declining balance method over its recovery period, except for 15- or 20-year property, for which the 150% declining balance method is used. Real estate may only be depreciated under the straight-line method.

Assets other than real estate are mostly assigned to the various recovery periods based on the old Asset Depreciation Range (ADR) "midpoint" class lives[2] which were published by the IRS back in the 1970s. These ADR class life guidelines vary from industry to industry in many cases and are far too voluminous, technical, and detailed to reproduce in a book of this nature. The new law, however, specifically assigns some types of assets to recovery classes. For example, autos and light trucks are now five-year property (they were three-year property under the old ACRS rules). The Modified ACRS provisions have further reduced the maximum annual depreciation deductions on so-called luxury automobiles as discussed in Section 8.6 in the preceding chapter.

One small ray of sunshine in this new tax depreciation nightmare is a liberalization of the former $5,000 first year expensing election for tangible personal property. After 1986, you may elect to expense up to $10,000 in cost of furniture, equipment, etc. in the year such assets are placed in service.[3] For example, if the only depreciable items you buy in 1991 are $10,000 of office equipment, you may be able to deduct the full $10,000 in 1991. Note, however, that this special deduction is no longer allowed to the extent that it would create a loss for your trade(s) or business(es) for the year. Also, the deduction is phased out if you acquire more than $200,000 of eligible property during the tax year.

The Old ACRS System

Here is a summary of the basic depreciation rules under the Accelerated Cost Recovery System (ACRS) of depreciation which applies to all tangible depreciable property acquired after 1980 and before 1987, except certain pre-1981 assets acquired from a related person or entity.

This included autos and light trucks, mainly, but also included tangible personal property used in connection with research and experimentation, plus certain special tools and dies used in manufacturing. Three-year property was depreciated according to this schedule.

Three-year Property

Year	Cost Deducted
1	25%
2	38%
3	37%

Almost any other machinery, equipment, or furniture bought for your business was five-year property and depreciated as noted below.

Five-year Property

Year	Cost Deducted
1	15%
2	22%
3	21%
4	21%
5	21%

This category rarely applies to small businesses, since it applies mainly to railroad tank cars, manufactured homes, theme park structures, and certain public utility property. Here is how ten-year property was depreciated.

Ten-year Property

Year	Cost Deducted	Year	Cost Deducted
1	8%	6	10%
2	14%	7	9%
3	12%	8	9%
4	10%	9	9%
5	10%	10	9%

The 15-year public utility property category is not relevant to most small businesses.

Fifteen-year Public Utility Property

The old ACRS system allowed buildings to be depreciated over 15, 18, or 19 years, compared to the 27.5 or 31.5 years required after 1986. Real estate acquired during the period from 1981 through March 15, 1984 is depreciable over 15 years. In general, real estate acquired or constructed after March 15, 1984 and before May 9, 1985 must be written off in 18 years. Real estate acquired or constructed on or after May 8, 1985 and before 1987 generally must be written off over a period of 19 years. A taxpayer could either elect straight-line depreciation or use one of the following accelerated depreciation tables for real property other than low-income housing.

Fifteen-, Eighteen-, or Nineteen-year Real Property

15-Year ACRS Real Estate Accelerated Depreciation Table (for Real Estate acquired between January 1, 1981 and March 15, 1984)

Percentage of Cost Deducted Annually

Year	Months in Service in First Tax Year											
	1	2	3	4	5	6	7	8	9	10	11	12
1	1%	2%	3%	4%	5%	6%	7%	8%	9%	10%	11%	12%
2	12	11	11	11	11	11	11	11	11	11	10	10
3	10	10	10	10	10	10	10	10	9	9	9	9
4	9	9	9	9	9	9	8	8	8	8	8	8
5	8	8	8	8	8	8	7	7	7	7	7	7
6	7	7	7	7	7	7	7	7	6	6	6	6
7	6	6	6	6	6	6	6	6	6	6	6	6
8	6	6	6	6	6	5	6	6	6	6	6	6
9	6	6	6	5	5	5	6	5	6	6	6	6
10	5	6	5	5	5	5	5	5	6	5	6	5
11–15	5	5	5	5	5	5	5	5	5	5	5	5
16	5	4	4	4	3	3	2	2	1	1	–	–

18-Year ACRS Real Estate Accelerated Depreciation Table[4] (for Real Estate acquired after March 15, 1984 and before June 23, 1984)

Percentage of Cost Deducted Annually

Year	Months in Service in First Tax Year											
	1	2	3	4	5	6	7	8	9	10	11	12
1	1%	2%	2%	3%	4%	5%	6%	6%	7%	8%	9%	10%
2	10	10	10	9	9	9	9	9	9	9	9	9
3	9	9	9	9	8	8	8	8	8	8	8	8
4	8	8	8	8	8	8	7	7	7	7	7	7
5	7	7	7	7	7	7	7	7	7	7	7	6
6	6	6	6	6	6	6	6	6	6	6	6	6
7	6	6	6	6	6	6	6	6	5	5	5	5
8–12	5	5	5	5	5	5	5	5	5	5	5	5
13	4	4	4	4	5	4	4	5	5	4	4	4
14–18	4	4	4	4	4	4	4	4	4	4	4	4
19	4	3	3	3	2	2	2	1	1	1	–	–

18-Year ACRS Real Estate Accelerated Depreciation Table (for Real Estate acquired after June 22, 1984 and before May 9, 1985)

Percentage of Cost Deducted Annually

Year	Months in Service in First Tax Year											
	1	2	3	4	5	6	7	8	9	10	11	12
1	0.4%	1%	2%	3%	4%	4%	5%	6%	7%	8%	9%	9%
2	10	10	10	9	9	9	9	9	9	9	9	9
3	9	9	9	9	8	8	8	8	8	8	8	8
4	8	8	8	8	8	8	8	7	7	7	7	7
5	7	7	7	7	7	7	7	7	7	7	7	7
6	6	6	6	6	6	6	6	6	6	6	6	6
7	6	6	6	6	6	6	6	6	5	5	5	5
8–12	5	5	5	5	5	5	5	5	5	5	5	5
13	5	5	4	4	4	5	4	4	5	4	4	4
14–17	4	4	4	4	4	4	4	4	4	4	4	4
18	4	4	4	4	4	4	4	4	4	4	3	4
19	3.6	3	3	3	3	2	2	2	1	1	1	–

19-Year ACRS Real Estate Accelerated Depreciation Table (for Real Estate acquired after May 8, 1985 and before January 1, 1987)

Percentage of Cost Deducted Annually

Year	Months in Service in First Tax Year											
	1	2	3	4	5	6	7	8	9	10	11	12
1	0.4%	1.1%	1.9%	2.7%	3.5%	4.2%	5.0%	5.8%	6.5%	7.3%	8.1%	8.8%
2	9.2	9.1	9.0	9.0	8.9	8.8	8.8	8.7	8.6	8.5	8.5	8.4
3	8.3	8.3	8.2	8.1	8.1	8.0	7.9	7.9	7.8	7.7	7.7	7.6
4	7.6	7.5	7.4	7.4	7.3	7.3	7.2	7.1	7.1	7.0	7.0	6.9
5	6.9	6.8	6.8	6.7	6.6	6.6	6.5	6.5	6.4	6.4	6.3	6.3
6	6.2	6.2	6.1	6.1	6.0	6.0	5.9	5.9	5.9	5.8	5.7	5.7
7	5.6	5.6	5.6	5.5	5.5	5.4	5.4	5.3	5.3	5.3	5.2	5.2
8	5.1	5.1	5.1	5.0	5.0	4.9	4.9	4.8	4.8	4.8	4.7	4.7
9	4.7	4.6	4.6	4.5	4.5	4.5	4.5	4.4	4.4	4.3	4.3	4.2
10–19	4.2	4.2	4.2	4.2	4.2	4.2	4.2	4.2	4.2	4.2	4.2	4.2
20	4.0	3.7	3.3	3.0	2.6	2.3	1.9	1.6	1.2	0.9	0.5	0.2

Internal Accounting Controls

One area in which many new or small businesses are deficient is in the area of internal controls and recordkeeping procedures. Lax procedures are frequently to blame when a secretary or bookkeeper departs for Brazil with thousands of dollars of stolen or embezzled funds belonging to their employer. Ideally, you would consult a good accountant to set up and review your internal financial controls; however, that will cost you a good deal of money, so before you do so, you may want to do your own review of your internal controls, utilizing this checklist.

Internal Controls Checklist

☐ The same person who handles your cash receipts should not be the same person who makes the bank deposits. Cash is too easily misappropriated. Don't tempt an employee by letting him or her handle both of these duties.

☐ The person who writes checks should not also sign them or have the authority to sign checks. A different person should sign checks.

☐ Whoever signs checks, you or another person, should only sign them when the bill that is being paid is presented at the time for scrutiny, and the check number should be written on the bill at the time, to avoid double payments or payments to a nonexistent vendor that is actually your employee's Brazilian bank account. When you sign the check, be sure you know what the bill is for.

☐ Consider using some type of mechanical check imprinting equipment for all checks that are written, as a further means of preventing unauthorized payments. Such machines keep a record of the amount of any checks written.

☐ Use only prenumbered checks and keep all of the cancelled or voided checks in your records. This will help make it readily apparent if any additional checks are written without your knowledge.

(continued)

Internal Controls Checklist (continued)

☐ Do a monthly bank reconciliation yourself or have your outside accountant do it, if you have one. Never let the person who writes checks do the reconciliation.

☐ Deposit your daily cash receipts in the bank each day. Do not let cash collections for one day get mingled with the next day's collections.

☐ Use a petty cash fund and voucher system for stamps, small bills, and other small cash outlays. Do not use cash from the day's receipts to pay bills! Put a voucher or bill in the petty cash box each time money is taken out. When the fund is depleted, write a check to bring it back up to the maximum amount (say $50), and record all the vouchers at the time the check is cashed to replenish the fund.

☐ Use prenumbered sets of sales checks, invoices, and receipts to keep control of payments made and received. Duplicates will be kept track of by the individuals making sales, etc., and the master copy will enable you to make sure they account for all of their transactions.

☐ Maintain a master or control account for all of your accounts receivable, and reconcile it each month to the subsidiary accounts receivable. If someone is stealing money from customer payments, it will be easier to spot if the master and subsidiary accounts are reconciled regularly.

9.3 Cash Flow Management

Cash flow is the lifeblood of any business organization. Yet all too many small business operators are so concerned with other matters that they fail to pay proper attention to managing their cash resources properly. Good cash management can make a significant contribution to the competitiveness and profitability of your business. Poor cash management is one of the main causes of business failures, particularly among smaller firms, since a cash shortage due to poor planning can set off a chain reaction of disastrous consequences, even in a profitable business.

Cash flow management has two aspects — projecting future cash flow and controlling and maximizing the cash available from operations at all times.

Projecting Cash Flow

Perhaps the most important part of cash flow management is projecting your business' near- and long-term cash needs accurately and making your business decisions reflect and take into account those needs. Often it will be necessary to rely on what has happened in the past in order to project what your sales will be in coming months, what percentage will be credit sales, and when your receivables are likely to be collected. Similarly, you have to estimate and project what you will have to pay out in the way of payroll, rent, taxes, servicing debts, purchasing inventory, and paying off existing payables, plus extraordinary outlays you can anticipate.

The purpose of making these detailed projections of expected cash inflows and outflows is to bring to your attention any point in the future when you might incur a cash shortage or deficit, so that you can take steps in advance to prevent that occurrence. For example, if your projections indicated that you were going to experience a severe cash crunch in about three months, you might take any of a number of steps to avert it, such as seeking to raise new capital, borrowing money, cutting prices in order to liquidate some of your inventory, or cutting back on planned expenditures. If you have a computer, be aware that there are microcomputer models available to assist in preparing projections of cash flows. If you don't own a computer, your CPA may have such models available to assist you.

PSI Research's Successful Business Software has developed an inexpensive and simple-to-use program that can help a small business owner–manager manage all financial aspects of the business. *Financial Templates for Small Business* lets the owner–manager monitor cash flow; generate financial statements; track monthly, quarterly, or three-year cash flow and income; and plan for the future by analyzing past and present performance. These multipurpose templates run on either IBM PC or compatible, or with Macintosh computers, along with spreadsheet programs, such as Lotus 1-2-3, Excel, or PSI's own spreadsheet program, available separately or in a package with *Financial Templates for Small Business*. For more information, contact The Oasis Press, (800) 228-2275.

Controlling and Maximizing Cash Flow

If you are able to increase available cash by speeding up collections, delaying payments, or by other means, you can use the extra cash to reduce your borrowings — thus saving interest expenses — or can invest the surplus cash to earn interest. Either way, improving your cash flow should increase your net earnings and should also help to avert cash shortages.

Here are some basic ways to improve your business' cash flow.

- Bill your customers promptly. The later they receive the bill, the later you will collect for a particular sale, in general.
- If you know that certain large customers must receive bills by certain days of the month in order for you to get paid that month, try to bill them before those deadlines if possible.
- Deposit your cash receipts in the bank daily, if possible.
- Keep close tabs on credit customers. Send them past due notices as soon as payments become overdue.
- If you can do so without hurting business, add late charges to overdue accounts.

- Never pay bills until just before they become due, unless there is a worthwhile discount for quick payment.
- Try to keep inventories as lean as possible. Even if you occasionally lose a small sale because you are temporarily out of an item, you should be far ahead of the game by substantially reducing the amount of cash you have tied up in inventory.
- Look for items in your inventory that are moving slowly or not at all. Consider slashing the price on those articles to convert them to cash and also to reduce the cost of storing them or taking up valuable shelf space.
- Consider leasing equipment items instead of buying.
- Be sure that you are not paying more on your estimated income taxes than you have to. You may qualify under one or more exceptions that will allow you to delay paying much of your tax for the year until the tax return is due, without incurring interest charges or late payment penalties. If you realize that you have already overpaid your corporate estimated tax for the year, there is a procedure for obtaining a refund prior to the time when you can file a return.[5]
- If your business has a net operating loss for tax purposes that can be carried back to prior years, a procedure exists for filing a claim for a quick refund of the prior years' taxes. And file it as early as you can, since the IRS no longer pays interest on these refunds.
- Instead of keeping all your business cash in a local bank account, consider putting a significant portion of your cash in an out-of-town money market-type fund that pays interest and allows you to write checks against the account. Since you continue to earn interest on funds on deposit until the checks clear, consider using a fund in a distant part of the country, since it will take longer for your checks to clear when you make payments to local firms.

9.4 Protecting Your Assets

Starting a new business is almost always a risky proposition, and you should not overlook the fact that, if the business fails, you may be forced into bankruptcy and could lose everything except what the bankruptcy laws allow you to keep. This is one reason why many small businesses incorporate at the outset, since a corporation will generally limit your liability to business creditors to the amount you invest in the corporation, plus any loans to the corporation you guarantee.

Accordingly, if you incorporate you should be cautious about unnecessarily committing too much of your personal assets to the business. For example, instead of putting a building or piece of land you own into the corporation, it may be better (and may save income and property taxes) for you to keep the property and lease it to the corporation.

Even if you incorporate, the leases or bank loans you find it necessary to guarantee on behalf of the corporation could still wipe out your personal assets if the business folds. Thus, it often makes sense to have your corporation set up a tax-qualified pension or profit-sharing plan and to have it contribute as much as possible to the plan on your behalf. Not only does this provide substantial tax savings and deferral, but the law in most states will in many cases protect your account under such a plan from your creditors or the corporation's creditors. Thus if, over a period of years, you build up a significant retirement fund in your corporation's pension plan, you have at least some degree of assurance that the failure of the business or a disastrous lawsuit will not touch that nest egg, — but in a divorce, your spouse may be able to claim his or her share of the pension plan account.

9.5 Protecting Trade Names and Trademarks

If you intend to use some type of distinctive trade name for your business or trademark for your product or in advertising your services, it will usually be advisable to consider taking steps to protect the use of the name or mark by registration under state or federal law or both. Also, it may be necessary to perform a search, which can be expensive, to determine whether someone else has already registered the same or a very similar name or symbol, so that you will not open yourself up to a lawsuit for infringement. Since not every trade name can be registered, you will need to consult a trademark attorney if you are interested in protecting a particular name used by your business. Federal registration of a name confers a number of significant benefits, including:

- Nationwide notice to others of your exclusive right to use the name or mark.

- Prima facie evidence of the validity of the registration and your exclusive right to use the mark throughout the country.

- With certain exceptions, registration gives you an unquestionable right to use the name or mark.

- If you prove in court that someone violated your rights under the Trademark Act of 1946,[6] you will be entitled to recover their profits from its use and damages, in some cases, treble damages.

- The right to sue in federal court for trademark infringement regardless of the amount at stake and whether or not there is diversity of citizenship, e.g., regardless of whether you and the defendant operate in the same or different states.

- The right to have customs officials halt importation of counterfeit goods using your trademark.

The Oasis Press' *How to Develop & Market Creative Business Ideas* can explain, step-by-step, how to protect your idea. To obtain this book contact your book source or The Oasis Press, (800) 228-2275.

9.6 Section 1244 Stock

If you invest directly in a small corporation by transferring money or property (other than securities) to the corporation in exchange for its common stock — or preferred stock, if issued after July 18, 1984 — the stock will usually qualify as section 1244 stock.[7] If it does, and the stock later becomes worthless or you sell it at a loss, Section 1244 of the Internal Revenue Code permits you to deduct up to $50,000 of your loss — $100,000 for a couple filing a joint return — as an ordinary deduction instead of as a capital loss for that year.

This can be very important, since you can fully deduct an ordinary loss from your taxable income, while capital losses can only be used to offset capital gains, if you have any, or $3,000 of ordinary income per year until your capital losses are used up.[8]

Any stock issued by a "small business corporation" will generally qualify as section 1244 stock unless the corporation obtained half or more of its gross receipts from passive kinds of income, such as interest, dividends, and the like, in the five years before your loss is incurred.[9] A corporation qualifies as a small business corporation if the total invested in its stock is $1 million or less.[10]

In the recent past, it was necessary for a corporation to adopt a plan to issue section 1244 stock in order for its stock to qualify for this special tax treatment. This is no longer required. If the stock issued by your corporation meets the requirements of Section 1244 described above, it will automatically qualify for ordinary loss treatment in your hands, up to the first one million dollars of stock issued. However, you should be aware that capital contributions you make, where no stock is received by you for such money, will not qualify for ordinary loss treatment.[11]

Note that the $50,000/$100,000 limit on the amount of loss that can qualify for ordinary loss treatment is an annual limitation. Thus, if you sell part of your stock for a loss in each of several years, you could theoretically claim up to $50,000 or $100,000 of your loss each year[12] as an ordinary deduction under Section 1244. See Section 11.9 as to whether state law also provides favorable tax treatment for losses on stock in a small business corporation.

9.7 SBA and Other Government Loans

If you need to borrow money for your business and cannot obtain regular bank financing, you should not overlook the possibility of obtaining a loan through the federal Small Business Administration (SBA). While many small business owners are under the impression that it is virtually impossible to obtain an SBA loan unless you are a member of a minority group, this is not the case. Although the SBA does make special efforts to provide financing for minority-owned businesses, only a relatively small percentage of SBA loans (13% in a recent year) are made to minority firms. Furthermore, a very high percentage of applications for SBA loans are approved when applications are properly submitted.

If you intend to apply for an SBA loan or a conventional loan, you can obtain *The Loan Package* by Emmett Ramey and Alex Wong, which gives you step-by-step instructions on how to lay out and present a professional-looking loan application package that will create a favorable impression with most loan officers. This comprehensive workbook is available from your book source or The Oasis Press, (800) 228-2275.

SBA Loan Programs

The SBA, an agency of the U.S. government, guarantees intermediate and long-term loans to small firms and, to a limited extent, also makes direct loans to some small businesses. The SBA is not allowed to grant such financial assistance unless the borrower is unable to obtain private sector financing on reasonable terms. The SBA does not compete with banks or other lenders. Instead, it works with private lenders to assure availability of capital to potentially profitable small firms.

For your firm to qualify for SBA financial assistance, it must come within the current definition of a "small business." In general, these are the types of small businesses eligible for SBA financing.

- Manufacturers with a maximum of 250 to 1,500 employees, depending upon the industry in which the applicant is engaged.
- Retailers with less than $2 million in annual sales — up to $7.5 million for some types of retailers.
- Wholesaling firms with gross annual sales ranging from $9.5 million to $22 million, depending on the industry.
- General construction firms, whose annual sales have averaged less than $9.5 million for the last three fiscal years. Lower limits apply to various special trade construction firms.
- Service firms with annual receipts not in excess of $2 million to $8 million, depending on the industry.
- Other definitions apply for businesses engaged in activities such as agriculture and transportation.

Private lenders that are eligible to make SBA-guaranteed loans or participate in SBA financing packages include banks, savings and loans, and certain other lenders such as SBICs and MESBICs (see below). The SBA has several types of loan programs for small businesses.

Guaranteed Loans

Most SBA financing actually consists of loans by banks or other lenders that are guaranteed by the SBA, which enables the small business to obtain such loans at reasonable interest rates, since the bank's risk is largely eliminated. The borrower must put up a reasonable amount of equity or collateral. These loans are usually secured by fixed assets, real estate, and inventory and are limited in term to seven years for working capital loans or 10 years for purchasing fixed assets. Construction loans can be for as long as 25 years.

Under this program, the bank or other private lender deals with the SBA — you deal with the bank, not the SBA. However, you will need to do the following in applying for such a loan or any other SBA financing:

- Define the amount you need to borrow and the purposes for which the funds will be used.
- Describe the collateral you will offer as security.
- Determine from a bank that a conventional loan is not available.
- Prepare current financial statements, preferably with your CPA's assistance. These would include, at a minimum, a relatively current balance sheet and an income statement for the previous full year and for the current year up to the date of the balance sheet.
- Prepare personal financial statements for the owners, partners or stockholders owning more than 20% of the stock of the company.

Direct Loans

If you are unable to obtain sufficient conventional financing or SBA guaranteed loan funds, you may in some cases be able to obtain a direct loan from the SBA of up to $150,000; however, these direct loans are hard to get, and can only be made if the SBA has funds available. In recent years, the funds available for lending by the SBA have been quite limited, so that eligible borrowers are frequently turned away because the SBA simply doesn't have any money to lend. When made, these loans are usually made on a participation basis with a bank or other lender, where the bank oversees the loan payments and loan servicing on behalf of itself and the SBA.

Other SBA Programs

New legislation frequently adds to and modifies the number and scope of SBA loan programs. Such other programs include seasonal lines of credit, economic opportunity loans for entrepreneurs who are physically handicapped or members of a minority group, short-term contract loan guarantees, energy loans to small firms to install, sell, service, develop, or manufacture solar energy or energy-saving devices, and disaster recovery loans to firms harmed by natural disasters. Since the nature, scope, and availability of funds under these numerous programs are constantly changing, you should consult your bank or local SBA offices, if you think your firm may qualify under one of these special financial assistance programs.

The U.S. Department of Housing and Urban Development (HUD) makes Urban Development Action Grants (UDAG) to cities in economically-distressed areas. The cities are then able to use these UDAG funds to make second-mortgage loans to private developers who are able to leverage these loans by borrowing at least five times such amounts (three times in small towns) from private sources. The purpose of such loans is to encourage new investment and development in depressed areas.

U.S. Department of Housing and Urban Development

The Economic Development Administration (EDA) of the U.S. Department of Commerce makes direct loans and offers loan guarantees to businesses in areas with low family incomes or suffering from high unemployment, to promote creation or retention of jobs for residents of such areas. To qualify for such financing, your business must be located in an EDA redevelopment area, and you need to demonstrate that the venture will directly benefit local residents and will not create over-capacity locally for the industry in question. Application for EDA loan assistance is a long and complex process, taking much longer for processing than typical SBA loans.

U.S. Department of Commerce

The Farmers Home Administration (FmHA) can perhaps be thought of as an SBA for rural areas. It offers insured and guaranteed loans to develop business and industry in nonurban areas with populations of under 50,000. Like the SBA program, FmHA loan guarantees are for up to 90% of the total amount of the loan and are made for up to 30 years for financing real estate acquisition, 15 years for machinery and equipment, and 7 years for working capital. FmHA loan guarantees are not available for agricultural production.

Farmers Home Administration (FmHA)

Unlike SBA loan guarantees, there is no dollar limit on FmHA loan guarantees, nor does the FmHA make direct loans. Applicants for FmHA loan guarantees must not only have adequate collateral and good business histories, but must also demonstrate that the project will have a favorable economic impact and will create new jobs in the area and not merely result in shifting business activity and jobs from one area to another.

Preference is given to business expansions rather than transfers, to projects in open country areas or towns with populations of under 25,000, and to business owners who are military veterans.

Other major federal loan programs include Federal Land Bank Association loans to businesses providing services to farmers, for purchasing land and equipment, and for start-up working capital; and a similar loan program

Other Federal Loan Programs

through the Production Credit Association and the Federal Intermediate Credit Bank provides loans of up to seven years.

SBICs and MESBICs

In addition to direct loans and guarantees from government agencies, you should not overlook possible loans or equity financing from Small Business Investment Companies (SBICs) and Minority Enterprise Small Business Investment Companies (MESBICs) as possible sources of financing. Both are licensed and regulated by the SBA to provide equity capital, long-term loans, and management assistance to small businesses.

SBIC and MESBIC loans are usually subordinated to loans from other creditors and are typically made for five- to seven-year terms. Both types of investment companies are privately-owned and thus tend to favor loans to established companies with significant net worth rather than new business start ups.

MESBICs serve only those small firms that are owned by members of economically- or socially-disadvantaged minority groups.

Business Development Corporations

Business Development Corporations are Local Development Companies (LDC), SBA Section 502, and Certified Development Companies (CDC), SBA Section 503, organized by local residents to promote economic development in their particular communities. These entities do not make working capital loans or loans to purchase free-standing equipment. Instead, LDCs or CDCs will arrange for SBA-guaranteed bank loans and sale of SBA-guaranteed debentures for up to 90% financing for 25 years for land acquisition, building construction, or renovation and purchase of fixed assets such as machinery and equipment. Refer to Section 11.9 for information regarding state business loan programs.

9.8 Mail Order Sales

If your business involves selling goods by mail order, you need to be aware of a regulation of the Federal Trade Commission that deals with mail order sales, Rule 435.1.[13] This federal regulation requires any business soliciting mail order sales to be prepared to ship the merchandise within 30 days after an order is received, unless it has clearly stated in its solicitation that orders will not be shipped for a longer period, such as 60 days. Otherwise, the solicitation will be considered as an "unfair and deceptive trade practice."

In addition, if you receive an order and for some reason you cannot ship it within 30 days, or the period stated in your solicitation, you must:

- Immediately notify the customer and offer the customer the option to either cancel the order and receive a refund or consent to the delay in shipment.

- Indicate when you will be able to ship or that you do not know when you will be able to ship the order.
- Provide other required information to the customer, which will vary in content depending upon when you expect to be able to ship.

Rule 435.1 is fairly complex and difficult to understand, but you need to understand and be familiar with it if you sell goods by mail order. If you are going into the mail order business and want a single source of information on state and federal mail order laws, obtain the *Mail Order Legal Manual*, by Erwin J. Keup, from your book source or The Oasis Press, (800) 228-2275.

Note that if you sell across state lines to customers in states where you have no offices, employees, or other presence, the sale is usually not subject to sales tax in either state, since it is an interstate sale; however, technically, such sales are subject to use tax in the customer's state. A use tax is sort of a "shadow" of the sales tax and, in most states, applies where the sales tax doesn't.

The U.S. Supreme Court and other courts generally have not supported attempts of the various states to force out-of-state retailers to collect use tax on mail order or other sales made to residents of the taxing state, so that most mail order firms tend to treat such interstate sales as being tax-free, or tell the customers that it is up to them to report the purchase and pay the use tax, which they rarely do.

Unfortunately, in the last few years, many states have enacted new and broader sales and use tax laws that require out-of-state retailers who advertise in the local media or send substantial amounts of direct mail/catalog solicitations into the state to register as retailers subject to sales or use tax in the state, and treating such direct sales as taxable. Some states are aggressively enforcing these new laws, which will definitely cramp the style of many mail order firms if these laws stand up in court.

Even if these new state laws are held to be unconstitutional, a bill has been working its way through Congress in recent years that would specifically grant states the right to require out-of-state sellers to collect use tax on sales made into the state, with certain restrictions. The bill, as it currently stands, would provide exceptions for small businesses, since having to file and pay sales or use taxes to all 50 states would be extremely expensive and onerous for small firms, and would effectively put small mail order firms out of business if they are not exempted. Note that, unlike the proposed federal legislation, the new state laws adopted in recent years do not generally make an exception for small firms.

Don't assume that interstate sales are still "sales tax-free," at least in many states. If the proposed federal legislation passes, you will probably be required to collect and pay over sales or use tax in all 50 states fairly soon after any such enactment. Some states, like Massachusetts, have

State Sales and Use Taxes

The Bottom Line

already passed such legislation, but because of doubts as to its constitutionality, will not attempt to enforce it until the proposed federal legislation is enacted into law.

9.9 Toxic Substances and Hazardous Wastes

If your business is one that engages in the manufacturing, processing, or distribution of chemical substances, you should be aware that you may be required under the Federal Toxic Substances Control Act[14] to report certain information regarding chemical substances and mixtures you use to the Environmental Protection Agency (EPA). There can be severe penalties for failing to make the required reports to the EPA, including civil and criminal penalties of $25,000 and up to a year's imprisonment for each violation. Each day the violation continues is considered a separate violation for purposes of the fines.

In addition, there is a rapidly growing body of federal and state laws regulating (and taxing) the disposition of hazardous waste substances. The primary federal law regulating hazardous waste disposal is the Resource Conservation and Recovery Act[15] (RCRA), which is also administered by the EPA. The RCRA focuses its regulations on generators of toxic or hazardous wastes, rather than merely the disposal sites. Its rules apply to any business that generates more than 100 kilograms of hazardous wastes a month.[16] For example, petroleum products have been added to the RCRA's hazardous substance list. Owners or operators of underground storage tanks, such as a gas station, can now be held personally liable for leakage that could contaminate groundwater.

If you feel that one or more of these laws may apply to your business, consult your attorney immediately.

9.10 Truth-in-Lending and Usury Laws

If your business activities involve lending money, or if you sell to consumers on credit terms, you may have to comply with the Federal Truth-in-Lending Act[17] and state laws that prohibit the charging of usurious interest rates on loans or other credit transactions.

Truth-in-Lending Requirements

If you regularly lend money, or if you sell goods or services to consumers on credit and either impose a finance charge or provide in a written agreement for them to make payment in four or more installments, you will generally be subject to the Truth-in-Lending disclosure requirements. Regulations under the Truth-in-Lending Simplification and Reform Act provide that a business is not subject to the Truth-in-Lending rules unless it extended consumer credit more than 25 times in either the previous year or the current calendar year.[18] For loan transactions, required disclosures include:

- The annual percentage rate of interest;
- When the finance charge begins to accrue;
- The total amount of the finance charge;
- The number of payments to be made and the dollar amount of each payment;
- When payments are to be made;
- The total dollar amount of all payments;
- How any prepayment penalty and any late charges are to be computed;
- The amount of any prepaid finance charges and any deposit, plus the sum of the two;
- The amount financed;
- The existence of any balloon payment and its dollar amount;
- Annual statements of billing rights;
- Other information regarding security interests and rights to rescind;
- Periodic billings to credit customers must include a number of disclosures regarding outstanding balances, how finance charges have been computed, and other items.

The rules regarding Truth-in-Lending are far too complex to cover satisfactorily in a book of this nature, and it can only alert you to the possibility that you may be required to comply with those rules and to give you some sense of what will be required if you are. If you plan to extend credit to consumers — other than sending out bills requesting payment in full, without interest charge, after you have provided goods or services — you need to consult an attorney experienced in this area.

Fortunately, recent legislation has considerably simplified the Truth-in-Lending rules, and the Federal Reserve Board has published model disclosure statements and billing rights statements that can be used to satisfy the requirements of the Truth-in-Lending regulations.

Cash Discount Act

One other fairly recent development you need to be aware of is the Cash Discount Act (Public Law 97-25), which now permits sellers to offer a discount of any amount to customers who pay in cash or by check without running afoul of the Truth-in-Lending rules, if the discount is clearly disclosed and made available to all customers.[19] In the past, if you offered more than a 5% cash discount, you were considered to be imposing a finance charge on credit customers and had to give them all the required Truth-in-Lending disclosures.

Usury Laws

See Section 11.9 for the maximum legal rate of interest you may charge in this state and a brief description of how the state's usury laws may apply to your business.

9.11 Employee or Independent Contractor?

As was pointed out in Chapter 5, Section 5.2, there are some major advantages in hiring independent contractors rather than employees to work in your business. Not only do you effect considerable payroll tax savings by retaining independent contractors, but there are far fewer administrative headaches, since you don't have to withhold income and payroll taxes from payouts to an independent contractor, provide workers' compensation coverage for them, or cover them in your retirement plan or other employee fringe benefit plans.

Unfortunately, just because you agree with someone you hire that they will be an independent contractor does not make it so for tax and legal purposes.

Thus, before you hire anyone to work for you as an independent contractor, you need to take a hard look at whether the IRS or a court of law would consider that person to be your employee rather than an independent contractor. While the IRS uses a 20-factor test to evaluate whether a person is or is not an employee, there are a few major warning flags that will tend to indicate that the person is your employee:

- The person works mostly or only for your firm. That is, the employee is not like, for example, a lawyer who has a number of clients besides you that he or she works for.
- The worker is subject to your control, and you have the right to direct how the work is done, not just to demand a particular result.
- The person works in your office or establishment, and does not have his or her own place of business, business cards, business name, etc.
- The kind of work the person does for you is of a kind normally done by employees, such as secretarial work.
- The person is not a licensed professional of any type.

Cautionary Note!

Unless you are quite clear that the work relationship will not be considered that of employer–employee, be very careful about hiring someone as a so-called independent contractor. The consequences of being wrong can be quite severe. Here are just a few of the things that can happen if your independent contractor is held to be an employee:

- You are liable for not only the employer payroll taxes you failed to pay, but also for a portion of the employee taxes you failed to withhold (income taxes, FICA). If you treat someone as an independent contractor, you should report payments of $600 or more a year to that person on IRS *Form 1099-MISC*. If you do, and the IRS later determines that the person was really an employee, the back taxes you are liable for are limited to: (a) the employer payroll taxes, (b) 20% of the employee's FICA tax you failed to withhold, and income tax withholding equal to only 1.5% of the wages you paid the person. If you do not file *Form 1099-MISC* and the person is reclassified as an employee, you are liable for 40% of the employee's FICA tax and income tax withholding equal to 3% of the wages — twice as much as if you would have filed *Form 1099-MISC*. Furthermore, there is now a $100 penalty for failure to file *Form 1099-MISC* and you will owe interest on the taxes due. It is no longer a bargain to "borrow" from the IRS. You may also be assessed other penalties if you did not have a reasonable basis for treating the person as a nonemployee and may be liable for up to 100% of the employee's FICA and income tax which you failed to withhold.

- If the person is hurt on the job and you have not provided workers' compensation insurance coverage, you will be liable for extensive legal damages.
- If your firm has a qualified retirement plan and you have not contributed to the plan on behalf of the person because he or she was not thought to be an employee at the time, the retirement plan could be disqualified for tax purposes for failing to cover the employee in question.

Thus, do not get stampeded into the independent contractor game by your friends and business associates who tell you how simple it is to avoid all those payroll taxes — not unless you are planning to become part of the subterranean economy.

Note that the foregoing discussion of independent contractors summarizes federal rules only. Many states take an even more restrictive view than the IRS on the employee–independent contractor issue.

9.12 Whether You Should Incorporate Outside the State

For most small businesses, there is little reason to consider incorporating your business under the laws of some state other than where you live. In fact, there are a few very good reasons why you should not incorporate in a different state:

- Your corporation may have to pay a qualification fee to transact business in your home state as a foreign corporation. See Section 11.9 on this point.
- If your attorney is a local lawyer, he or she is likely to be much less familiar with the corporate law rules of some other state than those of this state. Thus, your attorney is likely to either charge you more for

corporate law advice if he or she has to research the law of an unfamiliar jurisdiction or give you less accurate advice than he or she could about this state's corporation laws.

- In many states, your corporation will have to pay some sort of minimum annual franchise tax or capital tax to the state of incorporation, even if you do no business there.

Also, don't believe the newspaper ads that tell you to incorporate in wonderful, tax-free Nevada or some other state and avoid your state's corporation income or franchise taxes. It doesn't work. If your corporation does business in your state, it pays the same taxes on its taxable income regardless of whether it is incorporated in your state, Nevada, or in the Grand Duchy of Luxembourg.

Perhaps the only valid reason why a business might incorporate elsewhere would be to take advantage of some particular provision or flexibility available under the corporate laws of a particular state, such as Delaware, in particular. If you own all the stock of your company, it is unlikely you would ever need to take advantage of any such provisions, which are usually more important where different groups are struggling for control of a corporation's board of directors or the like.

Footnotes

1. I.R.C. § 168.
2. I.R.C. § 168(i).
3. I.R.C. § 179(b)(1).
4. Notice 81-16, I.R.B. 1981-40.
5. I.R.C. § 6425.
6. 15 U.S.C. §§ 1051–1127.
7. I.R.C. § 1244(c); The Tax Reform Act of 1984, § 481(a).
8. I.R.C. § 1211(b).
9. I.R.C. § 1244(c)(1)(C).
10. I.R.C. § 1244(c)(3).
11. I.R.C. § 1244(d)(1)(B).
12. I.R.C. § 1244(b).
13. 16 C.F.R. § 435.
14. 15 U.S.C. § 2601–2629.
15. 42 U.S.C. § 6901, *et seq.*
16. 42 U.S.C. § 6921(d)(1).
17. 15 U.S.C. § 1601, *et seq.*
18. 12 C.F.R. § 226.2(a)(17).
19. 12 C.F.R. § 226.4(c)(8).

Chapter 10

Sources of Help and Information

"If you're going to sin, sin against God, not the bureaucracy.
God will forgive you, but the bureaucracy won't."

— Admiral Hyman G. Rickover

10.1 General Considerations

There are numerous services and publications provided free or at low cost to small businesses by government and private organizations. Unfortunately, most small business owners only find out about a few of these sources and then only on a haphazard basis. This chapter summarizes many of the services and publications that you may need to draw on as an owner or operator of a small business.

10.2 Professional Services

Select your accountant carefully, for this is the one person outside your business who is most likely to be closely in touch with almost everything going on in your operation. Besides helping to set up your books and to establish systems for handling cash receipts and disbursements, a good accountant can provide a wealth of practical advice on a wide range of subjects that are important to your business, including taxes, managing your money, obtaining financing, and evaluating business opportunities. Attorneys and bankers are often in a good position to know accountants whom they can recommend to a small business.

Accountant

Attorney

Unless you are starting out as a sole proprietor, you will usually need an attorney to prepare a partnership agreement or to set up a corporation. You will probably do well to consult an attorney anyway to make sure you are obtaining necessary licenses and permits or to help you obtain them in some cases. In most parts of the country, local bar associations have lawyer referral services that can put you in touch with attorneys in your area practicing in various fields. In most cases, however, you will do better to ask an accountant or banker to recommend a good business lawyer. If you need highly-specialized legal advice or representation, ask an attorney you know to recommend a specialist.

Banker

Establishing a good relationship with officers of the bank branch where you open an account for your business is strongly recommended. While you may find it tough to borrow from your friendly banker when you first go into business, he or she will be interested in keeping an eye on your business to see how it develops. It pays to cultivate the relationship to create a good impression before you want to apply for a business loan from the bank. Ask around before opening an account, to find out if there is a bank in your area that is well known for lending to small businesses. Many of the large banks tend to be more interested in larger accounts, although different branch managers of the same bank may have very different ideas about working with small businesses.

Your banker is usually very well "plugged-in" to your community and can be a useful source of free advice at times when you need practical financial advice or to make connections with other businesses or people in your vicinity.

Benefit Consultant

If you intend to establish a corporate pension or profit-sharing plan (or Keogh plan, if you have a number of employees), you may want to seek out a benefit consulting firm and obtain their proposals as to the type of benefit plan you need and how it should be structured. Since many such firms are primarily engaged in selling insurance products, such as life insurance, annuities, and investment contracts, designed for pension plans, the plan those firms design for you will almost invariably involve building in their products. Since an insured retirement plan may not necessarily make sense in your particular situation, you should ask your attorney or accountant to recommend a benefit consulting firm that does not have a product like insurance to sell other than their consulting and plan administration services.

10.3 Small Business Administration

The federal Small Business Administration (SBA) is one government agency that is genuinely helpful to small businesses. The SBA not only guarantees financing for many small businesses (see Section 9.7) but it also provides a number of valuable services.

One service you might find helpful is Service Corps of Retired Executives (SCORE). This is a program in which retired executives with many years of business experience volunteer their services as consultants to small businesses and charge only for their out-of-pocket expenses.

In addition, SBA offices put on a variety of seminars and workshops on topics of interest to people who are starting or operating small businesses. Here are some of the seminars recently offered by the SBA.

- *Small Business Seminar with IRS*
- *Pre-Business Workshop*
- *Starting Your Own Business: A Seminar for Women*
- *Export Workshop*

Contact your local SBA office for more information.

The SBA and several other government agencies maintain toll-free telephone hotline information services to assist businesses:

Telephone Hotlines

- SBA Answer Desk: (800) 368-5855 or (202) 653-7561 from within Washington, D.C.

  This is the toll-free number of a new small business information/referral service offered by the SBA, which you can call from anywhere in the continental United States, except Washington, D.C.

  This telephone answer desk is staffed from 9:00 A.M. to 6:00 P.M., Eastern standard time, by experts from the SBA's Office of Advocacy, who will handle your questions regarding problems connected with your firm and the government.

- Small Business Hotline: (800) 424-5201

  This toll-free line is a specialized free service offered by the Export-Import Bank to small exporters needing general information or problem-solving assistance relating to doing business abroad. It provides information on export credit and on assistance available from other government agencies and the private sector.

- EPA Small Business Ombudsman: (800) 368-5888 or (202) 382-4538 in Washington, D.C.

  Like certain Scandinavian countries, the Environmental Protection Agency now has a Small Business Ombudsman to give easier access to the EPA, help you comply with EPA regulations, and make sure you are fairly treated in any disputes with the EPA.

10.4 Publications Regarding Small Business Operations

SBA

The SBA has more than 100 helpful booklets and other publications on subjects of importance to new and existing small businesses. The publications, which sell for a nominal fee (usually about $0.50 [50 cents] or $1.00 each — and never more than $2.00), can be obtained through your nearest SBA office or by calling the Small Business Administration Answer Desk and asking for a list of publications.

- SBA Answer Desk: (800) 368-5855 or if calling from within Washington, D.C.: (202) 653-7561

You can also use the preaddressed post card in the back of this book to request lists of SBA publications.

The Oasis Press

The publisher of this book, The Oasis Press, also has a number of how-to business guides targeted toward small businesses. A free catalog of these related resources can be obtained by calling:

- The Oasis Press: (800) 228-2275

Magazines

Here are some magazines that provide continuing information for businesses in general, and small businesses in particular. There are also a number of specialized publications you may find helpful. Most of these publications can be located through your local library, or you can contact them at the addresses below.

Nation's Business 1615 H. Street, N.W. Washington, D.C. 20062 (202) 463-5650	**INC.** Subscriber Service P.O. Box 54129 Boulder, CO 80322-4129 (800) 525-0643	**In Business** 419 State Ave. Emmaus, PA 18049 (215) 967-4135
Success Magazine 230 Park Ave. New York, NY 10169 (800) 234-7324	**Small Business Opportunities** 1115 Broadway, 8th Floor New York, NY 10010 (212) 807-7100	**D&B Reports** 299 Park Avenue New York, NY 10171 (212) 593-6728
Entrepreneur Magazine Subscriber Service 2392 Morse Ave. P.O. Box 19787 Irvine, CA 92713-9441 (800) 421-2300 (800) 352-7449 (in CA)	**Family Business Magazine** Subscriber Service One Heritage Way P.O. Box 420265 Palm Coast, FL 32142-0265 (800) 423-1780 (800) 858-0095 (in FL)	**Independent Business** National Federation of Independent Business Membership Office 150 West 20th Ave. San Mateo, CA 94403 (415) 341-7441
Business Week Subscriber Service P.O. Box 506 Hightstown, NJ 08520 (800) 635-1200	**The Wall Street Journal** 84 Second Ave. Chicopee, MA 01220 (413) 592-7761	**Business Month** Subscriber Service P.O. Box 55982 Boulder, CO 80322 (800) 825-2850

Some of the more important sources of statistical information that you will need if you do your own marketing research are:

Title	Additional Information	Publisher
Survey of Buying Power	Comprehensive data on population, retail sales, and consumer buying income for states, counties, and cities.	**Sales and Marketing Management** 633 Third Avenue New York, NY 10017-6706 (212) 986-4800
Publication List	Publishes titles on corporate relations, human resources, management, economic and business environments, and consumer research.	**Conference Board** 845 Third Avenue New York, NY 10022 (800) 872-6273
Survey of Current Business	U.S. Department of Commerce's monthly survey of business trends and conditions.	**Superintendent of Documents U.S. Government Printing Office** Washington, DC 20402 (202) 783-3238
The Complete Information Bank for Entrepreneurs & Small Business Managers, Second Edition	An excellent sourcebook which lists and describes hundreds of leading business books and other sources of help and information for small businesses.	**Center for Entrepreneurship and Small Business Management** P.O. Box 48, Wichita State University Wichita, KS 67208 (316) 689-3000

10.5 Do-It-Yourself Incorporation

If you want to form your own corporation and save several hundred dollars in legal fees, there are books that tell you how to do it and provide the forms you need. However, the author has mixed feelings about whether you should attempt this. In some cases, setting up a corporation is not that complicated, and if you precisely follow the instructions in a self-incorporation book (if one is available for your state), you should be able to do it properly. But you will have to spend many hours carefully figuring out and then doing all that is required. Your time might be worth much more than what you would save in legal fees if you concentrated instead on getting the business off to a good start. Check Section 11.10 to see if there is an incorporation book for your state.

10.6 Information Regarding Payroll Taxes and Withholding

Major offices of the Internal Revenue Service (IRS) frequently put on seminars for new employers regarding payroll tax requirements. Call your local IRS office for information as to when such seminars will be held in your area. In addition, you may want to obtain *Circular E,*

Employer's Tax Guide, from the IRS. *Notice 109, Information about Depositing Employment and Excise Taxes*, can be obtained from the IRS or by using one of the preaddressed post cards at the end of this book.

In addition, the Matthew Bender publishing company puts out an excellent book called the *Payroll Tax Guide*, which covers almost every aspect of federal payroll tax returns. Refer to Section 11.10 for information about useful publications on state payroll and other taxes.

10.7 Other Useful Tax Publications

The publications below can also be obtained at your local IRS office:

Publication	Subject
Publication 587	Business Use of Your Home
Publication 334	Tax Guide For Small Business Income and other Federal Taxes
Publication 552	Recordkeeping Requirements
Publication 510	Federal Excise Taxes
Publication 349	Federal Highway Use Taxes on Heavy Vehicles
Publication 463	Travel, Entertainment, and Gift Expenses

The IRS also puts on free small business workshops nationwide. To call for a reservation, use the IRS nationwide toll-free number: (800) 424-1040.

10.8 ERISA Compliance

If your business has a pension or profit-sharing plan and you wish to handle your own ERISA filings for the plan, you should at least obtain a copy of Charles D. Spencer & Associates' annual *Form 5500 Guide*, which explains how to complete the forms. The price is $55. It can be obtained by writing to:

Charles D. Spencer & Associates, Inc.
250 S. Wacker Drive, Suite 600
Chicago, IL 60606
(312) 993-7900

10.9 Managing Your Own Keogh or IRA Investments

If you want to set up a canned Keogh plan or an Individual Retirement Account (IRA) and have the ability to manage the plan or account's investments for yourself, you can do so through certain stockbrokers.

Check with your local bank or stockbroker to compare services and prices. Discount brokers, such as Charles Schwab & Co. and Fidelity Brokerage Services, provide such accounts at competitive rates.

10.10 Information on Franchising

Title and Author	Additional Information	Publisher
Franchise Bible Erwin J. Keup	1990. 340 pp., paperback	**The Oasis Press** 300 North Valley Drive Grants Pass, OR 97526
Miscellaneous titles on Franchise topics	Write for a catalog.	**International Franchise Association** 1350 New York Ave., N.W., Suite 900 Washington, DC 20005
Business Franchise Guide	Published monthly.	**Commerce Clearing House, Inc.** 4025 W. Peterson Avenue Chicago, IL 60646
The Chain-Restaurant Industry D. Daryl Wyckoff & W. Earl Sasser	The Lexington Casebook Series in Industry Analysis. 1978. 270 pp.	**Harvard University** Cambridge, MA 02138
The Complete Handbook of Franchising David D. Seltz	1981. 247 pp.	**Addison-Wesley** General Books Division Reading, MA 01867
Directory of Franchising Organizations	Revised annually.	**Pilot Industries, Inc.** 103 Cooper Street Babylon, NY 11702
The Franchise Annual	Published annually.	**Info Press** 736 Center Street Lewiston, NY 14092
Miscellaneous titles on Franchise topics	Write for a catalog.	**Pilot Books** 103 Cooper Street Babylon, NY 11702
Franchise Opportunities Handbook	1985. 380 pp. Survey lists about 1,000 franchisors with basic information as to cost of franchise, capital required, number of franchises, etc. Other franchise information is also available. Write for list of publications.	**U.S. Department of Commerce** **U.S. Government Printing Office** Washington, DC 20402
The Franchisee Option DeBanks M. Henward, III & William Ginalski	1980. 186 pp.	**Franchise Group Publishers** 4350 E. Camelback Road, S-140B Phoenix, AZ 85018

Title and Author	Additional Information	Publisher
Franchise Restaurants		**The National Restaurant Association** 311 1st Street, N.W. Washington, DC 20001
Franchisee Rights — A Self-Defense Manual For The Franchisee Alex Hammond	1980.	**Hammond & Morton** 1185 Avenue of the Americas New York, NY 10036
Franchising Gladys Glickman	1979 Revision. 4 volumes, 15, 15A, 15B, 15C of the Business Organization Series.	**Matthew Bender & Co., Inc.** 235 East 45th Street New York, NY 10036
Franchising Dr. Alfred J. Modica	1981. 159 pp.	**Quick Fox** — distributed by: **Acidom Publishing Co.** P.O. Box 22 Scarsdale, NY 10583
Franchising: Its Nature, Scope, Advantages, and Development Charles L. Vaughn	1979. 288 pp.	**D.C. Heath & Co.** 125 Spring Street Lexington, MA 02173
Franchising: Regulation of Buying and Selling A Franchise Philip F. Zeidman, Perry C. Ausbrook & H. Bret Lowell	CPS Portfolio #34.	**Bureau of National Affairs** 9435 Key West Avenue Rockville, MD 20850
How To Get Started In Your Own Franchised Business David Seltz	320 pp.	**Farnsworth Publishing Co.** 78 Randall Avenue Rockville Center, NY 11578
The Info Franchise Newsletter	Published monthly. Subscription.	**Info Press** 736 Center Street Lewiston, NY 14092
International Franchising: An Overview		**Science Publishing Co., Inc.** P.O. Box 1663, Grand Central Station New York, NY 10163
Legal Aspects of Selling and Buying	32 pp.	**Shepard's/McGraw-Hill** P.O. Box 1235 Colorado Springs, CO 80901
Survey of Foreign Laws and Regulations Affecting International Franchising. Compiled by the Franchising Committee of the Section of Antitrust Law of the American Bar Association		**Publications Planning and Marketing** **American Bar Association** 705 N. Lake Shore Drive Chicago, IL 60611

10.11 Estate Planning

How to Save Taxes Through Estate Planning
Robert J. Pinto

Estate planning for the layperson, complete with charts and illustrations and written in understandable terms.

Dow-Jones Irwin
1818 Ridge Road
Homewood, IL 60430

Retirement & Estate Planning Handbook
Chuck Tellalian with Walter Rosen

A do-it-yourself workbook, complete with worksheets, forms, and step-by-step instructions for developing retirement plans.

The Oasis Press
300 North Valley Drive
Grants Pass, OR 97526

10.12 OSHA Publications

If your business will be subject to these laws (see Section 5.6), you should obtain the following free booklet on OSHA requirements from your local office of the U.S. Department of Labor, Occupational Safety and Health Administration:

- *Recordkeeping Requirements for Occupational Injuries and Illnesses.*

10.13 Mail Order Sales Regulations

If you intend to sell goods by mail order, you need to be familiar with Federal Trade Commission Rule 435.1 (see Section 9.7). For a complete treatment of federal and state laws (all 50 states) affecting mail order businesses, you can obtain the *Mail Order Legal Manual*, by Erwin J. Keup, from The Oasis Press, (800) 228-2275.

10.14 "Expert" Software for Small Businesses

As a business owner or prospective owner, you may be interested in a new kind of computer software program, designed to aid and advise small- to medium-sized businesses with respect to tax, legal, and other business questions. *The Small Business Expert*, developed by Michael D. Jenkins, the principal author of this book, is a "smart" or "expert" program that provides such a capability.

This easy-to-use software is a bit like having a high-powered business, tax, and legal consultant on retainer, available day or night. The program allows you to simply type in a question or a key word or two about various business-related subjects and immediately responds by giving you textual information on that subject. Or you may quickly scan through a lengthy subject index and simply hit one key to view information on any item in the index. The software covers a wide range of subjects applicable to small businesses, with a primary emphasis on tax and legal information relevant to the state you do business in.

The program will first prompt you for numerous details about your business or proposed business. It will then create — and you may print out — detailed checklists of state and federal government regulations and other items your particular business must deal with. The program will also give you specific tax planning suggestions, all tailored specifically to your business. The program does quick calculations of both personal and corporate income taxes (allowing you to do instant "what if" projections) and will also compute federal estate taxes to assist you in income and estate tax planning.

The Small Business Expert also provides a number of consulting session topics, where you engage in a question-and-answer sequence with the program, regarding such subjects as whether or not you should incorporate your business, what accounting method can or should your new business adopt, and other topics. After you answer a series of questions, the program will offer you recommendations or advice regarding your specific situation, as well as its reasons for such advice.

Among other useful features, built-in worksheets are also provided for you to simply fill in the blanks on screen and print out a business plan outline, marketing feasibility study, or personnel policies summary for your business. *The Small Business Expert* is available from The Oasis Press which also publishes other economical software to streamline business activities. These and other related resources can be purchased through your book or software source or by calling The Oasis Press, (800) 228-2275.

Part IV

State Laws & Related Resources

Notes to New York State Section

PSI Research/The Oasis Press is committed to providing the most accurate, up-to-date information possible. Readers of this publication, however, should be aware that constant changes occur in the legislative, organizational, and public affairs activities of government agencies used as reference for this book.

PSI Research, whenever possible, has listed state agencies, throughout this chapter, for readers to contact for more information; however, phone numbers and mailing addresses of state offices also change, sometimes, more than the laws and regulations themselves. If changes have occurred that this particular revision has not noted, we advise readers to contact the following state office for assistance:

Small Business Division
New York State Department of Economic Development
52 Chambers Street
New York, NY 10007
(212) 827-6180
(516) 334-2500
(800) STATE NY (in New York State)

This office will also be able to direct you to the proper agency.

About the Author

The co-author of the 1990 state revision of *Starting and Operating a Business in New York* is Jacob Weichholz.

Mr. Weichholz is a tax partner and Director of Tax of the Metropolitan Office of Ernst & Young in New York. Mr. Weichholz specializes in serving small- and medium-sized businesses and their principals. He is also involved with international clients who invest and operate in the U.S. marketplace. He is a member of the American Institute, New York Society of Certified Public Accountants, and other professional organizations.

Acknowledgments

Mr. Weichholz wishes to thank Ms. Kathleen Swift, Mr. Joshua Markman, and Mr. Corey Rosenthal, who are state and local taxation specialists with Ernst & Young, for their help in developing this chapter.

The publisher would like to thank the many individuals, too numerous to mention, in the state agencies and organizations, who have contributed to the research of this book.

Chapter 11

State Laws and Taxes

11.1 Introduction

New York offers unparalleled opportunities for businesses to prosper. All the conditions favorable to business creation and growth are available in this state: a well-educated and skilled labor force, an abundance of natural resources, a vast transportation network, an enormous marketplace, and a government committed to encourage businesses within the state.

The strength and overall resiliency of the New York economy is largely attributable to a strong small business sector located throughout the state. Small businesses account for 98% of the more than 460,000 businesses in New York, and of these, 79% or more have fewer than 10 employees.[1]

New York is home to a full complement of industries, all with the potential for enormous growth and job creation. New York City is acknowledged as the corporate and financial capital of the world. The city's economy, while hurt by a recent decline in the financial services industry, is expected to rebound. New York City is also a major manufacturing center with almost 15,000 manufacturers. The largest manufacturing employer in New York City is the apparel industry. Although always a huge magnet for foreign investment, New York City has significantly increased the number of foreign-based firms within its boundaries. There are now more than 3,000 such firms operating within the city.

The city is also located at the heart of the nation's largest consumer market with more than 78 million people — 35% of the entire U.S. population — all within one day's delivery. The New York City metropolitan area encompasses 8.5 million people, and by itself, represents one of the largest effective buying-income areas in the country.[2]

Whether your business will be located in New York City, or some other location in New York State, the New York State Department of Economic Development has resources aimed at making your business successful. The New York State and City governments are fully committed to supporting the development and expansion of all industries throughout the state. The state administers special economic development programs through state-created authorities and corporations. For example, the New York State Department of Economic Development, Small Business Division, is particularly active in helping small businesses grow.

New York State has also empowered local governments to create and promote their own development agencies, thus enabling them to respond quickly to opportunities in their areas. New York City's Office of Business Development is a central source of assistance on various available city programs and incentives.

On the tax front, New York State clearly imposes a high tax cost of doing business. It has both an individual and corporate income tax structure and a sizable sales and use tax system. These are the state's three main sources of tax revenues. At approximately 52% of the total, personal income taxes are by far the largest single source; however, sales and use taxes follow closely behind, at approximately 21%.[3]

In the sections that follow, two specific jurisdictions in New York State — New York City and the upstate city of Rochester — are discussed. These locales are fairly representative of the entire state. New York City's tax structure is almost identical to the state's, while Rochester is typical of all other areas; it has no separate income tax.

11.2 Choosing the Legal Form of the Business

There are three basic types of business structures generally used in New York State. They are the sole proprietorship, the partnership, and the corporation. The general business considerations for selecting one of these structures are discussed in Section 2.1–2.4 of this book. Listed below are the particular New York State tax and legal considerations for each.

Sole Proprietorships

The simplest form, and one chosen by many small business owners, is the sole proprietorship. In organizing an enterprise as a sole proprietorship, there are no special legal requirements in New York State; however, you may be required to obtain a license if engaged in certain professions, trades, and occupations (see Section 11.4). If you intend to operate the business under a name other than your own, i.e., a fictitious name, that name must be registered with the county clerk of each county in which your business is located to enable creditors and other interested parties to determine actual ownership. To register, obtain a certificate of doing business under an assumed name from any New York business stationery store. The certificate must be completed in triplicate and the signatures notarized. After registration, the county clerk will keep one copy of the form and return the other two copies to you. One copy is for the bank where you establish your business checking accounts. The other copy is for display at the business premises. The registration fee is currently about $33 and must be paid in cash, by certified check or postal money order. For more information, call the county clerk's office in the county where your principal office is located.

Tax Treatment

New York State no longer imposes an additional tax on a sole proprietor's business income; rather the income earned from the business is taxed directly on the owner's federal and state personal income tax returns. A copy of federal *Form 1040, Schedule C,* is used for this purpose. The tax benefits of owning your own business flow through onto your personal return. All the income, deductions, and credits related to the business are reported on your personal return. A New York State resident should use *Form IT-201.* If you are a nonresident of New York State, your tax will be based on the business income allocable to the state, even if you are not otherwise taxable in the state. In this instance, *Form IT-203* and *Form NYC 203* (if the business is in the city) are used. For more information, call the New York State Department of Taxation and Finance at (800) 225-5829 in New York State.

Unlike the state, New York City imposes an unincorporated business tax on a sole proprietor's net business income. Currently, the tax rate is 4% applied to New York City taxable business income. New York City income is the net business income reported to the federal government with certain New York City statutory modifications. This modified base is then sourced in and out of New York City. Generally, this tax is only due when net business income exceeds $25,000. *Form NYC-202EZ* is used by individuals who are required to file a return, but do not pay tax. When taxable business income exceeds $25,000, *Form NYC-202* is filed to report and pay this tax. It is important to keep in mind that the city's unincorporated business tax is an additional tax, since the net business income from a sole proprietorship is also taxable on the owner's individual New York City income tax return, which is included on the individual's New York State income tax return. Further, although the city's unincorporated business tax is allowed as a deduction in arriving at federal taxable income, it cannot be deducted in computing New York State or City taxable income.

As a sole proprietor, you are not considered to be an employee of your business, as you would be if the business were incorporated. Because of this, there are certain employer tax savings in operating as a sole proprietorship — as well as the elimination of numerous payroll tax return filings and paperwork — if you are the only individual working in the business. These savings, however, do not continue as your business expands.

When you hire one or more employees to help operate the business, your reporting responsibilities to the federal, state, and certain local taxing jurisdictions expand significantly. See Section 11.5 for additional requirements for businesses with employees.

The individual tax rates in both New York State and City are quite high. While New York State has recently reduced its individual income tax rates, the highest state tax rate is 7.875% in 1990, 7.7% in 1991, and 7.55% in 1992. The rate continues to decline until it reaches 7.0% in 1994.

New York City's top rate for individual taxes with respect to residents has been reduced to 3.4%. Nonresidents of New York City are only taxed on their wages earned (0.45%), and net earnings from self-employment (0.65%) within the city. Under the current enabling legislation, significantly lower rates take effect in 1991; however, legislation is expected to be enacted to extend the current rates and to provide for a surcharge in 1991, and 1992.

Partnerships

Another common way of operating a business in New York State is through a partnership. This is an undertaking by two or more people to enter into a business for profit. Usually, this arrangement is governed by a written partnership agreement which specifies the rights, duties, and obligations of each partner. Although a written agreement is not required, the services of a lawyer are usually obtained, since this agreement is critical. In organizing a New York partnership, you must file a certificate of conducting business as partners and file the firm's name with the county clerk in each county where the business is located and doing business. The certificate for partnerships is available at most business stationery stores; and similar to sole proprietorships, it must be completed in triplicate and the partners' signatures notarized. After registration, the county clerk will keep one copy of the form and return the other two copies to you. Send one copy to the bank where you establish the business checking account; the other copy is for display at the business premises.

In New York, like most other states, there are both general and limited partnerships. General partners are usually liable for all the partnership's obligations. That is to say, each partner is potentially responsible for all debts of the partnership under most circumstances. In a limited partnership, the limited partners' liability is typically limited to their total capital contributions. Limited partnerships are frequently seen in real estate partnerships where passive investors may want to limit their partnership liability exposure. You should consult with a qualified attorney when forming either type of entity to make certain that the partnership agreement is valid under state laws. This is particularly true with respect to limited partnerships where state securities or "blue sky" laws may be applicable.

If you are planning to form a limited partnership, there are additional filing obligations in New York State. First, you will be required to file a certificate of limited partnership rather than a certificate of conducting business as partners. In addition to filing this certificate with the county clerk, etc., the partnership is required to publish a notice, regarding the limited partnership's formation, in two local newspapers where the partnership will be operating.

A partnership in New York State is not a taxable entity. As under the federal tax law, it is treated as a conduit. Each partner reports his *prorata* share of the partnership's income or loss on his or her own New York State tax return. Although the partnership is not taxable, it is required to file an information return. This information return annually reports to the state each partner's *prorata* share of income, loss, or any applicable tax credits from the partnership's operations. *Form IT-204* is used for this purpose.

Filing Requirements

It is important to note that a nonresident partner involved in a New York State general partnership is deemed to be doing business in New York and therefore will be required to file a New York State nonresident income tax return. This is true even if the partner is not active in the business. A New York City nonresident income tax return must also be filed if the partnership is doing business in New York City. This additional filing is often overlooked and frequently results in problems in later years.

Generally, a nonresident partner involved in a New York State limited partnership is also subject to New York State tax. If the limited partnership does not conduct a trade or business (e.g., trades for its own account), it is possible the nonresident, limited partner would not be subject to tax. In addition, in 1988, New York State opined that in certain instances ownership of a limited partnership interest did not cause a corporation to be subject to tax. Finally, a limited partner is not deemed to generate self-employment earnings from the partnership and thus is not subject to New York City nonresident tax.

Allocation of Income

When the partnership conducts business activities partly within and partly outside of New York State, some allocation of the income or loss generated in New York State will be necessary. Allocation of income within and without New York State is a major element in New York's tax system. There are three statutory methods allowed: 1) the specific-book method; 2) a three-factor apportionment formula method; or 3) any method specifically approved or mandated by the tax commission. While the specific-book method is preferred, the three-factor method is frequently employed. Under the three-factor method, the total business income is apportioned to New York State according to the partnership's business allocation percentage. The business allocation percentage measures the partnership's presence in New York by comparing the partnership's New York State property, payroll, and sales (numerators) to its total property, payroll, and sales (denominators). When using the three-factor method, the percentage of partnership net income taxed in New York State is figured by averaging the percentages of the three factors discussed below.

Property Factor

This is the average of the beginning and ending values of real and personal property employed in New York State over the average value employed by the business from all locations within and outside of the state.[4] In addition to assets owned, a rental factor determined by multiplying by eight the gross rental payments (or amounts paid in lieu of rent) paid for the use of real property in the taxpayer's business must be considered.[5] Rental payments also include annual amortization on leasehold improvements — which revert to the lessor at the termination of the lease.[6] Rental payments do not include rents paid for personal property, any rent paid to a partner, specific charges for utilities, or rent paid on property which is subleased and not used by the partnership.[7]

Payroll Factor

This is the total compensation paid or incurred by the business during the taxable year to nonpartner employees in connection with business carried on in New York State over the total of such compensation paid or incurred by the business from all sources within and outside of the state.[8] Payments to independent contractors, sales agents, etc., are not included.

Sales Factor

This is gross sales and service revenue performed through, or generated from, a permanent New York State business location over such gross sales and services revenue performed through or generated by the business from all sources within and outside of the state. Sales covering other states are also included in the New York State numerator if the employee, agent, or independent contractor is situated at, connected with, or sent from offices of the business (or its agencies) located in New York State.[9]

As with sole proprietorships, New York City, unlike the state, continues to impose the unincorporated business tax on partnerships engaged in business within its jurisdiction. The 1990 tax rate is 4% and is applied to the partnership's taxable business income. If the partnership has a place of business outside of New York City, the partnership is allowed to allocate income in and out of the city. The city's allocation rules are similar to the state's. *Form NYC-204* is used to report this tax.

Generally, an allowance for each active partner's services, equal to the lesser of 20% of net income or $5,000 per active partner, is permitted. There is also a specific exemption of $5,000 allowed against the combined net income from all business activities.

Corporations

Corporations are a more complicated form of doing business in New York State; however, they are the one most frequently used.

Organization

Unlike sole proprietorships and partnerships, the corporation is purely a creature of state law. Thus, you should follow the applicable rules governing its establishment and operation. In New York State, the process of incorporation begins with one, or a small number of, incorporator(s), who are frequently the lawyers for the corporation and play a purely formal and temporary role. The incorporators adopt the bylaws, which lay down the basic rules for the internal functioning of the corporation; these bylaws may subsequently be amended by the shareholder(s) or the board of directors.

A New York State corporation may be organized with only one stockholder, either a corporation or an individual, foreign or domestic. There is no minimum capital requirement, and the corporation may issue stock up to the amount of the shares authorized by its certificate of incorporation.[10] None of the shares have to be subscribed or paid for on formation of the corporation; the stock is issued by resolution of the board of directors, which determines the price of issue and the conditions of payment.

Unlike the rules for stockholders, directors must be individuals, and under New York State law, the board must have at least three members, unless there are fewer than three stockholders. Directors can be removed by stockholders at any time without cause. There are no requirements that stockholders, employees, or representatives of labor be represented on the board nor are the directors required to be American citizens or residents. Board of director meetings may be held outside of the United States, and the bylaws may permit absent members to participate by telephone.

A domestic corporation is created in New York State by filing a certificate of incorporation with the Department of State. Certificate of incorporation forms may be obtained from most business stationery stores.

Division of Corporations
New York State Department of State
162 Washington Avenue
Albany, NY 12231
(518) 474-6200

Under New York State law, a domestic corporation must use a name which is distinguishable from other corporate names on file. There are other technical restrictions on selecting a corporate name, so it is worth your while to request approval of a corporate name from the Department of State before preparing the certificate of incorporation. The Department of State charges a small fee for each name submitted for approval.

New York State also imposes an organization tax on each domestic corporation. This tax is $1/20$ of 1% on the par value shares the corporation is authorized to issue; or $0.05 (five cents) per share on no par stock. There is a minimum tax of $10 — whether or not the tax is on par or no par stock.[11] Because the organization tax is based upon the total number of authorized shares, not the number of shares issued, it normally is prudent to limit the initial number of authorized shares. This should produce a tax savings. If necessary, you can always increase the number of authorized shares at a later date and then pay the organization tax on the increased shares. For more information, call the New York State Department of Taxation and Finance at (800) 225-5829 in New York State.

The organization tax and filing fees are due and payable at the time the certificate of incorporation is filed. Payment is required to be made in cash, certified check, or money order; business checks and personal checks will not be accepted.

Foreign Corporations

In New York State, there is no distinction between a corporation incorporated in another state and one organized under the laws of a foreign country. Both are considered "foreign corporations" for authorization purposes. A corporation from another country, upon establishing an office or branch operation in New York State, will be permitted to conduct most types of activities with the same conditions as a corporation formed in any other state in the United States.

Whether a corporation is organized under the laws of another state or country, it should obtain the authority to do business in New York State from the secretary of state by filing the appropriate application. This requires a limited amount of basic information about the corporation and requires designating a registered agent in the state for the service of legal process, etc. A license fee, similar to the New York State organization tax imposed on New York corporations, is also required. This license fee is based upon the amount of capital employed by the corporation in New York State, and the fee is now imposed at a rate equal to the domestic corporation organization tax.

The definition of what constitutes doing business in New York State is not clearly defined. In practice, however, a foreign corporation may conduct only certain incidental and interstate activities without being deemed as doing business in the state.

Income Tax Treaties

A significant observation is that New York State does not recognize various income tax treaties which, for federal tax purposes, would exempt certain foreign income from U.S. taxation. Therefore, any industrial or commercial profits apportioned to a New York branch of a foreign corporation may be subject to New York State taxes, even though for federal tax purposes, the income may be exempt. Keeping this in mind, financial information regarding a corporation's worldwide operations may be required to be disclosed to the New York State tax authorities and questions may arise as to whether proper apportionments have been made. For this reason, as well as the fact that branch office liabilities are generally the liability of the foreign corporation, a New York branch may not be the desirable structure within which to conduct substantial business operations. Many overseas foreign corporations establish subsidiary corporations in the United States to eliminate these potential problems.

Please also note that when referring to a corporation in this chapter, the author is discussing a general business corporation. There are very special rules in New York which cover banking corporations, insurance companies, transportation and transmission companies, utilities, farmers and agricultural cooperatives, and nonstock corporations organized and operated for nonprofit purposes. The rules for these type of entities are quite complicated, and a qualified attorney should always be consulted.

New York State, but not New York City, has conformed its corporate tax law to the federal S corporation provisions — which are discussed in Section 2.5. At this point, there are no differences between the federal S corporations rules and those for New York State, except as noted below. A separate S corporation election, however, must be made for New York State tax purposes on *Form CT-6*, at any time during the preceding taxable year or within the first two months and 15 days of the current taxable year. If no election is made, the S corporation will not be treated as an S corporation in New York State.

Adopting New York S Corporation status will no longer completely avoid state tax at the corporate level. For tax years beginning after 1989, a tax equal to the greater of the fixed-dollar minimum tax, or the difference between the tax on income using the corporate rate and the tax using the personal income tax rate, is due. S corporations are subject to the temporary corporate surcharge (discussed below), but are not subject to the Metropolitan Transportation Business Tax Surcharge (discussed below). This tax replaces the annual filing fee.

An important point to recognize about S corporations is that all shareholders, resident and nonresident alike, must agree to the New York State elections. Before the election is made, it is critical to recognize the tax effects such election will have on any nonresident shareholder. If an election is made, the nonresident shareholder will be taxed in New York State based on the allocated New York income of the corporation, even if he or she has no direct contact with New York State. The corporation's business allocation percentage and investment allocation percentage would be used to obtain the New York State source income of the nonresident. The resident shareholder is taxed on all of the S corporation's income, regardless of the business or investment allocation percentages.

Since many new businesses incur losses in the initial years of operations it is equally important to recognize the effect tax losses or tax credits will have on the shareholders. Resident shareholders will be allowed to offset their other New York State income against the business loss and utilize the tax credit to reduce their overall tax liability to the state. However, nonresidents will not obtain any current tax benefits from the loss or the tax credits unless they happen to have other New York source income.

New York City does not recognize S corporations and it taxes S corporations in the same manner as it does any other corporation doing business in the city.

New York State and City Taxation

The New York State franchise tax and New York City general corporation tax are levied on all corporations employing capital, owning or leasing property, and/or maintaining an office in New York — unless specifically exempted or subject to some other New York franchise tax. Although the rates for New York State and City differ, the basic tax structures, including recent law changes, are quite similar.

The New York State corporation franchise tax and the New York City general corporation tax are computed on several different alternative bases. The taxpayer must pay the highest of the tax applicable to each base, and when necessary, a tax computed on allocated subsidiary capital.

Tax on Entire Net Income

The tax on net income is the most frequently applicable tax. This tax is measured by entire net income, an amount derived from federal taxable income, but adjusted for various statutory modifications. New York State has adopted the federal rules of income taxation, and that is the starting point; however, there are several significant differences primarily designed to limit loss of local revenues. For example, income taxes paid to other states, their political subdivisions, and the District of Columbia are not deductible. Another example of a New York statutory modification would be the adjustment for accelerated cost-recovery system (ACRS) or modified accelerated cost-recovery system (MACRS) depreciation taken as a deduction on the federal corporate income tax return. Before 1984, New York did not allow any ACRS depreciation method. Currently, New York State and City will accept federal ACRS and MACRS depreciation only as it relates to luxury automobiles and with respect to qualified property placed in service in New York State. In computing New York taxable income, any disallowed ACRS or MACRS depreciation must be added back to federal taxable income. Only the New York-allowed depreciation methods may be applied.

For taxable years beginning on or after January 1, 1989, New York State no longer requires an add-back to federal income for interest expense paid to shareholders. For New York City, this change was effective for taxable years beginning on or after January 1, 1988.

There are several other modifications which must be made. What is important to note here is that, although New York's system basically follows federal law, significant differences do exist, and their impact must be carefully considered.

After all statutory modifications have been made to arrive at New York State taxable net income, it is then necessary to allocate the income generated inside and outside of New York State. This is a beneficial provision and is permitted even if the business' sole location is in New York. A much stricter rule is applicable for New York City. Here, income can be allocated only if the corporation has a regular place of business outside of New York City. This is a significant difference.

Entire net income has two components: investment income and business income. Each component is allocated by, respectively, the investment allocation percentage and the business allocation percentage.

The business allocation percentage is basically a weighted average of the corporation's payroll, property, and receipts apportioned inside of the jurisdiction (New York State or City) compared with the corporation's total payroll, property, and receipts worldwide. Except with respect to the receipts and property factors, the apportionments are done in a manner similar to that discussed previously for partnerships.

With respect to the receipts factor, generally sales of tangible personal property are only treated as New York sales if delivery is made in New York State. This destination bases rule can be very beneficial in lowering the New York State receipts allocation factor. There is another important difference with respect to the receipts factor. In New York State, but not New York City, this factor is double-counted. Thus, it has extra weight over the other factors in deriving the New York State business allocation percentages.

It should also be noted that in computing the business allocation factor, owned real and tangible property are valued at their adjusted federal tax basis when calculating the property factor. Taxpayers were allowed a one-time revocable election to continue to use fair market value. Tangible personal property is now included, in addition to real property, when calculating rental property. Taxpayers were allowed to make a one-time election to phase in the inclusion of rented, tangible personal property over a five-year period.

The investment allocation percentage is obtained by multiplying the net average value of the taxpayer's qualified investment in corporate or governmental stocks, bonds, etc., by the New York State allocation percentage of that issuer. The results are added together and then divided by the total net average value of all the taxpayer's investments. When calculating the percentage, marketable securities are valued at average fair market value. To obtain net value the value of each investment is reduced for its share of average liabilities of the taxpayer attributable to investment capital.

For the purpose of calculating each issuer's New York State allocation percentage, the state tax commission annually releases the New York State allocation percentage of each corporation doing business or owning property within the state. One interesting technique used in recent years is to select stocks with low allocation percentages to New York, so as to decrease the taxpayer's overall investment allocation percentage. This is particularly helpful, because a corporate taxpayer can elect to allocate all investment income, including interest from bank accounts and other cash deposits, by using the overall calculated investment allocation percentage. Proper selection of investments could significantly reduce the New York tax; however, the tax authorities reserve the right to challenge this election, if in their opinion, its use does not result in a clear reflection of income. Clearly, a taxpayer, who invests only minimal amounts in corporate stocks and bonds and then makes this election, runs the risk of challenge by the tax authorities. It is, therefore, advisable for a taxpayer, wishing to utilize this election, to invest more than a minimal amount of his or her funds in corporate stocks since such a course of action lessens the likelihood that the tax authorities would argue that income was not clearly reflected.

Allocated business income and allocated investment income are then combined, resulting in New York taxable net income. The apportioned net income figure is subject to a corporate tax rate of 9% and 8.85% for New York State and New York City, respectively.

For qualifying small business corporations, the New York State rate has been reduced to 8% on income up to $200,000. Starting at $200,000, the regular 9% rate takes effect. If income exceeds $250,000, the benefit of the reduced rate is progressively recaptured and, at $290,000, the benefit is fully recaptured. A qualifying small business corporation is any corporation:

- which has an entire net income of no more than $290,000; and
- whose aggregate amount of money or other payments received for stock (either as a contribution to capital or as paid-in-surplus), does not exceed $1 million; and
- which is not part of an affiliated group of companies unless the group itself could qualify.

New York City does not allow a separate (lower) corporate tax rate for small businesses.

The following possible alternative taxes may also be levied in lieu of the apportioned net income tax. Remember that the highest tax is payable.

Flat Minimum Tax

New York State recently increased its fixed-dollar minimum tax to range between $325 and $1,500 per annum, based generally on gross payroll. The $325 figure is usually applicable if gross payroll is $1 million or less; the $1,500 figure is applicable if gross payroll is $6.25 million or more.

Be aware that New York State imposes a high annual minimum tax on shell corporations. This tax is $800 if a corporation's gross payroll, total receipts (both inside and outside the state), and average value of gross assets is $1,000 or less.

New York City has also increased its flat minimum tax of $125 per year. For tax years ending after June 30, 1989, the minimum tax is $300.

Tax Based on Capital

A capital tax at the rate of 0.178% and 0.15% is imposed on apportioned business and investment capital in New York State and City, respectively. There is also a maximum tax of $350,000 for each jurisdiction.

When computing the taxable capital base, both New York State and City allow average total liabilities to be deducted from average adjusted total assets.

For purposes of computing business, investment, and subsidiary capital, real property and marketable securities are valued at fair market value. Personal property, other than marketable securities, are valued at book value pursuant to generally accepted accounting principles.

Minimum Taxable Income

A new tax base has been instituted for New York State, but not for New York City. The minimum taxable income base for tax years beginning in

1989 and 1990, is 5%; for tax years beginning in 1991, it is 4.5%; and for tax years beginning after 1991, it reverts to 3.5%. The tax base for tax years beginning in 1990 and thereafter is the entire net income, plus certain federal, tax-preference adjustment items. In addition, for allocation purposes, a single, weighted modified receipts factor is used. Note: This minimum tax may not be reduced by any tax credits.

New York City's Alternative Tax

New York City still imposes an alternative tax measured by income plus officers' compensation at the rate of 8.85% (this tax was repealed by New York State for tax years beginning on or after January 1, 1987). To obtain the tax base, the corporation's entire net income plus officers' compensation, less a statutory exemption of $15,000, is multiplied by 30% and then apportioned. Note: Included in the above tax base is compensation to shareholders owning in excess of 5% of the capital stock of the corporation.

Tax on Subsidiary Capital

No matter which of the alternative taxes discussed above applies, the taxpayer must also pay a tax on allocated subsidiary capital, if applicable. Corporations, owning more than 50% of the issued and outstanding voting stock of other corporations, are subject to a subsidiary capital tax of .09% and .075% on apportioned subsidiary capital for New York State and City, respectively. Apportioned subsidiary capital is determined by calculating the subsidiary's net average value — average value of the subsidiary less the average liabilities of the taxpayer attributable to that subsidiary — and multiplying the result by the subsidiary's New York State or City issuer's allocation percentage.

Surcharge

A three-year surcharge applies to tax years ending after June 30, 1990 and before July 1, 1993. The surcharge, at the rate of 15% for the first two years, and 10% in the third year, applies to the tax liability after reduction for credits. The surcharge itself cannot be reduced by credits.

When computing a New York S corporation surcharge, special rules apply. Note, the surcharge applies to the tax computed before reduction for the personal income tax equivalent. An S corporation that qualifies as a small business taxpayer, and whose entire net income does not exceed $200,000, does not pay the surcharge. If entire net income exceeds $200,000, but not $290,000, the surcharge is prorated.

Anti-Takeover Provisions

In 1989, New York State and City legislation was enacted which eliminates various tax benefits upon certain corporate acquisitions, mergers, or consolidations. The new law is effective for tax years beginning on or after January 1, 1989. In general, the significant provisions are:

- For stock acquisitions where more than 50% of the voting power in the target corporation is acquired, all credit carryovers of the target are lost.
- For all highly leveraged stock acquisitions, any loss carryovers of the target corporation are lost. There is, however, recapture of the target's

credits previously taken as if there were a disposition, and up to 5% of the acquiring corporation's interest expense may be disallowed, if the value of the acquisition exceeds $5 million.

State and City Tax Rates

Under current statute, the New York City corporate franchise tax rates stated in this section do not apply to tax years beginning after 1990. If legislation is not enacted, the 1991 tax rates would decline significantly; for example, the tax on entire net income would be imposed at the rate of 6.7%; however, due to budgetary concerns it is not likely this reduction in rates will come to pass.

Acquisitions, mergers, or consolidations between members of an affiliated group are excluded from these rules.

In addition, the legislature has also passed a three-year corporate income tax surcharge, for taxable years beginning after June 30, 1990. The surcharge will be equal to 15% of the regular tax for the first two years and 10% for the third year, and will replace the final two years of the current 2.5% bank and insurance company surcharge. Also, a S corporation will now be subject to a corporate level tax (for years beginning after 1989) equal to the difference between the tax computed on the entire net income corporate income tax base and the tax computed using the highest personal income tax rate in effect for the taxable year — with a minimum tax of $325 on a S corporation. The new corporate surcharge will not apply to an S corporation with an entire net income of $200,000 or less.

Moreover, New York State has in effect a temporary surcharge that is based on the state tax calculated without the corporate surcharge. The *Metropolitan Transportation Business Tax Surcharge Report, Form CT-3M/4M*, is required to be filed by all corporations doing business in the Metropolitan Commuter Transportation District. For tax years ending on or after December 31, 1983, and ending before December 31, 1990, the surcharge equals 17% of the tax attributable to business carried on within the Metropolitan Commuter Transportation District.[12] Note: The surcharge has been extended through tax years ending before December 31, 1992. The counties of New York, Bronx, Kings, Queens, Richmond, Dutchess, Nassau, Orange, Putnam, Rockland, Suffolk, and Westchester are all within the Metropolitan Commuter Transportation District.

New York City has imposed a city income tax surcharge for tax years beginning in 1990, 1991, and 1992. The surcharge varies by year and filing status, generally ranging from 0.42% to 0.51% of city taxable income that is in excess of certain specified levels.

Thus, when you combine the two surcharges with the regular New York State corporate income tax rate of 9%, New York State's effective, corporate tax rate becomes 11.88%.

For a corporation operating entirely within New York City, its effective aggregate rate for the four corporate taxes (assuming all is based on income) is 19.674%. This 19.674% rate is determined by adding these four corporate taxes together.

- 8.85% — New York City
- 8.2% — New York State (i.e., 100% less 8.85% deductible New York City tax multiplied by 9%)
- 1.23% — corporate surcharge (i.e., 8.2% effective New York State rate multiplied by 15%)
- 1.394% — Metropolitan Commuter Surcharge

As noted previously, a corporate taxpayer is entitled to allocate business income by the business apportionment factors for New York State purposes but may not avail itself of these apportionment factors for New York City purposes, unless it maintains a regular place of business outside of New York City. If no bona fide office exists outside of New York City, the corporation would have a 100% business apportionment percentage for city purposes only, and accordingly, New York City's full tax would apply to the corporation's business income.

A second point to note is that both New York State and City require an allocation of direct and indirect expenses attributable to investment capital or investment income and to subsidiary capital or income. To determine investment and subsidiary capital the state and city specifically require direct and indirect attribution of all liabilities.

A third point concerns the calculation of the business apportionment factors for New York State and City purposes. The law provides that with respect to the payroll factor, only salaries paid to employees who are not general executive officers are taken into account. Thus, if the payroll consisted of salaries paid only to such officers, the payroll factor would not be used in the calculation of a total business apportionment factor. Refer to the earlier discussion under Partnerships regarding the payroll factor.

A fourth point to note is the availability of the small business exemption from tax under the business and investment capital base for the initial two years of operations. This is often helpful in the early stages of a new business. To qualify for the small business exemption, certain criteria must be met, such as:

- More than 50% of the number of its voting shares cannot be owned by one or more corporations;
- At least 90% of its assets (based on their cost) are located in New York;
- At least 80% of its employees are primarily employed in New York;
- It is not substantially similar in operation and ownership to another corporation; and
- The corporation qualifies as a small business corporation under Internal Revenue Code Section 1244.

New York State and City, to some extent, allow net operating losses to be carried back three years and forward 15 years. New York State and City have adopted a very stringent rule with respect to the carryback of a loss. For taxable years ending after June 30, 1989, only $10,000 of the current year's loss may be carried back to offset prior years' incomes. The remainder must be used solely on a carry-forward basis. The New York net operating loss deduction cannot exceed the federal deduction, even if this amount is greater, due to necessary adjustments for New York modifications.[13] This is important to remember, because if the corporation has a significant amount of New York statutory modifications, it may have to pay New York State and City taxes in years that it reports losses on its federal income tax return.

New York State has a separate dividend deduction which is calculated differently than the federal 80% dividends received deduction — discussed in Section 2.4. The following dividends are exempt from New York State and City tax:

- All dividends from a subsidiary — with the exception of dividends from a Domestic International Sales Corporation (DISC);
- 50% of dividends derived from nonsubsidiary corporations — this exclusion is limited to shares of stock which qualify for the federal dividend exclusion pursuant to Internal Revenue Service Code Section 246(c). Please note that real estate investment trusts and regulated investment companies are not allowed this deduction; and
- Foreign dividends — as grossed-up under Section 78 of the Internal Revenue Code.

Corporate Filing Requirements

There are several corporate filing requirements that both New York State and City impose on businesses. You should consult with your financial adviser or attorney to obtain more information on these requirements.

New York State

Corporations that are eligible to allocate income and capital generally file *Form CT-3, Corporation Franchise Tax Report*, which is due the 15th day of the third month following the year's end; however, an automatic six-month extension is available through filing *Form CT-5, Application for Extension for Filing Income Tax Report*. If the first six-month extension does not provide sufficient time to complete the return, two additional three-month extensions may be requested. Additional extensions are granted upon the taxpayer's request, if good cause for the delay in filing exists.

A qualified small business taxpayer may use the short *Form CT-4*. A corporation qualifies as a small business taxpayer if the following conditions apply:

- The business' entire net income before allocation is not more than $290,000.

- Capital stock does not generally exceed $1 million.
- The corporation is not part of an affiliated group.
- The business' entire net income base does not exceed $10,875.
- The capital base is not more than $488,750.

The *Metropolitan Transportation Business Tax Surcharge Return, Form CT-3M/4M*, discussed previously is filed with the corporation's franchise report; however, a separate extension request must be made for filing *Form CT-3M/4M*.

For more information on forms, call the Taxpayer Assistance Bureau at (800) 462-8100 in New York State.

S corporations file their New York State returns using *Form CT-3S*. *Form CT-3M/4M* is not required.

Every foreign corporation (including electing S corporations) authorized to do business in New York State must pay an annual maintenance fee of $300, which may be claimed as a credit against the regular, state franchise tax owed (noted above). *Form CT-245* is used for this purpose when forms CT-3, CT-4, or CT-3S are not required. New York City requires corporations that disclaim liability from tax, but who have an officer, employee or representative in New York City, to file a similar information return — *Form NYC-245*.

New York City

Corporations that are eligible to allocate income and capital, generally file *Form NYC-3L*, but can obtain an automatic, six-month extension by filing *Form NYC-6*. New York City may grant, upon the taxpayer's request, two additional discretionary, three-month extensions by filing *Form NYC-3L*. A separate *Form NYC-6.1* must be filed for each additional, three-month extension that is requested. A simplified, *Form NYC-4S*, which parallels the New York State *Form CT-4*, is also available.

Combined Reports

New York State and City may allow, or even require, the filing of combined tax reports when two or more corporations are controlled by the same interests and are part of one unitary business. *Forms CT-3A* and *NYC-3A* are used for this purpose. A combined report may or may not be advantageous. This will depend on the particular facts. Clearly, however, this could be beneficial if one corporation generated a profit and another incurred a loss. Permission to file combined reports should be requested on a timely basis. New York State *Form AU-2.1* and New York City *Form 3A-REQ* are used for this purpose.

Although New York State and City can require combined reports so as to clearly reflect income, not a unitary tax system is employed. Alien (non-U.S.) corporations are not included in the combined reports nor are non-taxpayers, unless they have significant inter-company dealings with other corporations filing in the state of New York.

11.3 Buying an Existing Business — State Legal Requirements

When buying an existing business, one of the key factors to determine is whether any claims, liens, etc. on the property need to be acquired.

Bulk Sales Law

New York, like most states, has a special law that prevents creditors of an existing business from being cut off by a sale of the business, or its assets, to a cooperative third party. Such laws are referred to as bulk sales laws, since sales made in the ordinary course of business are not covered. Generally speaking, businesses subject to bulk sales laws are those whose principal business activity is the sale or rental of merchandise.

Commonly, a bulk sale is considered to be a sale of a major part of the materials, supplies, or other inventory, not in the ordinary course of the seller's business. It should be noted that the terms 'bulk sale' and 'major portion' do not connote the sale of business assets in excess of 50%.

Usually, sales of service enterprise's assets are not affected by the bulk sales laws; however, there are exceptions. For example, there are special rules with respect to sales of restaurants. Sales that are exempted from the bulk sales laws are generally those which are intended to benefit the creditors of a seller.[14]

New York enacted bulk sales laws to protect a seller's creditors, who hold claims based upon transactions or events which occurred before the bulk sale, and who rely on the seller's inventory to secure payment. New York's bulk sales law is substantially the same as Article 6 of the Uniform Commercial Code. The business purchaser's failure to comply with bulk sales law results in the bulk sale being ineffective against the seller's creditors' claims.

To comply with bulk sales law provisions, the buyer must obtain from the seller, a list of the seller's creditors, their addresses, and the amount owed them. This list must be signed and sworn by the seller, even if the claims are subject to dispute.[15] The parties to the sale must also prepare a detailed schedule of the property to be transferred in the sale.

Any bulk sale, except one made by auction sale, will be ineffective against the seller's creditors, unless the purchaser provides notice to the creditors at least 10 days before the purchaser either takes possession of the goods, or pays for them, whichever happens first.[16] The notice should be personally delivered, or sent by either registered or certified mail, to all creditors shown on the list. This notice should state that a bulk sale is about to be made and include a property schedule, the names and business addresses of the seller and the purchaser, all other business names and addresses used by the seller within the past three years, and the address to which creditors should send their bills.[17] The buyer must then either file the list and property schedule with the department of state, or preserve the list and property schedule for the next six months following the sale, permitting inspection and copying of the list by any of the seller's creditors.[18]

Specific rules govern purchases dealing with bonds and debentures and whether the debts of the seller are not expected to be paid in full. A qualified attorney should be consulted regarding these types of situations.

Recorded Security Interests

The purpose of a security interest in real or personal property is to secure payment, or performance of an obligation, for a creditor's protection. A security interest becomes binding when it attaches to the property. In New York State, this is accomplished by the creditor recording a security interest. Before purchasing a business, find out if there are any security interests attached to the business property; otherwise, you could loose the property to secured creditors who have the right to sell the property to pay previously-owed debts. To determine whether or not security interests exist, follow the steps listed below:

- Security interests in real property can be discovered by conducting a title search in the county clerk's office, in the county where the real property is located.
- Security interests in personal property, such as consumer goods or farm-related property, farm products, farming operation equipment, farm accounts, or general intangibles relating to the sale of products by a farmer, will generally be found in the county clerk's office, in the county where the property is located.[19]
- Security interests on fixtures (or property expected to become a fixture) will generally be found in the county clerk's office, in the county where the real property (to which the fixture is to be attached) is located.[20]
- Security interests affecting all other types of property will generally be filed in the secretary of state's office.[21]

It is strongly recommended that a search for security interests be conducted by an attorney or other qualified professional, before you purchase any business.

Employment Tax Release

The purchaser should confirm that the seller has paid the required taxes withheld from the employees' wages to New York State.

A purchaser can discover whether the required payments have been made by requesting the seller to send a Statement of Open Items of Accounts Receivables and Transcripts of Withholding Tax to:

Processing Division, Withholding Tax Unit
New York State Department of Taxation and Finance
Building 8, Room 304
W. A. Harriman Campus
Albany, NY 12227
(518) 438-8581

The New York State Department of Taxation and Finance generally furnishes the information within three weeks after receiving the request.

Sales Tax Release

The purchaser in a bulk sale transaction is required to notify the New York State Department of Taxation and Finance of the purchase by filing *Form AU-196.10* at least 10 days before taking possession of the business, the transfer or assignment for the business, or the payment for the business, whichever occurs first. When notice is not given, the purchaser is liable for all sales taxes owed to the state by the seller, up to the higher of the purchase price or fair market value of the acquired property.

The Department of Taxation and Finance is required by law to give the purchaser notice within 90 days of the total amount of any tax due from the seller's business. If the department does not notify the purchaser within the 90-day period, the purchaser is cleared from any further obligation or liability to the state. As a practical matter, the state will generally furnish the information within 60 days after receipt of *Form AU-196.10*. Given this situation, you should be cautious about paying for the business in full until either the seller's sales tax account status is verified by the state or the 90-day period has expired.[22]

Note: There are no significant tax releases which should be secured other than those mentioned above.

Sales Tax on the Purchase of Assets

New York State imposes a sales tax on tangible personal property which is sold as a part of the business. Local sales taxes may also apply. These sales taxes are the primary responsibility of the purchaser. Due to the general sales tax exemption for property sold for resale, the tax would not apply to the inventory sold with the business, as long as the buyer is still planning to sell the inventory after acquiring the business, and does not use it for another purpose.

Unemployment Tax Rating

Under New York State's unemployment insurance law, a transfer of the prior owner's unemployment tax experience rate will occur automatically when any of the following four conditions are met:

- The purchaser assumes any of the transferring employer's obligations;
- The purchaser acquires any of the transferring employer's good will;
- The purchaser continues or resumes the business of the transferring employer, either in the same establishment or elsewhere;
- The purchaser employs, in connection with the business, substantially the same employees the transferring employer had.

Generally speaking, the above conditions are the usual situation for most business purchases. Therefore, a prudent business person should consider an unfavorable, tax experience rate as a condition which may warrant further discussion on the purchase price of the business.

It is also important to recognize that a tax experience rate is based upon prior employment activity, and the rate can be reduced by "voluntary contributions" to the state unemployment fund. See Section 11.5 for a more complete discussion of voluntary contributions and how this may save on unemployment taxes.

11.4 Requirements that Apply to Nearly All New Businesses

State Licenses

New York licenses just about all business activity in the state, regardless of a business' legal form. In addition, because separate agencies have been established to license the various businesses, professions, and occupations, a great deal of red tape has been created. The state has attempted to reduce this problem by establishing a specialized department of licensing and permit experts. A simple phone call to the New York State Office of Business Permits & Regulatory Assistance should alleviate much of the tedious footwork needed in licensing a New York business. See Section 11.6 for a selection of the businesses and occupations required to be licensed in New York as well as a listing for the Office of Business Permits & Regulatory Assistance.

Estimated Income Taxes

Any individual taxpayer who operates a sole proprietorship; is a partner in a partnership; or is a shareholder in an S corporation that conducts business in New York State; and who expects to owe the state more than $100 in taxes, after withholdings; is expected to pay estimated tax payments.

The required annual payment of estimated tax is 90% of the tax shown on the return for the taxable year. Generally, individual estimated tax payments are due quarterly in four equal installments on April 15, June 15, September 15, and January 15. If the 15th day of the month falls on a Saturday, Sunday, or holiday, the next business day becomes the due date.

Combined New York State and City payments are made together on the same form. Estimated tax payments should be made on *Form IT-2105* and mailed to one of the offices below:

Outside of New York City Area

NYS Estimated Income Tax
Processing Center
P.O. Box 1195
Albany, NY 12201-1195
(518) 938-8581

Inside New York City Area

NYS Estimated Income Tax
Processing Center
P.O. Box 2111
New York, NY 10008-2111
(800) 225-5829 (in NY State)

Unincorporated Business Tax

Estimated taxes for New York City's Unincorporated Business Tax may also be necessary if the expected taxable business income is greater than $15,000. *Form NYC-5UBTI* (individuals) and *Form NYC-5UB* (partnerships) are required quarterly. The payment dates are identical to those generally required for a calendar-year taxpayer: April 15, June 15, September 15, and January 15. Declarations with remittances should be filed with the New York City Department of Finance.

New York City Department of Finance
Box 1155
Wall Street Station
New York, NY 10005
(718) 935-6000

Corporate Estimated Income Tax

New York State — Estimates of New York State corporate income taxes are required by corporations with an expected tax liability greater than $1,000. Estimates are generally due as follows:

- 25% of the prior year's liability or estimated liability (if in excess of $1,000) is due on the 15th day of the third month of the current taxable year and is filed either on *Form CT-3* (the corporation's tax return for the prior year) or *Form CT-5* (an extension of time for filing the tax return) covering the prior year.
- One-third of the remaining estimated liability for the year is due on the 15th day of the sixth, ninth, and twelfth month from the beginning of the taxable year and is filed on the *Estimated Tax Form CT-400*.

If the annual estimated taxes do not equal 90% of the tax shown due on the taxable year's return, penalties may be imposed. Mail the estimated tax payment *Form CT-400* to the New York State Corporation Tax Processing Unit.

New York State Corporation Tax Processing Unit
P.O. Box 1909
Albany, NY 12201
(518) 438-8581

Notice that the first estimated tax payment for a corporation already in business is included with the corporation's tax return or extension request if the prior year's tax exceeds, or is expected to exceed, $1,000.

New York City — Estimates of New York City corporate income taxes are also required by corporations with an expected tax liability greater than $1,000. Like New York State, a payment of 25% of the preceding year's tax is due the 15th day of the third month following the close of the corporation's year end and like the state, payment is made on either the prior year's corporation tax return or on the extension request. Estimated tax payments for the remaining installments are made in a parallel manner to New York State; however, the third and fourth installments for New York City have different filing dates. They are due on the 15th day of the tenth month and on the 15th day of the first month of the following year, rather than the ninth and twelfth month. The form needed to make these payments is *Form NYC-400.* This is filed with the New York City Department of Finance.

New York City Department of Finance
Box 3900
Church Street Station
New York, NY 10008
(718) 935-6000

Sales and Use Tax Permits

Sales and use tax is a transaction cost imposed on a retail customer purchasing taxable property or services or both from the seller. Retail sales are essentially sales made to an "end-user" or a "true" consumer of the product or service.[23] There are numerous exemptions to this tax. The most significant is the sale for resale; that is, sales of tangible personal property to a purchaser, who in turn will resell the property.

The resale exemption is fundamental to the statutory plan of imposing a tax on the "retail" sale of tangible personal property or specified services; however, note that it is critical to apply for a resale number if you are claiming exemption and to ask for a resale certificate, *Form ST-120,* from any purchaser claiming exemption on a sale you are making to them.

Although the sales tax liability is primarily that of the purchaser, the seller assumes the role of an agent for the state in collecting this tax and therefore is liable to the state for either having not collected the tax or for not remitting the collected tax to the state. The burden of proof that a sale is not subject to tax is placed on the seller. Therefore, maintain adequate records of your business transactions to ensure that you collect and remit the required amount of tax due. This includes the timely obtaining of the purchasers' exemption certificates. The state requires maintenance of your records for audit purposes for a minimum of three years; however, failure to file a tax return, or filing a fraudulent tax return, will extend the three-year statute of limitations indefinitely.[24]

New York State imposes a sales tax on the retail sale (or rental) of tangible personal property, on the sales of food and drinks by restaurants and caterers, on hotel and motel occupancy charges, on admission charges to certain amusement places, and on social and athletic club dues and fees. It also imposes this tax on many services. Sales tax is imposed on services only if New York State tax law specifically taxes them. Taxable services include information services and services in processing, printing, installation, maintenance, storage, parking, interior decorating and design, protective and detective, and telephone and telegraph.

The New York State use tax complements the sales tax in that it covers transactions that would not otherwise be taxed because the sale took place outside of New York State. In other words, if property is purchased outside of New York State, but is transported into New York State for use, the use tax would apply, rather than the sales tax. The use tax is designed to protect vendors located in New York State from the competition of out-of-state vendors who are not required to collect the New York State tax.

New York State sales and use tax rates are 4% of the total sale's price. An additional $1/4$ of 1% (.0025) is added for sales within the Metropolitan Commuter Transportation District (MTCD). New York City and Yonkers currently impose an additional 4% tax for a combined tax rate of 8 $1/4$% within these jurisdictions.[25] Other cities outside of the MTCD, such as Rochester, impose an additional tax of up to 3% for a combined tax rate of 7%. The state collects all of these taxes from businesses on a single form and handles remitting the local sales taxes to the appropriate jurisdictions. For more information, call the Taxpayer Assistance Bureau at (800) 225-5829 in New York State.

At first glance, the sales and use tax law with its extensive statutory definitions may appear straightforward; however, its application requires careful interpretation because the statutory language is sometimes susceptible to multiple interpretations.

Inquiries concerning the application of sales tax law to unusual transactions may be directed to the New York State Department of Taxation and Finance or may be forwarded to the Advisory Opinions Unit on *Form AD1.8* at the same address.

Technical Services Section
New York State Department of Taxation and Finance
Building 9
State Campus
Albany, NY 12227
(518) 438-8581

If your business requires you to collect New York State sales tax, you must register with the state at least 20 days in advance of your opening business.[26] To successfully register the business, you must file the following forms:

- *DTF-17, Certificate of Registration*
- *DTF-17.1, Business Description*
- *DTF-17.2, Schedule of Business Locations*
- *DTF-17.3, Certificate of Registration Affidavit*

These forms should be filed with the New York State Department of Taxation and Finance.

Sales Tax Registration Unit
New York State Department of Taxation and Finance
W. A. Harriman Campus
Albany, NY 12227
(518) 438-8581

After these forms are processed, the New York State Department of Taxation and Finance will validate and return *Form DTF-17A*,

Certificate of Authority, to you. This validated certificate gives you authority to charge and collect sales tax. It should be displayed in plain view at your place of business.

After registration, any vendor with less than $250 of annual sales tax liability for the sales tax year ending May 31, should annually file on *Form ST-101*. Vendors, with taxable sales of less than $300,000 in any quarter of the preceding four quarters, are required to file *Form ST-100* quarterly. The due dates for filing *Form ST-100* are the 20th of March, June, September, and December for the quarterly periods ending on the last day of the preceding month. Large vendors, with $300,000 or more in taxable sales per quarter, are required to file a monthly *Form ST-809* within 20 days after the end of the month for which they are being filed. Every year, by March 20th, large vendors filing monthly returns must also file an estimated return on *Form ST-803*, for the month of March. No monthly returns are required for the months that end a sales tax quarter — February, May, August, and November. Large vendors who file *Form ST-809* on a monthly basis must also file quarterly returns on *Form ST-810*. The purpose of the estimated March return is to accelerate the March sales tax payment to help balance the state budget by its fiscal year end of March 31.

The states of New Jersey and Connecticut have entered into an agreement with New York State to administer and collect sales and use taxes on merchandise crossing the borders of each state. The agreement between the states, which became effective April 1986 with New Jersey, and October 1, 1988, with Connecticut, will impact businesses selling taxable property and services between New York and the other state. The agreement has been constructed to close the gap where a seller only conducts business in one state and thus is not required to collect sales tax on out-of-state sales.

The states will initially ask businesses to voluntarily register and collect the correct tax on merchandise shipped into the other state. A business will only be required to file in one state (their own) and to remit the sales and use tax collected for both states. The receiving state will then take the responsibility to remit the gross sales tax collected to the other state. As a final note, all three states intend to exchange sales tax information gathered in the audits of businesses which do not voluntarily register or claim nontaxable sales into the other state.

Property Taxes
Assessments and Rates

Property taxation in New York State is limited to taxes on real estate only. All personal property, either tangible or intangible, is specifically excluded from taxation by state constitution and statutory provisions. There are no tax return filing requirements, and taxes are levied and collected only by local governments pursuant to provisions within their local real property tax laws.

For the current year, the following approximate assessments and rates apply to New York City:

Rates for Each Class	$100 of Assessed Value
Class 1	$9.452
Class 2	9.229
Class 3	12.903
Class 4	9.539

Class 1 – Residential property containing up to three family dwellings.
Class 2 – All other residential property (except hotels and motels).
Class 3 – Utility real property.
Class 4 – All other property (essentially commercial and industrial realty, hotels, and motels).

The city of Rochester has different tax rates for commercial real estate as opposed to residential property. The current statutory tax rate for commercial property per $1,000 of assessed value is as follows:

Rochester School District — $21.27 (including Monroe County tax of $11.60).

New York City Commercial Rent & Occupancy Tax

In addition to taxing real property, New York City levies a commercial rent and occupancy tax on all businesses renting commercial space within any of its five boroughs. The tax is imposed on the annual gross rent paid by the tenant, when the tenant's base rent equals or exceeds $11,000. When a business subleases any of its rental space for the year, the annual rent on which the business pays tax is reduced by the sublease income received if the sublessee is subject to tax. The sublessee is required to file its own commercial rent and occupancy tax return with the city. The tax rate is 6% of the taxpayer's base rent.

The city will supply you with the necessary quarterly form, *Form CR-Q*, for filing the commercial rent and occupancy taxes. Returns and payments are due March 20, June 20, September 20, and December 20 for the preceding three-month period. The June 20 return is the annual return for this tax (*Form CR-A*). The annual return must be filed by every tenant subject to tax, even if base rent is less than $11,000.

Fictitious or Assumed Business Name

As discussed in Section 11.2, under New York State law an individual, partnership, corporation, or unincorporated association is not allowed to carry on or transact business in New York under a name or designation other than its own name, unless an assumed name certificate is filed. For unincorporated businesses, the certificate must state the name of the business and the address within the county where the business is conducted, the full name(s) of the person(s) conducting the business, including the names of all partners, with the residence address of each person, and the age of any person under 18 years of age. The certificate is required to be signed and notarized by all persons conducting the business.[27]

A corporation must file a certificate with the office of the secretary of state stating the name or designation the business is carried on under, its corporate name, and the address(es) of the corporation's place of business in the state. The certificate must be signed and notarized by an officer of the corporation, and a check for $50 must be attached. The certificate and filing fee are mailed to the Division of Corporations.

Division of Corporations
New York State Department of State
162 Washington Avenue
Albany, NY 12231
(518) 473-2492

The Department of State will certify a copy of the certificate, which must be displayed on the business' premises.[28]

Anyone carrying on, conducting, or transacting business under an assumed name, and fails to comply with the filing requirements, is prohibited from maintaining any action or proceeding in any court in New York on any contract, account, or transaction made in a name other than its real name until the assumed name certificate has been properly executed and filed. Also, misdemeanor penalties may apply.[29]

Sole Proprietorship Requirements

A sole proprietor is required to attach a copy of federal *1040 Schedule C* to state *Form IT-201, Resident Income Tax Return* or to state *Form IT-203, Non-Resident and Part-Year Resident Income Tax Return*. One of these two forms will also reflect your taxes for either New York City or City of Yonkers, if required.

If the business is located in New York City, it is also required to file *Form NYC-202* as an unincorporated business. See Section 11.2.

An automatic four-month extension is available by using *Form IT-370* and an additional extension for good cause can be obtained by completing *Form IT-372*.

Partnership Requirements

A partnership is required to file an informational return, *Form IT-204*, by the 15th day of the fourth month following the close of the taxable year.

Partnerships doing business in the City of Yonkers and having nonresident-of-Yonkers partners must also attach *Form Y-204* to their state *Form IT-204*.

If an extension of time is needed to file the New York State partnership return, *Form IT-370-PF* and *Form IT-372-PF* should be used. The type of return, *IT-204*, should be indicated on the form.

As with the sole proprietorship, each individual partner's share of the partnership's items should be reported on his or her *Form IT-201* or *Form IT-203*.

A New York City partnership is also required to file an *Unincorporated Business Tax Partnership Return, Form NYC-204.* As discussed in Section 11.2, the partnership must pay this tax on its taxable business income.

Corporation Requirements

All corporations incorporated or doing business in New York State must file an annual franchise tax report with the state. The due date for all of the franchise tax reports listed below is 2 ½ months after the close of the taxable year — March 15 for a calendar year end. *Form CT-3* is generally used and must be filed when any of the following conditions exist:

- The tax is greater than $1,000.
- A claim is made for any tax credits.
- A deduction is claimed for an optional depreciation, net operating loss, or capital loss.
- The corporation is a REIT, a DISC, or DISC stockholder.
- Subsidiary capital is owned by the corporation.
- Investment or business income or capital allocation is claimed.
- Investment is made in nonsubsidiary securities, including those issued by both domestic and foreign governmental agencies.
- A claim is made for exemption from the franchise tax based on business and investment capital of a new small business corporation.
- The corporation was involved in a merger, acquisition, or consolidation in the current year.

A corporation that makes an election under state law to be treated as an S corporation is required to file *Form CT-3S.*

The filing date can automatically be extended for up to six months for the above listed forms by filing *Form CT-5, Application for Automatic Six-Month Extension for Filing.*

Corporations required to file any of the above listed corporate tax forms may also be required to file *Metropolitan Transportation Business Tax Surcharge Return, Form CT-3M/4M.* See Section 11.2 for more details on this return.

The due dates for filing the *New York City General Corporation Return, Form NYC-3L,* are the same as New York State. A simplified *Form NYC-4S,* which parallels the New York State *Form CT-4,* is also available. Extensions for either of these forms is requested on *Form NYC-6.*

11.5 Additional State Requirements for Businesses with Employees

Withholding Taxes

All employers maintaining an office, transacting business within New York State, or making payments to employees performing services within the state, are required to deduct and withhold New York State (and City, if applicable) taxes whether or not a "paying" agency is maintained within the state. *Booklet IT-2100*, *Employer's Withholding Tax Tables*: *Methods and Instructions*, explains how to do this.

The New York State Tax Commission administers all of the payroll tax withholdings for New York State personal income tax, City of New York resident tax, City of New York nonresident earnings tax, City of Yonkers resident tax surcharge, and the City of Yonkers nonresident earnings tax. Therefore, an employer only needs to file and remit the withheld tax on one report, *Booklet IT-2101*, *Employers Return of Tax Withheld*, for the required filing period.

New employers are required to file their first withholding return for the period in which they begin to pay wages and compensation. The frequency of filing withholding tax returns depends upon the total amount of tax withheld in a six-month period. See the chart on the required filing frequency, shown later in this section. To obtain the necessary forms and instructions, write or call the Taxpayer Assistance Bureau.

Taxpayer Assistance Bureau
New York State Department of Taxation and Finance
W. A. Harriman Campus
Albany, NY 12227-0125
(518) 438-1073 (outside New York State)
(800) 462-8100 (in New York State)

For general business tax information, call:

(518) 438-8581 (outside New York State)
(800) 225-5825 (in New York State)

For convenience purposes, the federal employer identification number assigned by the IRS is used for all New York State and City purposes. See Section 5.2 regarding application for a federal employer identification number.

All wages and compensation paid to an employee which are subject to federal withholding are also subject to New York State and City and City of Yonkers withholding, unless the income is allocated outside of these jurisdictions or exempt from withholding.

The New York personal income tax withholding amount for state and city purposes is determined by using both the approved withholding tables printed in the New York *Booklet IT-2100* as well as the employee withholding exemption certificate discussed below. Federal provisions govern the withholding of tax on compensation paid to interstate transportation employees and seamen engaged in foreign, coastwise, intercoastal, interstate, or noncontiguous trade. You should refer to federal *Circular E* for information on these types of employees.

If the number of withholding exemptions claimed for New York purposes is different from the number claimed on the federal *Form W-4*, new employees are required to complete *Form IT-2104*, New York State and City and City of Yonkers withholding allowance certificate. Otherwise, the federal *Form W-4* number of exemptions is used to calculate the New York State and City withholding. See Section 5.2 for discussion on employee W-4s.

Employees may qualify for an exemption from the withholding tax requirement for state and city purposes when the following conditions apply:

- The employee is under 18 years of age, over age 65, or a full-time student under age 25, and had no income tax liability in the previous year and expects no income tax liability in the current year. If these conditions are satisfied, you must request, and keep as part of your employer records, a completed *Form IT-2104-E* certifying exemption from withholding in order to exempt the employee from withholding.

- Neither *Form IT-2104* nor *Form IT-2104-E* need be filed with the New York State Department of Taxation and Finance except where the number of allowances claimed by the employee exceeds 14 or, with respect to *Form IT-2104-E*, if the employee's weekly wage usually exceeds $200.

- All wages paid to a New York State and City or City of Yonkers resident are subject to state and city withholding, even though the work was performed outside the state or city.

- If the employee is a nonresident of the state, and all of the work was performed within the state (and city, if applicable), then tax is required to be withheld from all wages paid to the employee in accordance with the tables that apply to state residents. If applicable, New York City and City of Yonkers tax will also be withheld; however, in this instance, the employer must also obtain a certificate of nonresidence form for each applicable tax jurisdiction — *Form IT-2104.2* for New York City and *Form IT-2104.5* for the City of Yonkers.

- If a New York State and City or City of Yonkers nonresident employee performs services partly inside and partly outside of the state or city or both, only wages attributable to services inside the state and city are subject to withholding of personal income tax. Frequently, the portion of total wages allocable to the state or city is calculated by applying a ratio of the number of days worked inside the state or city to the total number of days worked both inside and outside of the state or city. When calculating this ratio, nonworking days such as Saturday or Sunday, holidays, leave of absence, vacation, sick days, and personal days are not included. In this situation, a state certificate of nonresidence, *Form IT-2104.1*, is also required of the employee.

The allocation becomes more difficult when calculating the earnings of a salesman, or other employee, whose compensation depends entirely on the volume of business transacted by the employee. A ratio is also used; however, rather than calculating the number of days inside and outside of the state or city, the volume of business transacted within the state or city over the volume of business transacted outside of the state or city is calculated. The ratio is applied to the employee's total compensation. The resulting amount is the portion of wages to withhold tax upon.

If a New York City or City of Yonkers nonresident is expected to work only a short period of time and earn less than $3,000 for the taxable year (prorate this amount for a short taxable year), then no withholding is required.

Filing Requirements

The frequency of filing *Form IT-2101 (PNS), Employers Return of Tax Withheld*, depends upon the expected total amount of New York State and City and City of Yonkers taxes required to be withheld in a semi-annual period ending June 30 or December 31. The appropriate due dates are as follows:

Total Tax Withheld in a 6-Month Period	Frequency of Filing IT-2101	Due Dates for Return and Remittance
$35,000 or more	Quarter-monthly	Within 3 banking days after the 7th, 15th, 22nd, and the last day of any month.*
$7,500 to 34,999	Semi-monthly	Within 3 banking days after the 15th and last day of each month.*
$800 to 7,499	Monthly	On the 15th day of the following month.*
$200 to 799	Semi-annually	July 31 and January 31
$0.01 to $199	Annually	January 31 of the following year
None	Annually	February 28 of the following year.

* Except that the return for the last week, last half, or 15th day of December is due January 31.

If there is a permanent decline in the amount of New York State and City or City of Yonkers taxes withheld, you must request a change in filing frequency by writing to the New York State Department of Taxation and Finance.

Withholding Tax Unit
New York State Department of Taxation and Finance
W. A. Harriman Campus
Albany, NY 12227

You must also file *Form WRS-2, Employer's Quarterly Report of Wages Paid to Each Employee*, four times a year. This form, due on the last day of the month following the end of the calendar quarter, is also filed with the New York State Department of Taxation and Finance.

WRS Report Processing Unit
New York State Department of Taxation and Finance
W.A. Harriman Campus
Albany, NY 12227

An employer is required by both the federal government and by New York State to provide each employee with a statement of annual earnings and withholdings. Generally speaking, employers use the federal *Form W-2* to comply with both of the jurisdictions; however, the employer may choose to complete both a W-2 for federal purposes and *Form IT-2102* for New York State and City purposes. The employer must provide the federal *Form W-2* to the employees by January 31 following the close of the year. New York State *Form IT-2102* is required to be furnished to the employee no later than February 15.

If an employee terminates employment before the close of the year and is not expected to return, either *Form W-2* or *Form IT-2102* is required to be furnished to them 30 days after employment is terminated.

Employers are required to annually file *Form IT-2103, Reconciliation of Tax Withheld* by February 28 following the close of the calendar year. The return is sent to the address listed above and must include the following:

- Federal *Form W-2* (state copy); or
- New York State *Form IT-2102* (copy 1) for each employee; and
- A listing (adding machine tape will suffice) of the total amounts of New York State and City tax withheld.

Filing on Magnetic Media

New York State requires employers who meet either of the following conditions to file on magnetic media:

- An employer having an aggregate of 250 or more employees in New York State during the calendar year for which *Form W-2/IT-2101* or *Form W-2P/IT-2102-P* is required; or
- An employer who files on magnetic media for federal purposes.

If hardship is shown, the magnetic media filing requirement will be waived. In addition, an employer can also voluntarily file on magnetic media, however, prior permission may be required. The following mailing address is used.

Withholding Tax Unit
New York State Department of Taxation and Finance
Building 8, Room 304
W.A. Harriman Campus
Albany, NY 12227
(518) 438-8581

Employers should retain all records relating to payroll tax for a period of four years. New York State requires the same records to be maintained as the federal government. See the federal *Circular E* for this information.

In addition, the state requires that you maintain all pertinent certificates of exemption, nonresidence certificates, and a record of withholding allocation used for New York State and City and City of Yonkers nonresidents.

Additional information regarding New York State withholding tax requirements can be obtained by contacting the New York State Department of Taxation and Finance.

State Unemployment Tax

A business owner employing one or more people may be liable to pay the New York State Unemployment Tax. Generally, this applies when you have gross payroll of $300 or more in a calendar quarter. You must register by using *Form IA-100*. The New York State Department of Labor administers New York State Unemployment Insurance Law and provides information, assistance, and enforcement of the law through multiple department sections. Booklets can be obtained by writing to the New York State Department of Labor or by using the preaddressed postcard at the back of the book.

Liability and Determination Section, Registration Section
New York State Department of Labor
State Office Building Campus #12, Room 359
Albany, NY 12240
(518) 457-4179

Unemployment tax is paid on the first $7,000 of each employee's earnings in a calendar year, if the employee is covered under the New York State unemployment tax law. Reporting and payment (if applicable) is required quarterly using *Form IA-5*. This form, due on the last day of the month following the end of calendar quarter, should be filed with the New York State Unemployment Insurance.

New York State Unemployment Insurance
P.O. Box 1589
Albany, NY 12249-0406

Not all employees are required to be covered by the New York unemployment tax law. For example, the services of the taxpayer's spouse and minor children would not be covered under the law, and therefore their wages would not be taxable. Payments to elementary and high school students as well as severance and dismissal payments are subject to New York State unemployment tax if the payments are also subject to FUTA tax. College students are covered under New York unemployment tax law, and therefore their earnings are taxable regardless of whether their employer is subject to FUTA.

Unemployment Tax Rate

A new employer, who begins a business, is assigned a tax rate of 2.6%. A new employer, who purchases the business of an already liable employer, will usually be assigned the prior owner's rate. See Section 11.3, Buying an Existing Business — State Legal Requirements. An employer, however, who is already involved in one or more existing businesses and purchases a similar existing business with employees, will usually have a new rate assigned to the business, combining and averaging the old unemployment tax rates.

Employers must pay unemployment taxes if wages of $300 or more were paid in a calendar quarter. New employers, as discussed above, are assigned a rate of 2.6% of wages until the employer acquires sufficient reporting experience to have the rate set under the experience rating system. The range of rates varies and depends upon the employer's individual account balance and the statewide size of fund-index percentages as calculated by the New York State Department of Labor. The tax rates are set annually by the New York State Department of Labor and remain in effect until the next annual rate adjustment, which usually occurs in March of each year. In 1990, the minimum rate was set at 0.3% and the maximum rate was 5.4%. Given the wide fluctuation in possible tax rates, it's a good idea for an employer to keep track of their assigned unemployment tax rating, especially preceding a year an increase in employees is contemplated.

The state maintains a system of voluntary contributions, whereby an employer may reduce his or her annual experience rate by additional contributions. You should contact the New York State Department of Labor by the first week in January for the year in which you want to reduce your experience rate. Ask the department for the preliminary information on your upcoming experience rating for voluntary contribution purposes. They will send you a two-page letter explaining your preliminary rate and provide detailed instructions on how to calculate your voluntary contribution to arrive at approximately the rate you require. For further information, an employer should contact:

Employer Account Adjustment Section
New York State Department of Labor
State Office Building Campus
Albany, NY 12240-0415
(518) 457-2169

Workers' Compensation Insurance

With few exceptions, New York State employers are required to carry workers' compensation insurance and disability benefits insurance to insure their employees against accidental injury, disability, or death which may occur in the course of their employment. Generally, this liability arises if you have one or more employees for 30 days in a calendar year. Rates vary according to the nature of the employment and the hazards involved.

Employers may satisfy the insurance requirement in one of three ways:

- Purchasing a workers' compensation policy from the State Insurance Fund.

The State Insurance Fund	**The State Insurance Fund**
15 Computer Drive West	199 Church Street
Albany, NY 12205	New York, NY 10007
(518) 485-8800	(212) 312-9000

- Purchasing a workers' compensation policy from an insurance company authorized to write such a policy in New York; or
- Providing the chairman of the workers' compensation board with satisfactory proof of ability to self-insure and providing security for payment which the chairman may require.[30]

The employer is required to post a notice of compliance which states the workers' compensation law, in each place of business. *Form C-105* is required for this purpose and may be obtained from the State Insurance Fund or your private insurance company.[31] To request *Form C-105* and other material from the State Insurance Fund, contact the New York City office on the previous page.

Employee Safety and Health Regulations

New York State has adopted the provisions contained within the federal Occupational Safety and Health Act of 1970 (OSHA); therefore, the obligation of employers to furnish their employees with a safe working environment falls under the jurisdiction of the U.S. Department of Labor's Occupational Safety and Health Administration. The Regional OSHA office is located in New York City.

Federal Occupational Safety and Health Administration
U.S. Department of Labor
201 Varick Street, Room 670
New York, NY 10014
(212) 337-2378

To obtain the necessary forms and posters to comply with OSHA standards, as well as other pertinent regulations for your particular business, write to the above address. In addition, the New York State Department of Labor provides New York businesses with on-site consultation by trained state personnel to advise employers on whether or not their business conforms to OSHA standards. The service is provided free to any business which requests it and the state consultants' report is not reported to the OSHA offices.

Information regarding OSHA guidelines as well as the consultation service are provided by the offices listed below.

Division of Safety and Health
New York State Department of Labor
One Main Street
Brooklyn, NY 11201
(718) 797-7646

Division of Safety and Health
New York State Department of Labor
State Campus, Building 12, Room 159
Albany, NY 12240
(518) 457-5508

Labor Laws

Employees in New York State, with certain exceptions, are protected by New York's Minimum Wage Act. The act currently provides for a minimum hourly wage of $3.80;[32] however, the federal minimum wage is currently $4.25.

Wage and Hour Laws

Generally, New York law states that eight hours constitute a legal day's work.[33] Employees are to be allowed time for a noonday meal with the allotted time varying with the occupation of the employee.[34] For example, factory workers are to be allowed at least 60 minutes for lunch and employees in mercantile establishments are to be allowed at least 45 minutes for lunch.

Employers are generally required to pay wages at specific intervals, depending upon the type of employee being compensated. For example, in most instances, manual workers must be paid weekly and no later than seven calendar days after the end of the week in which the wages are earned. Commission salespersons must be paid at least once per month. Clerical workers should be paid wages in accordance with their employment terms, but not less than semi-monthly.[35]

Wages are legally required in New York State to be paid in cash but may be paid by check, if the employer can furnish satisfactory proof to the commissioner of labor of both the employer's financial responsibility and that the checks may be cashed without difficulty by the employees for their full value.[36] To pay wages by check, it is necessary to file an application accompanied by a nonrefundable fee of $25, per location.

If the employee is terminated, the employer must pay the employee's wages no later than the regular payday of the period during which the termination occurred, and if requested by the terminated employee, the wages shall be paid by mail.[37]

State labor laws provide protection for workers under 18 years of age, restricting the maximum number of hours worked, etc.[38]

Employers are required to post a notice (on a form furnished or approved by the commission) stating the maximum number of daily hours of work, the beginning and stopping hours, and the time allowed for meals for those people protected by state labor laws.[39] Employers are also required to maintain records showing the names, addresses, and the hours worked daily by each of their employees.

Anti-Discrimination Laws

Under the New York Human Rights Law, it is unlawful for an employer to discriminate against an employee due to age, race, religion, national origin, color, sex, disability, or marital status.

In addition, an employer is prohibited from printing or circulating any publication, statement, advertisement, or job application which expresses directly or indirectly any type of discrimination listed above.[40] Further, an employer may not retaliate against an employee because the employee opposed the unlawful discriminatory practice or brought, testified, or assisted in any proceeding against the employer.[41] An employer may, however, terminate an employee who is physically unable to perform the required duties.[42] Under certain circumstances, an employer may institute affirmative action plans approved by the state Division of Human Rights. Discrimination based upon bona fide occupational qualifications is permissible; however, in light of recent court decisions, it is becoming extremely difficult to justify.

It is unlawful for an employer to force a pregnant employee to take a leave of absence, unless her condition prevents her from reasonably performing her job.[43]

At its offices, places of employment or employment training centers, every employer subject to the Human Rights Law must post and maintain notices, furnished by the Division of Human Rights, that indicate the substantive provisions of the Human Rights Law, the place where complaints may be filed, and other such required information. The notices are required to be posted conspicuously in easily-accessible, well-lighted places customarily frequented by employees and applicants for employment, or by applicants for or participants in apprenticeships, on-the-job training, or other training or retraining programs. The notice must also be posted at each location where employee services are performed.[44]

For questions pertaining to state anti-discrimination laws, contact:

Division of Human Rights
55 W. 125th Street, 13th Floor
New York, NY 10027
(212) 870-8400

11.6 State Licenses

The Office of Business Permits & Regulatory Assistance maintains up-to-date information on more than 1,100 required state permits, licenses, and approvals. The following is a list of selected businesses, occupations, industries, and items that require licensing in the state of New York. For more information, see the discussion in Section 11.4 on New York State and City licenses.

New York Licenses Required for:

Apartment information vendor	Commission merchants for food products	Funeral directors, undertakers, and embalmers
Attorneys	Explosives manufacturers, dealers, and stores	Hairdressing and cosmetology
Auctioneers		Hearing aid dealers
Barber shops	Feedstuffs, commercial	Horse racing
Boiler inspectors	Fertilizer, commercial	Insurance personnel
Boxing matches	Fishing and fishing vessels	Junk dealers
Canneries and processing plants	Food processing	Laboratories and blood banks
Certified Public Accountants and enrolled public accountants	Food salvagers	Liming materials
	Foreign banking corporation representatives	Milk dealers and brokers
Certified shorthand reporters		Milk gathering stations
Check cashiers	Frozen desserts	Motorboats
Collateral loan brokers	Fundraisers	

New York Licenses Required for: (continued)

Motor vehicle driver schools	Radiation installation	Soil and plant innoculant sales
Nursery schools	Real estate brokers and salespersons	Steamship ticket agencies
Nursery stock	Sales finance companies	Trade names, trademarks, and devices
Pesticides	Scrap processors	Trading stamps
Pharmacy, manufacturers, wholesalers, and retailers	Securities brokers, dealers, and salespersons	Upholstered furniture and bedding
Premium finance agencies		Vehicle dismantlers
Private investigators; watch, guard, and patrol agencies	Shellfish	Vessels
	Slaughterhouses	Warehouses
Private schools	Small loans	Weighmasters
		Wells

The New York State Office of Business Permits & Regulatory Assistance was established as a service to businesses operating, or planning to operate, in the state to help simplify the licensing procedures involved in operating a business in New York State. The office has experienced personnel to assist in the area of licensing and provides you with a personalized package — *Business Assistance Package* — which includes all necessary information, applications, and regulations for your particular type of business. You can request the *Business Assistance Package* by using the post card provided at the back of this book.

Questions pertaining to business permits can be directed to the Office of Business Permits & Regulatory Assistance.

New York State Office of Business Permits & Regulatory Assistance
Alfred E. Smith State Office Building, 17th Floor
P.O. Box 7027
Albany, NY 12225
(518) 474-8275
(800) 342-3464 (in New York State)

New York City Licensing Requirements

In addition to New York State licensing requirements, New York City imposes its own licensing requirements. Currently, New York City licenses 81 additional businesses and occupations. Some licenses require that you post a bond as security. For information and applications, contact:

License Issuance Division, New York City Department of Consumer Affairs
80 Lafayette Street, Fourth Floor
New York, NY 10013
(212) 577-0111

In New York City, certain licensed businesses and occupations may also require special permits to operate. For further information about businesses requiring New York City permits as well as application information, contact:

Division of Permits, New York City Department of Health
125 Worth Street, Main Floor
New York, NY 10013
(212) 566-8184

11.7 State Excise Taxes

State excise taxes are listed below, but note that rates are subject to change. Questions pertaining to tax information can be directed to the toll-free number of the Department of Taxation and Finance.

New York State Department of Taxation and Finance
(800) 225-5829

Sale, possession, production, and distribution of liquor and other alcoholic beverages are under the control of the New York State Liquor Authority. Local Alcoholic Beverage Control Boards exist to advise the authority on the issuance or refusal of retail licenses. Rules, regulations, and taxes are enacted and enforced by both the New York State Department of Taxation and Finance and the State Tax Commission. Licenses range in cost from $5 to approximately $9,400. The excise tax varies depending on the type of beverage sold. For example, beer is taxed at $0.21 (21 cents) per gallon, the tax on wine ranges from $0.01 to $0.25 (1 to 25 cents) per liter, and liquors are taxed at either $0.01 (1 cent), $0.67 (67 cents), or $1.70 per liter. Taxes due on sales must be reported and paid by the 20th day of each month and sent to the Miscellaneous Tax Bureau at this address.

Miscellaneous Tax Bureau
New York State Department of Taxation and Finance
State Campus
Albany, NY 12227

Alcoholic Beverage Taxes

A mineral severance tax is not applicable in New York State or City.

Severance Tax on Minerals

A real property gains tax is imposed on the gains derived from the transfer of real property located within the state. Whenever such property or an interest therein is transferred, the transaction may be subject to the real property transfer gains tax. A transfer of real property means the transfer of any interest in real property, by any method. An important application of this tax comes into play when a business with an interest in real property is acquired or even where a controlling interest in such business is acquired or transferred. In the case of a corporation, a controlling interest means 50% or more of the total combined voting power of all classes of stock, or 50% or more of the capital profits or beneficial interest in such stock. In the case of a partnership, association, trust, or other entity, a 50% or more interest in the capital, profits, or beneficial interest in such entity is considered a controlling interest. Transfers of condominium units and stock of a cooperative corporation are also covered.

The tax is imposed at the rate of 10% of the gain on the property when the consideration is $1,000,000 or more. Please note that in the case of a

Real Property Gains Tax

transfer of controlling interest, consideration is based on the fair market value of the real property. No tax is imposed if the real property is used solely as your residence or if the consideration is less than $1 million. In computing the gain, any depreciation previously taken for income tax purposes is also disregarded.

A pre-transfer audit procedure has been established for transfers where the consideration equals or exceeds $500,000. The procedure requires both the purchaser and seller to file a questionnaire that provides information concerning the details of the transaction. The questionnaire and any required information or documentation must be submitted together to the New York State Department of Taxation and Finance.

New York State Department of Taxation and Finance
P.O. Box 5045
Albany, NY 12205-5045
(518) 438-1073 (out of state)
(800) 225-5829 (in New York State)

The filing must be made at least 20 days prior to the date of transfer. If the Department of Taxation and Finance determines that tax is due on the transaction, a tentative assessment will be issued by the department within 20 days of receipt of the questionnaires and supporting documentation. This tax usually must be paid before the closing can take place; however, installment payments may be permitted where the tax due exceeds 50% of the cash consideration received on or before the date of the transfer and exceeds $10,000.

Real Estate Transfer Taxes

For every conveyance of real estate, New York State also imposes a separate real estate transfer tax of $2 for each $500 of consideration over $500. The concept of conveyance is very broad. It includes actual transfers by deed as well as all other conveyances of economic interests in real property. For example, the transfer or acquisition of a controlling interest (50% or more) in any entity which owns real property or an interest therein is covered by this tax. In addition, the transfer of residential property is also subject to tax.

There is an additional transfer tax imposed on each conveyance of residential real property, or interest therein, when the consideration is $1 million or more. The rate of tax is 1%, and it applies to both condominium and cooperative units. This tax is a true transfer tax since the concept of economic gain is not relevant: the tax is imposed if the consideration equals or exceeds $1 million irrespective of whether any gain was realized.

Form TP-584 is used to report the real estate transfer tax. This is a joint return which must be signed by both the transferor and transferee. For transfers that are recorded, the form is filed with the county clerk, otherwise, the form is filed with the New York State Department of Taxation and Finance.

Gasoline and Special Fuels Taxes

The state imposes an excise tax on all motor fuel sold by a distributor within the state and on the retail sale and use of diesel motor fuel from bulk storage for the operation of a motor vehicle within the state. The tax rate is either $0.0805 (8 1/20 cents) per gallon of motor fuel sold and $0.10 (10 cents) per gallon for diesel motor fuel. Every distributor must generally file a return on a prescribed form stating the number of gallons of fuel sold in the state during the preceding calendar month.

Quarterly or annual returns may be used for certain diesel motor fuel distributors. Returns may be filed with the office below.

New York State Department of Taxation and Finance
P.O. Box 1833
Albany, NY 12201-1833
(518) 438-1073
(800) 225-5829 (in New York State)

Cigarette and Tobacco Products Taxes

New York State imposes a stamp tax for all cigarettes held for sale in the state. The tax is assessed only once on the same package of cigarettes. On June 1, 1990, the New York legislature voted to increase the state cigarette tax from $0.33 (33 cents) to $0.39 (39 cents) per pack of 20 cigarettes.

Every agent licensed by the Commission of Taxation and Finance is required to file a return on the 15th day of each month that shows the number of unstamped cigarettes and stamps handled during the month; however, additional records indicating purchase, sale, or any other disposition of cigarettes handled are required from dealers, vending machine owners, and cigarette transporters. These required records must be maintained and made available for inspection by the tax commission for at least three years. All agents must file returns with the Transaction Transfer Taxation Bureau.

Transaction Transfer Taxation Bureau
New York State Department of Taxation and Finance
W. A. Harriman Campus
Albany, NY 12227
(518) 438-8581

A separate tax on tobacco products, other than cigarettes, is also imposed. This tax equals 15% of the products' wholesale price. Every distributor — a person who imports or manufactures any tobacco product, and who is authorized by the department to make returns and pay the tax on his or her sales in the state — is usually required to file a return and remit tax by the 20th day of the subsequent month. Other filing periods can be required.

Beginning January 1, 1991, every retail dealer and vending machine owner–operator, must register with the department. Registration covers the calendar year. The registration fee is $100 for each place of business and $25 for each vending machine.

Mortgage Recording Tax

This tax is imposed for the privilege of recording a mortgage on real property situated within the state. In most instances, the tax is 1% on the principal debt or obligation secured by the mortgage. The tax is generally due when the mortgage is recorded.

Motor Vehicle Registration Tax

Fees for the registration of motor vehicles are imposed annually and generally based on weight, as listed by the vehicle manufacturer. Rates begin at $1.08 for the first 3,500 lbs. and increase at a rate of $1.68 for each additional 100 lbs. All registration fees are paid to the commissioner of motor vehicles or his or her agent. Registration fees for omnibuses are based on seating capacity and start at $52. Under a tax proration and reciprocity agreement, registration fees for buses operating in New York and other contracting states may be apportioned on the basis of miles traveled within New York and other states.

The clerk of each county, except the counties of Albany, Westchester, Suffolk, Onondaga, Bronx, Kings, Queens, Richmond, and New York are designated as agents of the commissioner.

In addition to the registration tax, every owner of a vehicle in New York State must obtain a certificate of title; title fees range from $2.50 and up.

Highway Use Taxes

The state of New York imposes a highway use tax for the privilege of operating certain commercial motor vehicles on the public highways of the state. A carrier can choose between the gross weight method and unloaded weight method. Under the gross weight method, the tax is based upon the gross weight of each motor vehicle and the miles it operated on the public highways of the state. The tax is computed by multiplying the number of miles operated within the state by the appropriate weight group tax rate. For example, a vehicle weighing 21,000 lbs. and having traveled 10,000 miles would be assessed $70 in highway use tax. New York State does not tax vehicles weighing less than 18,000 lbs. under this method.

The carrier may elect to use the unloaded weight method in lieu of the gross weight method. The tax would be computed by multiplying the number of miles operated within the state by the appropriate weight group tax rate. For example, a truck weighing 18,000 lbs. and having traveled 20,000 miles would be assessed $280 in highway use tax. Note that trucks weighing less than 8,000 lbs. and tractors weighing less than 4,000 lbs. are exempt under the unloaded weight method.

The election to use the unloaded weight method must be made only on the first return filed during the calendar year and applies to all vehicles included in the return.

A supplemental tax is also imposed. Basically, the supplemental tax equals the taxpayer's highway use tax computed under the chosen method; however, excluded from the base is mileage on a thruway for which the thruway authority has made a charge.

An additional highway use tax is based on the amount of motor fuel and diesel fuel used in the state. This fuel use tax is computed by multiplying the net amount of motor fuel and diesel motor fuel used by a carrier in the state by the composite rates applicable for motor fuel and diesel motor fuels. This composite rate is based on the prevailing price of fuel established by the tax commission each calendar quarter unless the carrier elects the exact computation method to establish the average price for fuel purchased.

Highway use tax returns, *Form MT-903*, are filed and paid on the last day of each month following that month's highway use activity. Every carrier subject to fuel use tax must file quarterly returns reporting operations for the previous calendar quarter activity. Carriers with an average monthly highway use tax of $100 or less, and carriers filing fuel use tax returns, file on a quarterly basis; the returns are due January 31, April 30, July 31, and October 31. Returns for both highway use tax and fuel use tax must be submitted to:

State Tax Commission
P.O. Box 1913
Albany, NY 12201-1913

Hotel Occupancy Tax

New York State imposes a 5% occupancy tax on hotel occupancy where the daily room rate is $100 or more. The $100 amount is computed without taking into account any separately stated charges, such as meals, room service, telephone charges, etc.

New York City Excise Taxes

New York City excise tax rates are listed below. Questions pertaining to the items below can be directed to:

Taxpayer Assistance and City Collector's Office
(718) 935-6000

Beer and Liquor Excise Tax

In addition to New York State, New York City taxes distributors and non-commercial importers of beer and liquor for sale, or use within New York City at the rate of $0.12 (12 cents) per gallon on beer and $0.264 (26.4 cents) per liter on liquor. Since the beer and liquor excise taxes are administered by New York State, further information may be obtained from the State Tax Commission.

State Tax Commission
W. A. Harriman Campus
Albany, NY 12227
(518) 438-1073
(800) 225-5829 (in New York State)

Retail Alcoholic Beverage License Tax

New York City levies a tax for the privilege of selling liquor, wine, or beer at the retail level within the city. Any licensed business which sells liquor, wine, or beer at the retail level within the city is subject to the tax. The rate of tax is equal to 25% of the license fees imposed on retailers under the State Alcoholic Beverage Control Law. See Section 11.7.

For licenses issued on or before June 1 of the tax year, a return is due on or before June 25 of each year. For licenses issued after June 1 of the tax year, a return is due on or before 25th day of the month following the month in which the license was issued. All returns must be filed with the New York City Department of Finance.

New York City Department of Finance
25 Elm Place, 3rd Floor
Brooklyn, NY 11201
(718) 935-6000

Real Property Transfer Tax

This tax is imposed on each deed at the time of its delivery by a seller to a purchaser and when the consideration for the real property and any improvement exceeds $25,000. Although the seller is liable for the tax, the purchaser may be liable if the seller is exempt or fails to pay the tax.

The tax rate is assessed at 1% of the consideration with respect to a conveyance of a one, two, or three family house, or an individual residential co-op or condominium unit, where the consideration does not exceed $500,000.

The rate of tax on transactions where the consideration exceeds $25,000 was recently increased to:

- 1.425% of the consideration for conveyances — including leaseholds but excluding residential property — where the consideration is less than $500,000.
- 2.625% of the consideration for conveyances — including leaseholds but excluding residential property — where the consideration is $500,000 or greater.
- 1.425% of the consideration for residential conveyances — including residential leaseholds — where consideration is more than $500,000.

Certain types of persons, deeds, and conveyances are exempt. Further, the reach of this tax extends to transfers of controlling economic interests in real estate. For example, the transfer or acquisition of a 50% or more interest in the stock of a corporation that owns or leases real property in New York City would trigger tax.

A notarized return, signed by both the grantor and grantee, must be filed within 30 days after delivery of the deed, whether or not a tax is due. When a conveyance is not recorded, the return should be sent to New York City Department of Finance.

Real Property Transfer Tax Group
New York City Department of Finance
25 Elm Place, 3rd Floor
Brooklyn, NY 11201
(718) 935-6000

New York City also imposes a tax for the privilege of recording a mortgage on real property situated within the city. The tax rate varies depending on the type of property and amount of debt. For example, on nonresidential property where the debt equals or exceeds $500,000, the tax is 1.25% on the principal debt or obligation secured by the mortgage. Generally, the tax is due when the mortgage is recorded.

Mortgage Recording Tax

New York City imposes a tax at the rate of $0.01 (one cent) per gallon on the sale in New York City of motor fuel containing lead, which is payable by the distributor of the fuel. Because leaded motor fuel tax is administered by New York State, additional information may be obtained from New York State Tax Commission.

Leaded Motor Fuel Tax

This tax is payable on all cigarettes held for sale or used in New York City and is imposed only once on the same package of cigarettes by using a stamp. The cigarette tax is generally advanced and paid by an agent or distributor and collected from the purchaser. The tax is imposed at the rate of $0.04 (4 cents) for each 10 cigarettes or fraction thereof. Agents are required to file reports on or before the 15th day of each month with the Department of Finance

Cigarette Tax

Cigarette Tax Unit
New York City Department of Finance
345 Adams Street, 5th Floor
Brooklyn, NY 11201
(718) 403-4000

In addition to the cigarette tax, every wholesale and retail dealer must annually apply to the commissioner of finance for a license for each place of business.

See discussion in Section 11.4.

Commercial Rent Tax

New York City also levies additional taxes, such as:

Miscellaneous Taxes

- Coin-Operated Amusement Devices Tax
- Commercial Motor Vehicle Tax
- Foreign and Alien Insurers Tax
- Horse Race Admissions Tax
- Hotel Room Occupancy Tax
- Passenger Motor Vehicle Tax
- Taxicab License Transfer Tax
- Utility Tax
- Vault charges

Taxpayer Assistance
New York City Department of Finance
25 Elm Place, 3rd Floor
Brooklyn, NY 11201
(718) 935-6000

For Further Information

11.8 Planning For Tax Savings in a Business — State Tax Laws

In most states, tax planning is important in order to increase the business' cash flow by either deferring or eliminating taxable income. This is particularly true in New York State. Not only does New York State have far reaching tax statutes, but the combination of state and city rates are quite high. As noted previously, a corporation solely operating in New York City would be subject to a combined New York State tax rate on its income of 19.674% (for calendar year 1990). This is quite considerable even though these taxes will be deductible on the business' tax return for federal purposes.

On the state level, the major tax benefits will be derived by paying close attention to the various mechanics involved in calculating the apportionment percentage of your total business income to New York State.

Frequently, mistakes are made by including items which should not be considered and vice versa. Careful scrutiny of these calculations should better assist you in lessening the New York State tax burden.

Since both New York State and City generally follow the federal income tax system, most of the tax-saving ideas applicable at the federal level will produce beneficial results in New York.

Dividends Received Deduction

See discussion in Section 11.2 on the corporation dividends received deduction.

Office Outside New York City

Since a major savings may be derived by the ability to allocate income outside of New York City, it is advisable to consider whether the business economics and extra cost of establishing such office are not offset by the tax savings obtained.

Sheltering Profits on Export Sales

New York State has announced that it will treat Foreign Sales Corporations (FSCs) — discussed in Chapter 8 — basically the same as such corporations are treated at the federal level. Thus, establishing an FSC may be beneficial.

Since most of the FSC's sales will be for delivery outside New York State, this company should have a very low New York State sales allocation percentage. As such, the income allocated to New York State should be substantially reduced.

Investment Tax Credit

For tax years beginning in 1990, New York State offers an investment tax credit rate of 5% on the cost of qualifying tangible real or personal property on the first $425 million of investment tax credit base and 4% on amounts greater than $425 million. For tax years beginning after 1990, while the rate remains the same, the 5% investment tax credit rate applies to the first $350 million of the investment credit base and 4% on amounts greater than $350 million.

New York State also offers, at the option of the taxpayer, an investment tax credit of 9%, rather than the restricted rates prescribed above, on the cost of qualified research and development property. The qualified property must have a useful life of at least four years and be used for the purpose of research and development in an "experimental or laboratory sense." Examples of nonqualifying property would be equipment used in the testing and inspection of products for quality control, efficiency surveys, advertising, promotion, management-type studies, and other projects not directly related to research and development.

The investment tax credit base is defined as properties with a useful life of four years or more which are primarily used in manufacturing, processing, agriculture, assembly, refining, mining, research and development, and certain other activities. The credit is designed to provide incentives for the construction, purchase, or improvement of a qualified facility located and used by the taxpayer in New York. It is generally not available to service companies.

The credit is available to corporations as well as to individuals (through sole proprietorship or partnership activities) to reduce their tax liability to the state. Any unused credit may generally be carried forward for seven taxable years; however, tax credits acquired in tax years before 1987 may be carried up to 1994. It should be noted that the credit may not reduce a taxpayer's liability below the greater of the tax due on minimum taxable income base or the fixed dollar minimum tax.

A new business may elect to receive as a tax refund any unused portion of the investment tax credit earned. A new business includes any corporation other than the following:

- A corporation owned 50% or more by another New York corporation subject to New York State tax;
- A corporation which is essentially the same or similar in ownership and operation as other entities taxable or previously taxable in New York State;
- A corporation that has been subject to the New York State business corporation franchise tax for more than the previous four years.

Remember, upon a merger or acquisition, a target corporation might lose its credit carryover or be required to recapture the credits previously claimed.

New York State offers investment tax credit on the costs incurred to rehabilitate qualified real estate for use in retailing establishments. To qualify, the property must be eligible for the investment tax credit allowed under Internal Revenue Code Section 48(a)(1)(E). The taxpayer must also be a New York State vendor registered under the New York State sales and use tax laws, primarily engaged in consumer sales of tangible personal property. The rates and limitations are the same as those prescribed for investment tax credit. A merger or acquisition also limits the availability of this tax credit.

Employment Incentive Credit

New York State offers an additional employment incentive tax credit. For tax years beginning in 1990, if the average number of employees during the taxable year is less than 101.5% of the average number of employees in the base year, the additional Employment Incentive Credit (EIC) will be 2%. On the other hand, if the average number of employees in the taxable year is at least 101.5% of the average number of employees in the base year, the EIC will be 2.5% of the appropriate investment credit base. The term "base year" means the taxable year immediately preceding the year of the investment.

For tax years beginning after 1990, the following rules apply:

- If the average number of employees during the taxable year is less than 102% of the average number of employees in the base year, the EIC would be 1.5% of the applicable investment credit base.
- If the average number of employees during the taxable year is at least 102%, but less than 103% of the average number of employees in the base year, the EIC will be 2% of the applicable investment credit base.
- If the average number of employees during the taxable year is at least 103% of the average number of employees in the base year, the EIC will be 2.5% of the applicable investment credit rate.

It should be noted that if the optional rate applicable to research and development property is elected for investment tax credit purposes, then to the extent that such credit is claimed, no credit shall be allowed as Employment Investment Credit.

Furthermore, EIC may not reduce taxpayer's liability below the greater of the tax due on minimum taxable income base or the fixed-dollar minimum tax. Unused EIC may be carried forward in the same manner as unused investment tax credit.

At the local level, New York City offers a maximum tax credit — $500 for each industrial job and $300 for each commercial job — to any company that relocates to New York City from outside the state and creates 10 new jobs as a result. The credits are based on the actual relocation costs incurred and must be applied for and approved prior to any expenditure.

Further, any employer who relocates to New York City from outside the state and creates at least 100 jobs is also eligible for a general corporation tax credit calculated in the amount of the increased real estate taxes to be paid by the employer according to a written lease. The credits may be taken for either the term of the lease or 10 years, whichever is shorter. Approval of these credits must be obtained from the New York City Industrial and Commercial Incentive Board prior to the execution of the lease.

Remember, upon a merger or acquisition, a target corporation might lose its credit carryover or be required to recapture the credits it previously claimed.

Under New York State law, a spouse and certain minor children, who are hired as employees of a sole proprietorship, are exempt from New York State unemployment taxes and are not requested to pay disability benefits on their wages.

Hiring a Spouse as an Employee

11.9 Miscellaneous Business Pointers

New York follows the federal provisions contained in Section 1244 of the U.S. Internal Revenue Code, allowing ordinary loss deductions on stock of qualifying "small business corporations."

Section 1244 Stock

New York State and City administers a wide variety of economic development programs aimed at providing a stronger business climate for business location and expansion within New York. Some of the programs are run through the combined efforts and funding of the public and private business sectors. Information on available programs is discussed below.

Business Loan and Grant Programs

New York Business Development Corporation (NYBDC) — The NYBDC is a privately-owned company funded through a pool of money from New York financial institutions. It provides loans to businesses having difficulty securing financing. Loans range from $100,000 to $1 million at either a fixed interest rate or a floating interest rate up to 2.25% over the prime rate with terms of 5 to 15 years. Borrowers may use NYBDC loans for working capital, real estate acquisition, leasehold improvements, machinery and equipment, moving, debt restructuring, leveraged buyouts, sale leasebacks, leasing, purchase of a company, energy conversion, and pollution control.

Empire State Certified Development Corporation (ESCDC) — The ESCDC is a statewide nonprofit corporation licensed by the U.S. Small Business Administration and managed by the NYBDC. It processes federally-funded second mortgage loans for small businesses unable to obtain commercial loans for real property and equipment.

ESCDC loans are limited to 40% of the project's cost and cannot exceed $750,000. Financing is generally at a fixed rate below the prime rate for a term of 10 to 20 years, dependent on use of funds. For more information on NYBDC or ESCDC, contact:

New York Business Development Corporation
P.O. Box 738
Albany, NY 12201-0738
(518) 463-2268

New York Science and Technology Foundation, Corporation for Innovative Development (CID) — CID provides high-risk, start-up capital with flexible repayment structures designed to encourage the development of innovative technology-based ventures. Its assistance is targeted to supplement the needs of new business ventures.

Investments generally range from $50,000 to $150,000, which may be in the form of debt financing, equity financing, or a combination of the two. If you have further questions regarding CID, contact:

Corporation for Innovation Development Programs
New York State Science and Technology Foundation
99 Washington Avenue, Suite 1730
Albany, NY 12210
(518) 473-9741

New York Job Development Authority (JDA) — Through local nonprofit development corporations (LDCs), the JDA provides low-cost, fixed-rate second mortgage loans of up to 40% of project costs for industrial and certain commercial development projects. Nearly all businesses are eligible for assistance with the exception of retail establishments, hotels, and apartments.

The JDA also administers a Loan Guarantee Program which provides guarantees of up to 80% of project cost for loans made by banking organizations.

Bonding Assistance Program (BAP) — BAP is under the management of JDA. It assists small and minority contractors in securing payment and performance bonds on construction contracts of not more than $1 million with state agencies.

JDA Rural Development Loan Fund (RDLF) — The RDLF is designed to meet the special needs of small businesses located in the rural areas of New York State. Loans are generally made for up to 20% of the total project cost and usually range from $20,000 to $50,000. Interest rates are set at 3% below the prime rate at the time of the loan's closing, with a floor of 5% and a ceiling of 10%. For more information on New York JDA programs, contact the following two offices or use the preaddressed post card located at the back of this book.

New York Job Development Authority
605 Third Avenue, 26th Floor
New York, NY 10158
(212) 818-1700

New York Job Development Authority
1 Commerce Plaza, Room 1103
Albany, NY 12210
(518) 474-7580

New York State Urban Development Corporation (UDC) — The UDC manages a variety of programs aimed at supporting business expansion into both developed and underdeveloped urban areas.

Programs managed by UDC include the Small- and Medium-Sized Business Assistance (SAMBA) Program, Targeted Investment Program (TIP), the Regional Economic Development Partnership Program (REDPP), the Commercial Revitalization Program, and the Minority and

Women Revolving Loan Fund. These programs are designed to assist small and minority businesses as well as public and private developers to develop and expand into urban areas.

For additional information concerning the New York State Urban Development Corporation and its many programs, contact:

New York State Urban Development Corporation
1515 Broadway
New York, NY 10036-8960
(212) 930-9000

Office for Economic Development (OED) — The State of New York offers a wide range of business assistance, which include both commercial and industrial development programs, through the divisions within the OED.

For more information on the services offered by the OED, as well as information on additional OED offices within the five boroughs of New York State, write or call:

New York State Office for Economic Development
52 Chambers Street
New York, NY 10007
(212) 827-6100
(516) 334-2500
(800) STATE NY (in New York State)

New York City's Office of Business Development (OBD) — This office is the central source of assistance and information on the various city loan and grant programs. A selection of the incentives offered are discussed below.

- Low-Cost Financing — The city can provide low-cost subordinated loans through its Revolving Loan Fund. In addition, tax-exempt industrial bonds are available for both certain real property improvements or purchases of buildings, facilities, or equipment. Further information can be obtained by contacting:

Financial Services Corporation
110 Williams Street
New York, NY 10038
(212) 341-5900

- Relocation Employment Assistance Program — This program grants a 12-year, $500-per-employee credit on city business taxes to firms relocating from Manhattan south of 96th Street or from outside of the city, to Manhattan north of 96th Street or to any of the other boroughs. To be eligible, companies must relocate to new space receiving real estate tax abatements or space that has been improved by an investment of at least 50% of assessed value. Such eligible companies will also receive a 12-year exemption from the city's commercial rent tax.

- Human Resources Development Program — This program can show you how to take advantage of the various financial incentives offered when hiring eligible employees through the use of: 1) subsidized training programs that instruct new employees or upgrade the skills of current employees; 2) on-the-job training funds that reduce salary costs by up to 50% for 26 weeks; and 3) targeted job tax credits that pay up to $2,400 of the first $6,000 paid to an eligible employee in the first year of employment.

- Industrial Commercial Incentive Program (ICIP) — New York City's ICIP program provides tax incentives for businesses that wish to construct, rehabilitate, or expand their facilities. ICIP offers exemptions on the increase in real estate taxes from the construction or rehabilitation of industrial and commercial properties for up to 22 years.

Manufacturing facilities anywhere in the city are eligible for the full 22 years. Commercial facilities above 96th Street in Manhattan, and in the other four boroughs, are eligible for exemptions of 12 or 22 years, depending upon their exact location. In certain areas of Manhattan's central business district, commercial facilities can receive a seven-year tax deferral.

Owners of commercial and industrial property, who construct new buildings or improve existing buildings with an expenditure of at least 20% of their current assessed values, may qualify for the ICIP program, providing they apply before receiving their initial building permit.

- Energy Tax Credits/Cost Savings — Manufacturing companies qualify for an exemption of the 4.25% state sales tax on electricity, gas, and steam used directly in production or research and development. Such companies can also receive a refund on the state sales tax they pay on energy used in manufacturing over the past three years.

In addition, manufacturing companies qualify for a 4% tax credit or refund from the city's sales tax on electricity used directly in manufacturing. A refund for all such taxes paid since July 1, 1984 is also available. For more information, contact:

Office of Business Development
17 John Street, 14th Floor
New York, NY 10038
(212) 696-2442

- New York City Industrial Development Agency (IDA) — The IDA promotes and develops industry and commerce by administering a tax-exempt, low-interest, Industrial Revenue Bond program and by granting real property tax abatements and exemptions. Businesses eligible to participate in the IDA programs are industrial and manufacturing enterprises, warehousing, commercial and research facilities.

Project financing through IDA bonds is based on the company's financial position and the real estate involved. IDA bonds are generally placed with the lender, and title to the property is transferred to the

IDA which then eases the project back to the company for the term of the financing arrangement. At the end of the lease term, the "occupant" usually purchases the property back for $1. During the term of the lease, the project "occupant" is treated as the beneficial owner for both accounting and income tax purposes. For more information about the granting of real property tax abatements, contact:

New York City Industrial Development Agency
110 Williams Street, 3rd Floor
New York, NY 10038
(212) 341-5900

Usury Laws

Usury is the charging of an interest rate by a creditor in excess of the maximum legal interest rate as set annually by the New York State Banking Board. The current rate is 16% per year.[45] In many situations, banks, and other financial institutions are not subject to the 16% interest rate ceiling.

If a contract — other than a bank contract — is found to be usurious, it will be declared void and the creditor forfeits both the interest and principal due under the obligation. Banks will only forfeit the interest due unless the usurious interest on the obligation has been paid to the bank, in which case, the bank is then liable to the debtor for an amount equal to double the interest paid.[46] Inquiries regarding potential usurious transactions with such lenders should be directed to New York State Banking Department.

Consumer Services Division
New York State Banking Department
2 Rector Street, 18th Floor
New York, NY 10006
(212) 618-6220

11.10 State Sources of Help and Information

Do-It-Yourself Incorporation

Nolo Press offers an excellent publication on how to set up your own corporation. Entitled *How to Form Your Own New York Corporation*, it is written by Anthony Mancuso and Lewis R. Rosenbluth. Several other publications can provide insight into the process and should enable you to keep the legal fees involved in incorporating your business, if any, down to a minimum.

State Agency Assistance

New York State Department of Taxation and Finance — This department's Taxpayer Assistance Bureau has several hotline phone numbers that can assist you in answering business questions about taxes and tax forms. For general business tax information, call:

Taxpayer Assistance Bureau
New York State Taxation and Finance Department
W.A. Harriman Campus
Albany, NY 12227
(718) 935-6000 (in New York City)
(518) 438-8581 (outside New York State)
(800) 225-5829 (in New York State)

For ordering forms and publications, call the bureau at:

(718) 935-6739 (in New York City)
(518) 438-1073 (outside New York State)
(800) 462-8100 (in New York State)

In addition, both New York State and City jurisdictions of this department publish an equivalent of *Federal Package X*. New York State's equivalent is called *Publication 352* and can be obtained from the Forms Control Section of the Taxpayer Assistance Bureau at the address above. The New York City equivalent is entitled, *Booklet X*, and can be obtained from:

Bureau of Tax Operations
New York City Department of Finance
P.O. Box 029156
G.P.O. Brooklyn
Brooklyn, NY 11202
(718) 935-6000

New York State Department of Economic Development — This department offers one-stop shopping at its regional offices. Information on nearly all business-oriented programs (whether local, state, or federal) is available. Call (212) 827-6180; (516) 349-1266; or (800) STATE NY. This agency also prepares technical and statistical industrial development proposals for companies interested in relocating or expanding in New York State. This agency serves as a reference source on materials, plant locations, available buildings, mineral and agricultural resources, and water and utilities sources.

The International Division of this department encourages and assists foreign firms looking for branch offices or plant locations in New York State, as well as for other pertinent information, such as:

- Information on specific opportunities for overseas sales;
- Assistance in cutting through red tape;
- Technical assistance to state producers or suppliers interested in entering the international commerce field; and
- Identification of public and private funding sources.

The International Division maintains offices in New York City, Albany, Tokyo, London, Frankfurt, Montreal, Toronto, and Hong Kong. Additional inquiries about these programs may be directed to either one of these two offices:

Deputy Commissioner
New York State Department of Economic Development
1 Commerce Plaza
Albany, NY 12245
(518) 474-1431

Deputy Commissioner
International Division
New York State Department of Economic Development
1515 Broadway Avenue, 51st Floor
New York, NY 10036
(212) 827-6210

New York City Office of Business Development — The New York City Office of Business Development (OBD) provides a number of services to businesspeople, including expediting municipal services, providing business expertise, and referring questions, when necessary, to the appropriate city or state agency.

This office will help you find space, lower energy costs, access agreement funds to finance moving expenses, find and train new employees, and integrate security.

New York City Agency Assistance

New York City Office of Business Development
17 John Street, 14th Floor
New York, NY 10038
(212) 696-2442

Business Action Center — This business center provides assistance on how to eliminate red tape. It also provides information on city, state, and federal programs including regulatory requirements. In addition, it makes appropriate referrals. Contact the Office of Business Development for more information.

Executive Volunteer Corps — If you are starting a business, or need help in your present business, New York City has a group of experts ready to assist you: the Executive Volunteer Corps (EVC). The Executive Volunteer Corps is staffed by successful, retired businesspeople who have a wide range of management experience. They offer free advice and counseling on such matters as business planning (financial projections, cash flow, inventory control), sales and marketing (advertising, promotion, market analysis), and administrative issues (operating budgets, staff, recordkeeping).

All personal interviews are conducted at the Office of Business Development at the address shown above. Interviews are conducted from 10:00 A.M. to 4:00 P.M., Monday through Friday. No appointment is necessary, but it is advisable to call ahead to ensure an appointment with a counselor experienced in your area of interest. Phone interviews are also available.

Mayor's Office of Film, Theater, and Broadcasting — Staffed by industry specialists, this office provides fast and timely service to the entertainment industry. It works with both industry groups and individual producers to ease the process of obtaining special permits and other municipal services.

Assistance is provided to motion picture, television, radio, theater, photography, and video technology industries, including cable, pay television, and video disks. For information, write or call:

Mayor's Office of Film, Theater, and Broadcasting
254 West 54th Street, 13th Floor
New York, NY 10019
(212) 489-6714

New York City Convention & Visitors Bureau — New York City generates in excess of $9.7 billion each year from the tourism trade. There are estimates that more than 19.8 million people (including 4.5 million foreigners) visit New York City for its shops and department stores, sightseeing attractions, opera and ballet companies, museums and theaters, sports facilities, restaurants, parks, and beaches.

New York City Convention & Visitors Bureau is a private, membership-sponsored nonprofit organization serving as a marketing and promotional tool for the city's tourism and convention industry. It's the only service of its kind in the city and is recognized as the most successful tourism office in the world. The bureau works closely with travel agents, tour packagers, airlines, convention managers, trade associations, and journalists.

The bureau also has the following publications available to the public at no cost: *Calendar of Events*, *Visitor's Guide*, maps, hotel, shopping, and restaurant guides, and *Tour Package Directory*.

Businesses that are more likely to benefit most from New York City tourism should inquire about membership. For more information, contact:

New York City Convention and Visitors Bureau
2 Columbus Circle
New York, NY 10019
(212) 397-8200

State Business Journals

State business journals are a valuable source of news and information regarding the business climate in New York State. For your convenience, state business journals are listed below.

Business First: Newspaper
472 Delaware Avenue
Buffalo, NY 14202
(716) 882-6200

Business New York
152 Washington Avenue
Albany, NY 12210-2203
(518) 465-7511

Capital District Business
4 Central Avenue, 3rd Floor
Albany, NY 12206
(518) 432-1091

Central New York Business
4317 E. Genesee Street, #201
De Witt, NY 13214-2114
(315) 446-3510

Crain's New York Business
220 E. 42nd Street
New York, NY 10017-5806
(212) 210-0100

LI Business News
2150 Smithtown Avenue
Ronkonkoma, NY 11779-7348
(516) 737-1700

Long Island
80 Hauppauge Road
Long Island, NY 11725
(516) 499-4400

Manhatten, Inc.
420 Lexington Avenue
New York, NY 10170-0001
(212) 697-2100

Northeast International Business
401 Theodore Fremd Avenue
Rye, NY 10580-1422
(914) 921-1400

Orange County Business Journal
P.O. Box 339
Pine Island, NY 10969-0339
(914) 258-4008

Rochester Business Magazine
Rochester Business Journal
1600 Lyell Avenue
Rochester, NY 14606-2324
(716) 458-8280

Rockland County Business Journal
One Executive Boulevard, #205
Suffern, NY 10901
(914) 368-3696

Syracuse Business
208 N. Townsend¬ Street
Syracuse, NY 13203-2339
(315) 472-6911

Western New York
107 Delaware Avenue
Buffalo, NY 14202-2810
(716) 852-7100

Small Business Development Centers

The Small Business Development Centers (SBDCs) provide management and technical assistance to start-up and existing small business firms. They find private and government resources that will counsel and train small businesses in resolving organizational, financial, marketing, technical, and other problems small businesses might encounter.

SBDCs also offer programs such as business-plan development, small business start ups, organizational structures, accounting, financial planning, export assistance, cost analysis, loan information assistance, marketing, and training programs. These programs have a special emphasis on women, veterans, handicapped, and minority entrepreneurs. For the SBDC office nearest you, please review the list provided below.

SBDC: New York State
State University of New York
State University Plaza, South 523
Albany, NY 12246
(518) 443-5398
(800) 732-SDBC (in New York State)

SBDC: Corning Community College
24-28 Denison Parkway West
Corning, NY 14830
(607) 962-9461

SBDC: Greater Syracuse Incubator Center
1201 East Fayette Street, Room 10
Syracuse, NY 13210
(315) 475-0083

SBDC: Jamestown Community College
P.O. Box 20
Jamestown, NY 14702-0020
(716) 665-5220

SBDCs (continued)

SBDC: Jefferson Community College
Outer Coffees Street
Watertown, NY 13601
(315) 782-9262

SBDC: Monroe Community College
1000 East Henrietta Road
Rochester, NY 14623
(716) 424-5200, ext. 3030

SBDC: Niagara County Community College
c/o Technical Assistance Center
3111 Saunders Settlement Road
Sanborn, NY 14132
(716) 693-1910

SBDC: State University College at Albany
Draper Hall, Room 107
135 Western Avenue
Albany, NY 12222
(518) 442- 5577

SBDC: State University College at Binghamton
Vestal Parkway East
Binghamton, NY 13901
(607) 777-4024

SBDC: State University College at Buffalo
1300 Elmwood Avenue, BA 117
Buffalo, NY 14222
(716) 878-4030

SBDC: State University College at Plattsburgh
c/o Technical Assistance Center
Plattsburgh, NY 12901
(518) 792-1113

SBDC: State University College of Technology Utica/Rome
P.O. Box 3050
Utica, NY 13504-3050
(315) 792-7546

SBDC: Long Island University
Humanities Building, 7th Floor
One University Plaza
Brooklyn, NY 11201
(718) 852-1197

SBDC: Manhatten College
Farrell Hall
Riverdale, NY 10471
(212) 884-1880

SBDC: Pace University
Pace Plaza, Room W480
New York, NY 10038
(212) 488-1899

SBDC: Rockland Community College
145 College Road
Suffern, NY 10901
(914) 356-0370

SBDC: State University of New York
Harriman Hall 306
Stony Brook, NY 11794-3775
(516) 632-9070

SBDC: State University College of Technology at Farmingdale
Laffin Administration Building, Room 007
Farmingdale, NY 11735
(516) 420-2765

SBDC: Ulster County Community College
Main Campus
Stone Ridge, NY 12484
(914) 687-5272

SBDC: York College
The City University of New York
Jamaica, NY 11451
(718) 262-2880

Footnotes

1. Office of the Department of Economic Development, Small Business Division.

2. Id.

3. State Government Tax Collections in 1988, U.S. Dept. of Commerce, Bureau of the Census.

4. 20 N.Y.C.R.R. §131.15(d)(1).

5. 20 N.Y.C.R.R. §131.15(d)(2)(i).

6. 20 N.Y.C.R.R. §131.15(d)(2)(ii).

7. 20 N.Y.C.R.R. §131.15(d)(2)(iii).

8. 20 N.Y.C.R.R. §131.15(e).

9. 20 N.Y.C.R.R. §131.15(f).

10. BUS. CORP. LAW §401 (McKinney).

11. N.Y. TAX LAW §180.1 (McKinney).

12. N.Y. TAX LAW §209-B (McKinney).

13. N.Y. TAX LAW §208.9(f) (McKinney).

14. N.Y. TAX LAW §6-103 (McKinney 1964).

15. N.Y. TAX LAW §6-104(1)(a),(2) (McKinney).

16. N.Y. TAX LAW §6-105 (McKinney).

17. N.Y. TAX LAW §6-107(1) (McKinney).

18. N.Y. TAX LAW §6-104(1)(c) (McKinney).

19. N.Y.U.C.C. §9-401(1)(a).

20. N.Y.U.C.C. §9-401(1)(b).

21. N.Y.U.C.C. §9-401(1)(c).

22. N.Y. TAX LAW §1141(c) (McKinney).

23. 20 N.Y.C.R.R. §525.2(b).

24. N.Y. TAX LAW §1147(b) (McKinney) and 20 N.Y.C.R.R. §535.3.

25. N.Y. TAX LAW §§1107 and 1109 (McKinney).

26. N.Y. TAX LAW §1134 (McKinney).

27. N.Y. GEN. BUS. LAW §130.1(ii)(a) (McKinney).

28. N.Y. GEN. BUS. LAW §130.4 (McKinney).

29. N.Y. GEN. BUS. LAW §130.a (McKinney).

30. N.Y. WORK. COMP. LAW §50 subd. 1–3 (McKinney).

31. N.Y. WORK. COMP. LAW §229 (McKinney).

32. N.Y. LAB. LAW §652 (McKinney).

33. N.Y. LAB. LAW §160 subd. 3 (McKinney).

34. N.Y. LAB. LAW §162 subd. 2 (McKinney).

35. N.Y. LAB. LAW §191 (McKinney).

36. N.Y. LAB. LAW §192 subd. 1 (McKinney).

37. N.Y. LAB. LAW §191 subd. 1d.3 (McKinney).

38. N.Y. LAB. LAW §161 subd. 1 (McKinney).

39. N.Y. LAB. LAW §178 subd. 1 (McKinney).

40. N.Y. EXEC. LAW §296 subd. 1(d) (McKinney).

41. N.Y. EXEC. LAW §296 subd. 1(e) (McKinney).

42. N.Y. EXEC. LAW §296 subd. 3(g) (McKinney).

43. N.Y. EXEC. LAW §296 subd. 1(g) (McKinney).

44. N.Y. EXEC LAW §295 (McKinney).

45. N.Y. BANKING LAW §14-a subd. 1 (McKinney).

46. N.Y. GEN OBLIG. LAW §5-5 11 subd. 1 (McKinney).

Notes

Index

Appendix

Checklist of Tax and Other Major Requirements for Nearly All Small Businesses

Requirement	None	1–4	5–10	11–14	15–19	20–99	100+	Chapter–Section Reference
Federal estimated taxes	√	√	√	√	√	√	√	Sec. 4.3, 11.4
Federal income tax returns	√	√	√	√	√	√	√	Sec. 4.12
Form SS-4, Application for Federal I.D. Number:								
Sole Proprietorships		√	√	√	√	√	√	Sec. 5.2
Partnerships	√	√	√	√	√	√	√	Sec. 5.2
Corporations	√	√	√	√	√	√	√	Sec. 5.2
Form 1099 returns	√	√	√	√	√	√	√	Sec. 4.7
Federal payroll tax returns		√	√	√	√	√	√	Sec. 5.2, 5.3
Provide and file W-2's to employees at year-end		√	√	√	√	√	√	Sec. 5.2
ERISA compliance:								
For unfunded or insured employees' welfare plan:								
Provide a Summary Plan Description to employees		√	√	√	√	√	√	Sec. 5.5
File a Summary Plan Description							√	Sec. 5.5
File *Form 5500, Annual Report*							√	Sec. 5.5
Provide a Summary Annual Report to employees							√	Sec. 5.5
File and provide to employees a Summary of Material Plan Modifications							√	Sec. 5.5
File a Terminal Report, if plan terminated							√	Sec. 5.5
For funded employee welfare plan:								
File and provide all items described in ERISA list		√	√	√	√	√	√	Sec. 5.5
For employees' pension or profit-sharing plan:								
Provide a Summary Plan Description to employees and file with U.S. Department of Labor		√	√	√	√	√	√	Sec. 5.5
File *Form 5500, Annual Report*							√	Sec. 5.5
File *Form 5500-C* or *Form 5500-R*		√	√	√	√	√	√	Sec. 5.5
Provide to employees and file a Summary of Material Modifications		√	√	√	√	√	√	Sec. 5.5
File a Terminal Report, if plan terminated		√	√	√	√	√	√	Sec. 5.5
Provide a Summary Annual Report to employees		√	√	√	√	√	√	Sec. 5.5
Bonding requirement for plan officials		√	√	√	√	√	√	Sec. 5.5
Federal Wage and Hour Laws and Regulations — coverage depends on nature of business and employee types not covered		√	√	√	√	√	√	Sec. 5.7
Federal Fair Employment Laws:								
Anti-discrimination laws regarding race, color, religion, sex, etc.					√	√	√	Sec. 5.8
Equal Pay Act for women		√	√	√	√	√	√	Sec. 5.8
Anti-discrimination laws regarding age						√	√	Sec. 5.8
Anti-discrimination laws regarding federal contracts		√	√	√	√	√	√	Sec. 5.8

Requirement	None	1-4	5-10	11-14	15-19	20-99	100+	Chapter-Section Reference
Federal Fair Employment Laws: (continued)								
File *Form EEO-1*							√	Sec. 5.8
Post notice regarding discrimination: racial, sexual, etc.					√	√	√	Sec. 5.8
Post notice regarding age anti-discrimination laws						√	√	Sec. 5.8
Post other anti-discrimination notices by certain federal contractors		√	√	√	√	√	√	Sec. 5.8
Immigration Laws:								
Complete *INS Form I-9* for each new hire		√	√	√	√	√	√	Sec. 5.9
OSHA Job Safety Regulations:								
Health and safety		√	√	√	√	√	√	Sec. 5.6
Post *Job Safety and Health Notice*		√	√	√	√	√	√	Sec. 5.6
Post *Employee Rights Notice* regarding OSHA		√	√	√	√	√	√	Sec. 5.6
Record industrial injuries and illnesses				√	√	√	√	Sec. 5.6
Report job fatalities or multiple injuries to OSHA		√	√	√	√	√	√	Sec. 5.6
Federal and State Child Labor Laws		√	√	√	√	√	√	Sec. 5.7, 11.5
Local business licenses	√	√	√	√	√	√	√	Sec. 4.3, 11.4, 11.6
Sales and use tax permit and returns, if selling tangible personal property	√	√	√	√	√	√	√	Sec. 11.4
Assumed name statement, if using fictitious business name	√	√	√	√	√	√	√	Sec. 11.4
State estimated taxes	√	√	√	√	√	√	√	Sec. 11.4
State income taxes	√	√	√	√	√	√	√	Sec. 11.2, 11.4
State Wage and Hour Laws and Regulations — most employees are covered, yet some types are not		√	√	√	√	√	√	Sec. 11.5
Workers' compensation insurance		√	√	√	√	√	√	Sec. 11.5
State Fair Employment Laws: General prohibition of discrimination		√	√	√	√	√	√	Sec. 11.5

Checklist of Official Government Posters and Notices Required to be Displayed by Businesses

Type of Poster or Notice	When required	Where to obtain
Local business license	Required to be obtained by nearly all businesses operating in a particular locality.	Local city hall or county courthouse
Sales tax permit	Required to be displayed at each place of business where tangible personal property is sold.	State tax office
OSHA poster regarding job safety and health	Required to be posted by all employers.	U.S. Department of Labor, Occupational Safety and Health Administration
OSHA poster regarding rights of employees	Required to be posted by all employers.	U.S. Department of Labor, Occupational Safety and Health Administration
U.S. Fair Labor Standards Act Wage and Hour poster, *Attention Employees,* (WH Publication 1088)	Required to be posted by employers with employees whose wages and working conditions are subject to the U.S. Fair Labor Standards Act.	U.S. Department of Labor, Employment Standards Administration, Wage and Hour Division offices
Federal Equal Employment Opportunity poster	Required to be posted by all employers with 15 or more employees 20 weeks of a calendar year or with federal contracts or subcontracts of $10,000 or more.	Federal Equal Employment Opportunity Commission offices
Federal Age Discrimination poster	Required to be posted by all employers with 20 or more employees, 20 or more weeks in a calendar year.	U.S. Department of Labor, Wage and Hour Division offices
Federal Rehabilitation Act poster regarding hiring of handicapped persons	Required to be posted by employers with federal contracts or subcontracts of $2,500 or more.	Assistant Secretary for Employment Standards, U.S. Department of Labor, Washington, D.C.
Poster regarding hiring of Vietnam-era veterans	Required to be posted by employers with federal contracts or subcontracts of $10,000 or more.	The government contracting officer on the federal contract

New York State and City General Tax Calendar for 1991

For your convenience, here is a year-round calendar of general tax payment and filing requirements — and their respective due dates — for both New York State and City. The calendar is divided into months with each month's requirements listed after the appropriate day action should be taken or payment is due. The number after some of the items refers to the Footnotes for 1991 Tax Calendar, which are located after the tax calendar. These footnotes provide more specific information for those returns and filings that have multiple due dates or need further explanation.

January 10 – New York State and City income tax withholding returns and payment where a quarter monthly return is due.[1]

16 – New York State and City income tax withholding returns and payment.[2]

16 – Final estimated tax installment on the prior year New York City general corporation income tax.[7]

16 – Final tax payment on the prior year of estimated New York State and City personal income tax.[10]

16 – Final tax payment on the prior year New York City estimated unincorporated business tax.[10]

16 – New York State and City income tax withholding returns and payments.[3]

20 – New York State monthly sales and use tax return and payment.[11]

31 – New York State and City semi-annual income tax withholding return and payment.[4]

31 – New York State and City annual income tax withholding return and payment.[5]

31 – New York property taxes generally come due.

31 – New York employer's report of wages paid for quarter ended December 31.

31 – Annual or quarterly unemployment contribution report for the quarter ended December 31.

February 15 – You are required to provide New York State personal income tax information and annual withholding returns to employees by now.

20 – New York State monthly sales and use tax return and payment.[11]

28 – New York State Employer's Reconciliation of Tax Withheld.

28 – You are required to file the annual employer's withholding return.[5]

March 15 – Corporate calendar year return and payment for New York state franchise (income) tax.[8]

15 – Corporate calendar year return and payment for New York City.[8]

20 – New York City commercial rent and occupancy tax return and payment for the quarter ended February 28.

20 – New York State sales and use tax return and payment for the quarter ended February 28.[11]

20 – New York State monthly sales and use tax return, estimate for March.[11]

April 15 – New York State and City personal income tax return.[9]

15 – New York City unincorporated business tax return.[9]

April 15 – Declaration and first tax payment on estimated New York State and City personal income tax.[10]

15 – Declaration and first tax payment on estimated New York City unincorporated business tax.[10]

15 – New York State and City Fiduciary Income Tax return.[9]

15 – New York State and New York City partnership information returns.[9]

15 – New York State Annual Gift Tax Return.

22 – New York State monthly sales and use tax return and payment.[11]

30 – New York employer's report of wages paid for the quarter ended March 31.

30 – Quarterly unemployment contribution tax report for the quarter ended March 31.

May 20 – New York State monthly sales and use tax return and payment due.[11]

June 17 – Tax payment on New York State and City estimated personal income tax.[10]

17 – Second tax payment on estimated New York City estimated unincorporated business tax.[10]

17 – New York State general corporation estimated tax declaration and payment.[6]

17 – New York City general corporation estimated tax declaration and payment.[7]

20 – New York City annual rent and occupancy tax return and payment.

20 – New York State sales and use tax returns and payments for the quarter ended May 31.[11]

20 – New York State monthly sales and use tax return and payment due.[11]

July 22 – New York State monthly sales and use tax return and payment.[11]

31 – New York State and City semi-annual income tax withholding return and payment.[4]

31 – New York employer's report of wages paid for the quarter ended June 30.

31 – New York unemployment contribution tax report for the quarter ended June 30.

August 20 – New York State monthly sales and use tax return and payment.[11]

September 16 – Tax payment on estimated New York State corporate franchise tax.[6]

16 – Tax payment on New York State and estimated personal income tax.[10]

16 – Tax payment on New York City estimated unincorporated business tax.[10]

20 – New York City commercial rent and occupancy tax return and payment for the quarter ended August 31.

20 – New York State sales and use tax return and payment for the quarter ended August 31.[11]

October 15 – Tax payment on estimated New York City general corporation income tax.[7]

22 – New York State monthly sales and use tax return and payment.[11]

31 – New York employer's report of wages paid for the quarter ended September 30.

31 – Quarterly unemployment contribution tax report for the quarter ended September 30.

November 20 – New York state monthly sales and use tax return and payment.[11]

December 16 – Final tax payment on New York State corporate franchise (income) tax.[6]

20 – New York City commercial rent and occupancy tax return and payment for the quarter ended November 30.

20 – New York State monthly sales and use tax return and payment due.[11]

20 – New York State sales and use tax return and payment for the quarter ended November 30.

Footnotes for 1991 Tax Calendar

1. Returns and tax payments are due by the 3rd banking day after the 7th, 15th, 22nd, and the last day of each month if the expected withholding is, or exceeds, $35,000 for each calendar six-month period ending June 30 and December 31. The December 31 return and tax payment is due January 31 for quarterly-monthly filers. Remittances must be made via electronic funds transfer.

2. Returns and tax payments are due by the 15th day of the following month if the expected withholding is between $800 and $7,499, for each six-month calendar period. The December 31 return and tax payment is due January 31 for monthly filers.

3. Returns and tax payments are due by the 3rd banking day after the 15th and last day of each month if the expected withholding is between $7,500 and $34,999 for each six-month calendar period. The December 31 return and tax payment is due January 31 for semi-monthly filers.

4. Returns and tax payments are due by January 31 and July 31 if the expected withholding is between $200 and $799 for each six-month calendar period.

5. Returns and tax payments are due by January 31 if the expected withholding is under $200 for each six-month calendar period.

6. Any fiscal year corporations file and pay estimated tax installments on the 15th day of the 6th, 9th, and 12th month of the fiscal year.

7. Fiscal year corporations file and pay estimated tax installments on the 15th day of the 6th, 10th, and 13th month following the close of the fiscal year.

8. Corporate tax returns are due 2 1/2 months after the close of the fiscal year.

9. Personal income tax, fiduciary income tax, and unincorporated business returns and payments are due on the 15th day of the 4th month following the close of the fiscal year.

10. Estimated tax installments for income tax are due on the 15th day of the 4th, 6th, and 9th month of the year, and the 13th month following the close of the fiscal year.

11. Returns and tax payments are due by the 20th of each month following the sale if taxable receipts, in any four preceding quarters, were $300,000 or more. Monthly filers are required to estimate for the month of March; see Section 11.4 – Sales and Use Tax. Businesses with taxable receipts under $300,000 in any four preceding quarters file quarterly returns on the 20th of the month following the end of the quarter. As an added note, quarters are not standard calendar quarters; see Section 11.4 – Sales and Use Tax for more information.

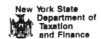

New York State
Department of
Taxation
and Finance

Publication 751 (10/88)

Sales and Use Tax Registration Information

If you sell tangible personal property, collect admissions or amusement charges, rent out hotel or motel rooms, or provide services, you must register with the New York State Department of Taxation and Finance and collect any New York State and local sales tax due on these transactions.

If you meet **any** of the following conditions you are required to be a registered vendor:

- You are required to collect sales tax.

- You buy or sell for resale (e.g., as a wholesale distributor).

- You want to issue exemption certificates (Resale Certificate, Exempt Use Certificate, etc.).

To register as a vendor you must complete the following forms:
DTF-17, *Certificate of Registration*
DTF-17.1, *Business Description*
DTF-17.3, *Certificate of Registration Affidavit*

If you operate from more than one business location, you must submit information for each additional location by completing Form DTF-17.2, *Schedule of Business Locations.*

Depending on how you choose to file your sales tax returns, you must submit the following information or forms:

- If you choose to file a consolidated return (one return for all locations), attach Form DTF-17.2 to Form DTF-17 along with DTF-17.1 and DTF-17.3.

- If you choose to file a separate return for each location, submit forms DTF-17, DTF-17.1 and DTF-17.3 for each location, and complete the attached Form DTF-17.2.

At least twenty days before the opening of your new business, send all required forms to:

NYS Tax Department
Sales Tax Registration Unit
W. A. Harriman Campus
Albany, N.Y. 12227-0155

After we receive your completed forms, we will send you a validated *Certificate of Authority*, authorizing you to collect the required state and local sales tax. However, the issuance of a Certificate of Authority is not automatic; the department may refuse to issue a certificate depending on your answers to the question on the *Certificate of Registration Affidavit* (DTF-17.3).

If you operate at more than one location, you will receive a separate *Certificate of Authority* for each location. The certificate must be prominently displayed at each place of business.

For more information, see Form ST-150, *General Instructions for State and Local Sales and Use Taxes in New York State.*

The Omnibus Tax Equity and Enforcement Act of 1985 provides, in part, that if you are required to register for sales tax purposes and fail to do so, or if you fail to properly display your validated *Certificate of Authority,* you will be subject to substantial penalties. You should also be aware that there is a minimum penalty of $50 for failure to file a required sales tax return, even if there is no tax due. For more information, see Publication 400.

Publications you may find helpful:

Publication 70
Record Keeping for Small Businesses

Publication 701
Sales and Use Tax Bracket Schedules for State and Local Sales Tax Purposes

Publication 717
New York State Communities

Publication 718
New York State and Local Sales Tax Rates by Community

Publication 752
Record Keeping for Sales Tax Vendors

Publication 765
Purchasing a Business —
Sales Tax Information for the Buyer

If you need additional help...

For forms or publications

Call toll free (from New York State only) 1 800 462-8100.

From areas outside New York State call (518) 438-1073.

For Information

Call toll free (from New York State only) 1 800 CALL TAX (1 800 225-5829).

From areas outside New York State call (518) 438-8581.

**Telephone assistance is available
from 8 a.m. to 5 p.m.
Monday through Friday.**

If you prefer to write, address your letter to:

NYS Tax Department
Taxpayer Assistance Bureau
W.A. Harriman Campus
Albany, NY 12227

To make sure that New York State employees give courteous responses and correct information to taxpayers, a department supervisor sometimes monitors telephone calls. No record is kept of any taxpayer's name, address or social security number.

Notes

DTF-17 (6/88)

New York State Department of Taxation and Finance — Sales Tax

Certificate of Registration

Read instructions before completing - Print or Type

SAMPLE

1. Legal name

2. ...me, if any, of business (if different from item 1)

3. Address of principal place of business (Number and street)

4. City, State   ZIP Code   5. Telephone number
                                                  (   )

6. County of principal place of business

7. Type of organization   Individual   Trust   Partnership   Other (specify)
                             Governmental   Exempt organization   Corporation

8. Reason for applying   Started new   Purchased   Other (specify)
                             business   going business

Department use only

9. Identification number

10. Mailing address, if different from business address
    Street
    City, State and ZIP Code

11. Date you will begin business in New York State (see instructions on back)

12. If you have ever registered as a sales tax vendor before   Name   Identification number
    with New York State give information as shown on the
    last sales tax return you filed:

13. If you acquired this business from a registered vendor, did you file a Notification of Sales, Transfer or Assignment in Bulk, Form AU-196.10,
    with the Tax Department?   Yes   No

    Give former
    owner's name   Address   ID#

14. a Will you operate more than one place of business?   Yes   No

    b If yes, check the appropriate box to the right and attach a completed Schedule of   Consolidated return will be filed to cover all places of business
       Business Locations, Form DTF-17.2   Separate return will be filed for each location

15. Do you expect to collect any sales or use tax or pay any sales or use tax directly to the Department of
    Taxation and Finance?   Yes   No

16. Name and address of banking institutions at which your business maintains or will maintain accounts for your business. Give branch office if applicable.

17 Owner's/officer's name		Title		Social security number	
Home address	City	State		ZIP Code	Telephone no. ( )
Owner's/officer's name		Title		Social security number	
Home address	City	State		ZIP Code	Telephone no. ( )
Owner's/officer's name		Title		Social security number	
Home address	City	State		ZIP Code	Telephone no. ( )
Owner's/officer's name		Title		Social security number	
Home address	City	State		ZIP Code	Telephone no. ( )

18. a Does your business currently have tax accounts with New York State for the following taxes?

    1. Corporation Tax   Yes   No
       If yes, enter Identification number

    2. Withholding Tax   Yes   No
       If yes, enter Identification number

    3. Other Tax(es) (please specify)
       Identification number(s)

       If you have a federal employer identification number (EIN) other than that entered above,
       enter it here

    b If you are an employer who withholds or will withhold New York State and local tax from your employees,
       do you need forms or printed information concerning such taxes?   Yes   No

Department use only

Mail code	Certificate NO
Type	Status	Sch. Ind.	Aux. sch.
SIC			

19. I certify that the above statements are true.

Signature   Title   Date

INSTRUCTIONS

Please complete Form DTF-17 and DTF-17A, *Certificate of Registration* and Form DTF-17.1, *Business Description*. Mail them in the enclosed envelope or to: New York State Tax Department, Sales Tax Registration Unit, W. A. Harriman Campus, Albany, N.Y. 12227. These forms must be filed at least 20 days before you begin doing business in New York State. All numbered items (1-19) must be completed in full.

1. Enter the exact legal name of the business which you are registering or for which you are changing the registration on line 1 and on the appropriate line of the certificate of authority attached to the bottom of this form. For a corporation, the legal name will be the name as it appears on the Certificate of Incorporation filed with the New York State Department of State. In the case of a business which is not incorporated, the legal name shall be the name in which the business owns property or acquires debt. Where the business entity is a partnership, the legal name shall be the partnership name. In the case of a sole proprietor the legal name shall be the name of the individual owner of the business.

2. Enter the trade name, doing-business-as name, or assumed name if different from 1 above on line 2 and on the appropriate line of the Certificate of Authority attached to the bottom of this form. For a corporation, this name shall be that name which appears on the trade name certificate filed with the New York State Department of State. In the case of a business which is not incorporated, this will be the name filed with the county clerk's office pursuant to Section 130 of the General Business Law.

3-6. Enter the actual street address and telephone number (including area code) of your business. In case of a business with more than one location refer to instruction for line 14.

7. Indicate how your business is organized by placing a check in the box which is the most accurate description.

   A governmental organization is an entity formed by the Federal Government, the State of New York (or any of its agencies, instrumentalities, public corporations or political subdivisions). This category includes political subdivisions of New York State such as a county, town, city, village, school district, fire district, etc.

   An exempt organization for purposes of this application is an organization as defined in Section 1116 of the Tax Law. Refer to ST-150 for further instructions with respect to exempt organizations.

8. Indicate the reason you are submitting this registration form by placing a check in the appropriate box. Specify the reason if you indicate "other".

9. Enter your federal employer identification number (EIN) in block 9. If you do not have an EIN, leave block 9 blank. You will be assigned a temporary number by our Department.

11. Enter the date you will begin making taxable sales or providing taxable services within New York State and/or issuing or accepting New York State exemption certificates.

14. If you will be operating from more than one business location, a separate Certificate of Authority is required and will be issued for each location, therefore a separate DTF-17 and 17.1 is required for each location. Indicate if you will operate from more than one business location by placing a check in the appropriate box.

   List all your business locations on the schedule provided (DTF-17.2). Indicate if you will be filing a consolidated return for all locations or separate returns for each location by placing a check in the appropriate box on the schedule. Return Form DTF-17.2 with this certificate.

   If a consolidated return will be filed, a suffix C will be assigned after the identification number. In the case of separate returns for each location, numerical suffixes (such as 01, 02) will be added to the identification number to indicate the different locations for which separate returns will be filed. Refer to ST-150 for instructions on filing returns.

15. If you are a manufacturer or wholesaler whose activities are such that you are not required to collect any sales tax and use tax or pay any sales and use tax directly to the Department of Taxation and Finance, check "No". Because you are registering only in order to accept or issue exemption certificates, you need to file only an annual information return. There are other instances when you may file an annual return. Refer to ST-150 for instructions on filing returns and for what constitutes a taxable sale. You will, of course, still have to collect sales or use tax and to pay sales or use tax on any taxable retail sale or purchase. The tax should be remitted with the annual return.

17. Enter the required information for all owners or officers of the business. In this regard, identify the individuals who are responsible for the day-to-day operations of the business, to include but not restricted to the responsiblity for:

   (a) the signing of checks on the company's bank account

   (b) the signing of the business' tax returns

   (c) the payment of creditors

   d) the hiring and discharging of employees

   (e) the final determination as to which bills are to be paid

   (f) the general financial affairs of the business

   In the case of a partnership, enter the required information for all general partners and for those limited partners who are active in running the business. Indicate whether the partner is a general partner or a limited partner by entering (GP) or (LP) after the partner's name.

   Notice: The authority to require personal information, including identifying numbers (Social Security numbers, etc.), is found in Section 1134, 1136, 1137-A, 1142, 1251 and 1253 and Articles 28 and 29 of the Tax Law in general and the regulations for Sales and Use Taxes in subchapter J, Title 20 NYCRR. The principal purpose for collecting this information is to assist the Department of Taxation and Finance in determining New York State and local sales and use tax liabilities under Articles 28 and 29 of the Tax Law.

   The information will be used for tax administration purposes and as necessary under Tax Law Sections 1145 and 1250 and for any other purpose authorized by law.

   Failure to provide the requested information may result in civil and/or criminal penalties under Sections 1145 and 1250 of the Tax Law and Parts 533 and 536 of the regulations for Sales and Use Taxes.

   This information will be maintained by the Director, Accounting and Records Management Bureau, Processing and Revenue Management Division, Department of Taxation and Finance, W. A. Harriman Campus, Building 8, Room 905, Albany, New York 12227, (518) 457-2260.

   The authority to maintain this information is found in Sections 1146(e) and 1250 of the Tax Law.

18. (a) Indicate if you have any other New York tax accounts by placing a check in the appropriate box. If the response to (3) is yes, enter the identification number and the tax type on the line provided.

    (b) Indicate if you need withholding tax information by placing a check in the appropriate box.

If you have a question regarding Sales Tax Registration:

From within New York State, call toll free . . . . **1 800 CALL TAX (1 800 225-5829)**

From outside New York State, call **1 518 438-8581**

NOTICE TO PROSPECTIVE PURCHASERS OF BUSINESS AND BUSINESS ASSETS

THE PURCHASER OF A BUSINESS OR BUSINESS ASSETS (FURNITURE, FIXTURES, EQUIPMENT, MERCHANDISE INVENTORY, LAND AND BUILDINGS) **MUST NOTIFY** THE COMMISSIONER OF TAXATION AND FINANCE OF SUCH PURCHASE BY REGISTERED MAIL, RETURN RECEIPT REQUESTED, AT LEAST TEN DAYS BEFORE THE PURCHASE DATE OF OR PAYMENT FOR THE BUSINESS OR ASSSETS, WHICHEVER IS EARLIER. THE PURCHASER MAY BE LIABLE FOR ALL SALES TAXES OWED BY THE SELLER UNLESS, AFTER NOTIFYING THE COMMISSIONER, YOU ARE INFORMED THAT YOU ARE NOT LIABLE.

FORMS AND INSTRUCTIONS (FORM AU-196.10) ARE AVAILABLE AT ANY DISTRICT TAX OFFICE OR THE BULK SALES UNIT, SALES TAX SECTION, W. A. HARRIMAN CAMPUS, ALBANY, N.Y. 12227.

INSTRUCTIONS TO SELLER: Every seller who intends to sell his business assets including furniture, fixtures, equipment, merchandise inventory, land and buildings, must give each prospective purchaser a copy of this notice. Additional copies are availabe at the address set forth in the notice.

THIS NOTICE SHOULD BE MADE A PERMANENT PART OF YOUR FILE FOR FUTURE REFERENCE IN THE EVENT YOU SELL YOUR BUSINESS.

DTF-17.1 (3/90) New York State - Department of Taxation and Finance - Sales Tax

Business Description

(Print or type in blue or black ink)

	Department Use Only	
Legal name of business	Identification number	
DBA/Trade name *(if different from legal name above)*	Name code	
Address of principal place of business *(number and street)*	SIC	%
City State ZIP code	Add'l SIC	%
Business phone number ( )		

SAMPLE

Please complete this Business Description form and return it with your Certificate of Registration (Form DTF-17) or your Application for Registration Renewal (Form PR-27) to the address shown on that form.

1 Enter your business name, address, and telephone number in the space provided above.

Check the appropriate box in answer to the following questions:

2 Do you participate **solely** in flea markets, antique shows, etc.? . . . . . . ☐ Yes ☐ No

3 Are you a sidewalk vendor? . . . . ☐ Yes ☐ No

4 Do you sell from door to door? . . . . ☐ Yes ☐ No

5 Do you sell party plan merchandise? . . . . ☐ Yes ☐ No

6 Do you sell: . . . . ☐ Food? ☐ Non-food items?

7 Is this a seasonal business? . . . . ☐ Yes ☐ No (If Yes, from month _____ , to month _____)

8 A complete description of business activities **must** be written in the space below:

_____

_____

_____

_____

_____

_____

_____

_____

_____

_____

_____

_____

_____

_____

_____

_____

9 Check the box from one of the **divisions** listed below which best describes your major operation. If you are a manufacturer deriving more than fifty percent of your receipts from your own retail outlets, check "G. Retail trade".

☐ A. Agriculture, forestry, fishing   ☐ E. Transportation, communications, electric, gas, sanitary service   ☐ H. Finance, insurance, real estate

☐ B. Mining   ☐ I. Services

☐ C. Construction   ☐ F. Wholesale trade   ☐ J. Public administration

☐ D. Manufacturing   ☐ G. Retail trade

10 Locate on the back of this form, within the **division** that you checked above, the four digit code which best describes your principal product or service and enter the code number here: _____

Business Description Codes

Code

A. Agriculture, Forestry, and Fishing
- 0100 Agricultural production crops
- 0200 Agricultural production livestock
- 0750 Animal husbandry
- 0780 Landscaping
- 0800 Forestry
- 0900 Fishing, hunting and trapping

B. Mining
- 1000 Metal mining
- 1200 Coal mining
- 1300 Oil and gas extraction
- 1400 Nonmetalic minerals, except fuels

C. Construction
- 1500 General building contractors
- 1600 Heavy construction, ex. building
- 1711 Plumbing, heating, air conditioning
- 1721 Painting and paper hanging
- 1731 Electrical work
- 1741 Masonry and other stonework
- 1742 Plastering, drywall, and insulation
- 1743 Terrazzo, tile, marble, mosaic work
- 1751 Carpentry work
- 1752 Floor laying and floor work, not elsewhere classified
- 1761 Roofing, siding, and sheet metal work
- 1771 Concrete work
- 1781 Water well drilling
- 1794 Excavating and foundation work

D. Manufacturing
- 2010 Meat products
- 2030 Canned, frozen, and preserved fruits and vegetables
- 2040 Grain mill products
- 2050 Bakery goods
- 2060 Sugar and confectionary products
- 2070 Fats and oils
- 2080 Beverages
- 2100 Tobacco products
- 2200 Textile mill products
- 2300 Apparel and other textile products
- 2400 Lumber and wood products (except furniture)
- 2411 Logging camps and logging contractors
- 2500 Furniture and fixtures
- 2600 Paper and allied products
- 2711 Newspapers: Publishing or publishing and printing
- 2721 Periodicals: Publishing or publishing and printing
- 2731 Book: Publishing or publishing and printing
- 2800 Chemicals and allied products
- 2900 Petroleum refinery and related industries
- 3000 Rubber and plastics products
- 3100 Leather and leather products
- 3200 Stone, clay, glass and concrete products
- 3300 Primary metal industries
- 3400 Fabricated metal products (except machinery & transportation equip)
- 3500 Industrial and commercial machinery & computer equip
- 3600 Electronic & other electrical equip & components - (except computer equipment)
- 3700 Transportation equipment
- 3800 Measurement, analysis & control instruments; photographic, medical and optical goods; watches and clocks

E. Transportation, Communications, Electric, Gas, and Sanitary Services
- 4000 Railroad transportation
- 4100 Local and interurban passenger transit
- 4200 Motor freight transportation and warehousing
- 4400 Water transportation
- 4500 Transportation by air
- 4600 Pipelines (except petroleum)
- 4700 Transportation services
- 4800 Communications
- 4911 Electric services
- 4925 Gas production and distribution
- 4950 Sanitary services

F. Wholesale Trade
- 5010 Motor vehicles & motor vehicle parts and supplies
- 5020 Furniture and home furnishings
- 5030 Lumber and other construction materials

Code

- 5040 Professional and commercial equipment and supplies
- 5050 Metals and minerals (except petroleum)
- 5060 Electrical goods
- 5070 Hardware and plumbing & heating equipment and supplies
- 5080 Machinery, equipment and supplies
- 5110 Paper and paper products
- 5120 Drugs, drug proprietaries and druggists' sundries
- 5130 Apparel, piece goods and notions
- 5140 Groceries and related products
- 5150 Farm-product raw materials
- 5160 Chemicals and allied products
- 5170 Petroleum and petroleum products
- 5180 Beer, wine and distilled alcoholic beverages

G. Retail Trade

Building Materials & Garden Supplies
- 5211 Lumber and other building materials dealers
- 5231 Paint, glass & wallpaper stores
- 5251 Hardware stores
- 5261 Retail nurseries, lawn and garden supply stores
- 5271 Mobile home dealers

General Merchandise Stores
- 5311 Department stores
- 5331 Variety stores

Food Stores
- 5411 Grocery stores
- 5421 Meat and sea food markets incl. freezer provisioners
- 5431 Fruit and vegetable markets
- 5441 Candy, nut and confectionery stores
- 5451 Dairy products stores
- 5461 Retail bakeries

Automotive Dealers & Service Stations
- 5511 Motor vehicle dealers (new and used)
- 5521 Motor vehicle dealers (used only)
- 5531 Automotive supply stores
- 5541 Gasoline service stations
- 5551 Boat dealers
- 5561 Recreational vehicle dealers
- 5571 Motorcycle dealers

Apparel & Accessory Stores
- 5611 Men's and boy's clothing and accessory stores
- 5621 Women's clothing stores
- 5632 Women's accessory and specialty stores
- 5641 Children's and infant's wear stores
- 5651 Family clothing stores
- 5661 Shoe stores

Furniture & Home Furnishings Stores
- 5712 Furniture stores
- 5713 Floor covering stores
- 5714 Drapery, curtain and upholstery stores
- 5722 Household appliance stores
- 5731 Radio, television and consumer electronics stores
- 5734 Computer and computer software stores
- 5735 Record and prerecorded tape stores
- 5736 Musical instrument stores

Eating & Drinking Places
- 5812 Eating places
- 5813 Drinking places
- 5816 Sidewalk vendor - food

Miscellaneous Retail
- 5912 Drug stores and proprietary stores
- 5921 Liquor stores
- 5932 Used merchandise and antique stores
- 5934 Flea markets
- 5941 Sporting goods and bicycle stores
- 5942 Book stores
- 5943 Stationery stores
- 5944 Jewelry stores
- 5945 Hobby, toy and game shops
- 5946 Camera and photographic supply stores

Code

- 5947 Gift, novelty, card and souvenir shops
- 5948 Luggage and leather goods
- 5949 Sewing, needlework and piece goods stores
- 5961 Catalog and mail-order houses
- 5962 Automatic merchandising machine operators
- 5963 Direct selling establishment operators
- 5983 Fuel oil dealers
- 5984 Liquefied petroleum gas dealers
- 5991 Non-food peddlers
- 5992 Florists
- 5993 Tobacco stores and stands
- 5994 Newsdealers and newsstands
- 5995 Optical goods stores

H. Finance, Insurance, Real Estate
- 6000 Depository institutions
- 6100 Nondepository credit institutions
- 6200 Security & commodity brokers, dealers, exchanges & services
- 6300 Insurance carriers
- 6400 Insurance agents, brokers & services
- 6500 Real estate
- 6700 Holding and other investment offices

I. Services

Hotels & Other Lodging Places
- 7011 Hotels, motels
- 7021 Rooming and boarding houses
- 7030 Camps and recreational vehicle parks
- 7041 Organization hotels & lodging houses, membership basis

Personal Services
- 7211 Power laundries, family and commercial
- 7213 Linen supply
- 7215 Coin operated laundries and dry cleaning
- 7216 Dry cleaning plants, except rug cleaning
- 7217 Carpet and upholstery cleaning
- 7218 Industrial launderers
- 7221 Photographic studios, portrait
- 7231 Beauty shops
- 7241 Barber shops
- 7251 Shoe repair shops and shoe shine parlors
- 7261 Funeral service and crematories
- 7291 Tax return preparation services

Business Services
- 7310 Advertising
- 7320 Consumer credit reporting agencies
- 7330 Mailing and reproduction
- 7335 Commercial photography
- 7336 Commercial art and graphic design
- 7338 Stenographic services
- 7342 Disinfecting and pest control
- 7349 Building cleaning and maintenance services
- 7350 Misc. equipment rental and leasing (except computer)
- 7361 Employment agencies
- 7371 Computer programming services
- 7373 Computer integrated systems designs
- 7374 Computer processing & data preparation & processing
- 7377 Computer rental and leasing
- 7378 Computer maintenance and repair
- 7379 Computer consultants
- 7382 Security systems services
- 7383 News syndicates
- 7384 Photofinishing laboratories

Auto Repair, Services & Parking
- 7510 Automotive rentals, and leasing without drivers
- 7521 Automobile parking
- 7532 Body repair shops
- 7533 Exhaust system repair shops
- 7538 General automotive repair shops
- 7542 Car washes
- 7549 Automotive services (except repairs)

Miscellaneous Repair Services
- 7622 Radio and television repair
- 7623 Refrigerator and air conditioning
- 7629 Electrical and electronic repair
- 7631 Watch, clock and jewelry repair
- 7641 Reupholstery and furniture repair
- 7692 Welding repair

Code

Motion Pictures
- 7810 Motion picture and video tape production
- 7820 Motion picture and video tape distribution
- 7832 Motion picture theaters
- 7833 Drive-in theaters
- 7841 Video tape rentals

Amusement & Recreation Services
- 7911 Dance halls, studios and schools
- 7922 Theatrical producers and theatrical services
- 7929 Bands, orchestras, and entertainers
- 7933 Bowling alleys
- 7940 Commercial sports
- 7991 Physical fitness facilities
- 7992 Public golf courses
- 7993 Coin operated amusement devices
- 7996 Amusement parks
- 7997 Membership sports and recreation clubs

Health Services
- 8011 Offices and clinics of doctors of medicine
- 8021 Offices and clinics of dentists
- 8041 Offices and clinics of chiropractors
- 8042 Offices and clinics of optometrists
- 8043 Offices and clinics of podiatrists
- 8050 Nursing and personal care facilities
- 8060 Hospitals
- 8071 Medical laboratories
- 8072 Dental laboratories

Legal Services
- 8100 Legal services

Educational Services
- 8211 Elementary and secondary schools
- 8221 Colleges, universities, and professional schools
- 8222 Junior colleges and technical institutions
- 8231 Libraries
- 8240 Vocational schools

Social Services
- 8322 Individual & family services
- 8331 Job training & related services
- 8351 Child day care services
- 8361 Residential care

Museums, Botanical, Zoological Gardens
- 8400 Museums, art galleries, botanical, zoological gardens

Membership Organizations
- 8611 Business associations
- 8621 Professional membership organization
- 8631 Labor unions and labor organizations
- 8641 Civic, social and fraternal associations
- 8651 Political associations
- 8661 Religious organizations

Engineering & Management Services
- 8711 Engineering services
- 8712 Architectural services
- 8713 Surveying services
- 8721 Accounting, auditing and bookkeeping services
- 8731 Commercial physical and biological research
- 8732 Commercial economic, sociological & educational research
- 8733 Noncommercial research organizations
- 8734 Testing laboratories
- 8741 Management services
- 8742 Management consulting services
- 8743 Public relations services
- 8744 Facilities support management services
- 8748 Business consulting services

Private Households
- 8800 Private households (domestic service)

J. Public Administration
- 9100 Executive, legislative and general government
- 9200 Justice, public order and safety
- 9223 Correctional institutions
- 9224 Fire protection
- 9300 Finance, taxation and monetary policy
- 9400 Administration of economic programs
- 9500 Environmental quality and housing
- 9600 Administration of human resouces
- 9700 National security and international affairs

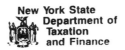

New York State Department of Taxation and Finance

Collection Charts
for
State and Local Sales and Use Tax

Publication 701 (6/90)

4% Sales and use tax collection chart

Amount of sale	Tax to be collected	Amount of sale	Tax to be collected	Amount of sale	Tax to be collected	Amount of sale	Tax to be collected
$0.01 to $0.12	$.00	2.63 to 2.87	.11	5.13 to 5.37	.21	7.63 to 7.87	.31
.13 to .33	.01	2.88 to 3.12	.12	5.38 to 5.62	.22	7.88 to 8.12	.32
.34 to .58	.02	3.13 to 3.37	.13	5.63 to 5.87	.23	8.13 to 8.37	.33
.59 to .83	.03	3.38 to 3.62	.14	5.88 to 6.12	.24	8.38 to 8.62	.34
84 to 1.12	.04	3.63 to 3.87	.15	6.13 to 6.37	.25	8.63 to 8.87	.35
1.13 to 1.37	.05	3.88 to 4.12	.16	6.38 to 6.62	.26	8.88 to 9.12	.36
1.38 to 1.62	.06	4.13 to 4.37	.17	6.63 to 6.87	.27	9.13 to 9.37	.37
1.63 to 1.87	.07	4.36 to 4.62	.18	6.88 to 7.12	.28	9.38 to 9.62	.38
1.88 to 2.12	.08	4.63 to 4.87	.19	7.13 to 7.37	.29	9.63 to 9.87	.39
2.13 to 2.37	.09	4.88 to 5.12	.20	7.38 to 7.62	.30	9.88 to 10.00	.40
2.38 to 2.62	.10						

5% Combined sales and use tax collection chart

Amount of sale	Tax to be collected	Amount of sale	Tax to be collected	Amount of sale	Tax to be collected	Amount of sale	Tax to be collected
$0.01 to $0.10	$.00	3.10 to 3.29	.16	6.10 to 6.29	.31	9.10 to 9.29	.46
.11 to .27	.01	3.30 to 3.49	.17	6.30 to 6.49	.32	9.30 to 9.49	.47
.28 to .47	.02	3.50 to 3.69	.18	6.50 to 6.69	.33	9.50 to 9.69	.48
.48 to .67	.03	3.70 to 3.89	.19	6.70 to 6.89	.34	9.70 to 9.89	.49
.68 to .87	.04	3.90 to 4.09	.20	6.90 to 7.09	.35	9.90 to 10.00	.50
.88 to 1.09	.05	4.10 to 4.29	.21	7.10 to 7.29	.36		
1.10 to 1.29	.06	4.30 to 4.49	.22	7.30 to 7.49	.37		
1.30 to 1.49	.07	4.50 to 4.69	.23	7.50 to 7.69	.38		
1.50 to 1.69	.08	4.70 to 4.89	.24	7.70 to 7.89	.39		
1.70 to 1.89	.09	4.90 to 5.09	.25	7.90 to 8.09	.40		
1.90 to 2.09	.10	5.10 to 5.29	.26	8.10 to 8.29	.41		
2.10 to 2.29	.11	5.30 to 5.49	.27	8.30 to 8.49	.42		
2.30 to 2.49	.12	5.50 to 5.69	.28	8.50 to 8.69	.43		
2.50 to 2.69	.13	5.70 to 5.89	.29	8.70 to 8.89	.44		
2.70 to 2.89	.14	5.90 to 6.09	.30	8.90 to 9.09	.45		
2.90 to 3.09	.15						

6% Combined sales and use tax collection chart

Amount of sale	Tax to be collected	Amount of sale	Tax to be collected	Amount of sale	Tax to be collected	Amount of sale	Tax to be collected
$0.01 to $0.10	$.00	2.59 to 2.74	.16	5.09 to 5.24	.31	7.59 to 7.74	.46
.11 to .22	.01	2.75 to 2.91	.17	5.25 to 5.41	.32	7.75 to 7.91	.47
.23 to .38	.02	2.92 to 3.08	.18	5.42 to 5.58	.33	7.92 to 8.08	.48
.39 to .56	.03	3.09 to 3.24	.19	5.59 to 5.74	.34	8.09 to 8.24	.49
.57 to .72	.04	3.25 to 3.41	.20	5.75 to 5.91	.35	8.25 to 8.41	.50
.73 to .88	.05	3.42 to 3.58	.21	5.92 to 6.08	.36	8.42 to 8.58	.51
.89 to 1.08	.06	3.59 to 3.74	22	6.09 to 6.24	.37	8.59 to 8.74	.52
1.09 to 1.24	.07	3.75 to 3.91	.23	6.25 to 6.41	.38	8.75 to 8.91	.53
1.25 to 1.41	.08	3.92 to 4.08	.24	6.42 to 6.58	.39	8.92 to 9.08	.54
1.42 to 1.58	.09	4.09 to 4.24	.25	6.59 to 6.74	.40	9.09 to 9.24	.55
1.59 to 1.74	.10	4.25 to 4.41	.26	6.75 to 6.91	.41	9.25 to 9.41	.56
1.75 to 1.91	.11	4.42 to 4.58	.27	6.92 to 7.08	.42	9.42 to 9.58	.57
1.92 to 2.08	.12	4.59 to 4.74	.28	7.09 to 7.24	.43	9.59 to 9.74	.58
2.09 to 2.24	.13	4.75 to 4.91	.29	7.25 to 7.41	.44	9.75 to 9.91	.59
2.25 to 2.41	.14	4.92 to 5.08	.30	7.42 to 7.58	.45	9.92 to 10.00	.60
2.42 to 2.58	.15						

On sales over $10.00, compute the tax by multiplying the amount of sale by the applicable tax rate and rounding the result to the nearest whole cent.

See reverse side for 7% and 8% collection charts

7% Combined sales and use tax collection chart

Amount of sale	Tax to be collected	Amount of sale	Tax to be collected	Amount of sale	Tax to be collected	Amount of sale	Tax to be collected
$0.01 to $0.10	$.00	2.93 to 3.07	.21	5.79 to 5.92	.41	8.65 to 8.78	.61
.11 to 20	.01	3.08 to 3.21	.22	5.93 to 6.07	.42	8.79 to 8.92	.62
.21 to .33	.02	3.22 to 3.35	.23	6.08 to 6.21	.43	8.93 to 9.07	.63
.34 to 47	.03	3.36 to 3.49	.24	6.22 to 6.35	.44	9.08 to 9.21	.64
.48 to 62	.04	3.50 to 3.64	.25	6.36 to 6.49	.45	9.22 to 9.35	.65
63 to 76	.05	3.65 to 3.78	.26	6.50 to 6.64	.46	9.36 to 9.49	.66
77 to 91	.06	3.79 to 3.92	.27	6.65 to 6.78	.47	9.50 to 9.64	.67
.92 to 1.07	.07	3.93 to 4.07	.28	6.79 to 6.92	.48	9.65 to 9.78	.68
1.08 to 1.21	.08	4.08 to 4.21	.29	6.93 to 7.07	.49	9.79 to 9.92	.69
1.22 to 1.35	.09	4.22 to 4.35	.30	7.08 to 7.21	.50	9.93 to 10.00	70
1.36 to 1.49	.10	4.36 to 4.49	.31	7.22 to 7.35	.51		
1.50 to 1.64	.11	4.50 to 4.64	.32	7.36 to 7.49	.52		
1.65 to 1.78	.12	4.65 to 4.78	.33	7.50 to 7.64	.53		
1.79 to 1.92	.13	4.79 to 4.92	.34	7.65 to 7.78	.54		
1.93 to 2.07	.14	4.93 to 5.07	.35	7.79 to 7.92	.55		
2.08 to 2.21	.15	5.08 to 5.21	.36	7.93 to 8.07	.56		
2.22 to 2.35	.16	5.22 to 5.35	.37	8.08 to 8.21	.57		
2.36 to 2.49	.17	5.36 to 5.49	.38	8.22 to 8.35	.58		
2.50 to 2.64	.18	5.50 to 5.64	.39	8.36 to 8.49	.59		
2.65 to 2.78	.19	5.65 to 5.78	.40	8.50 to 8.64	.60		
2.79 to 2.92	.20						

8% Combined sales and use tax collection chart

Amount of sale	Tax to be collected	Amount of sale	Tax to be collected	Amount of sale	Tax to be collected	Amount of sale	Tax to be collected
$0.01 to $0.10	$.00	2.57 to 2.68	.21	5.07 to 5.18	.41	7.57 to 7.68	.61
.11 to .17	.01	2.69 to 2.81	.22	5.19 to 5.31	.42	7.69 to 7.81	.62
.18 to .29	.02	2.82 to 2.93	.23	5.32 to 5.43	.43	7.82 to 7.93	.63
.30 to 42	.03	2.94 to 3.06	.24	5.44 to 5.56	.44	7.94 to 8.06	.64
.43 to 54	.04	3.07 to 3.18	.25	5.57 to 5.68	.45	8.07 to 8.18	.65
.55 to .67	.05	3.19 to 3.31	.26	5.69 to 5.81	.46	8.19 to 8.31	.66
.68 to .79	.06	3.32 to 3.43	.27	5.82 to 5.93	.47	8.32 to 8.43	.67
.80 to .92	.07	3.44 to 3.56	.28	5.94 to 6.06	.48	8.44 to 8.56	.68
.93 to 1.06	.08	3.57 to 3.68	.29	6.07 to 6.18	.49	8.57 to 8.68	.69
1.07 to 1.18	.09	3.69 to 3.81	.30	6.19 to 6.31	.50	8.69 to 8.81	.70
1.19 to 1.31	.10	3.82 to 3.93	.31	6.32 to 6.43	.51	8.82 to 8.93	.71
1.32 to 1.43	.11	3.94 to 4.06	.32	6.44 to 6.56	.52	8.94 to 9.06	.72
1.44 to 1.56	.12	4.07 to 4.18	.33	6.57 to 6.68	.53	9.07 to 9.18	.73
1.57 to 1.68	.13	4.19 to 4.31	.34	6.69 to 6.81	.54	9.19 to 9.31	.74
1.69 to 1.81	.14	4.32 to 4.43	.35	6.82 to 6.93	.55	9.32 to 9.43	.75
1.82 to 1.93	.15	4.44 to 4.56	.36	6.94 to 7.06	.56	9.44 to 9.56	.76
1.94 to 2.06	.16	4.57 to 4.68	.37	7.07 to 7.18	.57	9.57 to 9.68	.77
2.07 to 2.18	.17	4.69 to 4.81	.38	7.19 to 7.31	.58	9.69 to 9.81	.78
2.19 to 2.31	.18	4.82 to 4.93	.39	7.32 to 7.43	.59	9.82 to 9.93	.79
2.32 to 2.43	.19	4.94 to 5.06	.40	7.44 to 7.56	.60	9.94 to 10.00	.80
2.44 to 2.56	.20						

On sales over $10.00, compute the tax by multiplying the amount of sale by the applicable tax rate and rounding the result to the nearest whole cent.

For additional copies of this publication (or card forms for each individual rate), please write to NYS Tax Department, Taxpayer Assistance Bureau, W. A. Harriman Campus, Albany, NY 12227; **or** call toll free 1 800 462-8100 (within New York State only). From areas outside New York State, call (518) 438-1073.

The Tax Department also has card charts for ½%, 1%, 1½%, 2%, 2½%, 3%, 3¼%, 3½%, 3¾%, 4¼%, 4½%, 5¼%, 5½%, 5¾%, 6¼%, 6½%, 6¾%, 7¼%, 7½%, 8¼%, 10%, 10¼%, 14% and 18¼% (for New York City parking only). If you need any of these, please contact us.

**New York State
Department of
Taxation
and Finance**

PUBLICATION 718 (12/90)

New York State and Local Sales Tax Rates by Community

Effective December 1, 1990

Counties

The following list includes the state sales tax rate combined with any county sales tax rate currently in effect. Jurisdictions whose rates and/or codes have changed from the previous version are noted in **bold italics.**

County	% Rate	Reporting Code	County	% Rate	Reporting Code	County	% Rate	Reporting Code
Albany	7	0172	Herkimer	7	2100	Richmond *	#	8009
Allegany	8	0215	Jefferson	7	2202	Rockland *	6¼	3902
Bronx *	#	8009	Kings *	#	8009	St. Lawrence	7	4092
Broome	7	0312	Lewis	7	2303	Saratoga	7	4103
Cattaraugus	8	0499	Livingston	7	2402	Schenectady	7	4234
Cayuga	7	0502	Madison	7	2582	Schoharie	6	4302
Chautauqua	7	0602	Monroe	7	2602	Schuyler	7	4402
Chemung	7	0792	Montgomery	7	2792	Seneca	7	4512
Chenango	6	0803	Nassau *	8	2803	Steuben	7	4682
Clinton	7	0992	New York *	#	8009	Suffolk *	7½	4709
Columbia	7	1008	Niagara	7	2902	Sullivan	7	4812
Cortland	7	1102	Oneida	7	3002	Tioga	7	4905
Delaware	6	1202	Onondaga	7	3102	Tompkins	7	5092
Dutchess *	7¼	1303	Ontario	7	3272	Ulster	7	5112
Erie	8	1415	Orange *	6¼	3324	Warren	7	5292
Essex	7	1502	Orleans	7	3472	Washington	7	5302
Franklin	7	1602	Oswego	4	0002	Wayne	7	5402
Fulton	7	1706	Otsego	6	3602	Westchester *	5¾	5508
Genesee	7	1892	Putnam *	7¼	3714	Wyoming	7	5602
Greene	7	1912	Queens *	#	8009	Yates	7	5702
Hamilton	7	2002	Rensselaer	7	3878			

* Rates in these counties include ¼% imposed for the benefit of the Metropolitan Commuter Transportation District.

\# New York City includes the counties of Bronx, Kings (Brooklyn), New York (Manhattan), Queens and Richmond (Staten Island). The combined tax rate in New York City is 8¼%.

Cities

The rates shown below include the combined state, county and city sales tax currently in effect. For reporting purposes, vendors must keep separate records of sales made within the cities listed. Listings of street addresses for the cities shown below are available upon request from the Taxpayer Services Division, W. A. Harriman Campus, Albany, New York 12227.

City (County)	% Rate	Reporting Code	City (County)	% Rate	Reporting Code
Amsterdam (Montgomery)	7	2712	New York City * (See # above)	8¼	8009
Batavia (Genesee)	7	1822	Norwich (Chenango)	7	0844
Canandaigua (Ontario)	7	3232	Ogdensburg (St. Lawrence)	7	4012
Corning (Steuben)	7	4612	Olean (Cattaraugus)	8	0419
Elmira (Chemung)	7	0712	Oneida (Madison)	7	2526
Fulton (Oswego)	7	3532	Oswego (Oswego)	7	3542
Geneva (Ontario)	7	3242	Plattsburgh (Clinton)	7	0912
Glens Falls (Warren)	7	5212	Rome (Oneida)	7¼	3039
Gloversville (Fulton)	7	1715	Salamanca (Cattaraugus)	8	0429
Hornell (Steuben)	7	4622	Sherrill (Oneida)	7	3048
Ithaca (Tompkins)	7	5012	Utica (Oneida)	7	3055
Johnstown (Fulton)	7	1724	White Plains * (Westchester)	7¼	5560
Mount Vernon * (Westchester)	8¼	5513	Yonkers * (Westchester)	8¼	6578
New Rochelle * (Westchester)	7¼	6585			

* Rates in these communities include ¼% imposed for the benefit of the Metropolitan Commuter Transportation District.

Reporting Codes

The reporting codes listed above are those used on the sales tax returns. These codes, rather than ZIP codes, should be used for identifying customer location for tax collection purposes. (Postal zones usually do not coincide with political boundaries and the use of ZIP codes for tax collection purposes results in a high degree of inaccurate tax collection.) See Publication 717, *New York State Communities,* for the alphabetical list of localities, followed by the counties in which they are located (in parentheses), ZIP codes and postal addresses, if different from the locality names.

This listing is intended to indicate **only** the enactment and effective dates of sales and use tax rates imposed, increased or decreased by the various localities. Since certain cities and counties have preempted an existing tax imposed by the other, **the rates indicated cannot be added to determine the combined state, county and city tax rate.** Refer to the front of this form for combined rates. Any items changed from the previous version are noted in **bold italics**.

JURISDICTION	%	ENACTED	EFFECTIVE
New York State	2	Apr 14, 65	Aug 1, 65
	3	Mar 29, 69	Apr 1, 69
	4	Apr 2, 71	Jun 1, 71
COUNTIES			
Albany	2	Dec 11, 67	Mar 1, 68
	3	Dec 15, 69	Mar 1, 70
Allegany	2	Nov 16, 67	Mar 1, 68
	3	Oct 14, 75	Mar 1, 76
*s	4	Oct 14, 86	Dec 1, 86
Broome	2	Jul 13, 65	Aug 1, 65
	3	Feb 19, 74	Jun 1, 74
Cattaraugus	3	Nov 21, 67	Mar 1, 68
*q	4	Dec 30, 85	Mar 1, 86
Cayuga	3	Mar 19, 68	Jun 1, 68
Chautauqua	3	May 10, 68	Sep 1, 68
Chemung	2	Jul 12, 65	Aug 1, 65
	3	Dec 12, 67	Mar 1, 68
Chenango	2	Dec 2, 68	Mar 1, 69
Clinton	3	Nov 24, 67	Mar 1, 68
Columbia	2	Nov 29, 71	Mar 1, 72
	3	Dec 8, 82	Mar 1, 83
Cortland	3	Nov 24, 67	Mar 1, 68
Delaware	2	Jun 13, 90	Sep 1, 90
Dutchess *e	1	Dec 9, 75	Mar 1, 76
	3	Dec 11, 89	Mar 1, 90
Erie	2	Jul 27, 65	Aug 1, 65
	3	Nov 30, 71	Mar 1, 72
	4	Dec 10, 84	Mar 1, 85
	4	Dec 18, 86	Jan 1, 87
	3	Effective 1/1/88-1/9/88	
*l	4	Jan 7, 88	Jan 10, 88
Essex	3	Dec 4, 67	Mar 1, 68
Franklin	2	Aug 22, 67	Dec 1, 67
	3	May 29, 68	Sep 1, 68
Fulton	3	Dec 11, 67	Mar 1, 68
Genesee	2	Jun 25, 65	Jan 1, 66
	3	Nov 26, 80	Mar 1, 81
Greene	2	Mar 22, 68	Jun 1, 68
	3	Feb 1, 77	Jun 1, 77
Hamilton	3	Jan 4, 68	Jun 1, 68
Herkimer	3	Dec 14, 87	Mar 1, 88
Jefferson	2	Jul 12, 65	Aug 1, 65
	3	Nov 14, 67	Mar 1, 68
Lewis	2	Aug 24, 81	Dec 1, 81
	3	Jan 6, 87	Mar 1, 87
Livingston	3	Nov 30, 67	Mar 1, 68
Madison	2	Dec 15, 67	Mar 1, 68
	3	Aug 28, 84	Dec 1, 84
Monroe	3	Jul 20, 65	Aug 1, 65
Montgomery	3	Dec 5, 67	Mar 1, 68
Nassau	2	Dec 9, 68	Mar 1, 69
	3	Nov 29, 71	Mar 1, 72
	4	Jul 16, 76	Sep 1, 76
*e/d	3	Jul 16, 76	Sep 1, 77
	4	Apr 25, 83	Jun 1, 83
*j	4	Sep 10, 84	Jan 1, 85
*m	3¾	Sep 10, 84	Jan 1, 86
Niagara	3	Dec 3, 68	Mar 1, 69
Oneida *k	3	Oct 27, 82	Dec 1, 82

JURISDICTION	%	ENACTED	EFFECTIVE
Onondaga	2	Sep 11, 67	Dec 1, 67
	3	Oct 11, 68	Dec 1, 68
Ontario	2	May 26, 67	Sep 1, 67
	3	Mar 12, 70	Jun 1, 70
Orange *e	1	Sep 10, 82	Dec 1, 82
	2	Oct 26, 83	Dec 1, 83
Orleans	2	Nov 30, 67	Mar 1, 68
	3	Jun 4, 70	Sep 1, 70
Otsego	2	Dec 7, 67	Mar 1, 68
Putnam	1	Feb 10, 77	Jun 1, 77
*e	2	Oct 14, 80	Mar 1, 81
	2½	Oct 17, 83	Dec 1, 83
	2	May 5, 87	Sep 1, 87
	3	Nov 1, 88	Mar 1, 89
Rensselaer	2	Jul 24, 68	Dec 1, 68
	3	Oct 27, 82	Dec 1, 82
Rockland *e	2	Dec 20, 83	Mar 1, 84
St. Lawrence	3	Nov 13, 67	Mar 1, 68
Saratoga	3	Apr 22, 82	Jun 1, 82
Schenectady	½	Sep 29, 88	Dec 1, 88
	3	Jan 24, 89	Mar 1, 89
Schoharie	2	Jan 20, 84	Jun 1, 84
Schuyler	3	Nov 27, 67	Mar 1, 68
Seneca	1	Jan 12, 82	Mar 1, 82
	3	Jul 13, 82	Sep 1, 82
Steuben	2	Nov 27, 67	Mar 1, 68
	3	Nov 22, 71	Mar 1, 72
Suffolk	2	Dec 2, 68	Mar 1, 69
*e	3	Feb 8, 72	Sep 1, 72
*h	3¼	Sep 12, 84	Dec 1, 84
Sullivan	2	Dec 20, 67	Mar 1, 68
	3	Jan 6, 75	Mar 1, 75
Tioga	2	May 27, 68	Sep 1, 68
	3	May 14, 84	Sep 1, 84
Tompkins	3	Nov 28, 66	Mar 1, 68
Ulster	1	Feb 13, 69	Jun 1, 69
	3	Dec 9, 76	Mar 1, 77
Warren	3	Nov 27, 67	Mar 1, 68
Washington	3	Feb 25, 70	Sep 1, 70
Wayne	2	Nov 15, 67	Mar 1, 68
	3	Feb 20, 68	Jun 1, 68
Westchester *e	1	Dec 22, 71	Sep 1, 72
	1½	Dec 28, 81	Jun 1, 82
Wyoming *r	3	Nov 25, 80	Mar 1, 81
Yates	3	Nov 20, 67	Mar 1, 68
CITIES			
Amsterdam *a	1½	Mar 15, 68	Mar 1, 69
Batavia *a	1½	Jul 14, 80	Mar 1, 81
Canandaigua	1	Jul 13, 65	Aug 1, 65
*a	1½	Jul 13, 67	Mar 1, 68
Corning *a	1½	Aug 5, 74	Dec 1, 74
Elmira *a	1½	Sep 29, 71	Mar 1, 72

*a —City preempted county tax; within city, county tax rate is 1½%.
*b —County preempted 1%.
*c —Within city; County rate is 1½%.
*d —Expiration of 1% emergency tax.
*e —Additional tax of ¼% imposed in these localities for benefit of Metropolitan Commuter Transportation District; enacted July 11, 1981, effective on and after September 1, 1981.
*f —County preempted ½%.
*g —County preempted 1½%.
*h —¼% to expire on November 30, 2000, unless extended.
*i —Within city; county rate is 2%.
*j —Effective 1/1/85 through 12/31/85, the additional 1% rate is not subject to preemption.
*k —**3% to expire on 11/30/92 unless extended.**
*l —1% to expire on 2/28/91 unless extended.

JURISDICTION	%	ENACTED	EFFECTIVE
Fulton	2	Dec 5, 67	Mar 1, 68
	3	Dec 9, 71	Mar 1, 72
Geneva	1	Jun 14, 67	Sep 1, 67
*a	1½	Jun 14, 67	Mar 1, 68
Glen Cove *e/n	1½	Oct 9, 79	Mar 1, 80
*o/p	2	Jun 28, 83	Mar 1, 84
	—	Repeal effective Mar 1, 1988	
Glens Falls *a	1½	Jun 19, 68	Mar 1, 69
Gloversville *a	1½	Jun 23, 87	Mar 1, 88
Hornell	1	Apr 1, 69	Jun 1, 69
*a	1½	Jun 23, 70	Mar 1, 71
Ithaca *a	1½	Jun 25, 69	Mar 1, 70
Johnstown *a	1½	Jun 29, 87	Mar 1, 88
Mechanicville *f	2	Jun 10, 70	Sep 1, 70
	—	Repeal effective June 1, 1985	
Mount Vernon	1	Feb 23, 72	Jun 1, 72
*e/f	2	Jun 27, 74	Sep 1, 74
	2½	Aug 28, 84	Dec 1, 84
Newburgh	1	Oct 27, 86	Dec 1, 86
	—	Repeal effective Mar 1, 1988	
New Rochelle *e/f	2	May 4, 76	Sep 1, 76
New York City	3	Jul 22, 65	Aug 1, 65
*e	4	Jun 27, 74	Jul 1, 74
Norwich *a	1½	Jun 27, 89	Mar 1, 90
Ogdensburg *a	1½	Jun 13, 68	Mar 1, 69
Olean *a	1½	Apr 23, 68	Mar 1, 69
Oneida	1	Jun 13, 72	Dec 1, 72
*a	1½	Jun 13, 72	Mar 1, 73
Oswego	2	Nov 27, 67	Mar 1, 68
	3	Jan 10, 72	Mar 1, 72
Plattsburgh *f	2	Jul 15, 65	Aug 1, 65
Poughkeepsie *e	1	Jul 7, 65	Aug 1, 65
	2	Jan 9, 69	Mar 1, 69
	—	Repeal effective Mar 1, 1990	
Rome *c	1½	Oct 22, 80	Dec 1, 80
*t	1¾	June 27, 90	Sept 1, 90
Salamanca *a	1½	May 27, 68	Mar 1, 69
Saratoga Springs	1	Feb 3, 69	Jun 1, 69
	2	Aug 3, 70	Dec 1, 70
*g	3	Jul 28, 80	Sep 1, 80
	—	Repeal effective June 1, 1985	
Schenectady	3	Oct 28, 82	Mar 1, 83
	2½	Dec 5, 83	Mar 1, 84
	—	Repeal effective March 1, 1989	
Sherrill *i	1	Dec 27, 76	Jun 1, 77
Troy	1	Dec 5, 68	Mar 1, 69
*a	1½	Jun 4, 70	Mar 1, 71
	0	Oct 27, 82	Dec 1, 82
White Plains *e/f	2	Apr 30, 73	Sep 1, 73
Utica *c	1½	Apr 8, 82	Jun 1, 82
Yonkers	1	Dec 30, 67	Jun 1, 68
	2	Dec 10, 68	Mar 1, 69
*b	3	Jan 3, 70	Mar 1, 70
*e/f/c	4	Nov 25, 75	Jan 1, 76

*m —Effective 1/1/86 through 12/31/91, the additional rate is ¾% and is not subject to preemption.
*n —City preempted county tax. Within city, the county rate is 2½%
*o —City preempted county tax. Within city, county rate is 2% for the period 3/1/84 through 12/31/84.
*p —Effective 1/1/85, county rate is not subject to preemption. City rate is 1½% for the period 1/1/85 to the date of repeal.
*q —1% to expire on 2/28/91 unless extended; the additional 1% rate is not subject to preemption.
*r —3% extended indefinitely.
*s —Additional 1% to expire on 11/30/92 unless extended.
*t —¼% to expire on 8/31/2000 unless extended.

Business Formation and Planning

Starting and Operating a Business in... series
Book available for each state in the United States, plus District of Columbia

One-stop resource to current federal and state laws and regulations that affect businesses. Clear "human language" explanations of complex issues, plus samples of government forms, and lists of where to obtain additional help or information. This book helps seasoned business owners keep up with changing legislation. It also guides new entrepreneurs step-by-step to start the business and do what's necessary to stay up and running. Includes many checklists and worksheets to organize ideas, create action plans, and project financial scenarios.

Starting and Operating a Business: U.S. Edition
Set of eleven binders

The complete encyclopedia of how to do business in the U.S. Describes laws and regulations for each state, plus Washington, D.C., as well as the federal government. Gives overview of what is involved in starting and operating a business. Includes lists of sources of help, plus post cards for requesting materials from government and other agencies. This set is valuable for businesses with locations or marketing activities in several states, plus franchisors, attorneys, accountants, and other consultants.

Surviving and Prospering in a Business Partnership
Book

From evaluation of potential partners, through the drafting of agreements, to day-to-day management of working relationships, this book helps avoid classic partnership catastrophes. Discusses how to set up the partnership to reduce the financial and emotional consequences of unanticipated disputes, dishonesty, divorce, disability, or death of a partner.

Corporation Formation Package and Minute Book
Book and software for IBM-PC, available for Texas, Florida, or California

Provides forms required for incorporating and maintaining closely-held corporations, including: articles of incorporation; bylaws; stock certificates, stock transfer record sheets, bill of sale agreement; minutes form; plus many others. Addresses questions on regulations, timing, fees, notices, election of directors, and other critical factors. Software has minutes, bylaws, and articles of incorporation already for you to edit and customize (using your own word processor).

Franchise Bible: A Comprehensive Guide
Book

Complete guide to franchising for prospective franchisees or for business owners considering franchising their business. Includes actual sample documents, such as a complete offering circular, plus worksheets for evaluating franchise companies, locations, and organizing information before seeing an attorney. This book is helpful for lawyers as well as their clients.

How To Develop & Market Creative Business Ideas
Paperback Book

Step-by-step manual guides the inventor through all stages of new product development. Discusses patenting your invention, trademarks, copyrights, and how to construct your prototype. Gives information on financing, distribution, test marketing, and finding licensees. Plus, lists many useful sources for prototype resources, trade shows, funding, and more.

The Successful Business Plan: Secrets & Strategies
Book

Start-to-finish guide to creating a successful business plan. Includes tips from venture capitalists, bankers, and successful CEOs. Features worksheets for ease in planning and budgeting with the Abrams Method of Flow-Through Financials. Gives a sample business plan, plus specialized help for retailers, service companies, manufacturers, and in-house corporate plans. Also tells how to find and impress funding sources.

The Small Business Expert
Software for IBM-PC & compatibles

Generates comprehensive custom checklist of the state and federal laws and regulations based on your type and size of business. Allows comparison of doing business in each of the 50 states. Built-in worksheets create outlines for personnel policies, marketing feasibility studies, and a business plan draft. *Requires 256K RAM and hard disk.*

Related Resources from PSI Successful Business Library

Acquiring Outside Capital

The Loan Package
Book

Preparatory package for a business loan proposal. Worksheets help analyze cash needs and articulate business focus. Includes sample forms for balance sheets, income statements, projections, and budget reports. Screening sheets rank potential lenders to shorten the time involved in getting the loan.

Venture Capital Proposal Package
Book

Structures a proposal to secure venture capital. Checklists gather material for required sections: market analyses, income projections, financial statements, management team, strategic marketing plan, etc. Gives tips on understanding, finding, and screening potential investors.

Financial Templates
Software for IBM-PC & Macintosh

Software speeds business calculations including those in PSI's workbooks, *The Loan Package, Venture Capital Proposal Package, Negotiating the Purchase or Sale of a Business, The Successful Business Plan: Secrets & Strategies.* Includes 40 financial templates including various projections, statements, ratios, histories, amortizations, and cash flows. *Requires Lotus 1-2-3, Microsoft Excel 2.0 or higher, Supercalc 5, PSI's Spreadsheet (described in the Financial Management section of this resource list), or Lotus compatible spreadsheet and 512 RAM plus hard disk or two floppy drives.*

Managing Employees

A Company Policy and Personnel Workbook
Book

Saves costly consultant or staff hours in creating company personnel policies. Provides model policies on topics such as employee safety, leave of absence, flextime, smoking, substance abuse, sexual harassment, performance improvement, grievance procedure. For each subject, practical and legal ramifications are explained, then a choice of alternate policies presented.

Software for IBM-PC & compatibles and Macintosh

The policies are on disk so the company's name, specific information, and any desired changes or rewrites can be incorporated using your own word processor to tailor the model policies to suit your company's specific needs before printing out a complete manual for distribution to employees. *Requires a word processor and hard disk and floppy drive.*

Staffing A Small Business: Hiring, Compensating and Evaluating
Book

For the company that does not have a personnel specialist. Clarifies the processes of determining personnel needs; establishing job descriptions that satisfy legal requirements; and advertising for, selecting, and keeping good people. Over 40 worksheets help forecast staffing needs, define each job, recruit employees, and train staff.

Managing People: A Practical Guide
Book

Focuses on developing the art of working with people to maximize the productivity and satisfaction of both manager and employees. Discussions, exercises, and self-tests boost skills in communicating, delegating, motivating people, developing teams, goal-setting, adapting to change, and coping with stress.

Mail Order

Mail Order Legal Manual
Book

For companies that use the mail to market their products or services, as well as for mail order businesses, this book clarifies complex regulations so penalties can be avoided. Gives state-by-state legal requirements, plus information on Federal Trade Commission guidelines and rules covering delivery dates, advertising, sales taxes, unfair trade practices, and consumer protection.

To order these tools, use the convenient order form at the back of this book or call us toll-free at: 800-228-2275

Marketing & Public Relations

Marketing Your Products and Services Successfully
Book

Helps small businesses understand marketing concepts, then plan and follow through with the actions that will result in increased sales. Covers all aspects from identifying the target market, through market research, establishing pricing, creating a marketing plan, evaluating media alternatives, to launching a campaign. Discusses customer maintenance techniques and international marketing.

Customer Profile and Retrieval (CPR)
Software for IBM-PC & compatibles

Stores details of past activities plus future reminders on customers, clients, contacts, vendors, and employees, then gives instant access to that information when needed. "Tickler" fields keep reminders of dates for recontacts. "Type" fields categorize names for sorting as the user defines. "Other data" fields store information such as purchase and credit history, telephone call records, or interests.

Massive storage capabilities. Holds up to 255 lines of comments for each name, plus unlimited time and date stamped notes. Features perpetual calendar, and automatic telephone dialing. Built-in word processing and merge gives the ability to pull in the information already keyed into the fields into form or individual letters. Prints mail labels, rotary file cards, and phone directories. *Requires a hard disk, 640K RAM and 80 column display. (Autodial feature requires modem.)*

Publicity and Public Relations Guide for Businesses
Book

Overview of how to promote a business by using advertising, publicity, and public relations. Especially for business owners and managers who choose to have promotional activities carried out by in-house staff rather than outside specialists. Includes worksheets for a public relations plan, news releases, editorial article, and a communications schedule.

Cost-Effective Market Analysis
Book

Workbook explains how a small business can conduct its own market research. Shows how to set objectives, determine which techniques to use, create a schedule, and then monitor expenses. Encompasses primary research (trade shows, telephone interviews, mail surveys), plus secondary research (using available information in print).

EXECARDS®
Communication Tools

EXECARDS, the original business-to-business message cards, help build and maintain personal business relationships with customers and prospects. Distinctive in size and quality, EXECARDS get through even when other mail is tossed. An effective alternative to telephone tag. Time-saving, EXECARDS come in a variety of handsome styles and messages. Excellent for thanking clients, following up between orders, prospecting, and announcing new products, services, or special offers. *Please call for complete catalog.*

How To Develop & Market Creative Business Ideas
Paperback Book

Step-by-step manual guides the inventor through all stages of new product development. Discusses patenting your invention, trademarks, copyrights, and how to construct your prototype. Gives information on financing, distribution, test marketing, and finding licensees. Plus, lists many useful sources for prototype resources, trade shows, funding, and more.

International Business

Export Now
Book

Prepares a business to enter the export market. Clearly explains the basics, then articulates specific requirements for export licensing, preparation of documents, payment methods, packaging, and shipping. Includes advice on evaluating foreign representatives, planning international marketing strategies, and discovering official U.S. policy for various countries and regions. Lists sources.

Related Resources from PSI Successful Business Library

Business Communications

Proposal Development: How to Respond and Win the Bid
Book

Orchestrates a successful proposal from preliminary planning to clinching the deal. Shows by explanation and example how to: determine what to include; create text, illustrations, tables, exhibits, and appendices; how to format (using either traditional methods or desktop publishing); meet the special requirements of government proposals; set up and follow a schedule.

Write Your Own Business Contracts
Book

Explains the "do's" and "don'ts" of contract writing so any person in business can do the preparatory work in drafting contracts before hiring an attorney for final review. Gives a working knowledge of the various types of business agreements, plus tips on how to prepare for the unexpected.

Complete Book of Business Forms
New Book available Fall 1991.

Over 200 reproducible forms for all types of business needs: personnel, employment, finance, production flow, operations, sales, marketing, order entry, and general administration. Time-saving, uniform, coordinated way to record and locate important business information.

EXECARDS®
Communication Tools

EXECARDS, business-to-business message cards, are an effective vehicle for maintaining personal contacts in this era of rushed, highly-technical communications. A card takes only seconds and a few cents to send, but can memorably tell customers, clients, prospects, or co-workers that their relationship is valued. Many styles and messages to choose from for thanking, acknowledging, inviting, reminding, prospecting, following up, etc. *Please call for complete catalog.*

PlanningTools™
Paper pads, 3-hole punched

Handsome PlanningTools help organize thoughts and record notes, actions, plans, and deadlines, so important information and responsibilities do not get lost or forgotten. Specific PlanningTools organize different needs, such as Calendar Notes, Progress/Activity Record, Project Plan/Record, Week's Priority Planner, Make-A-Month Calendar, and Milestone Chart. *Please call for catalog.*

Customer Profile & Retrieval (CPR)
Software for IBM-PC & compatibles

Easy computer database management program streamlines the process of communicating with clients, customers, vendors, contacts, and employees. While talking to your contact on the phone (or at any time), all notes of past activities and conversations can be viewed instantly, and new notes can be added at that time. *Please see description under "Marketing & Public Relations" section on previous page.*

Business Relocation

Company Relocation Handbook: Making the Right Move
New Book available Fall, 1991

Comprehensive guide to moving a business. Begins with defining objectives for moving and evaluating whether relocating will actually solve more problems than it creates. Worksheets compare prospective locations, using rating scales for physical plant, equipment, personnel, and geographic considerations. Sets up a schedule for dealing with logistics.

Retirement Planning

Retirement & Estate Planning Handbook
Book

Do-it-yourself workbook for setting up a retirement plan that can easily be maintained and followed. Covers establishing net worth, retirement goals, budgets, and a plan for asset acquisition, preservation, and growth. Discusses realistic expectations for Social Security, Medicare, and health care alternatives. Features special sections for business owners.

Career Recordkeeping

Career Builder
Book

This workbook collects all of an individual's career-related data in one place for quick access. From educational details, through work history, health records, reference lists, correspondence awards, passports, etc., to personal insurance policies, real estate, securities and bank accounts, this manual keeps it all organized. Gives tips on successful resumés.

To order these tools, use the convenient order form at the back of this book or call us toll-free at: 800-228-2275

Financial Management

Financial Management Techniques for Small Business
Book

Clearly reveals the essential ingredients of sound financial management in detail. By monitoring trends in your financial activities, you will be able to uncover potential problems before they become crises. You'll understand why you can be making a profit and still not have the cash to meet expenses, and you'll learn the steps to change your business' cash behavior to get more return for your effort.

Risk Analysis: How to Reduce Insurance Costs
Book

Straightforward advice on shopping for insurance, understanding types of coverage, comparing proposals and premium rates. Worksheets help identify and weigh the risks a particular business is likely to face, then determine if any of those might be safely self-insured or eliminated. Request for proposal form helps businesses avoid over-paying for protection.

Debt Collection: Strategies for the Small Business
Book

Practical tips on how to turn receivables into cash. Worksheets and checklists help businesses establish credit policies, track accounts, and flag when it is necessary to bring in a collection agency, attorney, or go to court. This book advises how to deal with disputes, negotiate settlements, win in small claims court, and collect on judgments. Gives examples of telephone collection techniques and collection letters.

Negotiating the Purchase or Sale of a Business
Book

Prepares a business buyer or seller for negotiations that will achieve win-win results. Shows how to determine the real worth of a business, including intangible assets such as "goodwill." Over 36 checklists and worksheets on topics such as tax impact on buyers and sellers, escrow checklist, cash flow projections, evaluating potential buyers, financing options, and many others.

Financial Accounting Guide for Small Business
Book

Makes understanding the economics of business simple. Explains the basic accounting principles that relate to any business. Step-by-step instructions for generating accounting statements and interpreting them, spotting errors, and recognizing warning signs. Discusses how banks and other creditors view financial statements.

Controlling Your Company's Freight Costs
Book

Shows how to increase company profits by trimming freight costs. Provides tips for comparing alternative methods and shippers, then negotiating contracts to receive the most favorable discounts. Tells how to package shipments for safe transport. Discusses freight insurance and dealing with claims for loss or damage. Appendices include directory of U.S. ports, shipper's guide, and sample bill of lading.

Accounting Software Analysis
Book

Presents successful step-by-step procedure for choosing the most appropriate software to handle the accounting for your business. Evaluation forms and worksheets create a custom software "shopping list" to match against features of various products, so facts, not sales hype, can determine the best fit for your company.

Financial Templates
Software for IBM-PC & Macintosh

Calculates and graphs many business "what-if" scenarios and financial reports. Forty financial templates such as income statements, cash flow, and balance sheet comparisons, break-even analyses, product contribution comparisons, market share, net present value, sales model, *pro formas*, loan payment projections, etc. *Requires 512K RAM hard disk or two floppy drives, plus Lotus 1-2-3 or compatible spreadsheet such as our program called "Spreadsheet" listed below.*

Spreadsheet
Software for IBM-PC & compatibles

Economically priced spreadsheet program. Compatible with Lotus 1-2-3® release 2.01 files. Creates and manipulates worksheets with up to 256 columns by 2,048 rows, and will automatically use Lotus 1A, 2.0, and 2.01 macros (even the most advanced). Comes with a detailed, yet understandable, reference manual. Requires 640K RAM and hard disk drive. This program doesn't have Lotus' fancy fonts, separate tutorial, or ability to use expanded memory, but it handles most of the calculations (even statistical) you'd ever require. A great business workhorse at an affordable price!

PSI Successful Business Library / Tools for Business Success Order Form (Please fill out other side also)

BOOKS - Please check the edition (binder or paper) of your choice.

TITLE	BINDER	PAPERBACK	QUANTITY	COST
Accounting Software Analysis	☐ $ 39.95			
Career Builder	☐ $ 34.95	☐ $ 12.95		
A Company Policy and Personnel Workbook	☐ $ 49.95			
Company Relocation Handbook	☐ $ 49.95	☐ $ 19.95		
Complete Book of Business Forms	☐ $ 39.95	☐ $ 19.95		
Controlling Your Company's Freight Costs	☐ $ 39.95			
Corporation Formation Package and Minute Book CA☐ TX☐ FL☐	☐ $ 39.95	☐ $ 24.95		
Cost-Effective Market Analysis	☐ $ 39.95			
Debt Collection: Strategies for the Small Business	☐ $ 39.95	☐ $ 17.95		
Export Now	☐ $ 39.95	☐ $ 19.95		
Financial Accounting Guide For Small Business	☐ $ 39.95			
Financial Management Techniques For Small Business	☐ $ 39.95	☐ $ 19.95		
Franchise Bible: A Comprehensive Guide	☐ $ 49.95	☐ $ 19.95		
How to Develop & Market Creative Business Ideas		☐ $ 14.95		
The Loan Package	☐ $ 39.95			
Mail Order Legal Manual	☐ $ 45.00			
Managing People: A Practical Guide	☐ $ 49.95	☐ $ 19.95		
Marketing Your Products and Services Successfully	☐ $ 39.95	☐ $ 18.95		
Negotiating the Purchase or Sale of a Business	☐ $ 39.95	☐ $ 18.95		
Proposal Development: How to Respond and Win the Bid (hardback book)	☐ $ 39.95			
Publicity & Public Relations Guide For Businesses	☐ $ 39.95			
Retirement & Estate Planning Handbook	☐ $ 49.95	☐ $ 19.95		
Risk Analysis: How To Reduce Insurance Costs	☐ $ 39.95	☐ $ 18.95		
Staffing A Small Business	☐ $ 39.95	☐ $ 19.95		
Starting and Operating A Business in... BOOK INCLUDES FEDERAL SECTION PLUS ONE STATE SECTION —	☐ $ 29.95	☐ $ 19.95		
SPECIFY STATES:				
STATE SECTION ONLY (BINDER NOT INCLUDED) — SPECIFY STATES:	☐ $ 5.95			
U.S. EDITION (FEDERAL SECTION — 50 STATES AND WASHINGTON, D.C. IN 11-BINDER SET)	☐ $295.00			
Successful Business Plan: Secrets & Strategies	☐ $ 39.95	☐ $ 19.95		
Surviving and Prospering in a Business Partnership	☐ $ 39.95	☐ $ 19.95		
Venture Capital Proposal Package	☐ $ 39.95			
Write Your Own Business Contracts	☐ $ 39.95	☐ $ 19.95		
BOOK TOTAL (Please enter on other side also for grand total)				

SOFTWARE - Please check whether you use Macintosh or 5-1/4" or 3-1/2"Disk for IBM-PC & Compatibles

TITLE	5-1/4" IBM Disk	3-1/2" IBM Disk	MAC	PRICE	QUANTITY	COST
Company Policy & Personnel Software	☐	☐	☐	☐ $ 69.95		
★ Company Policy Binderbook & Software	☐	☐	☐	☐ $ 129.95		
Corporation Formation Package Software CA☐ TX☐ FL☐	☐	☐		☐ $ 59.95		
★ Corporation Formation Binderbook & Software CA☐ TX☐ FL☐	☐	☐		☐ $ 89.95		
Customer Profile & Retrieval: Professional	☐	☐		☐ $149.95		
Financial Templates	☐	☐	☐	☐ $ 69.95		
The Small Business Expert	☐	☐		☐ $ 59.95		
Spreadsheet	☐	☐		☐ $ 99.95		
★ Special Combination Software: Financial Templates & Spreadsheet	☐	☐		☐ $129.95		
SOFTWARE TOTAL (Please enter on other side also for grand total)						

Please add above totals on other side to complete your order.

Sold to: PLEASE GIVE STREET ADDRESS NOT P.O. BOX FOR SHIPPING

Name _____

Title _____

Company _____

Street Address _____

City/State/Zip _____

Daytime Telephone _____

Ship to: (if different)   **PLEASE GIVE STREET ADDRESS NOT P.O. BOX FOR SHIPPING**

Name _____

Title _____

Company _____

Street Address _____

City/State/Zip _____

Daytime Telephone _____

Payment Information:

☐ Check enclosed payable to PSI Research (When you enclose a check, UPS ground shipping is free within the Continental U.S.A.)

Charge - ☐ VISA ☐ MASTERCARD ☐ AMEX ☐ DISCOVER   Card Number: _____ Expires ____

Signature: _____   Name on card: _____

EXECARDS

ITEM	PRICE EACH	QUANTITY	COST
EXECARDS Thank You Assortment (12 assorted thank you cards)	$ 12.95		
EXECARDS Recognition Assortment (12 assorted appreciation cards)	$ 12.95		
EXECARDS Marketing Assortment (12 assorted marketing cards)	$ 12.95		
EXECARDS TOTAL (Please enter below also for grand total)			$

Many additional options available. Please request complete catalog.

PLANNING TOOLS

ITEM		NUMBER OF PADS
Calendar Note Pad	☐ 1991	
	☐ 91/92	
	☐ 1992	
☐ Progress/Activity		
☐ Make-A-Month		
☐ Milestone Chart		
☐ Project Plan/Record		
☐ Week's Priority Planner		
Total number of pads		
Multiply by unit price:		x
PLANNING TOOLS TOTAL		$

UNIT PRICE FOR ANY COMBINATION OF PLANNING TOOLS

1-9 pads $3.95 each
10-49 pads $3.49 each
50 or more pads $2.98 each

SONY 9/24/91

GRAND TOTAL

BOOK TOTAL (from other side) $ _____

SOFTWARE TOTAL (from other side) $ _____

EXECARDS TOTAL $ _____

PLANNING TOOLS TOTAL $ _____

TOTAL ORDER $ _____

Rush service is available. Please call us for details.

Please send:

_____ Successful Business Library Book Catalog

_____ EXECARDS Catalog

_____ PSI Software Information